Geopolitics and International Relations

Geopolitics and International Relations

Series Editor

David Criekemans (*University of Antwerp*)

VOLUME 1

The titles published in this series are listed at *brill.com/geop*

Geopolitics and International Relations

Grounding World Politics Anew

Edited by

David Criekemans

BRILL
NIJHOFF

LEIDEN | BOSTON

Cover illustration: World map from the Atlas Mayor o Geographia, 1662, by the 17th century Dutch map maker and publisher Joannes Blaeu. Photo with kind permission by the Maritime Museum Rotterdam.

The Library of Congress Cataloging-in-Publication Data is available online at https://catalog.loc.gov
LC record available at https://lccn.loc.gov/2021049617

Typeface for the Latin, Greek, and Cyrillic scripts: "Brill". See and download: brill.com/brill-typeface.

ISSN 2666-6669
ISBN 978-90-04-43207-9 (hardback)
ISBN 978-90-04-43208-6 (e-book)

This book is printed on acid-free paper and produced in a sustainable manner.

Printed by Printforce, the Netherlands

Geopolitics has long attracted a sceptical response from scholars trained to be disdainful of ambitious theory. Whereas historians and political scientists have been educated to know more and more about less and less, and are professionally programmed to dissect phenomena, geopoliticians are committed to the all too rare activity of putting things together. It is a crowning glory of geopolitical theory that it seeks to connect, rather than disconnect; it is, in a word, holistic.

COLIN S. GRAY, 2004

Contents

PART 3
Empirical Studies: The Enduring Relevance of Territorially Embedded Factors in IR

PART 4
Conclusions

Background and Acknowledgements

This book has indirectly been in the making for over fifteen years. When I started my own doctoral dissertation at the University of Antwerp (Belgium) in 1998 on the history of the geopolitical schools of thought and their interrelationship with International Relations, some colleagues stated that Geopolitics was no longer relevant as an academic body of literature to understand international relations. Europe was coming together, borders were being abolished. Communication technologies would bring us together. Capitalism had so-called prevailed over Communism. The US constituted the sole and, at that time, undisputed superpower or even hyperpower. The European Union and NATO would further expand. The end of history, as coined by Francis Fukuyama, had arrived. *"Geopolitics was the nineteenth century"*, these colleagues claimed. At that time, I stubbornly pressed on in the conviction that somehow, we in International Relations, had forgotten some important tools in the toolbox of any analyst; the enduring importance of territorially embedded factors in many aspects and forms. Also highly relevant in my opinion was the holistic perspective of how geoeconomics, geopolitics and geostrategy all mutually support one another in 'feeding' the strategies of countries and other territorially embedded actors such as regions (Catalonia, Scotland and many others) or *sui generis* entities such as the European Union.

By the time I defended my PhD dissertation at the University of Antwerp in June 2005, academia in Europe and around the world had already started to reflect upon the changes in the global balance of power. 9/11 in 2001 and the American invasion to topple the regime of Saddam Hussein in Iraq in March 2003 showed that the 'unipolar moment' for the United States of America perhaps was much more brief than some would have anticipated. International Relations as a field was not completely able to both detect and correctly interpret these fundamental changes in the domains of politics, economics and strategy, as they were initially subdued. However, with the eyes and hindsight of today, we may state that already back then the tectonic plates of world politics had started to shift. But some in IR had in the past deliberately ignored territorially embedded variables or the unique added value of Geopolitics in its attempt to create a more holistic picture of world affairs. Referring to the mistakes of the 1930s, most notably the German school of Geopolitics around the symbolic figure of Karl Haushofer and the *'Zeitschrift für Geopolitik'*, it was denounced by many starting with Hans Morgenthau as a *'pseudo science'* or a form of geographical determinism. Those who claim this do not understand the intellectual richness of Geopolitics.

Geopolitics was developed as an academic field in 1899 in another period of rapid changes in the global shift of power. At that time, the world was dominated by European powers that encompassed the whole world, in the wake of the colonial age and industrialisation. But this wave of Globalisation started to collapse; European powers were vying for geoeconomic and geostrategic interests. The world, moreover, had become, in the words of the British geographer Halford John Mackinder, a 'closed political system'. Since all world territories belonged to some kind of sphere of influence, border skirmishes in faraway Africa could have an immediate effect upon the power balance among the European powers.

Geopolitics was developed by the Swede Rudolf Kjellén from a perspective to develop a scientifically based instrument that could also *advise* key decision-makers in foreign policy and defence to avoid war. That engagement with policymakers is something which distinguishes Geopolitics from the more descriptive and 'politically neutral' Political Geography. Others have called Geopolitics "applied Political Geography". Influenced by one of the first political geographers Friedrich Ratzel, Kjellén believed that the state is foremost a territorially embedded entity, and more than the sum of legal or constitutional articles. Kjellén proposed an 'organic Political Science' in which Geopolitics played a key role, an answer to academia in the period leading up to World War One. In this era, problems of international relations were studied by historians or specialists in international law.

International Relations as a field was only constituted after the First World War with the initial mission to study the causes of war, and the attempt to try to avoid new disasters in the future, with the first academic chairs to be set up in Aberystwyth (Wales) and Geneva (Switzerland). That mission already failed dramatically in the 1930s, which produced the ontological first debate between Idealists and Realists. Interestingly, the geopolitical scholar Halford John Mackinder, who was part of the British delegation at the Versailles treaty negotiations in Paris, became very pessimistic about the future. As early as 1919, he referred to this dilemma in his book *'Democratic Ideals and Reality: A Study of the Politics of Reconstruction'*. But mainstream IR, as it developed, seemed to have difficulty with grasping and integrating the importance and influence of territorially embedded explanatory variables or the 'bigger picture'. The dichotomic debate between Idealism/Liberalism and Realism also inhibited at a basic conceptual level, and in terms of the operationalisation of research designs, to see how the overall geoeconomic, geostrategic and geopolitical aims which nations pursue are mutually supporting one another. The failure by some, though definitely not all, to deal with territorially embedded factors left IR often with incomplete analyses.

When I defended my PhD dissertation at the University of Antwerp in Belgium on the intellectual history of Geopolitics (1890-2005) and its relation to Theory of International Relations (the manuscript was published in Dutch with the Belgian scientific publisher Garant under the title *"Geopolitiek, 'geografisch geweten' van de buitenlandse politiek?"*), academia itself was changing too. Having consulted the original key academic texts in German, French, English and Italian between 1890 and 2005, a new more nuanced debate could be reconstructed between various schools of thought in Geopolitics and IR about the relevance of territorially embedded factors and the way in which power shifts could be studied. As the years passed, I was working less and less on my own 'academic island'. In the 1990s, an interesting school of thought 'Critical Geopolitics' had been developed whose thinking can be traced back to the criticism on alleged geographic determinism, the French *Hérodote*-school starting in the 1970s and social constructivism. It critically put into question the 'naturalization' of geography in foreign policy and issues of world affairs. This school of thought distanced itself from analysing current events and was not always able to thoroughly analyse these issues. Moreover, since often political geographers embarked on a critical geopolitical analysis, the school of thought kept its distance to the analysis of the practice of foreign policy and world affairs (see Chapter 3 and 5). This kept the question of how to gauge the geopolitical changes in world politics. There was still a fundamental need to 'ground' world politics anew, as if it were.

As so often is the case in moments of the gradual development of new schools of thought, the confrontation of world events with the scholarly ontological and epistemological assumptions created what I can only call a form of "crisis". Whereas I sometimes felt I had been working stubbornly on my own academic island, as the 2000s evolved, I had the great fortune to meet and start collaborating with several colleagues abroad on various dimensions of these academic and policy-relevant questions. Several colleagues in different European countries had come to similar conclusions. We discovered each other and connected. Also new journals appeared – although often only focussing on one specific geopolitical perspective or school of thought.

At the time when I finished my PhD, I had the great pleasure to meet my colleague Gyula Csurgai in Geneva, who already had written several interesting publications on Geopolitics. As we met for a now 'historic' pizza somewhere at Gare Cornavin, it felt for me as if we had already known each other for many years. Both our analysis of the relationship between Geopolitics and IR, and the geopolitical position of the European countries in an increasingly difficult world ran parallel (increasing US unilateralism under George W. Bush, the isolation of Russia, the gradual rise of China, the destabilisation of the Middle

East as a result of the American invasion of Iraq – a true watershed moment, etc.). Dr. Gyula Csurgai had already set up the International Centre for Geopolitical Studies (ICGS) in Geneva, that had made some interesting publications and organised several conferences in which open and as Csurgai called it "non-conformist" debates were possible. The aim was "to think outside of the box" with regard to the rapidly changing geopolitical context and its implications for Europe but also other countries in the world. We believed the world was moving away from the unipolar moment. Geopolitics in combination with IR could offer us tools in the toolbox to better academically analyse the various dimensions of these changes, and the implications and foreign policy options for countries but also regions around the world. Gyula Csurgai and I decided to set up a summer course in Geopolitics and geopolitical analysis, which was an immediate success in 2005. Dr. Anselm Zurfluh, former director of the Swiss Domaine de Penthes, offered us our regular meeting place. Neutral Geneva in July attracted (PhD) students from around the world, as well as diplomats, specialists in defence and intelligence, company managers, some (future) politicians and interested individuals. That initial group also included scholars such as Dr. Alexandre Vautravers and Dr. Bernard Wicht. Later also scholars such as Dr. Alexandre Lambert, Dr. Goran Jovanovic and Dr. Manlio Graziano joined us.

ICGS meanwhile became GIGS, the Geneva Institute of Geopolitical Studies, and gradually earned an international reputation. GIGS also inspired two 'winter schools' in Geopolitics on the Dutch island of Curaçao in November 2016 and 2017 organised by the then Latin American and Caribbean Institute of Geopolitical Studies (LACIGS) together with the University of Curaçao and the University of the Caribbean, with many invited geopolitical scholars from Latin and Central America. This created a very rich academic mutual cross-fertilization. Our former Geneva participants Ambassador Roberto Palacios and my former Antwerp 'student' & diplomatic representative of Curaçao Humphrey Senior played a pivotal role in this unique initiative. While maintaining contacts in Europe, GIGS also developed a considerable international network in the field of geopolitics with scholars, research institutions, universities and international organisations in all continents of the globe. From our little personal 'academic islands' in Europe we now had gone global. Between 2005 and 2019, our summer course attracted a lot of interested individuals from around the world. Then a pandemic of the coronavirus hit the globe, which caused us to pause this initiative both in 2020 and 2021. In the summer of 2022 however, we will celebrate the fifteenth edition of the GIGS summer course, which by now has 600 or more alumni from all over the world, strengthening the academic and policy-relevant network and debate about the fundamental geopolitical shifts that affect our world and how to deal with them.

In parallel I also continued my own academic work on the triangle of Geopolitics, Foreign Policy and Diplomatic Studies, focusing also on sub-state entities around the world and the place of Europe in a changing world. In all these endeavours I met many scholars who also started integrating Geopolitics into their analytical frameworks, for instance Dr. Anders Wivel and Dr. Hans Mouritzen in Copenhagen. It deserves to be mentioned that also the Flemish regional government between 2007 and 2011 financed much of my academic work on geopolitics, which helped me to also open up the field to a geopolitical study of non-state actors such as regions. Further building upon this work, Dr. Manuel Duran wrote and defended his PhD *'Mediterranean Paradiplomacies. The Dynamics of Diplomatic Reterritorialization'*, published with Brill in 2005, under my guidance and that of specialist in Diplomatic Studies Dr. Jan Melissen. This project was a first realisation of our endeavour to connect the IR subfields of Foreign Policy Analysis and Diplomatic Studies more directly to Geopolitics. To this very day, Manuel Duran plays an important role as 'sparring partner' in our continued quest to open up the geopolitical literature and connect it to understanding today's world politics.

Antonios Nestoras came to me in 2014 as a former student of Jan Melissen with a proposal to understand Greece's foreign policy in a way that transcends the current classical/critical geopolitics divide, a manuscript that he successfully defended in 2020. His proposal for an 'Analytic Geopolitics' tries to overcome some of the ontological and epistemological problems in the current literature through analysing 'geopolitical myths'. Meanwhile also other doctoral students are currently working in this fashion on various aspects, and we find ourselves in a moment in which contacts all over the world are multiplying. Dr. Steven Spittaels, whom I had met a decade earlier at the International Peace Institute Service (IPIS) in Antwerp, defended a PhD with my Antwerp colleague Dr. Tom Sauer. He pioneered a new and integrated way to study the correlation between resources and conflict, most notably in Africa. His work showed once again the continued relevance of territorially embedded factors in current questions of world politics. His approach to map and study greed deserves a wider global audience. In the past I had met Dr. Luis da Vinha, who contacted me on the basis of my work on 'mental maps', bringing together the intellectual heritage of Harold and Margaret Sprout and 'Cognitive Geopolitics' in a paper which I had presented at the International Studies Association Annual Convention in New York in 2009. We kept in touch and later worked together in a joint panel at WISC in 2011 in Porto. He continued his innovative thinking, which has further enriched the literature towards a nuanced analysis of the role of perception in geopolitics.

In 2019, I was asked to join Egmont, the Belgian Institute for International Relations in Brussels as a Senior Associate Fellow, with the programme 'World

Politics' under the guidance of Dr. Sven Biscop. Egmont had contributed widely on the institutional but gradually also more explicitly on the geopolitical dimensions of how Europe should adapt to this new world. Ambassadors Johan Verbeke and Marc Franco allowed me to join an initiative through which Belgian and Russian academics meet each six months to discuss current geopolitical events, explore ways of possible de-escalation, and 'compare notes' on issues of world affairs. I look forward to this developing new geopolitical dimension in my activities, which bring me as an academic closer to a better 'inside' view of the dilemmas of policy-making in geopolitics.

In many ways this book thus presents a reflection of my own intellectual voyage, taken together with many excellent colleagues over all these years. In the past I had worked together with Brill Academic Publishers for my book *'Regional Sub-State Diplomacy'* (2010). At that time, I had met and collaborated with Irene van Rossum at Brill with great pleasure. We went on our own personal voyages. Irene invited me to set up a new book series *'Geopolitics and International Relations'* with Brill. With humility but also great enthusiasm and academic curiosity, I immediately took up the gauntlet. Initial contacts with several colleagues in the various schools of thought in our field, but also the rapid geopolitical changes we are currently witnessing, led me to conclude that the time is right to set up this new book series. Over the past year, and in the middle of a global pandemic, I had the great pleasure to work together with Jason Prevost, Senior Acquisitions Editor Social Sciences & International Relations at Brill, as well as with Jennifer Obdam, Assistant Editor. Thanks to their professionalism and encouragement, we are together giving shape to the new book series. I am very much looking forward to our collaboration in the next years. We hope to offer authors a venue and stimulate academic debate.

Through my own intellectual voyage of the past twenty years, I have come to firmly believe that we need a platform where debate is possible between and within different schools of thought in Geopolitics and IR. Therefore this new and unique book series is conceived deliberately as a zone where Geopolitics and IR can connect with each other, rather than closing themselves off into existing publications in their respective fields. It also points to the increasing relevance of territorially embedded factors in the analysis of today's international relations. In addition, the new book series is also open to contributions from scholars in other fields, such as historians, geographers, economists, political scientists, psychologists, specialists in international law, etc. Today, more analysts are using the concept 'geopolitics', but they do not always clearly define it (sometimes it is merely used as a synonym for 'power politics'). *Geopolitics and International Relations* presents a clear opportunity to connect. The book series offers opportunities to academics, students and practitioners to learn from each other, as well as more comprehensive analyses on the geopolitical challenges which affect many dimensions of politics today and tomorrow (security, economy, energy, environment, technology, diplomacy & foreign policy).

Last but not least, the authors of this book would like to thank the team of Elizabeth Stone, and more in particular Judith Acevedo, for the indexing of this foundational book and their collaboration on several projects in this new book series.

Dr. David Criekemans
Antwerp (Belgium)
Spring 2021

Figures

Abbreviations

ACLED	Armed Conflict Location and Event Data Project
AIIB	Asia Infrastructure Investment Bank
ASEAN	Association of Southeast Asian Nations
BA	Bachelor of Arts degree
BDB	Benghazi Defence Brigades
BRI	Belt and Road Initiative, China
BRICS	Brazil, Russia, India, China and South Africa
BRSC	Benghazi Revolutionaries Shura Council
BTC	Bitcoin
CAT	Conventional Arms Transfer
CIS	Commonwealth of Independent States
CoR	Council of Europe
COVID-19	acronym used for the full name coronavirus disease first detected in 2019
CSBMS	Confidence and Security Building Measures
CSCE	Conference on Security and Cooperation in Europe
DDoS	Distributed Denial of Service
DPO	Department of Peace Operations
DPRK	Democratic People's Republic of Korea (aka North Korea)
DRRS	Document of Restructuring of the Sudanese State
EAEU	Eurasian Economic Union
EC	European Community
ECFA	Economic Cooperation Framework Agreement
EEAS	European External Action Service
EEZ	Exclusive Economic Zone
EI	Economic Intelligence
ET	Energy Technology
ETH	Ethereum
EU	European Union
FAZ	Forces Armees Zairoise
FLEC	Front for the Liberation of the Cabinda Enclave
FNLC	Front for the National Liberation of the Congo
FPA	Foreign Policy Analysis
G8	Group of Eight, an inter-governmental political forum from 1997 until 2014 comprising the industrial (western) countries Canada, France, Germany, Italy, Japan, United Kingdom, United States and the European Union. The Russian Federation was suspended in 2014, following the 'annexation' of the Crimea

GDP	Gross Domestic Product
GE	General Electric
GIGS	Geneva Institute of Geopolitical Studies
GIS	Geographic Information System
GNA	Government of National Accord in Libya
ICGS	International Centre for Geopolitical Studies
ICT	Information and Communication Technologies
IEA	International Energy Institute
IGO	International Governmental Organisation
ILO	International Labour Organisation
IMF	International Monetary Fund
IoT	Internet of Things
IPIS	International Peace Information Service
IR	International Relations
ISFEREA	Information Support for Effective and Rapid External Action
IT	Information Technology
JEM	Justice and Equality Movement
JMAC	Joint Mission Analysis Centre
KLA	Kosovo Liberation Army
LACIGS	Latin American and Caribbean Institute of Geopolitical Studies
LIFG	Libyan Islamic Fighting Group
LNA	Libyan National Army
LNG	Liquefied Natural Gas
M2M	Machine-to-Machine communication
MA	Master of Arts degree
MBFR	Mutual and Balanced Force Reductions
MCOP	Mission Common Operating Picture
MERCOSUR	Mercado Común del Sur / Southern Common Market
METI	Ministry of Economy, Trade and Industry
MIDLOC	Militarized Interstate Dispute Location
MPLA	Popular Movement for the Liberation of Angola
NAFTA	North Atlantic Free Trade Association
NATO	North Atlantic Treaty Organization
NCP	National Congress Party
NDC	New Dawn Convention
NDB	New Development Bank
NED	National Endowment of Democracy
NGO	Non-Governmental Organisation
NOC	Libyan National Oil Corporation
NSA	National Security Agency

NSC	National Security Council
NSR	Northern Sea Route
OAU	Organization of African Unity
OBOR	One Belt, One Road initiative (by the People's Republic of China)
OCHA	United Nations Office for the Coordination of Humanitarian Affairs
OECD	Organisation for Economic Co-operation and Development
OHCHR	Office of the United Nations High Commissioner for Human Rights
OSCE	Organisation for Security and Co-operation in Europe
PD	Presidential Directive
PFG	Petroleum Facilities Guard
PG	Political Geography
PhD	Doctor of Philosophy, a postgraduate doctoral degree
PPP	Purchasing Power Parity
PRC	Policy Review Committee
PRIO	Peace Research Institute Oslo
PRM	Policy Review Memorandum
QE	Quantitative Easing
R&D	Research and Development
RAS	Robotics and Automated Systems
REE	Renewable Energy
RMA	Revolution in Military Affairs
RMB	Renminbi
RSP	Revolution in Strategic Perspectives
SAF	Sudanese Armed Forces
SALT	Strategic Arms Limitation Talks
SCC	Special Coordinating Committee
SCO	Shanghai Cooperation Organization
SDI	Strategic Defence Initiative
SPLA	Sudan People's Liberation Army
SPLA-N	Sudan People's Liberation Army – North
SRF	Sudanese Revolutionary Front
SS	Schutzstaffel – the Protection Squadron that was a major paramilitary organization under Adolf Hitler and the Nazi Party (NSDAP) in Nazi Germany
UAV	Unmanned Aerial Vehicle
UK	United Kingdom
UN	United Nations
UNAMID	United Nations/African Union Mission in Darfur
UNASUR	Union of South American Nations
UNCLOS	United Nations Convention on the Law of the Sea

UNDESA	United Nations Department of Economic and Social Affairs
UNDSS	United Nations Department of Safety and Security
UNEP	United Nations Environment Programme
UNESCO	United Nations Educational, Scientific and Cultural Organisation
UNHCR	United Nations High Commissioner for Refugees
UNITA	National Union for the Total Independence of Angola
UNOCC	UN Operations and Crisis Centre
UNSC	United Nations Security Council
UPCD GED	Uppsala Conflict Data Program Georeferenced Event Dataset
US	United States
USA	United States of America
USSR	Union of Soviet Socialist Republics
WISC	World International Studies Committee
WMD	Weapons of Mass Destruction

Notes on Contributors

David Criekemans

Dr. David Criekemans is Associate Professor in 'International Relations' at the University of Antwerp and KULeuven (Belgium), Assistant Professor 'International Relations & International Security' at the University College Roosevelt (part of Utrecht University) in Middelburg (the Netherlands) and Senior Lecturer 'Geopolitics' at the Geneva Institute of Geopolitical Studies (GIGS) (Switzerland). In 2005, he established together with Dr. Gyula Csurgai the annual Summer Course in 'Geopolitics' in Geneva (GIGS), running each year in mid-July. Next to this, Dr. Criekemans is also a Visiting Professor at Blanquerna, Ramon Lull University in Barcelona (Spain). Since 2019, he is also a Senior Associate Fellow with Egmont, the Belgian Royal Institute of International Affairs, associated with the Belgian federal Department of Foreign Affairs in Brussels. Previously, Dr. Criekemans taught 'Geopolitics' at the Belgian Royal Military Academy (RMA) in Brussels (2007–2011), 'Regional Integration' at the Catholic University Brussels and at the Latin American and Caribbean Institute of Geopolitical Studies (LACIGS) on Curaçao. David Criekemans is often asked as an analyst and opinion maker on current problems of geopolitics and international relations for domestic and foreign media, both in the written press as on radio and television. He also often gives lectures and trainings on current geopolitical problems and on negotiations in an international context.

Gyula Csurgai

Dr. Gyula Csurgai obtained his Doctorate from the University of Geneva. His doctoral research focused on the development of the geopolitical analysis method and its application in different case study situations. He holds Degrees in Political Science from the University of Concordia (Canada) and the University of Toulouse (France). Dr. Csurgai earned Postgraduate Degrees in European Studies from the European Institute at University of Geneva and from the Department of Philosophy from the same university. He taught geopolitics, geoeconomics, strategy, international relations and diplomacy at different universities in Switzerland and abroad. He developed several university programs, organized international symposiums on different geopolitical issues and directed the publications of their proceedings. Dr. Csurgai also developed training programs in geopolitics and geoeconomics for professionals working for the public service and private corporations in Switzerland and elsewhere. He is co-founder and Director of the Geneva Institute of Geopolitical Studies and Academic Director of the Geneva-based University Program of the School for International Training in Multilateral Diplomacy and International Studies. He is also adjunct faculty member at the International University in Geneva and directs seminars on Geopolitics and Geoeconomics at the Geneva School of Diplomacy. He published several books and articles on the field of geopolitics, geoeconomics, economic intelligence, and international relations.

Luis Da Vinha

Dr. Luis da Vinha is Lecturer and Coordinator of the Master's program in International Relations at Flinders University (Adelaide, Australia). He received his Doctorate in International Relations from the School of Economics of the University of Coimbra (FEUC). Luis is a member of the Grupo de Estudos Avançados sobre Paz e Conflitos Internacionais (Grazil) and a guest researcher at the at the Centre of Studies on Geography and Spatial Planning – CEGOT (Portugal). He is author of *'Geographic Mental Maps and Foreign Policy Change: Re-Mapping the Carter Doctrine'* (De Gruyter) and *'Three Approaches to Presidential Foreign Policy-Making in the Twenty-First Century'* with Anthony Dutton (Peter Lang). Luis Da Vinha has published several papers on geography and international politics with *Routledge, Palgrave Macmillan, Presidential Studies Quarterly, Comparative Strategy, Journal of Policy History, Brown Journal of World Affairs*, and *European Journal of Geography*, among others.

Manuel Duran

Dr. Manuel Duran is a historian and specialist in International Relations and Geopolitics. He obtained his PhD at the University of Antwerp (Belgium) with a study on Mediterranean paradiplomacy. The manuscript was published by Brill in 2015 as *'Mediterranean paradiplomacies. Dynamics of Diplomatic Reterritorialization'*. Dr. Duran currently works as a scientific attaché for the national War Heritage Institute in Brussels (Belgium) and an associate collaborator of the research group International Politics at the University of Antwerp. His current research interests include geopolitics, military history and diplomatic history, particularly the role of military attachés in twentieth century Europe.

Alexandre Lambert

Dr. Alexandre Lambert holds a PhD in international relations from the Graduate Institute of International and Development Studies, Geneva. He has been an academic director and lecturer with SIT in Geneva since 2007. He has been lead researcher on the Organization for Security and Cooperation in Europe at the Graduate Institute, project officer at the Geneva Centre for the Democratic Control of Armed Forces, and a civil servant at the Swiss Federal Department of Defense. He belongs to non-profit civil society organizations including the Swiss Foreign Policy Association, the European Consortium of Political Research, and the European Research Group on Armed Forces and Society. He is a fellow of the Inter-University Seminar on Armed Forces and Society in Chicago and frequently provides policy advice to the OSCE Forum for Security Cooperation, often regarding operations in the Western Balkans, South Caucasus, and Central Asia. Alexandre has published on international politics and history, international security, and security sector governance.

Antonios Nestoras

Dr. Antonios Nestoras is Head of Policy and Research at the European Liberal Forum (ELF) and an adjunct professor at the Brussels School of Governance of the Free University of Brussels (VUB). Previously, he worked as a political advisor for policymakers in the European Parliament. He holds a double PhD in Social and Political Science from VUB and University of Antwerp. He is a laureate of the Huygens Scholarship for International Talent. Apart from geopolitics, his research also focuses on political myth, as well as disinformation and influence operations in cyberspace.

Steven Spittaels

Dr. Steven Spittaels is a conflict mapper, researcher and research manager on armed conflicts, specialized in the analysis of armed groups, conflict financing and war motivation. He served five mandates on UN Experts Panels focusing on the Democratic Republic of Congo (DRC) and Libya. Currently, he is the Team Leader for the Great Lakes Region at the European Institute of Peace, where his focus is more on mediation. He also remains associated with the International Peace Information Service, where he previously worked as a Senior Researcher on the DRC, the Central African Republic and both Sudans. Steven Spittaels holds a PhD in Political Science from the University of Antwerp and master degrees in political science and in conflict studies from the University of Leuven. He has authored, co-authored and edited over thirty reports commissioned by various clients including the UN Security Council, other UN agencies, the World Bank, the EU and various governments.

INTRODUCTION

The Need for a Renewed 'Grounding' of International Relations

David Criekemans

Some have in the past jokingly described geography as the 'unwanted stepchild' of International Relations. Whereas International Relations as an academic field was established after the First World War in 1919, Geopolitics is exactly twenty years older and rose to high prominence in continental Europe from the end of the 1890s onwards. Geopolitics is the scientific field of study belonging to both Political Geography and International Relations, which investigates the interaction between politically acting (wo)men and their surrounding territoriality (in its three dimensions; physical geography, human geography and the spatial dimension) (Criekemans 2007). After a tricky relationship of some geopolitical scholars with authoritarian regimes during the 1930s and 1940s in a number of continental European countries, Geopolitics became politically tarnished. But its core did not go away during the Cold War. In the 1950s, cognitive geopolitical analyses and mental maps were pioneered by such scholars as Harold and Margaret Sprout. From the 1970s onwards, scholars such as Yves Lacoste in France and Henry Kissinger in the US gradually started popularising the term 'geopolitics' anew, although their approaches sometimes lacked academic coherence. The field underwent an era of 'penance' when a constructivist wave, among others, gave rise to the school of Critical Geopolitics. This school of thought questioned the 'naturalization' of geography by and through politics.

Since the end of the 1990s, Geopolitics has again come to the fore as a subfield in International Relations and Political Geography. Geopolitics stresses the importance of territorially embedded factors such as physical geography (location, resources, energy, landscape, climate, etc.), human geography (religion, ethnic groups, etc.) and the spatial dimension (e.g. spheres of influence). Whereas at the beginning of the 1990s analysts believed the world would become one single entity thanks to, among others, technological advances (via the so-called 'geo-technical ensemble') and subsequent processes of 'space-time compression', today's international relations show tensions in between and among groups, regions, and countries. As a result of this, some of the

 | DOI:10.1163/9789004432086_002

academic work within International Relations became detached from reality and territorially embedded factors (physical geography, human geography and the spatial dimension). This dramatically reduced the explanatory power of some of the scholarship within IR. Today's world is showing a gradually different international picture compared to the globalisation wave of, say twenty five years ago. Territorially embedded factors seem to be gaining explanatory power through the rise of issues of scarcity versus abundance in subjects such as energy transition and the environment, (accompanying) changing geopolitical spheres of influence in the realm of geo-economics and geostrategy, processes of re-terrorialisation such as the stressing of identity in many places in the world as a counterbalance to de-terrorialising pressures (globalization seen from a geopolitical angle). Hence, some authors in the recent past reformulated this with a popular crede; the 'revenge of geography' (Robert D. Kaplan).

Whereas Geopolitics and International Relations were at best 'living apart together' during the past decades, empirical developments and intrinsic academic debates bring the two fields of academia gradually back together. Geopolitics already finds itself back in mainstream (popular) debates about the fundamental changes which individuals, societies and economies encounter early in the twenty first century. This book wants to contribute to the academic re-integration of both fields into a mutually beneficial, scholarly rewarding and fruitful journey. Judging by today's complex problems over energy, the environment and the economy, that intellectual endeavour is only getting started. Hence, IR will become better able to 'ground' world politics anew – a scholarly undertaking which we claim to be crucial in the further development of our thinking about the state of world politics and the foreign policy of nations and other territorially embedded actors within that world today. We therefore hope this book offers a modest, first orientation towards that ultimate academic goal.

Emanating from the theoretical work within the subfield of Geopolitics, many analysts of IR use implicit or explicit geopolitical analyses anew to study today's risks. Geopolitical risks can be analysed in multiple sectors; economy, environment, energy, strategy, technology. Moreover, most of these risks are interconnected. This book offers a more fundamental insight into the academic backbone of such an endeavour. As such, it serves as a foundational book in Brill's new and unique series *'Geopolitics and International Relations'* which we hope will further materialize in the years to come. *Geopolitics and International Relations* constitutes a new and unique platform where a debate is possible between and within different schools of thought in Geopolitics and IR. It is conceived deliberately as a zone where Geopolitics and IR can connect with each other, rather than closing themselves off into existing publications in their respective fields. It also points to the increasing relevance of territorially embedded factors in the analysis of today's international relations. In addition, the new book series is also open to contributions from scholars in other fields, such as historians, geographers, economists, political scientists, psychologists, specialists in international law, etc.

Today, more analysts are using the concept 'geopolitics', but they do not always clearly define it (sometimes it is merely used as a synonym for 'power politics'). *Geopolitics and International Relations* presents a clear opportunity to connect, it offers opportunities to academics, students and practitioners to learn from each other, as well as more comprehensive analyses on the geopolitical challenges which affect many dimensions of politics today and tomorrow (security, economy, energy, environment, technology, diplomacy & foreign policy).

This foundational book is organised in three main sections, each containing several chapters;

Section One devotes attention to the basic variables of geopolitical analysis.

> The first chapter by Gyula Csurgai develops an overview of the main components of geopolitical analysis. Moreover, the author focuses on the geopolitical method of analysis by briefly presenting the constant and variable factors, and their interaction, that have to be taken into account in a geopolitical approach. In terms of broad categories, one can make a distinction between three main dimensions within geopolitical analysis; physical geography, human geography and the spatial dimension. Csurgai further nuances and gives examples from geopolitics, geoeconomics and geostrategy. Through this chapter the reader gets a first glimpse of the continued relevance of territorially embedded factors in today's geopolitics.
>
> The second chapter by David Criekemans briefly zooms in on an often forgotten factor in geopolitical analysis; technology. Already early geopolitical scholars at the end of the nineteenth century and the first half of the twentieth century referred at least implicitly to technology, for instance Mahan, Mackinder and Spykman. According to Deudney however, the 'geo' in geopolitics has obscured the important role of technology in these earlier world order theories (Deudney, 1989, p. 2–3). Harold Sprout referred to 'geo-technic politics' (Sprout, 1963, p. 192). Deudney proposed to analyse the "geo-technical ensembles" (Deudney, 1989, p. 13). Inspired by his work, David Criekemans adapts this framework to today's world at the start of the 2020s. As technology advances and changes, territorially embedded factors are given new meaning. The author gives

examples from transportation, communication and energy, tapping into both classical geopolitical theories and more recent geopolitical developments in today's world, thereby referring to the recent technological struggle between, most importantly, the United States of America and the People's Republic of China over such technologies as 5G, quantum computing, social media and big data, artificial intelligence, robotization, etc.

Section Two devotes attention to theoretical approaches about the role played by territorially embedded factors in IR.

The third chapter by David Criekemans offers a concise overview of the history of geopolitical thought from 1890 till today. It explores the theoretical foundations of Geopolitics, which was proposed as a field of study in 1899 by the Swede Rudolf Kjellén. The author explores Classical Geopolitics' foundations with such authors as Friedrich Ratzel, Alfred Thayer Mahan, Halford John Mackinder. In addition, attention is devoted to the interwar geopolitical schools of thought. There is the German radicalised form of Geopolitics in the 1930s around Karl Haushofer, which, in the end, turned into geographical determinist thinking. As a counterpoint, the French geopolitical school of Possibilism was developed with such authors as Paul Vidal de la Blache and Alain Demangeon. Nicholas Spykman in the US tried to marry aspects of European geopolitical thinking with what later would become Realism in IR. Also authors such as Robert Strausz-Hupé and Hans Morgenthau introduced geopolitical analytical categories and arguments in Realism. A somewhat forgotten approach is cognitive behavioralism or 'Cognitive Geopolitics' from Harold and Margaret Sprout, which made an important distinction between the 'psycho milieu' and the 'operational environment' (see also chapter 4). Geopolitics returned to mainstream academia in the 1970s, first in France (Yves Lacoste) and later also in the United States of America (Kissinger). These approaches, however, focused on different aspects of the relationship between 'geo' and 'politics'. Finally, first emanating from a group of Anglo-American political geographers, a new school of 'Critical Geopolitics' developed which started from the assumption that 'geography' does not constitute an innocent product of nature. Rather, it is the result of the history of the battle between competing authorities over the power to organise, occupy and manage space. David Criekemans finally tries to offer an overview of the different schools of thought and how they could complement one another.

The fourth chapter by David Criekemans zooms in on the work by Harold and Margaret Sprout. In today's literature on Foreign Policy Analysis, the work of Harold and Margaret Sprout is being considered as "one of the three paradigmatic works/origins of Foreign Policy Analysis", most notably Harold and Margaret Sprout's *"Man-Milieu Relationship Hypotheses in the Context of International Politics"*. This article was first developed as an essay in 1956, and was later revised into an article in 1957. Based upon this article, Harold and Margaret Sprout developed a book in 1965 titled *"The Ecological Perspective on Human Relations with Special Reference to International Politics"*. Unique in the Sprouts' contribution was their statement that, to explain undertakings of foreign policy actors, one should look at the "psycho milieu" of the individuals and groups making foreign policy decisions. The psycho-milieu is the international and operational environment or context as it is perceived and interpreted by these decision makers. For those scholars who want to further study the contribution of Harold and Margaret Sprout, the available literature is rather scarce. This chapter tries to make a modest contribution to the existing lacuna in the literature. After an introduction to the life and academic work of Harold and Margaret Sprout, David Criekemans tries to gain a better insight into the ideas of the Sprouts. What did their suggested 'ecological triad' entail? What are the consequences of the distinction between the 'operational' and the 'psychological' milieu for the study of foreign policy? How is 'cognitive behavioralism' related to other possible epistemological appreciations regarding the relationship between 'territoriality' and 'foreign policy'? What does the distinction mean between 'foreign policy analyses' and 'capacity analyses'? Next, we will identify three ways in which Harold and Margaret Sprout influenced IR and FPA. Afterwards, the ontological, epistemological and methodological assumptions and traits of 'Cognitive Geopolitics' are discussed. Finally, some critiques on 'Cognitive Geopolitics' are formulated, while at the same time developing some ideas on the continued relevance today of the work of Harold and Margaret Sprout.

The fifth chapter by Antonios Nestoras tries to go beyond the current geopolitical schools of thought. The author states that the shift from Classical Geopolitics to Critical Geopolitics in the literature was largely ontological and epistemological in nature. It replicated the standard dualisms previously introduced in the discipline of IR with the advent of the postmodern condition. In ontological terms, the scientific materialism of Classical Geopolitics (i.e. the belief that there is a material reality that has essential properties) was overturned by the social constructivism of

Critical Geopolitics (i.e. reality has no essential properties, only relative, socially constructed properties). In epistemological terms, the positivism of Classical Geopolitics (i.e. through geographical survey and philosophical reflection we can know the essential properties of the material reality) was replaced with the interpretivist stance of Critical Geopolitics (i.e. without fixed essential properties, reality is relative to the ideological interpretation of the observer). According to Antonios Nestoras, these dualisms – materialism vs. idealism and positivism vs. interpretivism – outline a Classical/Critical divide in geopolitics that diverts scholarly attention from important research questions. Moreover it puts the field in an unfavourable position and reduces its potential to understand and explain patterns of behaviour in IR that may be grounded in geography. The chapter reviews the philosophical assumptions that underline geopolitics through the prisms of New Materialism and Critical Realism and, drawing from the growing literature on political myth, attempts to initiate a discussion on possible new research directions for geopolitics. The proposed approach is called 'Analytic Geopolitics'. It tries to offer a structural analysis of geopolitical myths into their constitutive elements, their historical emergence and their effect on patterns of state behaviour. This contribution suggests yet another, new 'grounding' of the discipline of IR, not only in geography, but also in history, culture and politics.

Section Three offers empirical studies which 'showcase' a specific innovative approach or method, hence further deepening our understanding of Geopolitics and geopolitical analysis. These chapters analyse various current problems of world politics and tap into several different schools of thought of both Geopolitics and IR, proposing a mutual enrichment of both:

The sixth chapter by Alexandre Lambert taps into a core concept of Classical Geopolitics; containment. While the literature often stresses the military interpretation of this, the author states that George Kennan in May 1947 rather essentially prescribed a non-military American strategy against the Soviet Union. The author uses this insight to revisit the talks in 1990 regarding the unification of Germany and membership into NATO *and* the alleged American pledge not to further expand NATO itself. He is critical of the liberal view that NATO membership spreads and deepens democracy, and compares to alternative frameworks such as the Council of Europe (CoR) and the Organisation for Security and Cooperation in Europe (OSCE) which, in his opinion, have produced more tangible results in this domain. Building upon this analysis and revisiting of a key classical geopolitical concept, the author makes a plea for more in depth expertise on the current situation in Russia, and the necessity of a more all inclusive Pan-European Security Architecture.

The seventh chapter by Gyula Csurgai discusses the term geoeconomics as it was initially introduced by Edward Luttwak (1990) and later also by Pascal Lorot (1999). In this chapter, the author examines the links between geopolitics and geoeconomics in the context of the growing importance of various economic means that are used as strategic instruments in contemporary power rivalries and discusses the role of the state in the organization of a national geoeconomic disposition. Geoeconomics can refer to the use of economic instruments to promote and defend national interests and achieve specific geopolitical goals. States can often implement a geoeconomic strategy that simultaneously advances multiple interests: geopolitical, diplomatic, political and economic. The author gives several historical and current examples to explain this further. In addition, some historical perspectives on the role of economic factors in power rivalries are integrated as well. Interestingly, Csurgai shows that in both peace and war, economic warfare has been applied against countries in order to weaken them economically. Global power shifts aggravate this process even further, and constitute an essential driver in this phenomenon.

The eighth chapter by Luis da Vinha brings us back to the school of thought of Cognitive Geopolitics and Foreign Policy Analysis. Earlier in chapter four, we learnt that Harold and Margaret Sprout had stated that *"what matters in the explanation of decisions and policies is how the actor imagined his environment to be, not how it actually was"* (Sprout & Sprout, 1960: 147). In this chapter, the author conducts an applied analysis of how to analyse geographic mental maps. Da Vinha defines 'geographic mental maps' as cognitive constructs *"which encompass an individual or group's beliefs about the geographic character of a particular place or places and their relationship to other places or spatial phenomena"* (da Vinha, 2019: 78). The author develops a rich analysis of a unique dimension of the foreign policy of the American President Jimmy Carter (1977–1981); most notably his administration's mental maps of Africa and the Persian Gulf. This study shows the richness of this type of analysis tapping into the way in which perception *mediates* between policymakers and the operational environment for which they devise policies. The chapter also shows some of the pitfalls with which policy-makers are confronted with regard to 'correctly' perceiving what is going on, and learning from their experiences in dealing with foreign policy crises and changes.

The ninth chapter by Steven Spittaels zooms in on analysing questions of conflict and security through a geopolitical lens. In this contribution, the author analyses the priorities of armed groups through the systematic analysis of their interaction with territorially embedded factors. By plotting both the actions of armed groups and the environment in which they operate on a map, the scholar is looking for correlations by visualising their interaction. This allows the analyst to establish, and show, links between conflict events and the geographic conditions within which they occur. When used in case studies, this can provide unique insights on armed group motivation as well as the opportunities for such groups to sustain themselves. The chapter by Spittaels focuses specifically on the question of greed as a cause of armed conflict. Greed refers to the pursuit of material gain, which can be a potential motivation of armed groups. Such material gain is usually closely linked to the territory that armed groups control or attempt to control. A methodology to assess to what extent greed motivations drive the actions of armed groups, is presented. Tools for such an analysis of armed groups' interests in material gain are available. The author applies these methodological tools on two recent cases; Sudan (2011–2013) and Libya (2014–2017).

The tenth chapter by Manuel Duran explores the connection between Geopolitics and Diplomatic Studies and History. We are used to think of diplomacy as the exclusive domain of the state. However, the author uses the original prism of 'neo-medievalism' to make us think twice. The author re-investigates the importance of territoriality as a guiding principle for political and diplomatic agency. He then canvasses the current international diplomatic environment, characterized by simultaneous and mutually influencing traditional and new territorial actors and modes of diplomatic practice and thinking. Duran claims that the confluence of traditional and new diplomatic actors can be regarded as a site of political re-territorialisation. In an original approach, the author compares medieval, pre-Westphalian diplomacy with contemporary diplomatic practice. From this confrontation between Geopolitics and History, the author states that contemporary diplomacy rather resembles medieval diplomacy, and that regions play a paramount role in this respect. Duran forces us to rethink some of our basic ontological assumptions about world politics, what entities are relevant in it, how diplomacy actually functions, and its further implications for the study of diplomatic practice.

Finally, this book will offer some conclusions about Geopolitics and International Relations, and how both fields relate to one another. Can we evolve from

'Living Apart Together' to 'Friends With Benefits'? What can both fields learn from each other, and which research agenda could accompany such a fascinating endeavour among political scientists, historians, geographers, economists, psychologists, specialists in international law, etc.? How can more local, non-Western approaches from all over the world (Central and Latin America, Africa, Russia and the post-Soviet sphere, Asia, etc.) be facilitated to also enter the mainstream debate? To what extent are territorially embedded factors relevant in understanding the key problems with which the world is being, or will be, confronted in such domains as security, economy, energy, environment, technology, diplomacy & foreign policy? With this first, not all encompassing but hopefully stimulating contribution, we hope to kickstart this book series *'Geopolitics and International Relations'*. We hope academics, students and practitioners alike may see it as a platform through which we can learn from each other, instead of closing ourselves off in our respective schools of thought. Enrichment of this academic debate is what this foundational book in the series hopes to foster, so as to once again 'ground' world politics anew.

PART 1

Basic Variables of Geopolitical Analysis

CHAPTER 1

The Main Components of Geopolitical Analysis

Gyula Csurgai

1 Introduction

Contemporary international relations have been characterised by a great complexity due to the increasing role of non-state actors, resource competition, identity conflicts, disinformation, geostrategic rivalries, tensions caused by contradictory effects of globalisation and a global power shift. To deal with this difficulty, the geopolitical method of analysis can be a useful tool, since it takes into account the strategic, historical, geographical, cultural and economic spheres in deciphering the complexity of current and potential future conflicts. The geopolitical approach is not only interdisciplinary but it integrates multiple causes and dimensions of conflicts. International relations theories often lack a multi-dimensional approach combined with an interdisciplinary framework. Theories such as Realism, Idealism/Liberalism, and Functionalism, among others, share a common feature in that they tend to constrain the interpretation of international relations to an oversimplified framework for analysis. This can result in the failure to analyse in depth the complexity of the contemporary world system. The inaccurate diagnoses of tensions, crises, or wars can lead to the implementation of inappropriate strategies that not only fail to bring about a remediation of the state of affairs, but can also exacerbate them. Many prominent theories of international relations are based on monocausality. These theories interpret political events through a limited ideological filter: for instance, Marxists emphasised the importance of class struggle while liberals underscored the expansion of the free market economy. In particular, followers of Liberalism and Marxism have considered that most problems in society, including political rivalries, are consequences of economic challenges, whether they are issues of competition between businesses or contradictions between social classes. For example, Marxists maintained that war between communist countries could not occur in spite of certain rivalries between these states. Nonetheless, in 1978 war broke out between the Khmer Rouge of Cambodia and the Vietnamese communists for control of a section of the

 | DOI:10.1163/9789004432086_003

Mekong delta. This conflict arose mainly due to the rival territorial interests of two communist countries; consequently, it was a geopolitical encounter. The logic of the geopolitical analysis method is multidimensional: it seeks to identify the interactions between the different enduring factors and variables on the internal and external levels of states in a time and space dimension. The notion of space refers to geography while the concept of time denotes retrospective and prospective methodologies. Retrospective is the historical dimension that a geopolitical approach integrates with other enduring factors and variables in order to make an assessment of a given situation at present.

Due to the rather rapid development of information and communication technologies, the permissible time for decision making has been considerably reduced; concurrently, the amount of information to process has multiplied. It is therefore a challenging task to select, analyse information and integrate the results in decision making processes. Prospective approach, also termed strategic foresight, is the projection of a current situation into the future. It is rather impossible to precisely tell what shall happen in the future; however, different scenarios can be elaborated on as regards the possible impending evolutions of a given geopolitical condition. The objective of the strategic foresight in geopolitical analysis is to anticipate different situations that may occur in order to help decision making processes on different levels, ranging from political, economic, and diplomatic to military.

In geopolitical analysis both objective and subjective factors have to be taken into consideration. Objective factors as such could include the size of a country or the demographic increase of a given population in a given geographic zone while subjective parameters could refer to the cognitive aspects of a geopolitical space or the symbolic meaning of a given territory for a nation. Subjective dimensions constitute the geopolitical representations that considerably influence the mindset of different actors seeking to control a given territory. Geographical or historical determinism is refuted in the geopolitical analysis approach presented in this book chapter. Geopolitical analysis is not the justification for control of a geographic zone by a given state due to a certain interpretation of history or religion disseminated through geopolitical representations. The geopolitical analyst has to take into consideration the different and often contradictory representations of diverse geopolitical actors seeking to claim a given territory or maritime zone.

1.1 *Geopolitical Analysis Method*

Geopolitics can be defined as the examination of interactions between political processes and geographic spaces in which these processes take place. Geopolitics is not a separate social science but rather an interdisciplinary method of analysis that integrates various branches of the social sciences; on the other hand, geopolitics is not the synthesis of the various disciplines in social sciences either. Geopolitical reasoning takes into consideration the geographical dimension that should be considered not only in its physical sense, but in terms of demographic, cultural and economic aspects as well. Furthermore, the external and internal factors related to the geopolitical situation in question need to be taken into account. These factors can be divided into constant, enduring and variable. Constant factors refer to some physical geographic factors such as location, enduring factors refer to cultural identity such as language or religion, and variable factors are those that change on both the internal level (inside of state borders) and external levels (interstate and global level). [1] These variable components refer to demography, socio-political structure, alliance configuration, strategic motivation, economic interest, and technological factors, among others. Also, historical factors have to be integrated into the analysis as these factors play an important role in the comprehension of a given geopolitical situation. The roots of power rivalries at present are very often to be found in the past. In conclusion, the geopolitical method can be defined as an analysis of the interactions between socio-political situations and their territorial dimensions, taking into consideration the historic, geographic, strategic, political, identity, demographic and economic factors related to these situations, at both the internal and external levels of states (Csurgai, 2005, p.19).

The main components of geopolitical analysis are the following:[2]

- Geographical configuration;
- Natural resources;
- Boundaries;
- Geopolitical representations;

1 While several physical geography factors such as location or shape of the territory can be considered as permanent factors, there are other factors in the category of physical geography such as climate change, different types of environmental degradations and natural resource depletion that are evolutive factors. For instance, due to relatively rapid process of melting ice in the Arctic due to climate change factors, the geopolitical landscape of the Artic region can change significantly in the near future. One example for this is the growing importance of *Northern Sea Route* (NSR), the shipping route extending from Europe across the top of Russia and exiting through the Bering strait to the Pacific Ocean. Melting Arctic ice caps are likely to increase traffic in and the commercial viability of the *Northern Sea Route* in the upcoming years. China has recognised the growing geopolitical significance of the Artic due to retreating ice, which offers potentially faster shipping route across the top of the world and easier access to energy resources and precious metals located in the Artic region. Beijing launched its *Polar Silk Road* project in 2018 as part of the Belt and Road Initiative.

2 There are other parameters including non-geographic factors that may impact geopolitics. For instance, international law is an important element in the examination of boundary issues and technological innovations can impact geopolitical power rivalries, among others.

- Geography of populations;
- Historical factors;
- Economic factors; and
- Strategy of Actors

The geopolitical method of analysis contains some elements of the so-called *systemic approach*. In this context, a geopolitical analyst has to first identify these parameters and then examine the interactions between these factors in different time and space considerations. The above-listed parameters are not isolated and are often overlapping. Each of the listed factors can interact with each other; a given geopolitical configuration is shaped by the interactions between these factors (Dussuoy, 2009, p. 224). The examination of the interrelations between these factors is carried out on different geographic scales:

- Within the state: on local, regional and national levels (internal geopolitics)
- Between states: on macro-regional, continental and global levels (external geopolitics)

A geopolitical analyst can be compared to an observer in a hot-air balloon who is permanently zooming in and out with a binocular from micro to macro and from macro to micro, in order to observe a given situation on the globe. A local geopolitical event is often influenced by external influences; a power rivalry between regional and global powers can impact the internal geopolitical configuration of a given country at a given moment in history due to its strategic location or its natural resources, amongst other factors. For instance, the geopolitical evolution of Kosovo has at the outset some local dimensions: the status of the Serb minority in that territory that also impacts the territorial organisation of Kosovo and its power sharing mechanism between the different communities, among other things. Secondly, the 2008 unilaterally declared independence of Kosovo can have some regional geopolitical implications, for instance for Macedonia, which has a considerable Albanian minority. On a continental level, the Kosovo independence experience may influence other nationalist movements across European states. On a global level, the Kosovo question has played an important role in power rivalries between major geopolitical actors such as the United States and Russia. The US gained an important strategic position in the southeast of Europe by supporting the independence of Kosovo while Russian regional influence weakened in the process. (Csurgai, 2005, pp.180–187)

1.2 *The Main Motivations of Geopolitical Actors to Control a Geographic Zone*

In geopolitical analysis, the strategies of different actors seeking to control or exercise some kinds of influence over a given geographic zone have to be examined. The area under examination can be a territorial or maritime zone. In some cases, the control of a given airspace can also become a geopolitical stake between different states. This for instance is the case between Greece and Turkey.[3]

States and non-state actors seek to control a given geographic zone and counter the strategies of rivals to control the same sector due to the perceived value considerations related to the contested area. The major value considerations in geopolitics that can influence the motivations of the different actors for control of a given geographic zone are the following:

- Wealth
- Strategic
- Cognitive factors
- Representation
- Regrouping of a same identity group

Wealth can refer to the objective of controlling an area rich in natural resources.[4] The specific location of a geographic zone such as the Golan Heights or Gibraltar can provide an advantageous position from a strategic perspective. Motivations related to representations for control of an area are largely influenced by the role of a given geographic zone in the collective identity of ethnic groups and nations. These representations are part of collective identity constructions and have an important psychological dimension for a given community. Therefore, these representations refer to the cognitive dimension of geopolitics. Symbols, myths, and certain interpretations of religion and national history are closely connected to given geographic zones contested by different groups. The question of Jerusalem, the perceptions of the Serbs and Albanians on Kosovo and the view of Lebanon in the collective mentality of Syrians, are all examples of rivalries related to geopolitical representations. Motivation for regrouping the same identity groups refers to uniting the same type of populations separated by political boundaries into one state: the struggle of the Kurds to create a *Kurdistan* is a typical example of this category.

Each geopolitical situation differs from another; consequently, the perceived value of contested areas varies from one to the other and varies for various actors. For instance, in a given case, one actor could have economic and strategic considerations while another actor's motivations can be related

3 Power rivalries in outer space and conflicts in the cyberspace impacting geopolitics can be mentioned as well; however, due to the limited length of this book chapter these issues are not discussed.

4 Further building upon this, Chapter 9 offers a compelling analysis of mapping 'greed' as a conflict motivation, with two illustrative case studies in Africa.

to geopolitical representations. The geopolitical analyst has to identify each actor's motivations: those who are already involved in a given geopolitical rivalry and those who can become potential actors as well. The elaboration of scenarios on the future involvement of potential actors is part of the geopolitical perspective.

2 The Main Components of Geopolitical Analysis

In the following parts of this book chapter the main parameters of geopolitical analysis are discussed. Each factor is explained and concrete examples on their influence on geopolitics are provided.

2.1 *Geographical Configuration*

Geographical configuration refers to factors of physical geography that should be taken into consideration in a geopolitical approach. These factors are the following: location, size, relief and shape of the territory, including its vegetation, hydrographical characteristics and natural resources.[5] Physical structure includes elements of topography and as well refers to surface features of a given geographic zone indicating their relative position, size and elevation. The geopolitical function of a given geographic zone – including a maritime space – derives from its perceived strategic importance held by pertinent geopolitical actors as regards its capacity for control of a given region and the potential for enhancing the defence capabilities of a country, increasing its geopolitical power and/or assuring control over vital communication lines. Therefore, the geopolitical function of a given territory in relation to its physical characteristics is an important factor in geopolitical analysis.

There are both constant and variable factors in the category of physical geography as it was mentioned earlier in this chapter. The size of a given state can change depending on historical circumstances. Moreover, climate change and environmental degradation are important variables that can impact considerably geopolitical power rivalries. Other physical elements of geography refer to permanent factors in geopolitics that can influence the foreign policy and military strategy of states over long periods of time. These constant factors should be examined as conditioning determinants interacting with other variables of geopolitics and should not be considered from a point of view of geographic determinism as the only component impacting states' foreign policies.

5 The natural resources factor will be discussed in the following section of this chapter.

Without presenting an exhaustive list, some examples are offered below in order to illustrate the influence of physical geography configurations of territories including their associated geopolitical functions perceived by different geopolitical actors.

The location of a country on the globe determines its ambit vis-à-vis important geographic zones: axes of road communication, harbours, rivers, important cities and regions, are just some examples. The geographic position of a state in a given historical period indicates the neighbouring states in its immediate geopolitical environment and distances from regional and extra-regional powers. The issue of distance held a major strategic consideration during the Cold War in Europe. The Warsaw Pact forces had a strategic advantage as they were concentrated in proximity to Western Europe. On the other hand, NATO forces on the continent had to be supplemented by US and Canadian detachments that would naturally take longer to deploy in case of a war. The distance between Europe and North America was not in favour of NATO forces but rather advantaged the Warsaw Pact countries in case of hostilities between these two military alliances. Moreover, location also defines the climate. Climatic conditions have a major impact on geopolitics in periods of peace as well as in times of war. Climate also influences socioeconomic activities of human communities and impacts their ways of life. The way of life is part of the collective identity structure of a given community and influences its mentality. Climate change is playing a growing influence on geopolitics. It can impact food security and livelihoods and can influence the evolution of collective identity factors of a given community. Desertification processes, the rise of sea levels, and natural resource depletion are major geopolitical risk factors that can significantly impact migration dynamics and conflicts related to the access of arable lands and natural resources such as fresh water.

Constant geographic factors can contribute to an advantageous power position for a state in a certain period of history while at other times it can lead to strategic vulnerability. The location of Switzerland at the crossroads of Europe is a very advantageous one from an economic and commercial point of view. However, the country found itself in a rather difficult situation during the Second World War when it was surrounded by countries with hostile political leanings: Nazi Germany, Fascist Italy, and a France occupied by Germany.

There are 48 landlocked nations in the world. Access to the sea can provide for the possibility of exploiting various natural resources (such as seafood/oil and gas) and furthermore offer the chance to integrate international trade with greater efficiency, increase tourist revenues, gain a potential military advantage and increase political influence (Gourdin, 2010, p.28). Conversely, losing access to the sea is of huge strategic loss for a state. Landlocked countries have always searched for ways to gain access to the open seas in order to expand their strategic and economic advantages. For example, with the independence of Eritrea in 1993, Ethiopia lost its access to the Red Sea. As political and economic relations with Eritrea have ever since been blocked due to hostility between the two states, Ethiopia has had to rely exclusively on Djibouti for seaport transit, conditions which have inhibited its economic development. The landlocked situation of Ethiopia, caused by its loss of control over Eritrea in 1993, resulted in the waning of its geostrategic position and contributed to its economic decline. The possibility cannot be excluded that tensions can re-escalate between these two countries as Ethiopia wants to regain access to the sea through a land corridor currently under the sovereignty of Eritrea.

Being in a buffer zone position can often mean geopolitical vulnerability for a country located between two or more competing powers. When relations are hostile between those powers or if extra-regional powers want to modify their zones of influence in the region, countries situated in buffer zones can be directly impacted by the rivalry of geopolitical forces to control them. The internal situation of Lebanon, located between Syria and Israel, has been greatly influenced by the hostility of these two countries towards each other. The location of Poland between Russia and Germany was a significant factor in the evolution of the territorial changes of the Polish state in the last couple of centuries. Territorial and border modifications and displacement of populations were greatly influenced by the geopolitical rivalry related to the control of Poland by Germans and Russians. Such an example was the 1939 *Nazi-Soviet Non-Aggression Pact* which resulted in the invasion of Poland by the Germans and Russians and led to the division of the Polish state into spheres of interest for these two powers.

The geopolitical function of mountains refers to their potential role in enhancing the defensive position of a given state. The mountains of Afghanistan offered refuge and an important element of defence for the guerrillas fighting the Soviet army in the 1980s and Western forces following the US-led invasion of this country in 2011. Afghanistan represents as well a strategic depth for Pakistan. In the eventuality of an Indian attack, Pakistani forces would be able to retreat to the mountainous region adjacent to their border with Afghanistan. Consequently, Afghanistan has an important geopolitical function in Pakistani strategic perceptions.

The maritime dimension is an important factor in the study of Geopolitics. Control of the seas and oceans has always represented an important strategic stake to geopolitical players. The competition between continental and maritime powers has been an essential part of geopolitical thinking and practises.[6] The increasing exploration of natural resources in maritime zones, in particular petroleum and gas, contributes to the growing geopolitical importance of seas and oceans. In this context for instance, the Arctic zone deserves special mention. Global maritime routes pass through specific locations corresponding to passages, canals, capes and straits. These major routes are utilised for the transport of raw materials (namely different minerals), some food products (such as grains, cocoa, and sugar), petroleum (and its by-products), and recently an increasing quantity of LNG (Liquefied Natural Gas) (Rodrige, Comtois & Slack, 2009, p.12). The potential disruption of these trade flows could negatively affect the increasingly globalised economy. In periods of war, the possibility of closure of an important maritime chokepoint represents an important strategic advantage over an adversarial power. For instance, the Iranian threat to close the Strait of Hormuz if Iran is attacked by Western powers or Israel is an illustration of the strategic importance of the security of maritime routes.

The strategic location of Gibraltar highlights its geopolitical function from a maritime strategy point of view. This territory, claimed by Spain, is under British sovereignty. It is located on the southern end of the Iberian Peninsula (and Europe) at the entrance of the Mediterranean Sea, overlooking the Strait of Gibraltar. Its territory covers 6.843 square kilometres and shares a land border with Spain to the north. Gibraltar has historically been an important base for the British armed forces and is the site of a Royal Navy base. Gibraltar's strategic location, in a connecting zone between the Atlantic Ocean and the Mediterranean Sea, is an important asset for Great Britain, a maritime power. During the Second World War, Gibraltar was used by the Anglo-American forces to deny the Italian and German fleet access to the Atlantic Ocean.

In spite of technological advances, the characteristics of physical structure of a given territory continue to exercise influence on the relations that a given human group has with its socioeconomic and political space. The constant factors of geography influence the way of life of populations, therefore these are also constituents of collective identity. Factors of physical geography can provide opportunities and signify vulnerabilities in periods of peace and war. These constant factors can influence the power of states; therefore, their interactions with different variables have to be examined in a geopolitical analysis. States can elaborate efficient strategies to seize the opportunities provided by favourable geographic factors and reduce the vulnerabilities caused by certain geographic constraints.

6 This question is discussed in chapter 3 on *Geopolitical Schools of Thought*.

2.2 *Natural Resources*

The control of geographic zones possessing natural resources has represented an important geopolitical stake throughout history. Rivers, such as the Nile and Euphrates, have played an important role in the emergence of the first agrarian and urban civilisations. The power of the Phoenician city states was based on the commerce of wood. The control of pepper played a considerable role in Portuguese colonial expansion in the 1500s, while for centuries, gold was an important element of commerce, linking the West to the Orient. Oil became a factor of military power during the First World War and its strategic importance has grown even more ever since. At present, the prosperity of highly industrialised countries of the North cannot be maintained without permanent access to those raw materials that are indispensable for economic production. In addition, one has to take into consideration the rapid economic growth of the so-called *emerging powers*,[7] mainly China and India. These countries have a growing need for natural resources in order to sustain the augmentation of their economic production and the rising levels of consumption by their growing middle-class population.

Demographic growth, combined with rapid industrialisation and the diffusion of consumer society in many parts of the world, has led to an ever-increasing demand for natural resources. This is especially the case, since in the last fifty years the global population has increased by three billion people. Even though, economic growth that resulted from industrialisation of the Southern Hemisphere did not benefit the entire population of developing countries, yet a considerable number of individuals found access to relatively high consumption levels.

Confrontation between the major powers over access and control of natural resources often directly influences the geopolitical situation in resource-rich areas of the South. For instance, rapidly increasing Chinese influence in a great number of African countries, efforts to maintain French troops in several nations in Africa, and foreign influence over conflicts occurring in the Democratic Republic of Congo, among other examples, illustrate the increasing importance of resource interests.

The motivation to sell arms and provide different types of support to a political regime, or to various kinds of non-state actors ranging from warlords

---

7 The concept of re-emerging powers may be used for the current rising powers of China and India as these countries played an important role in earlier periods of history as well. For instance, China was the world's leading trading nation up to the eighteenth century, until control of its ports and trade were taken over by imperial nations of Europe.

to different ethnic groups fighting the central government, are largely influenced by resource considerations. This phenomenon particularly concerns the so-called *weak states*, and *de-structured* or *failed states*. As state authority weakens or partially disappears, grey zones can emerge in resource-rich areas controlled by sub-state actors. These actors, varying from ethnic secessionist movements to organised criminal groups and terrorist organisations, seek control over natural resources, as the resulting profit from their exploitation and commerce serves to maintain their power, finance their military activities, and enrich them. External state and non-state actors can become involved in such kinds of internal geopolitical state of affairs, relating to states, by manipulating different groups due to the economic significance of resources.[8] External actors can be neighbouring and/or extra-regional states, or non-state actors, such as, enterprises, private military forces, or ethnic groups from neighbouring countries, motivated by gaining access to resources. Resources such as diamond, cobalt and gold, have played a considerable role, for instance, in the internal conflicts taking place in the Democratic Republic of Congo, Angola, or Sierra Leone, in recent years. Sapphires and rubies were an important source of revenue for the Khmer Rouge in Cambodia (Le Billon, 2005, p. 9). The growing activities of enterprises of those states which have rapidly growing economies, such as China, India and others, in resource-rich areas, have led to an ever-increasing level of competition with big Western mining interests. This process has often resulted in the increase in interference by both Western and non-Western companies into the internal affairs of resource-rich countries, and in some cases, to the militarisation of resource sectors (Le Billon, 2013, p. 3).

In the context of the growing need for natural resources, the issue of limited availability has to be taken into consideration. This is particularly relevant as concerns petroleum and water. According to certain estimations, in the second-half of the 21st century, the world might confront serious shortages of oil and water, due to insufficient supply, and the need to meet an ever-increasing global demand (Klare, 2013). Certain natural resources are considered strategic by states as access to them is vital for economic function and military capacity. Therefore, states want to maintain permanent access to these resources. The supply route security of these resources is a vital geopolitical stake for states. In this context, the following resources can be mentioned: water, oil, natural

8 On this subject, one can consult the books of Le Billon, P. (Ed.) (2005). *Geopolitics of Resources Wars, Resource Dependence, Governance and Violence.* New York: Routledge, and Le Billon, P. (Ed.) (2013). *Wars of Plunder, Conflicts, Profits and the Politics of Resources.* Oxford University Press.

gas, and certain minerals. (Minerals, such as, chrome, vanadium, beryllium and tungsten, for instance, are used in the production of aeroplanes). In his book, *Resource Wars*, Michael T. Klare argues that geopolitical rivalries related to control of natural resources will be the most likely causes of war in the 21st century (Klare, 2001). According to Klare, the main causes of these resource-related conflicts originate from:

- Escalating demand by rapidly growing populations for scarce resources;
- Uneven geographic distribution of resources;
- Location of these resources in regions torn by ethnic and political unrest; and
- Influences of competing global powers in these resource-rich regions.

One of the most important characteristics of natural resources is their uneven geographic distribution. The issue of controlling certain geographic zones can lead to geopolitical rivalries, due to the high concentration of natural resources in these areas. To illustrate, it can be mentioned that the "volatile" Middle East holds about two-thirds of the world's proven oil reserves. The fact that there are geographic zones with high natural resource concentration, while there are other deficient regions, or those lacking resources altogether, leads to the need for the *flow of resources*. States are forced to import necessary resources from resource-rich geographic regions, making control of the flow of such resources a major strategic imperative. For example, the transport of oil can be mentioned here: assuring the security of maritime transport routes is a geostrategic imperative for the *great powers*, as an important quantity of oil is shipped to major consuming countries through these linkages. Concerning land routes, the geography of pipelines has innumerable strategic and economic dimensions. Geopolitical problems can arise in different types of situations in which the control of natural resources becomes an objective for the various actors. These kinds of situations can occur within states and/or between two or more of them. Geopolitical tension and conflict can arise over the allocation of a particular source of supply that crosses international borders, such as a large river, or an underground oil basin.

Another key issue facing the twenty-first century is food security. Demographic growth, environmental degradation, and water scarcity, are some of the major factors, among others, which may impact the capacity of states to assure adequate nutrition for their citizens. Increasing importance of fishing zones can be mentioned, as well as the control of these areas, are becoming important geopolitical stakes. The rise in the cost of foodstuff in the last decade has been a contributing factor to socioeconomic instability, and in certain cases, led to political upheavals. Rising food prices, for instance, contributed to the discontent that led to the so-called Arab Spring uprisings. As a matter of fact, arable land access has become a rather significant factor in natural-resource related rivalries, as the important contracts of land-lease in Africa and other parts of the world illustrate. Important shortages of other vital natural resources can be expected in the coming decades. The natural forest cover of the world has been shrinking at a rate of 0.5% a year. This process, combined with a gradual rise in average global temperature, can contribute to a number of environmental scarcity issues, threatening the survival of countless plant and animal species, which can further inflame competition between human communities over access to vital natural resources (Klare, 2001, p. 20). Due to its limited length, this book chapter cannot cover all aspects of natural-resource related issues; the following section discusses some aspects of the role of fresh water in geopolitics.

Fresh water is an indispensable resource. It is a vital element for human life, and any activity somehow relates to water. At present, an estimated quarter of the world's population does not have access to a satisfactory quality of water. Furthermore, 700 million people in 43 countries are affected by water scarcity, while this number is estimated to rise to 1.8 billion by 2025 (UNDESA, 2018). In the last one hundred years, consumption of water has grown by about 700 percent. The main causes of this evolution are to be found in demographic growth, industrialisation, changes in agricultural production, urbanisation, desertification, and modifications in consumption patterns. Currently, agriculture represents roughly 70% of the world's consumption of water, industry 20%, and human consumption, 10 percent (UNEP, 2018). In all, 30 countries are confronted with a serious fresh water scarcity problem. Demand for fresh water is expected to rise by another 40% by 2030. Moreover, the increase of water usage for unconventional gas production and oil drilling (oil sands, shale gas, and shale oil, among others) can be mentioned. Climate change then, may impact future patterns of fresh water availability and use, and consequently impact water security.

97% of all water on the Earth is saltwater. Even still, slightly over two-thirds of the remaining 3% is frozen in glaciers and polar ice caps. The remaining unfrozen freshwater is mainly located in underground reservoirs, with only a small fraction present above ground. Also, the uneven geographic distribution of freshwater reserves has to be taken into consideration. Ten countries possess an estimated 60% of the natural fresh water reserves of the world: Brazil, Russia, Canada, United States, Indonesia, China, Columbia, Peru, India, and the Democratic Republic of Congo. On the other hand, 30 countries are confronted with a serious fresh water scarcity problem. For instance, in the Middle East region, nine countries are confronted with a problem of fresh water scarcity.

Water scarcity incorporates water stress, water deficit, water shortage, and water crisis. The concept of water stress is relatively new. Water stress is the difficulty of obtaining sources of fresh water for use, because of depleting resources. Scarcity is assessed by hydrologists, typically by considering the *population-water equation*. An area is experiencing water stress when annual water supplies drop below 1,700 m3 per person.[9] When annual water supplies drop below 1,000 m3 per person, the population faces water scarcity, and below 500 cubic metres, "absolute scarcity".[10] A water crisis is a situation where the available potable, unpolluted water within a region is less than its demand. The concept of water scarcity may refer to physical water scarcity and/or economic water scarcity.[11] Physical water scarcity refers to a situation when there is not enough fresh water to meet the demands of a given population, including what is needed for ecosystems to function effectively. Arid regions frequently suffer from physical water scarcity. Symptoms of physical water scarcity include environmental degradation and declining groundwater.

Economic water scarcity can result from the lack of investment in water-related infrastructure or reduced socioeconomic capacity to satisfy the demand for fresh water. Symptoms of economic water scarcity include, a lack of infrastructure where people often have to *fetch* water from rivers for domestic and agricultural purposes. Economic water scarcity affects considerable geographic areas of Africa, creating obstacles for poverty-reduction and development. In certain situations, critical shortages of fresh water can occur when both economic and physical water scarcity are combined and affect populations.

According to Pacific Institute (Pacific Institute, 2019), the following water-related conflicts can occur:

- **Control of Water Resources** (state and non-state actors): where water supplies, or access to water, are at the root of tensions;
- **Military Tool** (state actors): where water resources, or the systems themselves, are used by a nation or state as a weapon of military action;

---

9 Definitions based on those provided by United Nations Department of Economic and Social Affairs, (UNDESA), http://www.un.org/waterforlifedecade/scarcity.shtml, accessed on the 11 January 2018.

10 Ibid.

11 Definitions on Economic and Physical Water Scarcity are based on The United Nations World Water Development Report, 2016, Published by the United Nations Educational, Scientific and Cultural Organisation, (UNESCO) Paris, 2016, p.18. available on: http://www.unwater.org.

- **Political Tool** (state and non-state actors): where water resources, or the systems themselves, are used by a nation, state, or non-state actor, for a political endgame;
- **Terrorism** (non-state actors): where water resources, or the systems, are either targets, or tools, of violence or coercion by non-state actors;
- **Military Target** (state actors): where water resource systems are targets of military action by nations or states;
- **Development Disputes** (state and non-state actors): where water resources, or systems, are a major source of contention and dispute, in the context of economic and social development.

The abovementioned categories can overlap as a specific water conflict situation can fall into more than one type of category. For example, intentional military attacks on water-supply systems can fall under both categories of *Targets* and *Tools* (Pacific Institute, 2019).

Geopolitical rivalries related to access and control of fresh water can take place both within states (intrastate) and between them (interstate). Intrastate conflicts can arise from competition over access to fresh water between sub-state entities (region, an ethnic group, etc.) and the central state authorities, or between different sub-state actors. Interstate freshwater-related geopolitical conflicts can result due to the fact that aquifers, lakes, and rivers, can be situated in transboundary regions. Since a river which extends along international boundaries arises in a certain country, or has sources in more than one country, while carrying water through other countries before reaching its egress in the sea, the *upstream states* can influence the flow to those *downstream*. Conflict often arises when the upstream state uses its capacity to increase its water allocations at the expense of those lying downstream. The Nile River extends through eleven countries. It is the longest river in the world (6695 km). The source of the White Nile is Lake Victoria in Uganda and that of the Blue Nile is Lake Tana in Ethiopia. The Nile's water resources are shared by 11 countries: Tanzania, Uganda, Rwanda, Burundi, Democratic Republic of Congo, Kenya, Ethiopia, Eritrea, Sudan, South Sudan, and Egypt. This river flows downhill from high mountains in Central Africa to the Mediterranean Sea. Its basin has a population of 450 million, one which is expected to rise rapidly due to high reproduction rates. Four countries share 85% of the total area of the Nile Basin: Ethiopia, Sudan, South Sudan, and Egypt. The main portion of Nile waters reaching Egypt originate from Ethiopia. The length of the Nile that flows through Egypt runs for 1200 kilometres and represents 98% of the fresh water supply for those Egyptians who live in its proximity (Galland, 2014, p.150). More than 90% of the population of the country lives in this area. Egypt is one of the most populous countries in Africa and the Middle East, with an estimated population of roughly 94 million (UN data, 2019). This number can surpass 100 million by 2025 and even reach 120 million by 2050, due to high reproduction rates. These demographic factors, and the fact that agricultural production is overwhelmingly concentrated in the Nile region, explain the importance of the Nile River for Egypt, a regional power and a downstream riparian state. Water shortages and limited availability of arable acreage result in the need for food imports by Egypt.

As well, it is important to recall the vital role that the Nile River has played in the birth and development of Egypt's civilisation and society, and resultantly, it has exercised a huge influence on the collective identity of Egyptians. The Nile River issue plays a very important role in the foreign policy and security perceptions of this country. Egypt is opposed to the construction of dams on the Blue Nile on Ethiopian territory due to its fears relating to the potential reduction of fresh water volume inflow unto its own territories. On the other hand, Ethiopia would like to use more water from the Nile for irrigation and therefore considers the construction of hydroelectric plants on the river as necessary tools for its own socioeconomic development. Only 2% of the rural population of Ethiopia has access to electricity while only 20% of the country's populace are urban (Dionet-Grivet, 2014, p. 164). The current population of Ethiopia is 101 million but it can reach well above 125 million by 2050. Consequently, food security is a key issue for this country. The relations between Egypt and Ethiopia have deteriorated considerably since the 1990s due to their dispute over the Nile River. Increased cooperation between Egypt and other riparian states of the Nile River is necessary in order to enhance stability and development, and prevent an armed conflict over water resources.

The debate is far from over among experts regarding prospects of the future evolution of freshwater-related conflicts. Will water-wars occur in the 21st century? It is important to recall that managing access to fresh water and developing water infrastructure can be sources of cooperation as well between different countries. Historically, tensions over access to fresh water have resulted in more water-sharing agreements than armed conflicts. For example, disputes between Pakistan and India over the Indus River system have been addressed through their bilateral Indus Water Treaty of 1960. The integration of an effective water resource management system is security imperative for most states. However, a rapidly growing fresh water demand that does not correspond to available supplies can put into question the existing water agreements between countries. Future scenarios, whereby powerful nations would impose their policies in various water-related geopolitical conflicts by the use of force to obtain enhanced control of fresh water, cannot be excluded either.

2.3 *Boundaries*

Frontier zones, representing the limits of the geographic extensions of powers, have been part of human history for a very long time. The "Limes", the frontier of the Roman Empire, had an important strategic role in the defence system of the Romans (Luttwak, 1999, p. 112). International boundaries[12] emerged in Europe and then spread throughout the world after the *Thirty Years' War*. The *Treaty of Westphalia* in 1648, marked the end of this war and established the modern state system. States had exclusive sovereignty over their territories delimited by borders. Boundary lines replaced frontier-zones with the emergence of the modern state system; this evolution meant a major distinction between frontiers and boundaries. Frontiers did not represent lines but rather zones with larger spatial extensions than boundary lines (Anderson, 1999, p. 127). Also, boundaries have a vertical dimension that enables the state to claim air and subterranean space (Anderson, 1999, p. 127).

Borders have three points of reference: the real, the symbolic, and the imaginary (Foucher, 1991, p. 38). The *Real Dimension* refers to spatial limits of the exercise of sovereignty of a given state in its proper modalities: open boundary lines, semi-open, and closed. The *Symbolic Dimension* refers to the role of borders in the collective identity of a given population, and their mental representations related to the limits of their territory. Often, these representations refer not only to the actual limits of the territory of the state, but also to limits of former territorial configurations. The *Imaginary Dimension* of the border refers to the relation with the "Other", the neighbour, friend or enemy, situated outside of the state borders (Foucher, 1991, p. 38).

A boundary is a line that forms the limits of the territory of a state. The sovereignty of a given state ends at the state border and the sovereignty of another state starts from there. Borders form a geographic zone of contact and separation between two or more states, except in certain cases of maritime boundaries. Whether a state boundary is open to different flows or represents a barrier to different types of exchanges between populations separated by this border depends on the nature of relations between states sharing the border. As Michel Foucher, French expert on the geopolitics of borders, states: "There are no border problems; there are only problems with regard to relations between states and people around borders" (Foucher, 2001, p. 162). Borders have political, administrative, and military functions. The *border* defines political competencies of a state over its territory. The *administrative role* is linked to the control and regulation of flows transiting state borders. The *military function*

12 The terms border and boundary are used in an interchanging way in this chapter.

refers to the role of boundaries in the defence of the territorial integrity of the state, and in the protection of its security.

The geopolitical analysis of borders seeks to understand the effects of boundary lines on the internal and external interactions that take place on territories separated by boundaries, on the political elites of states, and on peoples; it also takes into consideration geopolitical discourses and representations linked to the boundaries (Foucher, 2001, p. 48). There are not only political borders that separate states, but also borders that represent limits of a territorial entity within a state: for instance, an autonomous region, a federal unit, provinces and cantons, etc. The territorial organisation of a given state is an important factor in internal geopolitics, in particular in the case of states that are constituted of different types of communities in terms of language and religion. This is particularly the case when such groups represent a relative or absolute majority in a given geographic zone within a state. In some political and constitutional arrangements of the territorial divisions of a given state in different sub-state entities, delimiting the territories of different types of populations can be perceived as a satisfactory political arrangement for the populations living in these zones.

At times, a given community can contest the internal territorial arrangements of a state and seek to modify the territorial limits of its respective sub-state area for a multiplicity of reasons: to better increase its economic power; to gain increased access to natural resources; to regroup the same type of populations in a geographic area; and/or, to enhance the conditions for preserving its cultural identity. The establishment of the Canton of Jura provides a relevant example for modification of internal boundaries, as demonstrated in Switzerland. This canton, covering an area of 839 square kilometres and having a population of 72,000 habitants, officially became the 23rd canton of the Swiss Confederation in 1979. The predominantly Francophone Roman Catholic population of Jura wanted to separate from the mainly Protestant German speaking Canton of Bern, and hence, requested the creation of a new canton. This demand was accepted by a popular vote of the Swiss people and a constitutional change was made.

Borders can also refer to the limits of the spatial distribution of language, religion and ethnicity; for instance, the geographic distribution of: the Shia and Sunni communities in the Middle East; the Arab population in Africa; the different ethnic groups in Southeast Europe; and so on. Likewise, borders can refer to the limits of economic zones, such as the Eurozone, for instance, representing countries that adopted the Euro as their official currency. Yet, most of the spatial units that can be drawn on a given map to represent different characteristics of a particular territory (natural resources, spatial distribution of populations, relief shapes, distribution of languages and religions, and so on) have limits that do not coincide with limits of other spatial units; these different spatial units form a series of intersections (Lacoste, 2001, p. 157). This fact has a very important geopolitical dimension, in particular in the context of borders. In most of these cases, borders cross intersections which form the limits of the different spatial units (Foucher, 1991, p.31). In particular, this has geopolitical consequences when borders do not spatially coincide with geographic limits of populations. Territorial claims based on the fact that borders do not coincide with the limits of nations and ethnic groups can result in boundary conflicts. There are some nations that are divided by political frontiers. The case of the Albanians or Hungarians in Europe illustrates this problem. Significant portions of both of these nations live at present under the sovereignty of neighbouring countries. The geopolitical division of these communities results from the imposition of state borders during specific historical circumstances by different powers.

Most borders are results of a military balance of power between different nations, or group of nations, during a certain historical epoch. Territorial rivalries between states seeking border modifications can be suppressed for different lengths of time under the influence of other and more powerful states. From a geopolitical point of view, what has to be examined is whether a state, or states, accept(s) a territorial status quo with their border limits or not. This question should not only be examined for the present, but also be put into the context of a prospective analysis. If at present, a given state accepts its boundaries, under what circumstances may this state opt for a different policy and seek border modifications? How can power relations affect this intention of a given state? Are there other states in the region, or extra-regional powers that may support a policy of border modification?

An important reference is the border treaty that defined the current boundaries in a given geopolitical configuration. The process through which borders were demarcated and delineated is critical for understanding how they are managed and the extent to which they are more or less open to different flows (Newman, 2003, p. 13). Often borders were imposed on a given state by external powers as a result of the division of an area into spheres of influence among themselves. About 85% of the borders of Third World states were drawn by the end of the 19th century; in this process, the British and French played a considerable role by drawing-up about 40% of all boundaries outside of Europe (Foucher, 2001, p. 160). Boundary lines have frequently reflected the division of a geographic zone into different spheres of interest for the great powers.

Ethnic, geographic factors, and economic interests of the countries on which borders were imposed, were often neglected. This unilateral definition of borderlines was perceived as a temporary one by the state on which its borders were imposed and has often led to the contest of these borders at a later period. Approximately one-quarter of the world's land boundaries can be considered unstable, and two-thirds of the global maritime boundaries have to be settled (Anderson, 1999, p. 125).

The Durand Line refers to the border between Afghanistan and Pakistan, which is approximately 2,640 kilometres long. It was created after the 1893 Durand Line Agreement between the colonial government of British India (Pakistan was part of the British Indian Empire) and the Afghan Amir Abdur Rahman Khan, for fixing the limits of their respective spheres of influence. A joint British-Afghan demarcation survey commenced from 1894, covering some 800 miles of the border. The resulting Durand Line established the buffer zone between British and Russian interests in the region. This poorly marked border goes through the Pashtun Tribal Area and the zones inhabited by the Baluchi population, and as a result, it divides these communities. Although the Durand Line is shown on most maps as the international border between Pakistan and Afghanistan, it is unrecognised by the latter and remains a factor of instability between these two countries.

When analysing a given geopolitical configuration, a classification of the size of all the different spatial units has to be taken into consideration, whether these units are related to physical or human geography (distribution of natural resources, distribution of language and religion, limits of an ethnic group, and so on). This multi-map and multi-scalar approach is a very important part of the geopolitical analysis method (Foucher, 2001, p. 163). The representation of these different orders, varying from the local to the global as a series of superimposed plans with a map for each, showing the intersections of the groupings of related dimensions mapped on the same scale, is necessary (Lacoste, 2001, p.31). The data that appears at each of the different levels should be examined with the characteristics of intersections showing the differences between the limits of various units. For instance, the non-coincidence of limits between state borders and ethnic communities, or between natural resources and state borders, illustrates the issue of intersections between various units. Examination of the intersections is important to understand the geopolitical problems related to the control of a geographic zone, whether this is a matter of rivalries at global, national, regional, or local level (Lacoste, 2001, p.31).

Maritime boundary questions have gained considerable importance in recent decades, due in particular to the growing economic and strategic importance of maritime zones. The 1958 Geneva Convention on the Territorial Sea and the Contiguous Zone, recognised the rights of a coastal state over its continental shelf. As a result, the number of potential disputes over boundaries has grown due to the rivalry of maritime claims (Anderson, 1999, p.129). Under the 1982 United Nations Convention on the Law of the Sea (UNCLOS), coastal states may claim sovereign rights over the living and non-living resources of the sea and seabed in an Exclusive Economic Zone (EEZ) extending up to 200 nautical miles from their coastal baselines. The *continental shelf* claim by states can lead to the extension of their rights over maritime zones. Where the physical continental margin extends beyond 200 nautical miles, the states also have rights over the resources of the seabed to the outer limit of the continental shelf. State's continental shelf may exceed 200 nautical miles until the natural prolongation ends. However, it may never exceed 350 nautical miles from the baseline.[13] The shelf usually ends at a point of increasing slope (called the shelf break). The sea floor below the break is the continental slope. Below the slope is the continental rise, which finally merges into the deep ocean floor, the abyssal plain. The continental shelf and the slope are part of the continental margin.[14]

The Spratly Islands dispute is a relevant example of the increasing importance of maritime boundaries. China claims the entire Spratly Archipelago, as Beijing seeks to establish an Exclusive Economic Zone (EEZ) covering most of the South China Sea. This has led to tensions between China and other states claiming their respective EEZs, including Brunei, Indonesia, Malaysia, the Philippines, Taiwan and Vietnam. The Spratly Islands represent an important maritime zone, due to their strategic location and potential oil and gas production capacity. Moreover, the South China Sea fisheries are vital to the economies of the claimant states. The area holds at least 3,365 species of marine fish; 55% of global marine fishing vessels operate in the South China Sea and some 12% of global fishing catches take place here. Fish is an extremely important source of nutrition for the states claiming EEZ in the South China Sea as fisheries employ at least 3.7 million people (Fridtjof Nansens Institute, 2019). China has backed its expansive claims with island-building and naval patrols; a runway is also under construction on Fiery Cross Reef in the Spratly Islands. The reclaimed land is China's most important base in those waters and the runway would allow the Chinese military to conduct more air patrols meant to enforce

---

13 Source of definition of Continental shelf: http://www.worldatlas.com/articles/what-is-a-continental-shelf.html, accessed on January 2019.

14 Ibid.

its territorial ambitions. The US maintains an active military presence in the region in order to balance Chinese military power vis-à-vis the other states in competition with China over the delimitations of EEZs on Spratly Islands.

"According to historical situations and contingencies, a frontier can be a separating line, or, on the contrary, a contact area" (Ratti & Reichman, 1993, p. 23). In the majority of geopolitical situations, modification of borders cannot solve territorial questions between states as the spatial distribution of ethnic groups is heterogeneous, therefore, border limits cannot coincide with limits of the geographic distribution of different populations. Moreover, economic integration processes in different regions of the world lead to more intensified flows of goods and people in these geographic areas. Thus, the solution is not to modify borders but to alter their function (Foucher, 1991, p. 13). The opening of state borders can reduce or eliminate their 'border-barrier' effects. This happened gradually in Western European countries in the context of the European integration process. Border regions, for instance, in Central and Eastern Europe, can become contact areas, as has happened in the European Union.

2.4 *Geopolitical Representations*

To understand a geopolitical rivalry, it is necessary to examine the role of ideas which influence the mindset of different actors seeking control over a given territory (Lacoste, 2003, p. 4). These ideas, called representations in geopolitics, often refer to a subjective dimension of a given territory in the collective mentality of a human group, connected to national myths, symbols, religion, and a specific interpretation of history. These "mental maps" relate to the cognitive dimension of geopolitics and may considerably influence geopolitical situations, as they can refer to contradictory representations (Lassarre, Gonon & Mottet, 2016, p. 27). [15] For instance, the rivalry of representations related to Jerusalem in the three main monotheistic religions of Judaism, Christianity, and Islam, vis-à-vis their relevant political influences on the controversies over the political status of this city, provides a pertinent example of rivalries as concerns geopolitical representations.[16] The narratives of Serbs on Kos-

15 The concept of "mental maps" and Cognitive Geopolitics has a rich intellectual history and application, which is not always fully appreciated in the existing geopolitical literature. Chapter 4 of this book deals with the intellectual contribution of the American scholars Harold and Margaret Sprout in this area. Chapter 8 offers an applied analysis to the 'Carter Doctrine' of the American president Jimmy Carter between 1977 and 1981.

16 Building upon, though separate from the insights of Cognitive Geopolitics, the school of thoughts of Hérodote (Yves Lacoste) in France and Critical Geopolitics in the Anglo-Saxon literature have further conceptually and theoretically developed the function which geopolitical representations play in the dynamics of foreign policy and our analyti-

ovo emphasise the important role this region plays in their national identity. Although at present Kosovo is populated by a majority Kosovar Albanian population while having gained independence from Serbia, the Serbs still have a rather strong emotional attachment to this area, which is considered by them as the cradle of their civilisation. The influence of these cognitive, and consequently immaterial, factors, is an important parameter to study in geopolitical analysis as these representations can be exploited to become the foundations of geopolitical projects. Different mental maps of two or more competing groups can refer to the same territory, therefore geopolitical tension and conflict can arise in rivalry over these contradictory representations. A group can claim a given territory and justify its claim through a certain interpretation of religion and history, most often based on rather subjective factors. Another group can justify its own claim, using a counter representation that is most often also based on a subjective interpretation of historical and/or religious factors, in order to rationalise control over the same space.

Representations can be diffused through various narratives and discourses. By way of these discourses, political leaders, members of religious movements, and heads of nationalist parties, for example, can mobilise public opinion and exploit such geopolitical representations. There are various means for the transmission of geopolitical representations, in form of maps, narratives, discourses, songs and films; family, church, political parties, art and culture, education system, among others, can be agents of transmission of representations, narratives and discourses, as well. Interpretations of history of human groups are often based on myths and symbols in their geopolitical representations. These interpretations of history, accompanied by the use of rather subjective maps, serve to construct the arguments in favour of a territorial claim. There are often references made to a "*golden age*", when a nation controlled huge territories, while at present some of these same places are controlled by another state. This "*golden age*" is presented as a period of considerable progress, stability, and general well-being of the nation. The nation has a "*missionary role*" to expand its geopolitical influence over a contested geographic zone in order to regain its power and lost grandeur. The possession of a given territory appears in the geopolitical discourse as a solution to the problems of the nation. The narrative of the counter representations of the other nation transmits a similar message, with opposite

cal understanding of problems of international relations. These theoretical contributions built further upon, amongst others, the insights of Social Constructivism. They are further developed in Chapter 3 on the main geopolitical schools of thought. Furthermore, Chapter 5 develops a profound criticism of Critical Geopolitics and, in doing so, proposes an alternative 'Analytic Geopolitics' – combining both material and ideational factors.

arguments, to defend its own *"rights"* to a territory. It is not a coincidence if this kind of message can correspond to the expectation of a nation, in particular in a given socio-political and historical context. When a given nation finds itself in political turmoil, or goes through an identity crisis, the use of geopolitical representations and discourses can have considerable impact on a large portion of the population, due to their potential cognitive impact.

Images have a more important and almost immediate impact on people than written texts. Images of the *natural frontier*, the *lost territories*, the *strategically important zones*, and spatial distribution of ethnic groups, are instruments that can be used for the transmission of a geopolitical narrative through representations. Such maps presented in schools are often small and not very detailed; more than anything they represent a symbolic image of a given country rather than scientific geographic data. Maps are accompanied by manuals of history which are also important means of transmission of geopolitical discourses and narratives corresponding to a rather subjective interpretation of history. A selective version of the history of the nation is taught with the objective to diffuse the official geopolitical representations and narratives. These representations, transmitted through the educational system to younger generations as a given, would be considered very important by political elites concerned with raising "geographic and historical consciousness" in their citizens at a relatively early age. In a geopolitical analysis, the objective is to examine the impact of each different representation on the strategy of the actors, and not to justify territorial claims based on these representations. The representation of one actor, based for instance on the *"historical rights"* of the nation, should be examined as well as the counter representation of another actor based on its own perceived *"historical rights."* In this way, geopolitical understanding of events goes beyond a rather simplistic presentation of tensions, conflicts and wars, where the role of the *"good"* and *"bad"* sides is attributed according to a rather schematic way of thinking. In a geopolitical analysis, the objective is not to judge the rightness or wrongness of competing and contradictory geopolitical representations, discourses and narratives, but to understand the influence of these cognitive factors on the strategies of the actors. This multi-perspective approach is an important element of the understanding of a geopolitical rivalry.

A geopolitical analysis seeks to examine the construction process of these representations. In this context, the main constituents related to different identity factors should be examined. The interpretation of different historical and religious factors, myths and symbols, among others, should be taken into consideration. Also, the following question should be answered: *Why have certain geopolitical representations emerged in a given historical period?* Second, the meaning of these representations for a given population should be examined. Third, the different means of transmission of these representations should be analysed. Fourth, exploitation of these representations by the elite of a given country should be studied. In what kind of political situation geopolitical representations can become powerful instruments of political mobilisation? In this context, the timing related to the socio-political environment of a given society and the political impact of representations should be analysed. Fifth, the question should be asked: *Whether there is a geopolitical project behind the exploitation of the representations by a given political leadership?* Additionally, if the answer is yes, what is this project about?

2.5 *Geography of Population*

Ethnicity, language, religion and relevant cultural and historical factors constitute the main collective identity factors that influence geopolitical situations of human groups. Cultural and national identities influence perceptions, beliefs, norms, and values of a given community. Collective mentality is an expression of these identities and impacts the behaviours, attitudes, reasoning processes, and strategies of actors in a given geopolitical situation. Therefore, the study of ethnic, cultural and national identities in geopolitics is very important. There is a fundamental link between territory and identity. To divide and control territories has been a constant psychological factor in the organisation of human societies throughout history (Charnay, 1992, p. 166). These human societies can be classified as clans, tribes, ethnic groups, nations and civilisations.

Cultural, ethnic, and national identities, in a given geopolitical situation, can prevail over social, economic, and gender identities. In the disintegration process of the former Yugoslavia, ethno-cultural and national identity was a decisive mobilising factor. Croatian individuals, or groups, belonging to the working class (an important category for Marxists) or other professional categories did not ally with their fellow social class groups of Serbians but identified themselves primarily as Croatians, while the same happened to different socioeconomic groups of Serbs who primarily identified themselves as members of the Serbian nation. A similar phenomenon occurred with age and gender identities as these characteristics were not primary factors of identification for Croats and Serbs. Ethno-cultural and national identity was a superior force of cohesion and primary mobilising factor as compared with other sources of identity in the wars leading to the disintegration of the former Yugoslavia. Similar phenomena were observed in other crises and war situations in different parts of the world.

In a considerable number of states, there is a conflicting relationship between two identities: civic and ethno-cultural. The first refers to the situation in which all persons living on the territory of a state, delimited by its sovereignty, are citizens of that nation regardless of their ethno-cultural origin; this concept is frequently defined as the *civic-nation*. Nationhood is defined by common citizenship. The creation of the British nation state at the end of the 18th century, or the French nation state born out of the French Revolution, are examples of *Civic Nationalism*. In this kind of statehood, the state creates the nation. The second identity concept refers to the ethno-cultural origins of a national community, often called ethnic-nation or "Kulturnation". In this approach, nationhood is defined by shared language, religion, customs and traditions. Therefore, emphasis is placed on belonging to an ethno-cultural community that can stretch over state borders. The *Ethnic Nationalism* concept originated in Germany's reaction to the French ideal of the nation-state. From late 18th century on, German Romanticism emphasised the political legitimacy of the state based on the ethno-cultural unity of the people, contrary to the French nation state ideology based on *civic nationalism*. The German emphasis on the ethno-cultural origin of the nation-state influenced people in different parts of Eastern Europe, in particular from 19th century onward. These populations had often lived under the domination of various empires, and their elites assumed that their common ethno-cultural origin could be a significant force to unite them in struggling for their independence (Csurgai, 2005, p. 65). The mixture of these two concepts of the nation frequently creates tension in states composed of diverse ethnic communities. The situation of the Kurds in Turkey, or the Serbs in Bosnia Herzegovina, point to some of the examples vis-à-vis this issue.

One of the principal factors behind geopolitical tensions and conflicts lies in the inadequate territorial configuration pertaining to ethnic groups and states. This factor relates to the concept of *intersection*, discussed in the section on *Borders*, in this chapter. The first dimension of the non-coincidence of political limits of territories and geographic distribution of populations refers to the internal geopolitics of states (Lacoste, 2003, p. 15). Within states, an ethnic group, or groups, can seek more power to control territories where they reside and generally form the majority of the population. The contest of control over a territory in a given state by an ethnic group, or groups, representing a minority vis-à-vis the majority population of that state, can lead to the re-defining of the status of those minorities. This question is closely related to the power-sharing mechanism and territorial organisation of the nation-state. In certain cases, power rivalry with the central authorities of the state can lead to an armed conflict if an ethnic group seeks secession to create its own state.

The second dimension of the non-correspondence of territories of ethnic groups and states refers to the problem of contesting control of territories between states. A state can contest a given territory that is under the sovereignty of another state based on the fact that the territory in question is populated by the same ethnicity as the population of the contesting state. Territorial claims based on ethnicity can also result in boundary problems. A state contesting a territorial arrangement can seek border changes as it perceives the boundary-line as an injustice since the border divides the nation and consequently parts of the national community get dispersed in different neighbouring countries.

As the secession of Kosovo from Serbia illustrated, in Europe, movements of national emancipation that affect multi-ethnic and multi-national states and their neighbours, are confronted with crucial geopolitical questions: What sort of political sovereignty is to be sought? What will be the territorial arrangements and how will they be realised; through negotiation, attribution or conquest? (Foucher, 1991, p. 12). Kosovo's independence may have an impact on other multi-ethnic regions, not only in Southeast and Central Europe, but in Western Europe as well. For instance, the *Basque Question* in Spain, with possible future ramifications for France which also has Basque minorities, illustrates this dilemma.

In many parts of the world, nation and state are juxtaposed geographically, therefore, ethno-cultural identity does not coincide with political frontiers. Consequently, there are national communities (often called minorities) whose ethno-cultural identity does not correspond to the state in which they live. For instance, a Serb from Croatia is a citizen of the state of Croatia, but this person considers himself/herself a member of the *Serbian Nation*. This duality between being a citizen of a given state and the perception of belonging to an ethno-cultural community, refers to the differences between the Civic and Ethnic concepts of the nation state as presented in the previous segment of this chapter.

The fact that one part of a *nation* is under the sovereignty of another state can lead to the phenomenon of the *'Kin State'*. A *Kin State* can provide different kinds of support to the parts of its nation separated from it by political frontiers. These parts of the nation, living under the sovereignty of neighbouring countries and forming minorities there, can receive educational, cultural, economic and political support from the nation-state of their origin. In extreme cases, this help can even take the form of military support, as it happened in the 1999 Kosovo conflict when the Kosovo Liberation Army (KLA) used Albanian territory for training and logistics purposes.

The question of minorities can be exploited by different powers seeking to extend their influence in a given geopolitical zone. Tsarist Russia developed a strategy to influence the Slav populations of the Austro-Hungarian Monarchy prior to the outbreak of the First World War. The support of Slavic communities in the name of Pan-Slav ideology served the strategic objectives of Russia to gain a sphere of influence in Central Europe. France also supported the political aspirations of Slavs to gain statehood, as Paris wanted a new territorial order after the disintegration of the Habsburg Monarchy. One of the main French objectives was to reduce the German sphere of influence in Central Europe. As these examples indicate, in addition to the *Kin State*, the role of a '*Support State*' should also be taken into consideration when examining a local and/or regional ethnic tension or conflict. A *Support State* can be located far from a given geopolitical rivalry, while it might not even have any kind of religious, ethnic or linguistic affiliation with a given nation or ethnic community in the affected state; its role of support for a given actor is rather influenced by geopolitical and/or economic interests.

A *unitary* nation-state is usually defined as a state in which the majority of the population represents one nation. However, this type of state is based on the sovereignty of the majority, which in the case of multinational states leads to the domination of the largest ethnic group over the less numerous communities and cannot provide a framework for peaceful coexistence among various national groups. Unitary nation-states cannot reconcile the often conflicting nature of ethno-cultural and political identity. All aspirations of minority communities for autonomy are considered by the state to be a challenge to its unity and territorial integrity. On the other hand, frustration of ethnic communities with highly centralised state structures by which they feel oppressed can lead to the radicalisation of their demands; they may opt for violence and seek secession. Consequently, democracy can become the tyranny of the ethnic majority as the majority rule may represent their domination over the numerically inferior ethnic communities. Without an effective power sharing system, minority populations may perceive their political status as unsatisfactory and rather opt for the use of different means to achieve political change.

From a geopolitical point of view, the main causes of tension and conflict in multi-ethnic and multinational states originate from mainly two factors. First, the application of the concept of a unitary nation state which cannot satisfy the aspirations of ethnic groups, other than the majority cluster, for power sharing territorial models. Second, the actual process of self-determination and the application of the principle of territorial integrity do not provide a middle ground for these two opposing principles of the international system to coexist in order to find peaceful solutions to the problems related to ethnic tension and conflict. Moreover, in most cases, the modification of political frontiers according to an ideal boundary design is impossible while on the other hand in the case of the majority of new nation states, they cannot satisfy the aspirations of all national communities within their borders. Since the end of the bipolar system, a considerable number of these new states have come into existence as a result of the breakup of multinational states, such as the former Soviet Union and Yugoslavia. Latent and open conflicts are occurring in many parts of the world, caused by secessionist movements demanding the right to have their own state in the name of the principle of self-determination. Opposed to this claim, respective states in which these movements are operating defend their rights to territorial integrity and national unity.

Geopolitical situations can vary to a considerable degree based on the characteristics of the geographic distribution of the various populations over a given territory, factors of demography, and interethnic relations. In the case of minority situations, for instance, a minority group living in a border zone of the nation state, and representing a majority of the population in this area, can be perceived by central authorities as a potential threat to the territorial integrity and unity of the country. This, in particular, is the case when the minority group enjoys the support of a *Kin State*. On the other hand, if minorities are dispersed in different parts of the territory of the nation state, and form enclaves in which their proportion is not dense in relation to the majority population, their capacity to contest the central authority is reduced. Therefore, the perception of the nation-state vis-à-vis minority groups is different when those groups live in compact geographic zones, in particular in border regions.

After the factor of geographic distribution of communities, the most important demographic indicator is size/number. Thereby, population of each ethnic group, and nation, living in a given geographic area should be taken into consideration. Within a state, the size of the population of each ethnic group should be compared with that of the entire population of that state, as the relative ratio of the different communities constituting the population of a given country is an important geopolitical indicator. An ethnic group which represents 0.5% of the entire populace of a country does not have the same geopolitical leverage as another group that represents 20% of the population. Additionally, density of the population is an important demographic consideration to be accounted for in a geopolitical analysis. Population density is expressed in the number of habitants by square kilometre/mile. In addition to population density, the numbers and proportions of the different ethnic groups constituting the population of a given state, and their demographic growth, stagnation or decrease, are important indicators to be taken into consideration. The demographic evolution of a population depends on internal and external factors. *Internal factors* refer to the differences between the death and birth rates of a given population within a given time period. *External factors* refer to migration: migrants are those who have left a given geographic zone while immigrants are the ones who have arrived and settled (Mathieu, 2000, p. 22). The abovementioned factors of demography, combined with other variables, such as socio-economic, political, strategic, and natural resource issues, among others, can exercise an important influence on the evolution of geopolitical situations, not only within states (intrastate) but also in between states (interstate) (Dumont, 1995, p. 64).

After an examination of the demographic factors and ethnic composition of a given territory, interethnic relations have to be taken into consideration. *Interethnic Relations* refers to the relationship between ethnic groups forming a nation state. It is an important factor, as it directly influences the cohesion and stability of states. The following elements should be taken into consideration when interethnic relations are analysed:

- Cultural differences and similarities, in particular in terms of language and religion;
- Perception of one community by the other, and vice versa;
- Collective historical memory;
- Distribution of economic and political power among the different communities;
- Possibility to maintain and develop collective identity of a given community: language use, practise of religion, presence in media, and relevant school system, to maintain cultural identity.

For instance, Croatians and Serbians are both Slavic people in terms of ethnicity while there are no major differences in their linguistic identity, with the exceptions of orthography, some vocabulary and grammatical standards. In Serbia, the official script is Cyrillic, although Latin can be used. In Croatia, Latin is used. However, in terms of religion, Croatians are Catholic and the Serbians are Christian Orthodox. The two communities have a rather conflictive collective historical memory, mainly due to the events that happened during the Second World War when a large number of Serbs were massacred by Croats who had allied with Germany and Italy in order to obtain support for an independent Croatia. The exploitation of religious differences and conflictive historical memory played a significant role in the growing tensions between Serbs and Croats of the Yugoslav Federation in the 1980s, and also in the war that started in 1991, in which Croatian and Serbian forces fought over territories that both wanted to control.

The distribution of economic and political power can have an important impact on interethnic relations. Minorities, although numerically inferior to the majority group, can hold a dominant position in the political and economic structure of a given country. This dominance can be negatively perceived by the ethnic majority. For example, this same factor considerably influenced interethnic relations during the apartheid regime in South Africa, when the South Africans of European descent controlled the economic and political levers of power.

2.6 *Historical Factors*

To examine power rivalries over the control of a geographic zone at a given moment in history, the zone's past has to be taken into consideration. Most often, geopolitical problems originate from historical processes that impacted the evolution of a given territorial configuration, and the nation and state building processes of populations living on that territory. Starting with an examination of the evolution of the spatial dimensions of a given territory through history, the historical retrospective approach allows the geopolitical analyst to understand the different territorial changes that have affected the life of a nation or state (Thual, 1996, p. 65). The French expert in Geopolitics, François Thual, highlights the importance of carrying out a so-called *Outcome Assessment* of the territorial evolution of states in geopolitical analyses. This process refers to the examination of state formation processes on a given territory: territorial expansions and territorial contractions resulting as a consequence of boundary changes of states. This assessment of the geo-historical evolution of territories of states can help one better comprehend the intentions, motivations, perceptions and enduring logics, related to territories that these states controlled, control at present, or may want to control in the future (Thual, 1996, p. 55). For instance, gaining access to warm seaports has been a constant factor in crafting of Russian foreign policy and the territorial expansion cycles in Russian history, and continues to be so, still. This was illustrated by Russia's 2014 annexation of Crimea and her interest in maintaining military bases on Syria's Mediterranean coast.

Another important factor for the application of the historical context section of the analysis is the study of demographic patterns and the state and nation formation processes of human groups occupying a given territory. The evolution of demographic changes on a given territory that can result from differences in birth rates, migrations, colonisation, and conflicts that lead to population changes, among other elements, has to be examined for the different periods in history (Thual, 1996, p. 65). To analyse these processes, historical geography can be a valuable tool. Historical maps highlighting the different territorial changes and population variations of a given area during various time periods are useful instruments for this retrospective approach. The assessment of territorial modifications of a given state, focusing on boundary changes, means the examination of the changes of sovereignty over a territory within a given time period. The principle dynamics leading to territorial changes are occupation, annexation, secession, unification, partition, fragmentation, and split-up (Rosière, 2007). These dynamics influence the territorial expansion or contraction processes of states and can overlap. In a given geopolitical configuration, two or three types of these territorial dynamics can be manifested. Secession can lead to the fragmentation and territorial division of a state while at the same time result in unification and territorial enlargement for another state. It is important to study these territorial dynamics in their historical context in order to better understand the historical roots of current geopolitical tensions and conflicts in a given region.

Some examples which can be mentioned for demonstrating instances of territorial changes affecting geopolitical dynamics are explained as follows. Israel occupied the Golan Heights in 1967 and annexed it in 1981. The Israeli annexation was motivated by the strategic importance of this territory due to its geographic location and rich water reserves. As well, there are examples of gaining sovereignty over a territory by using financial means. For instance, the United States bought Alaska from Russia for 7.2 million dollars in the 19th century. Through this acquisition, about 1.7 million square kilometres of new territory was added to the landmass of the United States. The incorporation of Alaska into US territory became an important step in the United States' rise as a great power in the Asia-Pacific region. In the case of the split-up of multi-ethnic states (e.g. Yugoslavia, USSR), or empires (e.g. Ottoman, Habsburg), as a result, primary and successor states come to be recognised. *Primary State* refers to the former multi-ethnic state whose territory was fragmented. Most often, the primary state remains with a reduced territory size compared to its former space before the breakup and partition process. *Successor States* emerge from this process of disintegration and end up possessing territories formerly under the sovereignty of the *Primary State*. Geopolitical problems, such as, the delimitation of newly created boundaries between the *Primary* and *Successor States*, or among the successor states themselves, or the status of minority populations who find themselves under the sovereignty of new states, are but a few which these newly formed configurations have to deal with once they are reconstituted. For instance, 15 independent states emerged from the 1991 dissolution of the Soviet Union. As a result of this historical event, about 25 million ethnic Russians found themselves living outside of the boundaries of the newly independent *Primary State* of Russia, and inside the boundaries of the newly formed *Successor States* which had emerged after the end of the Soviet Union. For instance, in the Baltic States alone, there are more than one million ethnic Russians living at present: Russian minorities represent about 6% of the population in Lithuania, 24% in Estonia, and 25 % in Latvia.

The evolution of a territory, its demographic and ethnic structure, influenced by historical processes, has to be taken into consideration at different timeframes. The French historian, Fernand Braudel, makes a distinction between short-term, medium-term, and long-*longue durée* (long-term) timeframes (Braudel, 1990, p. 15). Short-term refers to episodic history or political history, medium-term conjuncture refers to economic cycles, for instance, and long-term refers to structural periods of long historical stretches. As Fernand Braudel states, explanation of historical events should take into consideration the long duration influence of cultural systems, geographic constraints, and economic cycles interacting with other structural factors.

The study of the geo-historical evolution of the territory of present-day Ukraine in the *longue durée* contributes to a better comprehension of the identity question in, and weak national cohesion of, the current Ukrainian state[17]. Indeed, the current divisions between the different regions of Ukraine have been impacted by the historical evolution of its territory. A rather late state formation process characterises Ukrainian history; on the present-day territory of Ukraine, there was, in essence, no unified and independent country in the longer term until the mid-20th century. The actual territory of Ukraine was incorporated into different empires and mediaeval kingdoms during varying eras of the last thousand years. The Ukrainian-Russian boundary began to emerge in the early 1920s under the auspices of the Soviet Union while Ukraine's present territory was formed by 1954 when Crimea was transferred to the Ukrainian Soviet Socialist Republic by Nikita Khrushchev, General Secretary of the Communist Party of the USSR at the time. It is necessary to take into consideration the influence exerted by the different powers that exercised sovereignty on the territory of present-day Ukraine during various historical epochs in order to comprehend the difference in perceptions between populations of the eastern and western parts of that country. While significant parts of Eastern Ukraine were incorporated into the Russian Empire, most of its western regions had been under the sovereignty of Poland, Lithuania or the Austro-Hungarian Empire, during various periods in history. These historical factors impact the current political divisions in Ukraine, where the western part of the country looks towards Central and Western Europe while the eastern part has closer ties with Russia.

17 On this subject, one can consult the geo-historical analysis on Ukraine in the following book: Kocsis, K., Rudenko, L. & Schweitzer, F. (Eds.). (2008). Ukraine in Maps, Institute of Geography of the National Academy of Sciences of Ukraine and the Geographical Research Institute of the Hungarian Academy of Sciences. Kyiv-Budapest.

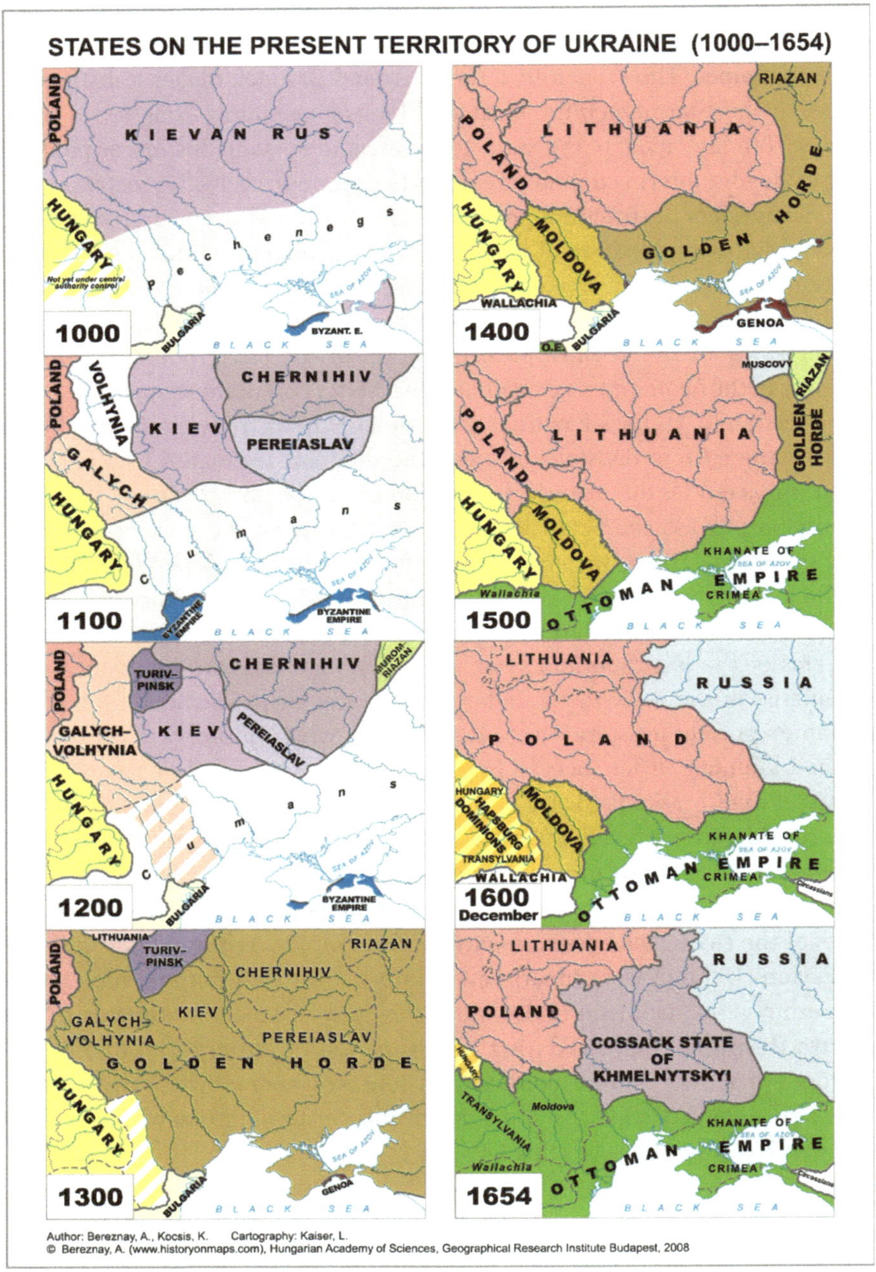

FIGURE 1.1 States on the present territory of Ukraine (1000–1654)

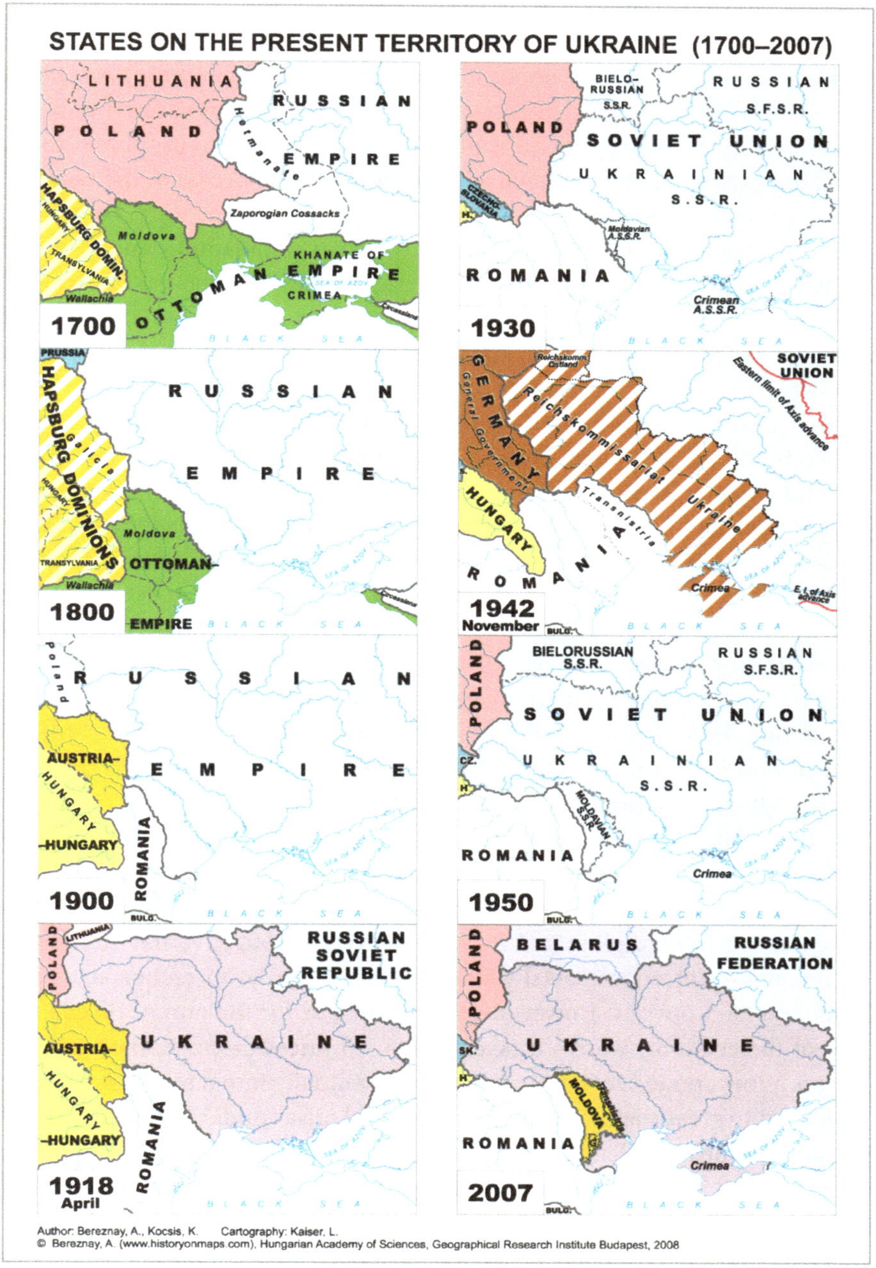

FIGURE 1.2 States on the present territory of Ukraine (1700–2007)

2.7 *Economic Factors*

Geographic factors, such as climate, vegetation, disposable land for agriculture, and natural resources, among others, influence the economic potential of states. Often, the economic activities of a state are shaped by centre-periphery dynamics. In the emergence of centres, which are the core economic zones of states, geographic factors such as location, distance, access to the sea, natural resources, or related aspects, have played an important role. These core economic areas are often characterised by high population density, dense transportation networks, and political significance (Cohen, 2009, p. 35). The economic development variances between the core areas and the less developed zones within a given state may impact the geopolitical cohesion of that state.

The power projection capacity of states in the international system also depends on their economic power. States cannot maintain an effective political and military strategy without economic power. Frequently, in contemporary international relations, the use of geoeconomic strategies to achieve various objectives of a given state – for instance, to enlarge its zone of influence, enhance its diplomatic strategies or weaken an adversary state, among others – can be more efficient than the use of military power.[18] The issue of diversification of the economy can directly impact the geopolitical power position of a given state. The current situation of Venezuela is a relevant example of this. This country used its oil revenues to support an active anti-US foreign policy after the election of President Hugo Chavez in 1998. The relatively high oil prices, in the first years of the 21st century, provided an important financial source for Chavez to carry out an active foreign policy, seeking Latin American integration through enacting bilateral trade and reciprocal aid agreements. Chavez sought to increase the geopolitical weight of Venezuela through "oil diplomacy". As well, the Venezuelan government used its oil income to introduce social welfare policies in order to reduce economic inequality and poverty. However, significant steps for the aim of diversification of the economy were not taken. When oil prices dropped, the Venezuelan economy entered into a recession and eventually into a major depression which led to great socioeconomic and political crises under the presidency of Nicolás Maduro who had been elected in 2013 after the death of Chavez. This crisis resulted in massive poverty and hyperinflation. Ultimately, this situation became the cause of important migration flows from Venezuela to neighbouring states, and in particular to Colombia, representing important challenges

18 This issue is further discussed in Chapter 7 on the increasing importance of Geoeconomics in Power Rivalries: from the past to the present.

for these nations. Further, the destabilisation of the economy of Venezuela impacted its capabilities to project geopolitical power in the Caribbean region and South America.

Dependence on one major trading partner versus diversification of trade relations can affect the geopolitical position of states as well. Trade relations, including regional integration processes, are often influenced by power rivalries to enhance respective spheres of geopolitical influence. The 2014 EU-Ukraine Association Agreement, with its *Deep and Comprehensive Free Trade Area* between the European Union and Ukraine, was perceived by Russia as a strategy to contain her sphere of influence in Ukraine, a geopolitically important country due to its function as a pivot state which can be used to contain Russia, from US sea power perspective.[19] Russia on the other hand, promoted a regional bloc between some of the post-Soviet states. Consequently, the Eurasian Economic Union Treaty was signed in 2014. Member states of the *Eurasian Economic Union* (EAEU) are the Republic of Armenia, the Republic of Belarus, the Republic of Kazakhstan, the Kyrgyz Republic, and the Russian Federation. Geopolitical motivations of Russia played a role in establishing the EAEU in order to enhance her influence in her neighbouring regions. (Popescu, 2014, pp.19–20)

The importance of a well-organised export-oriented economic structure, access to markets, and integration in the international trade system, can play important roles for states that do not have a sufficient natural resource base and/or territory for agricultural production. Japan and Switzerland are relevant examples of development of successful export-oriented economies, that are indispensable to those nations due to their geopolitical vulnerabilities. To develop its economic power, reduce the impact of geographical constraints, and profit from geographic advantages, a state must organise its own economic space. This engagement is translated by the strategic choices made by the state to develop its territory in order to ensure better socioeconomic cohesion and a better distribution of the wealth of its nation. Developing a canalisation system for irrigation, building desalinisation plants for enhancing freshwater supplies, transferring funds to peripheral regions to enhance road and railway networks, are some of the examples on how a state can intervene to increase the cohesion of its economic space.

19 Zbigniew Brzezinski emphasised the geopolitical pivot function of Ukraine is his book, *The Grand Chessboard* (Basis Books, New York, 1997), when he stated, *"Ukraine, a new and important space on the Eurasian chessboard, is a geopolitical pivot because its very existence as an independent country helps to transform Russia. Without Ukraine, Russia ceases to be a Eurasian empire"*. p. 46.

Subsequently, developing new technologies and innovations have impacted geopolitics as well.[20] Venice gradually became a powerful international actor from the 11th century on. In spite of its small geographic configuration, this city state became a considerable power, thanks to the mastering of advanced technologies in shipbuilding, and a well-developed financial sector, amongst other reasons. Innovations in shipbuilding during the Middle Ages contributed to the extension of maritime routes for Europeans. One of the more popular vessels for open sea travel was the *caravel*. Operated by navigators from Spain, Portugal, and England, the *caravel* was a small but fast merchant ship that typically carried few weapons. An improved version, the *Caravela Redonda*, was rigged with both *Square* and *Lateen* sails that increased its speed and manoeuvrability. Columbus's *Pinta* and *Niña* were these types of caravels and Magellan had one in his fleet that circumnavigated the world (Nautical Archaeology Program Texas University, 2019).

The development of a transportation infrastructure – fluvial, terrestrial (rail and road), and aerial – can contribute to the opening up of isolated regions and the reduction of socioeconomic development gaps between different areas of a given country, or between countries themselves. The Kerch Bridge, for instance, provides a direct link between the Krasnodar Krai and Crimea Peninsula. This bridge, inaugurated in 2018, not only directly links Crimea to the Russian mainland, but also strengthens Moscow's geopolitical control over that peninsula, annexed by her, following a referendum held in 2014.

Geopolitical analysis integrates the main elements of economic geography and various branches of economics, such as macroeconomics, political economy, and international economics, when analysing the influence of socioeconomic factors on the evolution of geopolitical situations (Savona, 2004, p. 9). Moreover, factors linked to socioeconomic development levels have to be taken into consideration as well; the assessment of purely macroeconomic and financial factors are not sufficient to critically assess a given situation in a country. For instance, a country can export natural resources such as oil and gas and its GDP growth per year can be significant, especially when oil prices are high. However, if there is no effective wealth distribution system in society, the gap between the rich and the poor can be widened and as a consequence the cohesion of the country may weaken, which in turn can impact the geopolitical position of that state.

Socioeconomic factors can impact both the internal and external geopolitical dynamics of states. For instance, major socioeconomic disparities between

20 The interactions between technology and geopolitics are further discussed in Chapter 2, through the concept of the 'geo-technical ensemble'.

different geographic zones in a given state can encourage autonomist or even secessionist movements in the economically well-developed regions. [21] These economically performant and prosperous regions do not always want to share the financial burden of assisting the poorer provinces. Such more developed regions, often located in the economic core areas of a given country, may contest the fiscal system of the national government and consider that they could participate in a more efficient way in a globalised economic system of competition by gaining more autonomy, and in certain cases even independence. Catalonia in Spain is a relevant example of this issue. Political, historical, identity and demographic factors are all important to help understand the current political deadlock in Spain with the Catalan demand for independence. In addition to the aforementioned factors, economic parameters should be taken into consideration as well. As the most prosperous of Spain's 17 regions, Catalonia boasts roughly 19 percent of the national economy, benefiting from tourism, export, manufacturing, and industry. While Catalans only account for about 16 percent of the Spanish population, Catalonia makes an important contribution to the overall Spanish economy of around 225 billion euros a year (Catalonia government, 2019). Moreover, Catalonia has an advanced healthcare system, efficient school system (including twelve universities), an innovative industrial system, and a good quality infrastructure. However, the Catalonian government contests the current fiscal system under the authority of the central government in Madrid.

Socioeconomic disparities between regions within a state can lead to important migration movements and affect the geopolitical cohesion of that state. The situation of China for instance illustrates this problem. China's economy has doubled every decade since 1979, and its foreign trade every five years since 1978. In 1978, China ranked as the 34th largest trading nation. By 2013, it had reached the top of that list. Its annual economic growth rate has been high, around 10% for several decades since the introduction of economic reforms in 1978 (Note: in the last few years its growth rate has steadily decreased to an average of 6–7%, which can still be considered as relatively high compared to most of the rest of the world). Then again, these significant growth rates did not benefit all regions of China uniformly. Although China has managed to lift more than 800 million people out of poverty since the start of its economic reforms (World Bank, 2019) disparity between urban areas and rural hinterlands remains significant. Geographic characteristics have played an important role

---

21 Chapter 10 further delves into the phenomenon of 'reterritorialisation' in which territorially embedded actors other than the national state regain relevance and prominence in internal and external political questions.

in coast/inland socioeconomic inequality (Sun, 2013). The preponderance of foreign investment in China, and the most important part of her foreign commerce, are centred in her coastal provinces. These regions played an important role in the gradual introduction of economic reforms within the framework of the so-called "Open Door Policy". As a result of coast/inland economic disparities, millions of people have left their impoverished rural zones and migrated to cities situated in the more developed economic regions of the coastal zones. One of the biggest challenges facing the internal geopolitical cohesion of China in coming decades is lessening socioeconomic disparities between the fast-growing coastal regions and the less developed rural districts. Development of the infrastructure, in particular road and rail networks, and increasing investments in economic development, can contribute to the reduction of the coast/inland wealth gap. The Belt and Road Initiative also favours the development of China's inland regions and can subsequently contribute to improving the geopolitical cohesion of the country.

Socioeconomic problems can be aggravated by high demographic growth of a given population of a state and lead to geopolitical tensions. This problem arises when the state cannot provide job opportunities for its growing population, in particular for the young generations. The situation can also become more serious when the state cannot assure food production levels corresponding to the alimentation needs of its growing population while it lacks the natural resources that are necessary to maintain sustainable socioeconomic development standards for them. Such situations have led to wars and/or major migration flows in human history as populations have wanted to obtain territorial extension of their respective geographic zones in order to satisfy their growing needs. Socioeconomic underdevelopment, often combined with high demographic rates and a scarcity of natural resources, constitutes the *push factors* that motivate populations to cross borders (often without authorisation as legal migration opportunities to Western countries have been decreasing) and reach countries with better socioeconomic situations. Higher development levels of the industrialised North represent the so-called *pull factors* that can attract people from the economically less developed South and influence their motivation to try to migrate to Western countries. Furthermore, the influence of globalised media networks on people, who live in poor socioeconomic conditions, has to be mentioned. Transmission of the Western lifestyle, with its high-level consumption models, through global media networks, can arouse frustration and motivate people to leave their country and try to settle in the West.

Land and maritime boundaries between states signify not only the division of territories between sovereign state entities but sometimes these borders also separate socioeconomic zones of great disparity. The Mediterranean Sea, separating Europe from Africa, provides a relevant illustration. Some North African countries, such as Algeria and Tunisia, are facing serious economic problems resulting in high unemployment rates, in particular among their younger populations. As the labour market in these countries does not absorb the young and often well-educated individuals, a considerable number of them seek to migrate to Europe. A major political challenge for both Southern and Northern Mediterranean countries is to develop a coherent strategic framework that integrates economic development with job creation in Northern Africa in order to reduce uncontrolled migration flows towards the EU (in particular to Spain, Italy and France). Youth unemployed rates are high in Maghreb countries. In Algeria, for instance, youth unemployment stands at 24.3%.[22] This country, with a population of 42 million, holds important oil and gas reserves. However, it has not been able to transform its resource-based economy into a more diversified structure that could provide jobs for its young population. Algerian youth, between the ages of 15 and 30, represent one-third of the country's population. The overall weight of the youth population is of great importance within its society as nearly 67% of Algerians are under 30 years old (Rarrbo, 2008, p. 10). In addition to the problem of job creation for the youth in Maghreb countries, the situation of Sub-Saharan Africa should also be mentioned. According to UN projections (World Population Prospects, 2015), the population of Africa may reach 1.7 billion by 2030 and 2.5 billion by 2050. The most significant demographic rise will take place in Sub-Saharan Africa. Job creation and socioeconomic development may not meet the challenges of this substantial rise in population; this in particular can be a problem for the rapidly growing number of young and active populations. Furthermore, this region has to confront political instability, climate change, desertification, water scarcity, and major problems with its public health and education infrastructure. All these *push factors* motivate young people to move towards other regions of the world, and in this context, Europe will remain a target location for African migration. Thereby, migration flows from Africa to Europe will most likely increase, due to these push factors. A major geopolitical challenge for Europe will centre on how to deal with increasing migration pressures and the resulting uncontrolled mass migration movements arriving from the African continent. Some experts propose the creation of a European Marshall Plan for Africa led by Germany in order to address the root causes of migration through massive investment in development projects and in the elimination

---

22 Data obtained from World Bank indicators (February 2019), https://data.worldbank.org/indicator/SL.UEM.1524.ZS

of poverty (German Federal Ministry for Economic Cooperation and Development, 2017).

2.8 *Strategies of Actors*

The strategy of actors as a part of geopolitical analysis refers to the geostrategic dimension: it examines how different state and non-state actors seeks to manage their geopolitical interests and achieve various objectives. *Strategy* in general is concerned with the relationships between ends and means, that is, between the results that an actor seeks and the resources at its disposal. Strategy also refers to a plan of action designed to achieve a particular goal, or goals. Furthermore, strategy can be defined as the combination of all means that a human entity disposes to achieve its defined objective, or objectives. *Means* refers to the different instruments of power, including military, economic, or cultural, among others, that can be used to achieve an objective or several objectives.

The *geostrategic dimension* in geopolitical analysis seeks to identify the actors, their intentions, motivations, objectives, means, alliances, and the timeframes for their actions, when examining the strategic framework of a situation. The following questions are to be asked in a strategic analysis (Thual, 1996, p. 23):

- *Who are the actors?*
- *Who wants what?*
- *With whom?*
- *Against whom?*
- *How?*
- *Why?*
- *What are the means?*
- *When?*
- *Where?*

By trying to respond to these questions, a geopolitical analyst tries to establish the *strategic framework* of a given geopolitical configuration by taking into consideration the different geographic scales, ranging from local, regional and national (internal geopolitics), to macro-regional (neighbouring countries, other countries in the region), continental, and global. For example, for the Syrian Civil War, instigated in 2011, interactions between, and the competing strategies of, the different groups in the country have to be examined in the context of the intentions of the regional powers (Iran, Saudi Arabia, Turkey, and Israel), and as well, on the global level, of the Russia-US geopolitical competition that impacts the evolution of this conflict.

Concerning the issue of *identification of actors* in a given geopolitical situation, the following observations should be taken into consideration. Despite the increasing influence of globalisation, the basic unit in contemporary international relations is still the state. Although the growing importance of non-state and sub-state actors and the transnational factors in contemporary international relations have altered the capacity of states to fully exercise their sovereignty, this has not resulted in the suppression of state sovereignty. A kind of hybrid system characterises contemporary international relations in which states and a wild variety of non-state actors interact. These non-state actors can be paramilitary groups, ethnic minorities, transnational criminal organisations, and big corporations, among other groups. There has come about a certain erosion of *state sovereignty* in which non-state actors may have more power capabilities in certain cases than a given state. In some cases, states do not control all parts of their national territory and therefore cannot fully exercise their sovereignty. The disintegration process of Libya, after the 2011 Western-led intervention, and the rather chaotic situation in Somalia, are some examples of weak or de-structured states whose territory is controlled by different non-state actors that are often linked to transnational criminal networks which find these zones fertile ground for their operations due to lack of state control over those given territories. On the other hand, states may transfer some parts of their sovereignty to regional blocs. Regional integration progressions, such as the European Union, illustrate this process which has led regional blocs to become geopolitical actors as well. These regrouping of states, often led by a dominant regional power, may direct the evolution of the 21st century world system towards *Großraum* ('Geopolitical Great Spaces'), as the German thinker Carl Schmitt had theorised.[23] In spite of the changing notion of sovereignty on the infra-state and supranational levels, and the growing power capabilities of non-state/transnational actors and regional blocs, states still remain the primary actors on the international relations stage as they are internationally recognised political and legal entities that claim sovereignty over a given territory (and any of its adjacent maritime zones), natural resources located therein, and the population which lives on the territory defined by the borders of that given state (Anderson, 1999, p. 126). Yet, geopolitical analysis is not state-exclusive as it takes into account the influence of the growing number of non-state, sub-state, and transnational actors.

---

23 On the theory of *Großraum*: Schmitt, C. (2006). *The Nomos of the Earth*. New York: Telos Press, Candor.

Strategies can be offensive and/or defensive. An *offensive strategy* has the objective to change the status quo of a given situation while a *defensive strategy* seeks to maintain the status quo. German diplomatic, economic, and military strategies after 1933 were offensive. The main objective of these strategies was to change the status quo in Europe, represented by the territorial order resulting from the Treaty of Versailles, which was contested by Germany. Countries such as Czechoslovakia and Poland developed defensive strategies in order to maintain the territorial integrity of their respective states due to the fear of the likelihood of German annexation of historically German territories still populated by Germans but under Czech and Polish sovereignty as a result of the peace treaties that ended the First World War.

Confrontation with an adversary can also be *direct* or *indirect*. The 2003 US-led invasion of Iraq is an example of a direct strategy. Indirect strategy seeks to avoid a direct confrontation and consequently the use of permanent and massive military force. One of the key authors of indirect strategy is Sun Tzu. In his book, *The Art of War* (Tzu, 2002), written in the 5th century BC, he advocates the use of psychological factors in warfare in order to minimise physical violence. He states as well that in war the most important concentration should be placed on disturbing the strategic plans of the enemy. Next, his alliances should be destroyed by diplomacy. According to Sun Tzu, supreme excellence is to beat the enemy without combat.

States possess diverse *strategic cultures*. China does not have the same strategic culture as European states and Russian strategic culture is different from that of the US. It is important to take into consideration these differences in order to understand the behaviour of states in various geopolitical situations. Strategic culture can be influenced by the characteristics of the physical geography of a territory of a given nation, historical and cultural factors, geopolitical representations, and national geopolitical schools of thought and doctrines.

Geopolitical analysis does not seek to only decipher the complexity of a given situation at present but also its possible evolutions in the future. In this context, geopolitical analysis integrates strategic foresight in order to anticipate what may happen. This projection towards the future of possible evolutions of a current situation can contribute to enhanced decision-making processes. Indeed, in the current era of complexity and uncertainty, decision-makers have to anticipate the possible evolutions of a wide range of geopolitical and geoeconomic situations and thereby integrate elements of strategic foresight in their decision-making processes. By not appropriately anticipating geopolitical and/or geoeconomic scenarios, decision-makers can be caught off-guard and accordingly not react well in an important emerging situation. *Strategic foresight* refers to a multidisciplinary approach on the study of how various actors in conjunction with enduring and variable factors may influence the outcome of given state of affairs in different timeframes: short, medium, and long term. Moreover, strategic foresight is the transformation of knowledge into informed decision-making processes in order to shape the future evolution of a current situation. Foresight is not the prediction of the future. The future is not predetermined, inevitable or fixed, and it is uncertain. To develop different hypotheses on the possible evolution of a current situation, *scenario building* can be employed. Building scenarios is an important constituent of strategic foresight. A geopolitical scenario is a description of what could possibly occur when examining different hypotheses with a range of possibilities for the future. Scenario building denotes the exploring and constructing of possible and preferable futures, but also the identification of different risks and worst-case scenarios, as well, which should be explored.

3 Conclusion

Every geopolitical configuration has its own characteristics which are based on history, geography, socioeconomic state of affairs, and cultural factors, among others. A geopolitical analyst can run into some difficulties since he/she has to take into consideration a great number of varying factors when performing a geopolitical analysis. For example, in certain situations, ethnicity or geopolitical representations can exercise a very important influence over the probable scenarios, while in other circumstances the control of natural resources and geostrategic motivations play a more important role than other factors. Therefore, in each situation to be analysed, one has to foremost establish a hierarchy of factors.

Some other difficulties that can affect a geopolitical analysis relate to rapid technological changes and their impact on geopolitics. Some other challenging areas to mention are unforeseen events such as natural disaster, rapid spread of disease, and the possible impact of an emerging charismatic leader on a given geopolitical configuration. Further to this point, there are also some subjective elements that are not quantifiable, such as the evolution of interethnic relations or the impact of geopolitical representations, amongst others. As well, there is no strategic analysis without some degree of imagination, speculation and intuition. Although these forms of reflection are mostly excluded from the Western perception of social sciences due to the influence of the major ideologies that have dominated Western thought in the last few centuries, yet they are a part of the Greco-Roman heritage of European thinking and are also present in Asian thought. Yet, geopolitics is not about predictions of the future.

The future is not predetermined, inevitable or fixed, but it is rather uncertain and complex. Nevertheless, geopolitical analysis can integrate foresight and scenario building in order to anticipate the evolution and potential outcome of a given geopolitical situation in the future.

To become a geopolitical analyst, one should go beyond one's own cultural representations and national filters, and instead, be able to put oneself in the position of any given country or populace in order to examine how local populations and ethnic groups perceive their own geopolitical environment and how these perceptions are influenced by geographic characteristics, historical and economic factors, and cultural identity. Indeed, the understanding of cultural diversity is indispensable to the geopolitical approach. Consequently, a geopolitical analyst should be able to enter into the mindset of the different actors in order to integrate the impact of the existent views on a given situation to be examined. One cannot become an expert in the geopolitics of a given region of the world without first spending some time there, being immersed in its host cultures, while learning some of its chief languages. This is because cultural diversity, particularisms, and the uniqueness of each geopolitical configuration, with the multiple perspectives and representations held by various state and non-state actors, are essential microelements to be taken into consideration in a geopolitical analysis. The objectivity of geopolitical analysis can be negatively prejudiced by beliefs and fixed ideas. A geopolitical analyst should reject fixed ideas and must instead question all things at all times while keeping a safe intellectual distance from events as he/she manages emotions. Therefore, a geopolitical situation should not be analysed according to personal preferences such as proclivity towards a country or a political leader, or otherwise.

Bibliography

Africa and Europe – A new partnership for development, peace and a better future, Cornerstones of a Marshall Plan with Africa. German Federal Ministry for Economic Cooperation and Development (2017). Bonn: BMZ. Retrieved from http://www.bmz.de/en/publications/type_of_publication/information_flyer/information_brochures/Materialie270_africa_marshallplan.pdf

Anderson, E. (1999). Geopolitics: International Boundaries as Fighting Places. In Gray, C., Sloan, G. & Cass, F. (Eds). *Geopolitics, Geography and Strategy.* London.

Braudel, F. (1990). *L'identité de la France.* Paris : Flammarion.

Brzezinski, Z. (1997). *The Grand Chessboard.* New York: Basis Books.

Charnay, J-P. (1992). *Stratégie générative.* Paris: PUF.

Cohen, S. (2009). *Geopolitics: The Geography of International Relations*. New York: Rowman & Littlefield Publishers.

Csurgai, G. (2005) *La nation et ses territoires en Europe centrale. Une approche géopolitique*. Bern: Peter Lang.

Dionet-Grivet, S. (2014). *Géopolitique de l'eau*. Paris: Ellipses.

Dumont, G-F. (1995). *Le monde et les hommes, Les grandes évolutions démographiques*. Paris: Litec.

Dussuoy, G. (2009). *Traité de relations internationales, Tome III. Les théories de la mondialité*. Paris: Harmattan.

Egypt (2019). UN Data. Retrieved from: http://data.un.org/CountryProfile.aspx?crName=egypt

Fish, not Oil, at the heart of the South China Sea Conflict. (2019). Fridtjof Nansens Institute, Retrieved from: https://www.fni.no/news/fish-not-oil-at-the-heart-of-the-south-china-sea-conflict-article1556-330.html

Foucher, M. (1991). *Fronts et Frontières*. Paris : Fayard.

Foucher, M. (2001). The Geopolitics of Front Lines and Border Lines. In Levy, J. & Cass, F. (Eds). *From Geopolitics to Global Politics*. London.

Galland, F. (2014). *Le Grand Jeu, Chroniques géopolitiques de l'eau*. Paris: CNRS Editions.

Gourdin, P. (2010). *Géopolitiques, Manuel Pratique*. Paris: Choiseul, 2010.

Government of Catalonia, Trade & Investment (2019). Retrieved from http://catalonia.com/catalonia-barcelona/catalonia-barcelona/Catalonia-facts-figures.jsp

History of the Caravel (2019). Texas A&M University, Department of Anthropology, Nautica Archaeology Program. Retrieved from: http://nautarch.tamu.edu/shiplab/01George/caravela/htmls/Caravel%20History.htm

Klare, M. (2001). *Resource Wars - The New Landscape of Global Conflict*. New York: Metropolitan books.

Klare, M. (2013). *The Race for What's Left, The Global Scramble for the World's Last Resources*. New York: Picador.

Kocsis, K., Rudenko, L. & Schweitzer, F. (Eds.). (2008). Ukraine in Maps, Institute of Geography of the National Academy of Sciences of Ukraine and the Geographical Research Institute of the Hungarian Academy of Sciences. Kyiv-Budapest.

Lacoste, Y. (2001). Rivalries for Territory. In Levy, J. (Ed.) (2001). *From Geopolitics to Global Politics*. London: Frank Cass

Lacoste, Y. (Ed). (2003). *Dictionnaire de Géopolitique*. Paris : Flammarion.

Lasarre, F., Gonon, E. & Mottet, E. (2016). *Manuel de Géopolitique, Enjeux de pouvoir sur des territoires*. Paris: Armand Colin.

Le Billon, P. (Ed.) (2005). *Geopolitics of Resources Wars, Resource Dependence, Governance and Violence*. New York: Routledge

Le Billon, P. (Ed.) (2013). *Wars of Plunder, Conflicts, Profits and the Politics of Resources*. Oxford: Oxford University Press.

Luttwak, E. (1999). *La Grande Strategia dell'Impero Romano*. Milano: Biblioteca Universale Rizzoli.

Mathieu, J-L. (2000). *La Population Mondiale*. Paris: Armand Colin.

Newman, D. (2003). On Borders and Power: A Theoretical Framework. In *Journal of Borderland Studies, Volume 18, n° 1*.

Popescu, N. (2014). *Eurasian Union: the real, the imaginary and the likely*, Paris: EU Institute for Security Studies. Retrieved from: https://www.iss.europa.eu/sites/default/files/EUISSFiles/CP_132.pdf

Rarrbo, K. (Ed.) (2008). *Studies on Youth Policies in the Mediterranean Partner Countries,* European Union, EUROMED program.

Ratti, R. & Reichman, S. (1993). *Theory and Practice of Transborder Co-operation*. Basel: Helbing & Lichtenhahn.

Rodrige, J-P, Comtois, C. & Slack, B. (2009). *The Geography of Transport Systems*, New York: Routledge.

Rosière, S. (2007). *Géographie politique & Géopolitique*. Paris : Ellipses.

Savona, P. (2004). *Geopolitica economica*, Milano: Sperling & Kupfer Editori.

Schmitt, C. (2006). *The Nomos of the Earth*. New York: Telos Press, Candor.

Sun, Z. (2013). Explaining Regional Disparities of China's Economic Growth: Geography, Policy and Infrastructure. Department of Economics, University of California, Berkeley. Retrieved from: https://www.econ.berkeley.edu/sites/default/files/Thesis_ZhengyunSun.pdf

The United Nations World Water Development Report (2016). United Nations Educational, Scientific and Cultural Organisation (UNESCO), Paris. Retrieved from: http://www.unwater.org.

Thual, F. (1996). *Géopolitique de l'Amérique Latine*. Paris: Economica.

Thual, F. (1996). *Méthodes de la géopolitique*. Paris: Ellipses.

Tzu, S. (2002). *The Art of War*. New York: Dover Publications.

United Nations Department of Economic and Social Affairs (UNDESA) (2018). Retrieved from: http://www.un.org/waterforlifedecade/scarcity.shtml

United Nations Environment Program (UNEP) estimations (2019). Retrieved from: http://www.unep.org/dewa/vitalwater/article48.html.

Water Conflict (2019). The World's Water, Pacific Institute. Retrieved from: http://worldwater.org/water-conflict

World Atlas (2019). Retrieved from: http://www.worldatlas.com/articles/what-is-a-continental-shelf.html

World Bank indicators (February 2019). Retrieved from: https://data.worldbank.org/indicator/SL.UEM.1524.ZS

World Bank Overview on China (2018). Retrieved from: https://www.worldbank.org/en/country/china/overview

World Population Prospects, The 2015 Revision. UN Department of Economic and Social Affairs, Population Division (2015). United Nations, New York.

CHAPTER 2

'Geotechnical Ensembles': How New Technologies Change Geopolitical Factors and Contexts in Economy, Energy and Security

David Criekemans

1 Introduction

This chapter explores a sometimes forgotten, yet very delicate dimension in geopolitical analysis; how the introduction, adoption or even contestation of *technology* generates *an effect upon territorially embedded factors and the wider geopolitical context*. As a result of new technologies in communication, transportation or production, some places in the world become more important compared to others. New economic relations may be forged between resource rich areas and consumer regions. For example, the evolution towards a world increasingly run on renewable energy will also mean that the needs of many countries will shift; from conventional oil over natural gas towards the critical materials that will power a renewable energy future. This could lead to scarcity & supply problems and geopolitical competition over key resources such as nickel, cobalt, copper, silver, scandium, lithium and rare earth elements (Criekemans, 2018). Cooperation is possible, but never a given. Some territories may be forced into a rivalry. In the United States of America for instance, new shale gas extraction & upscaling technologies have been developed since 2001. With it, gas molecules trapped in rock formations could now also be extracted. But the geopolitical consequence is that the US is trying to become a competitor for the Russian Federation in the European natural gas market. This explains why the former US president Donald J. Trump pressured Germany over the Nord Stream II pipeline, which is being built in the Baltic Sea.

The interaction between technologies and geopolitical factors may also have consequences for the foreign policy and diplomacy of nations; patterns of conflict and cooperation may be affected. At the same time, the introduction of new technologies may also have far-reaching geostrategic consequences and implications for whether and how nations have to be protected. Think for instance of the introduction of drones, 5G technology, the quantum computer, cyber threats, artificial intelligence, or even whole new domains

 | DOI:10.1163/9789004432086_004

such as cyberbiosecurity. New technologies may expose our vulnerabilities, or even change the nature of war itself. We may already be living in a *'grey zone'* between peace and war, ever more uncertain and precarious.

This chapter explores the unique relationship between technology and geopolitics:

First, it briefly goes back to some classical geopolitical thinkers such as Alfred Thayer Mahan and Halford John Mackinder, as well as to Harold Sprout. What we sometimes forget is that each of these authors took the technological factor into account when developing their respective geopolitical analyses.

Second, we will investigate the contribution by Daniel Deudney. According to Deudney, the 'geo' in geopolitics has obscured the important role of technology in these earlier world order theories (Deudney, 1989, p. 2–3). Harold Sprout already referred to 'geo-technic politics' (Sprout, 1963, p. 192). Daniel Deudney proposes to analyse the so-called "geotechnical ensembles" (Deudney, 1989, p. 13). We will connect this concept to Parag Khanna's more recent contribution in which he sees a 'Great Supply Chain War' developing (Khanna, 2016).

Third, inspired by the work of Deudney, we will investigate some recent examples of "geotechnical ensembles". How do new technologies change geopolitical factors and contexts in *economic*, *energy* and *security* relations? The thesis which emanates from this analysis is *that territorial entities (states, regions or cities) which invest in ground-breaking technological know-how, both fundamental and applied innovation, as well as in the industrial base that comes with it, will in many ways be able to shape tomorrow's world in its geo-economic, geopolitical and geostrategic dimensions*. Technologies come in many different shapes and forms. Nevertheless they act as force multipliers.

Finally, we develop some concluding thoughts on how today's technological trends could affect tomorrow's world politics from a geo-economic, geopolitical and geostrategic point of view. If power constitutes the 'currency' of global geopolitics, then technology could be seen as its 'conductor' and 'facilitator'. The world already finds itself in a geopolitical transition because of other explanatory factors. One potential scenario for the next decades is a new bipolar world with two power blocs; the United States of America and the People's Republic of China. Both are actively investing in technologies to try to gain an upper hand; 5G and 6G networks, quantum computing, big data artificial intelligence, robotization, etc. If the European countries still want to stay relevant geopolitically, they will need to catch up in terms of research & development, commercialization and the political acceptance of 'European champions' in key strategic sectors. From a European geopolitical point of view, a bipolar world order is something to avoid. Analysing these evolving 'geotechnical ensembles' can be helpful in nurturing a European debate on 'strategic autonomy'.

2 Classical Geopolitics and Technology

In his seminal article *'Geopolitical Hypotheses in Technological Perspective'*, Harold Sprout discussed the ways in which theorizers in geopolitical hypothesis-building had dealt with the continuing scientific and technological revolution (Sprout, 1963). [1] Whilst some had underestimated the possibilities and implications of continuing technological advances, others had built their geopolitical hypotheses expressly on the assumption that technological advances had become a "master variable" of international politics. Their criticism upon classical geopolitical authors stated that nearly all of them paid relatively little attention to institutional and other social factors that may set limits to projects and accomplishments of national political communities (Sprout, 1963, p. 187). Geopolitical hypotheses in this context are defined as *"propositions that purport to explain or to forecast the geographical distribution and patterning of political potential (power)"* (Sprout, 1963, p. 190). All geopolitical theorizing involves making or accepting estimates regarding the tools and skills (technology) available to interacting communities. It also involves making assumptions about the rate of future technological advance (Sprout, 1963, p. 192–193).

Harold Sprout identified several groups of geopolitical hypotheses dealing with technology:

> *First,* classical authors such as *Alfred Thayer Mahan* and *Halford John Mackinder* (Sprout, 1963, p. 193–196).[2] Mahan very much focused on how sea power technologies from traditional sailing boats over steel ships propelled by coal affected global power relations. Control over sea (lanes) was seen as a crucial step towards world political primacy (Stavridis, 2017, p. 62, 68). Mackinder focused on the mass introduction of railways on the Eurasian continent. This would 'unlock' the regional power potential in terms of natural resources and manpower. The political implications of constructing railroads was that it would favour land powers over sea powers. The latter would need containment strategies and buffer states in order to keep the *'Heartland'* in check. Critiques were voiced stating these authors combined Social Darwinism with environmental determinism in order to marry grand strategy with the expansion (and legitimization?) of imperial power (O'Lear, 2018, p. 11). However, the question remains whether such a blunt generalisation can be upheld.
>
> *Second,* there existed much speculation in the geopolitical literature around *climate in space and through time.* Such hypotheses could be

1 For more on the original geopolitical thinking by Harold and Margaret Sprout, read Chapter 4.
2 For more on the work of these classical geopolitical authors, read Chapter 3.

traced back to Hippocrates and Aristotle in 400 to 350 B.C. over philosophers, historians and geographers in the sixteenth through nineteenth centuries. More recent was the work of the geographer Ellsworth Huntington, who explained the rise and decline of civilisations in terms of the cyclic fluctuations of climate. Human and environmental variables then became crucial. Technologies that were able to cool or heat artificially, dehumidify or ventilate, were crucial for civilisational success. Education and the amount of capital available to (re)shape that environment to human needs, as well as other social factors, were deemed crucial in this specific body of literature (Sprout, 1963, p. 196–199).

A *third* type of geopolitical hypotheses in technological perspective dealt with the *uneven distribution of natural resources*. According to Harold Sprout, these geopolitical hypotheses generally start from the proposition that a nation's political position in international politics is significantly related to its capacity to provide military instrumentalities (Sprout, 1963, p. 201). That may have been true in the decades after the Second World War. However, today's literature also investigates how (the changing demand for) resources impacts the geo-economic and overall geopolitical position of territorial entities *other* than the state; sub-state entities such as a region, or for instance the European Union as an emerging foreign policy actor. More recent emanations of this body of literature tackle a wide range of issues. One can think of publications on resource war and the scramble for resources (Klare, 2001; Klare, 2012), oil geopolitics (Yergin, 1992), natural gas geopolitics (Grigas, 2017), the geopolitics of renewables (Criekemans, 2018b), the interconnection between energy and climate (Yergin, 2020) or even the geopolitics of the deep oceans (Hannigan, 2016). Technological advances may change once again the geo-economic and geopolitical situation and consequences. (see infra)

A *fourth* type of geopolitical hypotheses in technological perspective dealt with the *distribution of population*. This can be done in a quantitative way, but may also include qualitative variables, for instance in military affairs (Sprout, 1963, p. 203). One of the earlier publications on 'Technology and Geopolitics' was published by Ralph Turner in the journal *'Military Affairs'* in 1943. During the Second World War, he not surprisingly mentioned the invention of metallurgy on the transport of men and supplies. He stressed technological advances such as the internal combustion engine and the gun, as well as the tank and the airplane. Turner also noted a *socio-economic ecosystem* was needed in order to enable industries to produce these technologies in the first place. Each industry needs resources to cope with technological 'bottlenecks', has its own geographical extension, is in need of *a specialised labour force*, operates within a specific governmental system and forms the ecosystem *of* and depends *upon* other industries. Turner used these factors to examine the organisation and activities of a nation at war. Geopolitics could be understood as *"an effort to think about national existence in world terms"* (Turner, 1943).

A *fifth* type of geopolitical hypotheses in technological perspective dealt with *science and engineering*. Sprout quoted Blount's work on science as a factor in International Relations (Sprout, 1963, p. 205). Three variables were important; *whether* a nation had more "scientists of the highest grade" compared to other nations, *whether* engineering was pursued enough by the other scientists ('the much larger number of lesser scientists & trained technologists') in the nation. Finally he mentioned *whether* people, especially 'non-scientists' in the nation were sufficiently aware of the potentialities of new scientific knowledge *as well as* whether politicians and administrators were willing to rely on the advice of scientists. (Sprout, 1963, p. 205–206)

Each of these categories of geopolitical hypotheses represented attempts to identify one or a limited number of factors to account for the historic distributions of 'political potential' in the society of nations, or to provide a rational basis for predicting future distributions and patterns. Yet, the Sprouts were very critical and stressed that in 'Classical Geopolitics' nearly all geopolitical hypotheses were based on features of the *physical* environment (Sprout, 1963, p. 210–211). However, geopolitical hypotheses on technology needed to be more appreciative of the complexities in researching the impact of technology upon geopolitics, and perhaps also of geopolitics upon technology. Geopolitics as a field of science needed to better *"appreciate the magnitude of the continuing scientific revolution"*, as well as to *"anticipate the full political significance of engineering applications to scientific knowledge"*. Nevertheless, Harold Sprout did believe that science and technology transform and continue to 'radically change' the values and meanings of all the other variables, both non-human and human, in the environment of nations (Sprout, 1963, p. 211–212).

3 Daniel Deudney's "Geotechnical Ensembles"

There have been several other authors that have tried to bridge technology, geopolitics and strategy. In his book *'Global Communications since 1844. Geopolitics and Technology'*, Hugill explores the changes in information technology, telegraphy, telephony, radio telegraphy as well as the military applications of radar and military uses of radio and sattelites or fiber optics, and their impact upon command and control. Such communication system technologies have affected the world geopolitical system with different cycles of hegemony between the British, Germans, Americans, etc. Based upon his analysis of how the advancement of communication technologies benefitted states, Hugill predicted *"the end of the Mackinderian geopolitics of territorial states and a return to something more like the Mahanian geopolitics of trading states, in which blockading tactics will become ever more important."* (Hugill, 1999, p. 251). Butler was more interested in how transportation such as aviation had stimulated commerce and brought people in closer contact to one another. In a paper on the struggle for control of world air routes between 1910 and 1928, Butler coined the term *'technogeopolitics'*. Transportation and communication in his opinion can challenge fixed notions of geography by overcoming time and space. He complained that *"the process of technology is never incorporated directly into geopolitical theory"* (Butler, 2001, p. 637). [3]

Daniel Deudney constitutes one of the most interesting authors to further explore the relationship between geopolitics and technology, in a systematic way and over several decades. His innovative PhD tried to reconstruct, interpret and evaluate materialist world order theories of the late nineteenth and early twentieth centuries (Deudney, 1989). The hallmark of global geopolitical writings are the search for material explanations for human institutional outcomes (Deudney, 1989, p. 2–3). The "geo" in geopolitics "obscured" the important role of technology in the early world order theories. Classical geopolitical authors believed that geography-technology interaction plays a primary role in shaping an emerging world order (Deudney, 1989, p. 2). Deudney complained that *"none of the 'global geopoliticians' ever systematically spelt out the material assumptions, which are essential to understand them"* (Deudney, 1989, p. 6). The guiding assumptions of 'global geopolitics' are quite different from those of contemporary IR theories. Deudney was not claiming to have identified the "true" or "real" geopolitics, or some lost essence of geopolitics (Deudney, 1989, p. 7). However, he did claim that the factors which make up new world politics can best be understood as examples of such a materialist world order theory

3 In his analysis, Butler also referred to Gray and Sloan (Butler, 2001, p. 637). They saw the relationship between the geographical environment and the decision-making process as a dynamic one. They described geography as the mother of strategy (Gray & Sloan, 1999, p. 3). Many of the publications by Colin Gray explore the way in which geography is pertinent at the tactical, operational and strategic levels of conflict (Gray, 1977; Gray, 1996; Gray, 2004). Technology always has a role to play at each of these levels.

(Deudney, 1989, p. 7–8). 'Classical Geopolitics', in its simplest form, seemed to claim "that the largest physical features of the Earth in combination with capabilities of transportation, communication and destruction would *determine* the main features of world order. A 'handful of geographic features' (climate, fertility and resources, topography, and position) and techological capabilities (communication, transportation, and destruction) were the material forces making up the 'base' (Deudney, 1989, p. 9). The 'global geopoliticians' thought the 'base' or 'stage' of world politics is constituted by technology as well as geography. However, Deudney believed it is *erroneous* to picture them attributing primary causative weight to either geographical factors or technological factors (Deudney, 1989, p. 11).

Harold Sprout had already referred to *'geo-technic politics'* (Sprout, 1963, p. 192). Deudney believed that the important role which the 'global geopoliticians' attributed to technological factors had been *obscured* by the label "geopolitics" which suggests an almost exclusive emphasis on geography. Nevertheless, technology had always been part of geopolitical analysis, as early as in Mackinder's 1887 lecture 'The Scope and Methods of Geography", in which he referred to the *"state of knowledge and of material civilization"* (Deudney, 1989, p. 11). However, 'global geopoliticians' in his opinion had been *inconsistent* in applying the insight of technology's importance and dynamism (Deudney, 1989, p. 12).

In order to give unwarranted weight to either geographic features or technical capabilities, Deudney believed geopolitical scholars should describe the base or infrastructure as *combinations of particular geographic features and technological capabilities*. He termed these ***"geotechnical ensembles"***. Whereas 'global geopoliticians' treated combinations of geographical and technological factors as *exogeneous* factors acting upon or shaping human institutions, IR scholars primarily saw technology as *derivative* of human and political choice (Deudney, 1989, p. 13). Deudney believed that by incorporating technology, with some changes, into their concept of the base or non-social environment, 'global geopoliticians' were able to advance beyond the impasse of the naturalist theories (Deudney, 1989, p. 14). They were all theorists of change, looking at the impact of new technological forces and new aspects of geography. The writings of 'Classical Geopolitics' envisioned often, as a result of this, a 'period of turmoil' to be followed by the 'emergence of a more stable situation' (Deudney, 1989, p. 15). Think of the writings of Mahan on sea power or Mackinder on land power (Ball, 1985). Many other authors followed in their footsteps.

Deudney's innovative concept of ***"geotechnical ensembles"*** is a very useful one which can help today's geopolitical scholars to grasp the complexities of the interaction between 'geography' & 'technology' and how these can create new spaces of geo-economics, geopolitics and geostrategy. Deudney was of the opinion that in analysing technological impacts, it is important to distinguish between effects resulting from uneven access to technology and from the technology itself. Already 'Classical Geopolitics' dealt with the uneven acquisition of (industrial) technologies and organisations (Deudney, 1989, p. 26). 'Global geopoliticians' believed that a *master locale* or an *axial region* existed and tended toward unity, and that the fate of that axial region was of fundamental concern to states everywhere. If such a place were to be consolidated by one or more states, then the assets were brought together in order to be capable to support system-wide hegemony or empire (Deudney, 1989, p. 34). Only if interstate relations were able to contest such tendencies, could a plural world order be preserved (Deudney, 1989, p. 35). However, European overseas empires in large measure 'melted away' because the technologies of the Europeans became widely accessible (Deudney, 1989, p. 642). Deudney nevertheless remarks that 'global geopoliticans' often started their analysis from the alleged 'closure' of the world, Mackinder's 'Post-Columbian Epoch'. The world had become a 'closed political system'. [4] From this territorial closure, 'Classical Geopolitics' *"inferred that the existing natural resource base was fixed, subject only to the question of distribution – which might grow in a zero-sum environment"*. Deudney believed this inference was flawed. The continued growth of scientific knowledge and technical know-how has altered in many important ways the effective uses to which human institutions can put materials and energies drawn from the fixed or closed Earth (Deudney, 1989, p. 627). The same can be said of technologies today.

However, as Parag Khanna states, today's world localities such as cities and regions have also become geopolitical entities to which power is devolved. In such a world, *connectivity* has become intensely geopolitical (Khanna, 2016, p. 18). The march of connectivity will bring beliefs to collapse such as the idea that states are the main ordering entities in IR, or that *"national identity is the primary source of people's loyalty"*. In this context, Khanna mentions among others forces such as *devolution* (the fragmentation of authority towards provinces), *urbanization* (the growing size and power of cities), *mega-infrastructures* (new pipelines, new railways, and canals that morph geography), and *digital connectivity* (enabling new forms of community). They necessitate a re-imagination of how human life is organised on Earth. Central in his analysis are supply and demand as dynamic forces in search of equilibrium in all aspects of human life (Khanna, 2016, p. 19).

4 For more on the world as a 'closed political system' and the 'post-Columbian Epoch', read Chapter 3.

Supply chains between hubs in the world, often urban centres, are essential in the world in which we live. Khanna refers in this context to a 'Great Supply Chain War', a race not to conquer but to connect physically and economically to the world's most important supplies of raw materials, high technology, and fast-growing markets. In this 'Great Supply Chain War', Khanna believes that great powers (such as the United States of America and China) consciously seek to avoid costly military confrontations that could be 'self-defeating', because they disrupt these essential supply chains (Khanna, 2016, p. 28): *"In the Great Supply Chain War, infrastructure, supply chains and markets are as crucial as territory, armies and deterrence. The largest power does not always win; the most connected one does."*. While twentieth century territorial geopolitics was inspired by Mackinder, Khanna believes that in a supply chain world, it matters less who *owns* (or claims) territory than who *uses* (or administers) it. Instead of a de jure world *"This is my land"*, the motto of Khanna's de facto, supply chain world is *"Use it or lose it"* (Khanna, 2016, p. 28–29). For Parag Khanna, *connectivity* apparently constitutes both the main cause and effect of the current complexity in the world today. It is reshaping the human condition in the early twenty-first century around adapted geo-economic, geopolitical and geostrategic realities.

Deudney's insightful analysis of *'geotechnical ensembles'* together with Khanna's attempt at understanding the changed role of territory in which *supply chains* have become so central to both our lives and the fates of nations, offer us a stimulating conceptual framework. At the same time, this shapes and reshapes the wider geo-economic and geostrategic theatre within which to analyse the contemporary interaction between 'technology' and 'geopolitics'.

4 Technology & Geopolitics in Today's Economic, Energy and Security Relations

Let us now further analyse the relationship between technology and geopolitics in today's world. Inspired by Daniel Deudney, we will in particular discuss the new 'geotechnical ensembles' that are currently developing in economic, energy and security relations. A central theme will regularly return in some shape or fashion in this section; *territorial entities (states, regions or cities) which invest in ground-breaking technological know-how, both fundamental and applied innovation, as well as in the industrial base that comes with it, will in many ways be able to shape tomorrow's world in its geo-economic, geopolitical and geostrategic dimensions*. Hereafter, we will explore these new 'geotechnical ensembles' further.

4.1 *Economic Relations Faced with New 'Geotechnical Ensembles'*

Over the past decades, the advanced economies of the world have further developed and upgraded themselves into the *value chain of products and services*. We are witnessing the early stages of a 'Fourth Industrial Revolution', which is also affecting the new 'geotechnical ensembles' in the world. Traditional manufacturing and industrial practices are further automated, this time using modern smart technology. Large-scale machine-to-machine communication (M2M) and the internet of things (IoT) are integrated for increased automation, improved communication and self-monitoring. Smart machines are being developed that can analyse and diagnose issues without the need for human intervention. Countries such as Germany under Chancellor Merkel have developed governmental strategies as well as government-industry cooperation to increase domestic productivity and hence renew the place of the German industry in the world economy, as a 'hub' that still matters. Those countries that invest early in these kind of technologies, may very well develop a competitive edge that may later also translate into some 'geopolitical cloud' in world affairs. Czismadia stresses that, in the wake of industrial competition, the economic roles of regions and territorial units is appreciating. A rivalry amongst regions and even cities is taking shape (Czismadia, 2017, p. 17), in a race to attract the most capital, the best people and the greatest innovative ideas. Decentralisation fits well with this 'Fourth Industrial Revolution'.

Next to the industrial dimension, there is also *fintech, the financial-technological dimension*. Jose Miguel Alonso-Trabanco refers for instance to the financialization of the global economy. Today, many automated systems are amongst the top buyers and sellers of currencies, stock and bonds. Yet, *"their programming can be manipulated so that the high-speed algorithmic transactions they perform respond to geostrategic – rather than economic – imperatives, something that can unleash disturbances and widespread contagions of financial turmoil in order to undermine an enemy's financial nerve centres and circuits – attacks that can destabilize an entire economy. In other words, automation can change how financial warfare is carried out in the 21st century."* (Alonso-Trabanco, 2020). Pascal Vander Straeten confirms that 'financial weapons of war' have grown in importance, for instance in China. Insider trading schemes carry the mark of deliberate attack perpetrated by agents in another country. National security has become much more complicated and multifaceted. It can easily be compromised via nefarious infiltration of capital markets or clandestine activities aimed at disrupting critical components of a financial system. Financial warfare constitutes one of the tools of war in the arsenal of the Chinese to gain control and influence across the world without resorting to military engagement. *'Geofinance'* studies how geopolitics affect the world of global finance, but also how the realm of international finance is impacting world events, and their stakeholders, be it governments, businesses, or individuals. It covers the multi-faceted nature of the complex relationship between global finance and geopolitics in its broadest sense (Vander Straeten, 2018; Vander Straeten, 2020).

Another related phenomenon to watch in the future are *cryptocurrencies* such as Bitcoin (BTC) and Ethereum (ETH). These constitute a stateless medium of exchange that have challenged one of the essential attributes associated with national sovereignty: coinage. But, as Alonso-Trabanco rightly states, several national states are already undertaking ambitious research and development projects in order to launch their own digital versions of their national currencies (Alonso-Trabanco, 2020). In 2013, the Dutch financial investor and current fund manager Willem Middelkoop had already written about a coming *'Big Reset'* in the international financial system (Middelkoop, 2013). In 2020, the *World Economic Forum* and other institutions such as the International Monetary Fund (IMF) started to discuss a *'Great Reset'* to address global monetary instabilities. Digital currencies seem to become part of that future. The current massive 'money creation' also known as *'Quantitative Easing'* (QE) since the financial-economic crisis of 2008 and even more massive since the coronacrisis of 2020, create questions on the position of the current monetary system and the centrality of the American dollar as the world's reserve currency. In addition, there exists some degree of speculation amongst 'gold bull investors' that the current imbalances in the world economy, and the erosion of so-called 'fiat money' currencies, might lead to gold itself being re-valued upwards in the future. In this process, governments would embrace the technological advancements of digital currencies, and instrumentalize them so as to maintain or even reshape [5] the geo-financial underpinnings of the world economy.

---

5 In this context, the popular American author James Rickards refers to China and Russia having further expanded their gold reserves during the period between 2010 and 2020. Rickards and others believe a future upward 're-evaluation' of the gold price could form the basis for a new geo-economic system. It could even become the foundation of a new world order in which the United States of America in specific and the West overall could see its position relatively speaking diminished compared to that of Asia (Rickards, 2012; Rickards, 2016; Rickards, 2019). In his latest book *'The New Great Depression. Winners and Losers in a Post-Pandemic World'*, James Rickards believes that growth in the West will be persistently weaker because of the cumulated results of more than a decade of 'quantitative easing', structural governmental deficits and the liberal markets being disrupted and 'slowed down' by additional governmental regulation and taxation (Rickards, 2020).

A third aspect to take into account in the economic 'geotechnical ensembles' is *data* itself, which is becoming the new currency of the economy (Mayer-Schönberger & Ramge, 2018). Mayer-Schönberger and Ramge foresee a future in which 'financial capitalism' will gradually decline in favour of 'data capitalism'. Nowadays, we gradually see more and more examples of so-called free services in the cloud, in stock market brokerage and financial products, in health applications, etc. in which the consumer pays with his or her own data. Business models of companies hence are changed, in addition to the markets. Geopolitically, we are seeing that high tech societies start playing a geo-economic role as advanced tech and start up-hubs; in Singapore, Silicon Valley in California, Shenzhen in China, Tel Aviv in Israel.

In 1999, authors such as Ferguson and Mansbach still believed that 'new technologies' were somehow emancipating societies and world politics. They would spread 'modernity' and the secular culture that is associated with it. They erode "norms that previously had encouraged passivity and on which had been built the authority of traditional elites" (Ferguson & Mansbach, 1999, p. 19). With the eyes of the early 2020s, we know better and have lost some of our naivety. Centralised and authoritarian political systems such as those being strengthened in the People's Republic of China have instrumentalised the data revolution via apps, face recognition and social media to control or 'guide' their populations into subjugation. China's social credit system can be seen as of one of these experiments. Like with any technology in the past, 'big data' cannot only be used to better mankind, but also to advance the agenda of others. Even in democracies, there are concerns over the usage of data and surveillance technology, privacy and questions of individual freedom. The liberal world order itself seems to have been put under pressure, not only as a result of the alleged rise of more authoritarian regimes in the world, but also because of the gradual development of data technologies. Whereas Ferguson and Mansbach spoke of "technological change" leading to the "erosion of state capacity" and to the "declining importance of territory" in 1999 (Ferguson & Mansbach, 1999, p.23), we potentially see a rather juxtapositioning of these trends today. The latest technologies of big data in the hands of few can again strengthen the positions of centralised and populist governments. A debate will be needed on how each of these can be balanced and how to manage these new powers in the economy, but also in the political realm.

Sami Moisio has studied the *'geopolitics of the knowledge-based economy'* from a Critical Geopolitics-perspective.[6] Since the 1990s, material processes

6 The geopolitical school of thought of *Critical Geopolitics* is explained *and* criticised in chapter 3 of this book.

of the knowledge-based economy have been accompanied by politicians and scholarly literature on the development and nature of a 'new breed of territorial society'. Knowledge-based economization was extended from a world of production into a wider societal phenomenon. In this context, he refers to such terms as 'network societies', 'learning societies' or 'information societies'. Hence territorial entities from cities or regions to states and intergovernmental organisations have all articulated strategies on the knowledge-based economy (Moisio, 2018, p. 41–42).

Moisio believes the geopolitical in the context of knowledge-based economization boils down to three interlinked issues; 1°) *geopolitical discourses* on the production of business and management knowledge regarding inter-territorial competition and competitiveness in a post-Fordist [7] setting, 2°) *objectifying calculative practices*; cities, regions, states, supranational polities are seen as geopolitical objects locked into an inter-territorial competition, 3°) geopolitical subjects are produced. This for instance refers to the production of skilled labour in the knowledge economy, or the relationship between human creativity and urban space (Moisio, 2018, p. 44). As a critical geopolitical scholar, Moisio tries to question the 'naturalization' of such discourses. However, knowledge-based economization should be seen for what it is; *"knowledge-based economization takes place a relatively narrow faction of population in the driver's seat of societal development."* Moisio also believes it would be worthwhile to examine how knowledge-based economization is linked to democracy or socio-spatial-economic inequality (Moisio, 2018, p. 161).

In this context, one can also think of the global pandemic when the coronacrisis raged across the world. During 2020–2021, people around the world were in lockdown during several 'waves'. Thanks to the technological advances of the internet and network-societies, white collar workers could just continue their work. The blue collar workers were often called 'essential workers', but

---

7 In 'Fordism', large corporations make mass-consumer items with assembly line techniques. Production is standardized and, once begun, really rather difficult to reconfigure. The Fordist 'business model' thrives on the scale of production. It was pioneered in the early 20th century by the Ford Motor Company. By contrast, 'Post-Fordism' has three characteristics: (1) a focus on the transformative role of new technologies and practices regarding material and immaterial production, especially new information and communication technologies and their role in facilitating a new, more flexible, networked global economy; (2) a focus on the leading economic sectors that enable a transition from mass industrial production to post-industrial production; and (3) a focus on how major crisis tendencies of Fordism are resolved through the consolidation of a new and stable series of economic and extra-economic institutions and forms of governance that facilitate the rise and consolidation of profitable new processes, products, and markets (Encyclopedia Britannica).

were relatively speaking more affected than others by the virus and its myriad of consequences. Many others lost their jobs, or they still had to continue to go to work. Blue collar workers were, relatively speaking, much more affected by the global coronacrisis compared to their white collar colleagues. Since their housing conditions were often also less favourable compared to white collar workers, they again were more affected mentally by lockdown, which lasted for months on end. These realities showed the disparities that exist within societies. At the same time, it became quite apparent that even the white collar workers could not survive without the contribution of blue collar workers. This puts so-called knowledge-based societies somewhat in perspective. At a geopolitical level, some regimes such as Beijing tried to present their policy solutions to the crisis (severe lockdowns, restricting individual freedom through new technologies such as apps and surveying), as performing better compared to those utilized in Western societies. Some Western governments started mimicking some more rigid approaches that were heralded as successes in the East. The jury is still out on the wider geopolitical and geo-economic impact of the new technologies with which governments experimented during the global coronacrisis. In liberal democracies it may well spur debate over the constitutional and legal limits that should be imposed upon governments and corporations in 'crowd control'. *At the same time*, the coronacrisis has provoked a societal debate on technology and politics in affairs of health. Whilst some countries such as the Netherlands or the United Kingdom had disinvested in intensive care units and had applied neoliberal solutions, others such as Germany had protected their national health service. Countries such as Germany seemed to perform better, provoking a debate on *markets vs. politics* in health, and their consequences for Geopolitics.

4.2 *Energy Relations Faced with New 'Geotechnical Ensembles'*

A second case of new 'geotechnical ensembles' can be found in energy relations. The world is currently undergoing a fundamental *energy transition* from fossil forms of energy such as coal, oil and later natural gas towards a renewable energy future. The European Union and the United States under the Biden Administration both have the ambition to speed up this process, through the further development of *renewable energy technologies*. However, as these technologies will be further developed, it will also start to affect the geopolitical needs and partnerships of the EU and the US around the world.

First, changes to existing energy mixes might provoke geo-economic and geopolitical 'fall out'. *Second*, a growing need to get access to the critical materials that will power a renewable energy future could lead to scarcity & supply problems and geopolitical competition over key resources such as nickel, cobalt, copper, silver, scandium, lithium and rare earth elements. *Third*, a race over technological advances and intellectual property in the energy domain could erupt, most notably in the field of battery efficiency & recycling technologies. *In conclusion*, the US and the EU may very well have to develop their own 'strategic autonomy' in the domain of energy. Below we investigate these dimensions somewhat further.

4.2.1 Changes to Existing Energy Mixes and Geo-Economic & Geopolitical 'Fall out'

Many governments around the world are already changing their respective energy mixes. Conventional oil will in the coming decades diminish in *relative* importance. This may provoke crises in the business models of traditional oil producers such as in the Middle East, which could produce societal instability. Countries like for instance Saudi Arabia are already trying to diversify their respective business models, but it remains a race against time. [8]

The natural resource wealth of the past made the rulers of such countries more autonomous vis-à-vis their citizens. *Internally*, the decarbonization of the European energy market may put the social contract of in particular oil regimes under pressure (Scholten, Criekemans & Van de Graaf, 2020). *Externally*, such countries may fall into the sphere of influence of other powers, such as the People's Republic of China. Several geopolitical theatres around Europe may reconfigure as a result of decarbonisation and energy transition. As a consequence, Leonard et al. propose to *"help neighbouring oil and gas-exporting countries manage the repercussions of the European Green Deal"*. In their opinion, the EU should engage with these countries to foster their economic diversification, including into renewable energy and green hydrogen that could in the future be exported to Europe (Leonard, Pisani-Ferry, Shapiro, Tagliapietra & Wolf, 2021).

Natural gas will in the coming period grow in relative importance as a 'bridge fuel' towards a renewable energy future. Compared to oil & coal, natural gas is 'cleaner' provided there is no methane evaporation at production sites. On the demand side, a growing number of countries are therefore opting for an increased share of natural gas in their national energy mixes. Important changes are also taking place on the supply side. Thanks to innovative exploration techniques, novel supplies of natural gas are being discovered. This is

---

8 One option for Saudi Arabia could be to harness the power of the Sun and become a global hub for green hydrogen. With *'Helios Green Fuels'*, Saudi Arabia tries to become the world's largest hydrogen producer; 650 tons a day by electrolysis – enough for conversion to 1.2 million tons per year of green ammonia, to be shipped abroad (Ratcliffe, 2021).

prompting new shifts in geopolitical relations, causing the Russian Federation to be in a strategically less favourable position (Criekemans, 2018a).

Over the last decade, *innovative exploration techniques* have uncovered several substantial natural gas fields off the coast of Israel, Cyprus and Egypt. There are clear indications of more to come. This has caused severe geopolitical tensions between Turkey and Greece over their claim to natural gas deposits in the Eastern Mediterranean. This was a reason why Turkey started to support the GNA-government [9] in Libya militarily, in exchange for a deal with Libya over demarcating its Exclusive Economic Zone – which was in opposition to the UNCLOS-EEZ-interpretation [10] by Greece. Thus, energy transition may also 'fuel' new conflicts. Israel is likely to become a major natural gas exporter, which will also translate into geostrategic changes in Europe's near abroad. The *'Nord Stream 2'* natural gas pipeline between Germany and the Russian Federation caused tensions between Germany and other (Central-)European (also non-EU) nations. This case shows that sometimes even European internal solidarity may be 'ignited'. Europe's energy transition thus creates several new energy security risks. If Europe is to develop its own strategy in an age of increased competition, its altered energy needs will have to be taken into account in order to avoid dependence from other world actors.

4.2.2 Growing Need to Get Access to Critical Materials That Will Power Renewable Energy

A domain where new geo-economic and geostrategic security risks may also rise dramatically is the *import of the minerals and metals needed* for such

9 GNA refers to the Government of National Accord in Libya, formed under the Libyan Political Agreement, a United Nations–led initiative, signed on 17 December 2015. The GNA only controls a small western portion of the total Libyan territory. Its rival is the government led by General Haftar of the Tobruk-based Libyan National Army (LNA), and supported by other countries such as the Russian federation, Egypt, France, etc.

10 UNCLOS refers to the *United Nations Convention on the Law of the Sea*. It outlines the provisions relating to the definition of baselines along the coast, the spatial dimensions of claims to maritime jurisdiction, coastal and other state rights and responsibilities within such zones. Finally and importantly, UNCLOS also deals with the delimitation of maritime boundaries where overlapping claims occur. UNCLOS legally introduces Exclusive Economic Zones (EEZS), within which a Member State enjoys sovereign exploitation rights over natural (living and non-living) resources. The perimeter of an EEZ extends from land's low water line out 200 nautical miles. Foreign states may still navigate freely and fly overhead as well as lay underwater cables and submarine pipes. UNCLOS also formalized the Continental Shelf as a natural extension of the land territory (which is limited to 12 nautical miles, Article 3 UNCLOS), subject to the Member State's control. For legal application, the Continental Shelf can extend to the edge of the continental margin, the point at which the shelf descends to an abyssal plain on the ocean floor.

technologies as the manufacturing of solar panels, wind turbines, li-ion batteries, fuel cells and electric vehicles. As Leonard et al. state clearly, these minerals and metals have particular properties and few to no substitutes (Leonard et al, 2021, p. 8). A recent study by *The Hague Centre for Strategic Studies* delved into the policy options for the Netherlands and the EU with regard to securing critical materials (Patrahau, Singhvi, Rademaker, van Manen, Kleijn & van Geuns, 2021). It comes to the conclusion that China controlled in 2019 70% of renewable energy (REE) mining, 85% of REE oxide refining, 90% of REE metals and 90% of magnet production needed for wind energy and electric vehicles.

The electrification of transportation in the EU will change Europe's dependencies towards horizon 2030 and beyond. We may start witnessing scarcity and supply problems over key resources such as nickel, cobalt, copper, silver, scandium, lithium and rare earth elements. An urgent debate has emerged over the need for a European critical materials strategy. For the European Commission, critical raw materials have a high economic value and supply risk. Building on the EU's *Raw Materials Initiative* and in the wake of the COVID-19 health crisis, the Commission developed a document *'Critical Raw Materials Resilience: Charting a Path towards Greater Security and Sustainability'*. In it, the EU 2020 list of critical raw materials is developed. In addition, challenges are identified to enable a secure and sustainable supply of critical raw materials. Via implementing a wide range of actions, EU resilience and open strategic autonomy can be increased (European Commission, 2020). The European Commission already developed the *'Raw Materials Information System'* and will reinforce it, but more is needed. The Commission will strengthen its work with *'Strategic Foresight Networks'* to develop robust evidence and scenario planning on raw materials supply, demand and use for strategic sectors. The criticality assessment methodology may be reviewed for the next list (2023) to integrate the latest knowledge.

However, the question remains whether 'bureaucratic' desk planning will be enough. Such policy choices are inherently political. It seems that the needs of German or French industry do not always internally align yet. There is also an important diplomatic dimension to be considered. Berlin seems to prioritize good relations with Beijing, as suggested by its recent promotion in December 2020 of an *'EU-China Comprehensive Agreement on Investment'*. However, this agreement is mostly about sectors such as cloud services, financial services, private healthcare, environmental services, international maritime transport and air transport-related services. It steers far away from energy. It only asks China to effectively implement the Paris Agreement on climate change as well as to effectively implement the International Labour Organisation Conventions (ILO) it has ratified. Meanwhile in January 2021, China decided to strengthen regulation over the rare-earth metals industry from mining to exports in a new draft law of the Ministry of Transport and Information Technology. Commentators have suggested that Beijing could apply its new export control law (Tabeta, 2021). The move by Beijing should be seen in a broader context of geopolitical rivalry with the United States of America. China can use rare earths as strategic resources that can be leveraged as an advantage in international diplomacy.

Meanwhile, on 24 February 2021 the new American president Joe Biden signed an *'Executive Order on America's Supply Lines'* not only limited to critical materials but also essential goods, supply chains and key technologies also beyond but not limited to the energy sector (White House, 2021). Europe may well find itself in a world system in which the US-China rivalry may also affect its own options to develop its continental-wide geopolitical strategy in terms of renewable energy.

European countries will need to re-evaluate their relations with countries in Africa, Asia and the Americas in order to come to a balanced strategy. Increased competition may also mean that the US could sometimes be a competitor. We for instance see a recent effort by a US-led Canadian company *First Cobalt* to re-arrange part to the Congolese cobalt production towards Canada in order to refine it for the first time on North American soil, as well as to develop cobalt mines which will exclusively work for the American car industry. [11] The EU will need similar diversification strategies. In particular, Canada comes to the fore as a potential strategic partner for Europe. Canada may well stand at the cusp of a commodities boom with much expertise in such domains as nickel, copper, silver, etc. In addition, Canada is investing in sustainable mining and refining technologies that match the EU's climate ambitions. [12]

4.2.3 A Race over Technological Advances and Intellectual Property in the Energy Domain

The energy transition of the coming decades will also involve technology and intellectual property. The transition towards more renewable energy in countries and regions entails more than a mere change in the energy mix. The transition entails the conversion of an energy industry which was merely

11 For more on the strategy of the US-led Canadian company *First Cobalt*: https://www.first-cobalt.com/ .

12 Several Canadian companies are spearheading new sustainability techniques, which would make them very attractive. An example of such a company in the nickel sector is *FPX Nickel*: https://fpxnickel.com/ . Although located in faraway British Columbia, new advancements in sustainable mining may change these sectors.

based upon the extraction of fossil energy sources to an even more technology driven sector. This 'new energy' industry which is gradually taking shape will thus restructure technologically, combining new insights in sustainability with the decentralised character of the IT-sector of the nineties. That is why the evolution towards renewable energy is sometimes called an *"ET-Revolution"*, or *"Energy Technology-Revolution"* (Criekemans, 2018b). For instance, some authors stress that energy utility companies will be able to manage their energy input and output intelligently. Consumers will start using smart meters. Cyberspace technology may also enable changes in the energy infrastructure, operations and usage. Advances in energy storage technology are expected to become a 'game-changer' which will enable decentralised energy production to become more mainstream. Digital technology will upgrade the electricity infrastructure. This may very well change the geopolitical order in the years to come (Pandya, 2020, p. 74–75).

According to Guillaume Sainteny, there are also some other geopolitical dimensions in the global developments related to renewable energy. One can speak of a global struggle for the control over companies and the added value that they will produce. In order to determine the position of countries and regions, one could utilize three criteria; (1) how many patents are awarded; (2) the relative weight of the capital investments in renewable energy, and (3) the presence of leading companies in this new industry (Sainteny, 2010). An application of these parameters leads to similar countries popping up on the radar screen of the researcher. In 2010, Sainteny identified the three geographical REE-technology zones; the European Union with Germany as a core country, the United States of America and Asia (with China, India, South Korea and Japan as core countries). Meanwhile it seems that the People's Republic of China has developed substantially, both from a capital-intensive and technological point of view. The Dutch geopolitical risk think tank *The Hague Centre for Strategic Studies* reported in 2021 that Beijing is using its legal standardization efforts as a "geopolitically strategic instrument". It is trying to set the standards for basic features of such emerging technologies via a *Standardization Law* which entered into power in 2018 (Patrahau, et al., 2021, pp. 90–91). The country is also massively investing in research and development over many critical raw materials needed in the REE-sector. Whereas China's R&D expenditure in 2010 was less than half of that of the EU, the situation had changed drastically by 2015/2016. China overtook the EU in R&D expenditure and levelled with the US on most cited publications (Patrahau, et al., 2021, pp. 93–94). These are all clear indications that European countries will need to step up in the technology domain if they do not want to become dependent. In addition, China tries to diplomatically 'roll out' their know-how to their own sphere of influence in countries belonging to the *'One Belt, One Road'*-initiative (OBOR). That may have further repercussions down the road.

Key domains of geo-economic and even geopolitical interest for the EU, the US and China are clearly those new technologies involving the *circular economy* and *battery efficiency*. The latter may very well turn out to be the 'holy grail' for those wishing to roll out a renewable energy future. For the European Union, investments alone may not be enough. Strategic alliances will be needed as well, for instance with the United Kingdom and Japan. British companies such as *Ilika* [13] are developing the successors of lithium ion-batteries; solid state batteries. *Ilika* works closely together with the Japanese car manufacturer *Toyota*. These technologies could not only increase efficiency in transportation, offices & homes. They could also limit the Western dependence from China in terms of raw materials and technology. A similar American-European alliance has developed around another solid state battery developer; the American company *Quantumscape* is supported by *Bill Gates* and has an alliance with the German car manufacturer *Volkswagen*. Already in 1999, a French-Japanese *Renault-Nissan Alliance* was created around electric vehicles, of which *Mitsubishi* later became part. It is active in further driving down EV-costs. Inspired by such naturally developed cooperation at company level, the EU may well want to mature this further into an informal geo-economic alliance with like-minded countries. The *Organisation for Economic Co-operation and Development* (OECD) seems to be an ideal policy setting and platform to develop such a technological cooperation.[14] Its members share similar views both on economic development and values such as democracy and market economy. During the oil crises of the 1970s, it already played a role in coordinating the energy policy of its members through the creation of the *International Energy Institute* (IEA) in Paris. Coordinating research investment and standardization could also help the EU and US in creating a counterweight to the Chinese efforts in this domain. In addition, the IEA within OECD has in the past already published various reports on energy technology.

---

13 For more on the British pioneer in solid state battery technology *Ilika*: https://www.ilika.com/ .

14 The *Organisation for Economic Co-operation and Development* (OECD) is an intergovernmental economic organisation with 37 member countries, founded in 1961 to stimulate economic progress and world trade. It is a forum of countries describing themselves as committed to democracy and the market economy, providing a platform to compare policy experiences, seek answers to common problems, identify good practices and coordinate domestic and international policies of its members (Wikipedia).

4.2.4 New Energy Technology Necessitates a Debate on 'Strategic Autonomy'

What can we conclude based upon this analysis of the new 'geotechnical ensembles' in the domain of energy? As a result of the ongoing energy transition, one could state that the US and the EU may very well have to develop their own 'strategic autonomy' in the domain of energy. Decarbonization and energy transition is much more than adapting a country's energy mix to meet climate challenges. It requires a fundamental rethinking of the geo-economic position of countries in the world. It involves essentially changing our energy dependencies. It entails systematic and coordinated efforts at jointly developing renewable energy technologies. It is a process which needs to be structured and consolidated through standardization. There will be winners and losers. And those countries who feel they are losing could resort to naked power politics or changed alliances to push back. A debate on 'strategic autonomy' is a way of answering the challenges in a more strategic way. The EU and US will need an adapted energy diversification strategy and renewed technological alliances. At a more global level, both entities will need to engage in an active 'balancing' strategy in geo-economic and geopolitical matters. Their energy needs may ultimately also have to be defended geostrategically through a credible defence posture.

4.3 *Security Relations Faced with New 'Geotechnical Ensembles'*

As a third domain, let us now explore some of the new 'geotechnical ensembles' in the security domain. Over the past decades, security challenges have become much more interwoven; economic, societal, environmental and energy security challenges have become de facto interconnected (Collins, 2019). Nevertheless also in the defence and security sector new technological changes are impacting geopolitics and geostrategy.

In his analysis on *'Geopolitics and the Great Powers in the Twenty-First Century'*, Dale Walton stressed that the ongoing and interrelated revolutions in biotechnology, nanotechnology, robotics, computer science and others are laying the groundwork for a *next* 'Revolution in Military Affairs' (RMA) (Dale Walton, 2007, p.105–106). A revolution in military affairs was defined by the geopolitical author Colin S. Gray's as *"a radical change in the conduct and character of war"* (Gray, 2006, vi; Gray, 2009: 123). Dale Walton believed we are on the verge of a 'Revolution in Strategic Perspectives' (RSP). That will necessitate policy-makers to radically alter the way in which they think about politics. In some ways the last European RSP can be traced back to the European 'breakout' and the Age of Discovery. The last American RSP is of a more recent nature, and translated into their becoming a world power in the course of the twentieth century. The 'Second American RMA' essentially constituted a repudiation of the Nuclear American RMA. As Dale Walton stresses, an RSP constitutes a much more 'Epoch-shaping event' than a single RMA (Dale Walton, 2007, p. 90). Nevertheless, Dale Walton sees a combination of biotechnology, computer science (think of algorithms and quantum computers), robotics and many other fields changing the very nature of warfare (Dale Walton, 2007, p.105). If Dale Walton is correct, then the very nature of warfare itself may already be changing. We may already be living in a 'grey zone' between war and peace, ever more uncertain and precarious.

There are also fundamental geopolitical consequences to such a world. Instead of occupying spaces with conventional armies, or threatening annihilation with weapons of mass destruction (WMDs), war can now be waged in very different ways. Whereas the nuclear RMA raised the threshold for military conflict, the currently ongoing RMA may even lower that threshold. Perhaps we already find ourselves in a constant struggle over power with other means. Think for instance about the constant cyber warfare that is waged between Russia, China, the European countries and the United States of America. Increasingly, cyber warfare is also proliferating and being 'normalised' amongst other smaller state (and even non-state) actors. At the same time, this produces consequences for the foreign policy and diplomacy of nations which need to be dealt with in a more (pro)active way (Riordan, 2019, p. 72–82).

Current strategic doctrine is moving from 'defensive' towards 'offensive' strategic postures. Of all the companies in the world, Israel has some of the most important ones that are on the cutting edge of the current technological know-how. One could say that *cyber*, as an a-symmetric threat, *constitutes a kind of 'great equalizer' in geopolitics*. Think for instance about the very potent cyber capacities that were developed by the Democratic People's Republic of Korea (DPRK). Pyongyang has developed an extra capability that can threaten Western information networks, business infrastructure and government installations. Whereas in the past, these countries remained very well out of range of attack, this is no longer true today. The question of 'attribution' stands central; can the attacked entities prove whom is trying to destabilize them? Cyber threats may also foster uncertainty in the geopolitical landscape overall, and suspicion. Whilst a rival may engage in open trade relations and/or in diplomatic affairs, it may at the very same time as well try to gauge the vulnerabilities of its target and prepare for destabilisation actions. Current strategic thinking in the West, most in particular in the United States and in some other Western countries and Israel, seems to entertain the idea that the policy response is to develop 'offensive' cyber capabilities. Attackers should know that a price needs to be paid if they engage in cyber activities. However, the question remains whether such offensive capabilities themselves cannot contribute to scenarios in which the threshold between a cyber crisis and actual kinetic conflict is not lowered. Technology has brought capabilities and amassed the potential of even fewer people to affect others. At the same time it increases vulnerabilities and a deep sense of uncertainty in international relations. That uncertainty may increasingly affect or 'infect' geopolitical relations across the globe. There does not seem to be any obvious alternative than to continue this cyber race. And in that race itself, countries such as Israel have become major players. Of all the countries in the world, Israel boasts several major cyber security companies that are even selling their expertise and solutions of offensive capabilities and techniques.

In 2000, Steven L. Spiegel wrote the article *'Traditional Space vs. Cyberspace: The Changing Role of Geography in Current International Politics'*, in the journal *Geopolitics*. In it, he identified 'three tiers' in the international system (Spiegel, 2000). *First*, the 'high-technology states' of a 'twenty-first century style' (the US, Canada, Western Europe, Japan, Australia and the newly industrialised countries of Asia (South Korea, Taiwan and Singapore). *Second*, the 'nationalistic states' of a 'nineteenth century style' (with examples from the Middle East and Africa). *Third*, the 'transitional states' of a 'twentieth century style' (with examples such as the People's Republic of China, Brazil, Russia and Mexico). Seen with the eyes of the 2020s, these thoughts seems a reflection of their own time. Today, we see that some of Spiegel's 'transitional states' in fact have developed cyber capabilities that are quite advanced. They have developed hybrid strategies, and some have become quite nationalistic at the same time. The adoption rate of cyber capabilities, and in particular their 'weaponization' differs among countries. Earlier in 1998, Stanley Brunn proposed a 'Treaty of Silicon' as an analogy to the Treaty of Westphalia (Brunn, 1998). It would involve not only states but also IGOs and NGOs. It would deal with such issues as violations of electronic space, spying and electronic surveillance, policing and monitoring in the state, cyberterrorism, data banks, ownership issues of information and data (Brunn, 1998, p. 126–127). Almost a quarter century later, the world is still dealing with these questions. Westphalia's *'non-interference in the affairs of other states'* seems somewhat coming from another planet if we compare to today's information and data interdependence. Because there is no commonly agreed framework on how to deal with information technology vulnerabilities, geopolitical relations among nations are strained or sometimes undermined.

In addition, this constant struggle lowers the barriers between 'geo-economic' and 'geostrategic' concerns of states. It is not a coincidence that strategic thinkers are now much more concerned about a cyber infiltration into the critical infrastructure of their electricity and communication networks. Foreign operators may already lie dormant inside these networks. In the past, foreign actors used simple *Distributed Denial of Service* (*DDoS*) attacks. Today *botnets* [15] are used controlling several hundreds of thousands of 'zombie-computers', of which some may be located in Eastern-Europe, but also in the Americas, Africa, or even hacked computers in Western Europe. In the future as our societies will become even more technology-intensive, non-state and state-sponsored hackers will have even more 'attack surfaces' via new devices and connections. Why wage war when you can disrupt societies from the inside out? As a result, our strategic thinking will have to change. Buchanan believes state-sponsored hacking is becoming increasingly aggressive as modern cyber operations grow in capability. Developing these capacities is becoming a tool of geopolitical shaping. Hacking may be of direct use in joint operations with conventional military capabilities, such as demonstrated by the Russian Federation in their campaign against Georgia in 2008 (Buchanan, 2020, p. 306–307). Cyber espionage operations are also conducted by intelligence agencies, tapping into computers and networks. Next to *attack* and *espionage*, there is also the category of *destabilization* (Buchanan, 2020, p. 306–307). According to Buchanan, *hacking makes a difference in geopolitics*. Hackers achieve missions which are ever more varied and develop capabilities that are ever more powerful. They are motivated by the prospect of creating a geopolitical advantage for their states, largely uninhibited by norms, treaties or fears of retaliation (Buchanan, 2020, p. 319). Classical Geopolitics' social Darwinism [16] seems to be alive once again among all major powers, but now in a more high tech variation.

As Pandya underlines, many state or non-state actors would like to achieve political, economic, military and strategic security objectives without the use of military force. Information warfare increasingly is proving to be much more effective compared to traditional warfare tactics. The power of new information tools, techniques and targets to leak information and spread misinformation grows (Pandya, 2020, p. 168).[17] Increasingly, the military will need to

---

15 A *botnet* is an army of computers which all have, at an earlier stage, become infected with the same malware. This gives a 'botmaster' remote control of these computers. In this way, the botmaster can commandeer them, even without their owners' knowledge. They make use of so called 'zero-days'; computer-software vulnerabilities which are unknown to those who should be interested in its mitigation (including the vendor of the target software).

16 For more on social Darwinism, read Chapter 3 on geopolitical schools of thought by David Criekemans.

17 For more on (mis)information, geo-economics and increasing rivalry, read Chapter 7 by Gyula Csurgai.

work much more closely together with information specialists but also with intelligence services, both civilian and military. In the realm of 'Robotics and Automated Systems' (RAS), there are those countries that are reluctant, such as Belgium. Other countries such as the Netherlands, the United Kingdom and the United States of America are actively experimenting with it to see what works and what does not. This will change the battlefield itself.

Another example of how military technology changes the geopolitical impact of nations are *drones*. Over the past years, Turkey has become a major player in this domain. The drone producer Baykar Technologies has developed unmanned aerial vehicles (UAV) which are highly agile. Especially the Bayraktar TB2 [18] UAV is very nimble and accurate. Despite the UN embargo on Libya's ongoing civil war, it is suspected that at least three were being used over Tripoli by the GNA government forces in Libya, who were supported by the Turkish government of President Erdogan. In June 2020, Azerbaijani Defence Minister Zakir Hasanov announced that his country had decided to purchase Bayraktar drones from Turkey. During the Nagorno-Karabakh war in 2020, Bayraktar TB2s were used against the Armed Forces of Armenia with great success. Azerbaijan used TB2 to destroy Armenian artillery, infantry positions and military vehicles. With this technology, Turkey was able to support its geopolitical ally Azerbaijan against Armenia. This changed the geostrategic equation in the region. This geostrategic success apparently prompted the Ukrainian government to purchase 48 Bayraktar TB2 drones through a joint venture state-owned Ukrainian defence manufacturer. Incidentally, the Russian Federation stood on the other side of the crisis in every case; it supported the rivalling General Haftar in Libya. Russia however played a much weaker role vis-à-vis Armenia, and Moscow is pressurizing the Zelensky government in Ukraine. Via drone technology, Turkey seems to strengthen its own geopolitical ambitions in North Africa, the Middle East, the Caucasus and the Black Sea region.

Geopolitically, such technological revolutions may also aggravate the strategic challenges with which nations are confronted. Non-state actors such as terrorists may get hold of these technologies, or even start implementing their own adaptations such as miniaturization or simplification. Think for instance of the fighters of the Islamic State / Daesh in Syria. They were actively using rudimentary drones in combat and also waged an information campaign across borders via social media. Relatively cheap technologies then may be turned into a-symmetric tools of warfare, which spurs high tech counter-investments

18 The Bayraktar TB2 UAV is a surveillance and reconnaissance drone that can be armed with weapons such as anti-tank missiles, precision-guided missiles, and laser-guided rockets. It can fly up to 220 kilometres (136 miles) per hour and stay in the air for up to 27 hours.

in detection and eradication technologies by governments. A reverse arms race may hence be unleashed, de facto favouring the weaker side. Aside from that, the 'battlefield' may also become expanded into a psychological one, and may no longer be limited to the actual zone of combat. Social media technologies can be instrumentalised in new ways so as to undermine the existing geopolitical stability of countries. It becomes a struggle to win minds and souls, a fight over an idea instead of a battle between terrorists and state operatives. Geostrategically, governments still have not completely come to terms with this dimension in the so-called *'war on terrorism'*.

Dale Walton believes that the ongoing "super-revolution" in military affairs will result in "extraordinarily potent war-fighting innovations". He believes one can not do anything other than to embrace, shape and mould these developments. The combination of technological developments in this second American RMA will, in his opinion, inevitably lead to a revised strategic perspective (Dale Walton, 2007, p. 106):

> [...] resistance to the social and other changes that will result from technological innovation will disadvantage fundamentally a state in the highly competitive great power environment of the Post-Colombian Epoch.

For Dale Walton, the Post-Columbian Epoch must adopt a position of "judicious radicalism", boldly throwing itself into the maelstrom of social, economic, military, and political change that will define the early decades of this era (Dale Walton, 2007, p. 107). Not everyone is as enthusiastic as Dale Walton. From a political and social sciences perspective, one can expect many issues emanating from these trends. The introduction of new technologies make societies more complex, and some will be left out. If they are not in some way included into those rapidly modernising societies, the divides inside those societies may grow. The new 'machine age' will also create a new wave of labour expulsion, in an act of 'creative destruction' (Brynjolfsson & McAfee, 2014). Societal tensions could rise if these developments are not managed properly. Think for instance about the Capitol Crisis in Washington, D.C. of 6 January 2021, instigated by Donald Trump in the last days of his presidency. Many of his followers who trespassed into and violated the US Capitol building had been affected by 'creative destruction' in earlier waves of globalisation (for instance in the mining or car industry). Radicalised and isolated through social media 'echo chambers', they now also posed an unexpected security threat. Hence, as a result of the new 'geotechnical ensembles' in security the internal geopolitical stability of countries may produce additional unexpected security challenges.

From a geopolitical point of view, it is also important to realise that a technology development strategy for countries is determined by their geographical constraints, needs and existing infrastructure (Pandya, 2020, p. 190). For instance, due to Israel's harsh geography and scarce water situation, it has been forced to drive advances in technology, science and start-ups. For Japan's ageing population, emerging technologies constitute a compensation for lost labor (productivity) (Pandya, 2020, p.191–192), and still matter geostrategically. This may very well leave some countries more willing to explore new technologies in order to 'compensate' for their ex ante weaker or rapidly deteriorating geostrategic position.

5 Technology as 'Conductor' of Power and 'Facilitator' of Global Geopolitics

This chapter has explored the interconnection between technology and geopolitics. What concluding thoughts can be developed on how today's technological trends could affect tomorrow's world politics from a geo-economic, geopolitical and geostrategic point of view? If power constitutes the 'currency' of global geopolitics, then technology could be seen as its 'conductor' and 'facilitator'. The world finds itself already in a geopolitical transition because of other explanatory factors. Whilst Deudney's concept of 'geotechnical ensembles' helps us to better appreciate the complexities of the interaction between 'technology' and 'geopolitics', Khanna opens our eyes to a world in which the global struggle over supply lines becomes central. In addition, one could state that knowledge itself, both fundamental and applied, can be added to this mix. With it, the limitations of geography can be overcome, at least in some part and with the realization that there will always remain environmental limitations to humanity's activities on Earth. Today we nevertheless see increased global competition.

One potential scenario for the next decades is a new bipolar world with two power-tech blocs; the United States and China. Both are actively investing in technologies to try to gain an upper hand; 5G and 6G networks, quantum computing, big data artificial intelligence, robotization, etc. (Brown, 2019). The American think tank *Eurasia Group* has coined the term *'The Great Decoupling'* as one of the major risks for the 2020s (Eurasia Group, 2020, p. 7–8); the US and China would create their own separate geo-technical ecosystems. Ian Bremmer, president at *Eurasia Group*, had earlier coined the term of a *'Geopolitical Recession'* in world politics. In it, the alliances which the US had forged around the world were loosening. In fact, the US and UK themselves now retreated from these frameworks with Trump and Brexit. Technological evolutions will play a major role in reshaping the international world order.

In a final analysis, the recent developments in the interaction between 'technology' and 'geopolitics' also raise questions for European countries and for many other nations around the world today. The same can be said of regions and other hubs. If these still want to stay relevant geopolitically, they will need to catch up in terms of research & development and commercialisation. In the context of the EU, one would need more political acceptance of 'European champions' in key strategic sectors. It is not a coincidence that countries such as France and Germany have recently asked for a review of European competition law, which inhibits pan-European champions to rise. This has been good for the European consumer, but it now proves in key technological sectors a regulatory obstacle for the EU as a whole to play a role in those sectors where 'technology' is reshaping global geopolitics. As a result, the game is mostly played by the US and China, in regulatory terms, in terms of access to resources, supply lines and geopolitical reconfiguration. From a European geopolitical point of view, a 'decoupling world order' poses severe challenges. Analysing these evolving 'geotechnical ensembles' can be helpful in nurturing a (European) debate on 'strategic autonomy'. The same can be said for many other nations. Territorial entities (states, regions or cities) which invest in ground-breaking technological know-how, both fundamental and applied innovation, as well as in the industrial base that comes with it, will in many ways be able to shape tomorrow's world in its geo-economic, geopolitical & geostrategic dimensions.

Bibliography

Alonso-Trabanco, J. M. (2020). Geopolitical Impacts of the Fourth Industrial Revolution, *Geopolitical Monitor* 4 August 2020, Retrieved from: https://www.geopoliticalmonitor.com/geopolitical-impacts-of-the-fourth-industrial-revolution/, accessed: 15 April 2021.

Allison, G. (2017). *Destined for War. Can America and China Escape Thuciydides' Trap?* Boston & New York: Mariner Books & Houghton Mifflin Harcourt.

Ball, D. (1985). Modern Technology and Geopolitics., In: Zoppo, C. E. & Zorgbibe, C., *On Geopolitics: Classical and Nuclear.* Dordrecht, Martinus Nijhoff Publishers: 171–199.

Brown, E. (2019). *The Geopolitics of Technology. Big Data, Artificial Intelligence and 5G in a Multipolar World.* Toronto: Global Risk Institute in Financial Services, https://globalriskinstitute.org/publications/the-geopolitics-of-technology/

Buchanan, B. (2020). *The Hacker and the State. Cyber Attacks and the New Normal of Geopolitics.* Cambridge, Massachusetts & London, England: Harvard University Press.

Blouet, B. W. (Ed.) *Global Geostrategy. Mackinder and the Defence of the West.* Abingdon: Frank Cass.

Brunn, S. D. & Jones, J. A. (1994). Geopolitical Information and Communication in Shrinking and Expanding Worlds: 1900–2100, In Demko, G. J. & Wood, W. B. *Reordering the World. Geopolitical Perspectives on the Twenty-First Century.* Boulder, Colorado, Westview Press: 301–322.

Brunn, S. D. (1998). A Treaty of Silicon for the Treaty of Westphalia? New Territorial Dimensions of Modern Statehood. *Geopolitics*, 3(1): 106–131.

Brynjolfsson, E., & McAfee, A. (2014). *The Second Machine Age: work, progress, and prosperity in a time of brilliant technologies.* New York City: ww Norton & Company.

Butler, D. L. (2001). Technogeopolitics and the struggle for control of world air routes, 1910–1928. *Political Geography*, 20: 635–658.

Collins, A. (2019). *Contemporary Security Studies.* Oxford: Oxford University Press.

Criekemans, D. (2018a). Geopolitiek van aardgas: brug naar de toekomst? *Karakter : tijdschrift van wetenschap* (Katholieke Universiteit Leuven. Vlaamse Leergangen), 62(16): 25–27, Retrieved at: https://www.tijdschriftkarakter.be/geopolitiek-van-aardgas-brug-naar-de-toekomst/ .

Criekemans, D. (2018b). 'Geopolitics of the Renewable Energy Game and its potential impact upon global power relations', In Scholten, D. (et al.) (2018). *The Geopolitics of Renewables* (Lecture Notes in Energy, 61), Springer: 37–73.

Czismadia, N. (2017). *Geofusion. Mapping of the 21st Century.* Budapest: Pallas Athene Foundation.

Dale Walton, C. (2007). *Geopolitics and the Great Powers in the Twenty-first Century. Multipolarity and the revolution in strategic perspective.* Abingdon: Routledge.

Demarest, G. (1998). *Geoproperty. Foreign Affairs, National Security and Property Rights.* London, Frank Cass.

Deudney, D. H. (1989). *Global Geopolitics: A Reconstruction, Interpretation, and Evaluation of Materialist World Order Theories of the Late Nineteenth and Twentieth Centuries.* Princeton: Princeton University Press (unpublished Ph D.-manuscript).

Deudney, D. H. (1997). Geopolitics and Change. *New Thinking in International Relations Theory.* M. W. Doyle and G. J. Ikenberry. Boulder, Colorado, Westview Press: 91–123.

Deudney, D. H. (2020). Dark Skies. Space Expansionism, Planetary Geopolitics & the Ends of Humanity. Oxford: Oxford University Press.

Doboš, B. (2019). *Geopolitics of Outer Space. A European Perspective.* Cham, Switzerland: Springer.

Dolman, E. C. (2002). *Astropolitik. Classical Geopolitics in the Space Age.* London & Portland, Oregon: Frank Cass.

Eurasia Group, (2020). *Top Risks 2020.* New York: Eurasia Group.

European Commission, (2020). *COM(2020) 474 - Critical Raw Materials Resilience: Charting a Path towards Greater Security and Sustainability* (Brussels, March 9, 2020), 2, Retrieved from: https://eur-lex.europa.eu/legal-content/EN/TXT/?uri=CELEX:52020DC0474, accessed: 7 March 2021.

Ferguson, Y. H. & Mansbach, R. W. (1999). Technology and the Transformation of Global Politics. *Geopolitics*, 4(3): 1–28.

Fox, W. (1985). Geopolitics and International Relations, In Zoppo, C. E. & Zorgbibe, C. *On Geopolitics: Classical and Nuclear.* Dordrecht, Martinus Nijhoff Publishers: 15–44.

Frederick, H. H. (1993) *Global Communication and International Relations.* Belmont, California: Wadsworth Publishing Company.

Gilpin, R. (1972). Has Modern Technology Changed International Politics? The Analysis of International Politics, In Rosenau, J. N., Davis, V. & East, M. A. *Essays in Honor of Harold and Margaret Sprout.* New York, The Free Press: 166–174.

Gray, C. S. (1977). *The Geopolitics of the Nuclear Era: Heartlands, Rimlands and the Technological Revolution.* New York, Crane, Russak & Company, Inc.

Gray, C. S. (1996). A Debate on Geopolitics. The Continued Primacy of Geography, *Orbis: a quarterly journal of world affairs*, 40(2): 247–259.

Gray, C. S. (2004). In Defence of the Heartland: Sir Halford Mackinder and His Critics a Hundred Years On. *Comparative Strategy*, 23(1): 9–25.

Gray, C. S. (2006). *Recognizing and Understanding Revolutionary Change in Warfare: The Sovereignty of Context.* Pennsylvania: Strategic Studies Institute.

Gray, C. S. (2009). *National Security Dilemmas. Challenges and Opportunities.* Washington, D.C.: Potomac Books.

Gray, C. S. & Sloan, G. (Eds.) (1999). *Geopolitics. Geography and Strategy.* London: Frank Cass.

Grigas, A. (2017). *The New Geopolitics of Natural Gas.* Cambridge, Massachusetts & London, England: Harvard University Press.

Hannigan, J. (2016) *The Geopolitics of Deep Oceans.* Cambridge: Polity Press.

Henrikson, A. K. (2002). Distance and Foreign Policy: A Political Geography Approach. *International Political Science Review/ Revue internationale de science politique*, 23(4 (October)): 437–466.

Hugill, P. J. (1999) *Global Communications since 1844. Geopolitics and Technology.* Baltimore, Maryland: The John Hopkins University.

Johnson, E. & Morehouse, H. (Eds.) (2014). After the Anthropocene: Politics and Geographic Inquiry for a New Epoch, *Progress in Human Geography*, 38(1): 439–456.

Khanna, P. (2016). *Connectography. Mapping the Future of Global Civilization.* New York: Random House.

Klare, M. (2001). *Resource Wars. The New Landscape of Global Conflict.* New York: Henry Holt and Company.

Klare, M. (2012). *The Race for What's Left. The Global Scramble for the World's Last Resources.* New York: Picador.

Leonard, M., Pisani-Ferry, J., Shapiro, J, Tagliapietra, S. & Guntram, W. (2021). The geopolitics of the European Green Deal, *Policy Contribution,* 04/2021, Bruegel & European Council on Foreign Relations, 23 p., Retrieved at https://www.bruegel.org/wp-content/uploads/2021/02/PC-04-GrenDeal-2021-1.pdf

Legault, A. (1985). Geopolitics and the Conduct of Modern Warfare. In: Zoppo, C. E. & Zorgbibe, C. *On Geopolitics: Classical and Nuclear.* Dordrecht, Martinus Nijhoff Publishers: 201–215.

Libicki, M. (1996). A Debate on Geopolitics. The Emerging Primacy of Information. *Orbis: a journal of world affairs*, 40(2): 260–263.

Leonard, M., Pisani-Ferry, J., Shapiro, J., Tagliapietra, S. & Wolf, G. (2021). The geopolitics of the European Green Deal, *Policy Contribution,* 04/2021, Bruegel & European Council on Foreign Relations, Retrieved from https://www.bruegel.org/wp-content/uploads/2021/02/PC-04-GrenDeal-2021-1.pdf , accessed: 7 March 2021.

Locksley, G. (1991). Information technology and capitalist development. In: Little, R., & Smith, M. *Perspectives on World Politics.* London, Routledge: 339–351.

Mackinder, H. J. (1919). *Democratic Ideals and Reality: A Study in the politics of Reconstruction.* London, Constable and Company, Ltd.

Mackinder, H. J. (1943). The Round World and the Winning of the Peace. *Foreign Affairs,* 21(4): 595–605.

Mackinder, H. J. (1994 [1904]). The Geographical Pivot of History from Geographical Journal (1904), In: G. Ó Tuathail, S. Dalby & P. Routlegde. *The Geopolitics Reader.* London, Routledge: 27–31.

Mahan, A. T. (1890). The United States Looking Outward. *Atlantic Monthly,* LXVI (December): 816–824.

Mahan, A. T. (1897). *The Interest of America in Sea-Power, Present and Future.* London, Sampson, Low and Marston.

Mahan, A. T. (1900). *The Problem of Asia and Its Effect upon International Policies.* London, Sampson, Loe and Marston.

Mahan, A. T. (1957 [1890]). *The influence of sea power upon history, 1660–1783.* Boston, Little, Brown.

Mayer-Schönberger, V. & Ramge, T. (2018). *De Data-Economie.* Amsterdam: Maven Publishing.

Middelkoop, W. (2013). *De Big Reset. Gold Wars en het Financiële Eindspel.* Amsterdam: Amsterdam University Press.

Moisio, S. (2018). *Geopolitics of the Knowledge-based Economy.* Oxon & New York: Routledge.

O'Lear, S. (2018). *Environmental Geopolitics.* London: Rowman & Littlefield.

Pandya, J. (2020). *Geopolitics of Cybersecurity. Implications for the Future of Humanity.* s.l.: Risk Group LLC.

Patrahau, I., Singhvi, A., Rademaker, R., van Manen, H., Kleijn, R., & van Geuns, L. (2021). *Securing Critical Materials for Critical Sectors. Policy options for the Netherlands and the European Union.* The Hague: The Hague Centre for Strategic Studies.

Ratcliffe, V. (2021). Saudi Arabia's bold plan to rule the $700 billion hydrogen market, *The Economic Times* (India), https://economictimes.indiatimes.com/news/international/saudi-arabia/saudi-arabias-bold-plan-to-rule-the-700-billion-hydrogen-market/articleshow/81374199.cms?utm_source=contentofinterest&utm_medium=text&utm_campaign=cppst, accessed: 7 March 2021.

Rickards, J. (2012) *Currency Wars. The Making of the Next Global Crisis.* New York: Penguin Books.

Rickards, J. (2016) *The New Case for Gold.* New York: Penguin Books.

Rickards, J. (2019) *Aftermaths. Seven Secrets of Wealth Preservation in the Coming Chaos.* New York: Penguin Books.

Rickards, J. (2020) *The New Great Depression. Winners and Losers in a Post-Pandemic World.* New York: Penguin Books.

Riordan, S. (2019) *The Geopolitics of Cyberspace: a Diplomatic Perspective.* Leiden & Boston: Brill Academic Publishers.

Rona, T. P. (1982) *Our Changing Geopolitical Premises.* New Brunswick, USA and Londen, Uk: Transaction Books.

Sainteny, G. (2010). Les enjeux géopolitiques des énergies naturelles renouvelables, *Questions Internationales*, n°45, septembre-octobre.

Scholten, D., Criekemans, D., & Van de Graaf, T. (2020). An energy transition amid great power rivalry. *Journal of International Affairs* (New York: Columbia University), 73(1): 195–204.

Spiegel, S. L. (2000). Traditional Space versus Cyberspace: The Changing Role of Geography in Current International Politics. *Geopolitics*, 5(3): 114–125.

Sprout, H. H. (1963). Geopolitical hypotheses in technological perspective. *World Politics*, XV: 187–212.

Spykman, N., & Nicholl, H. R. (1969 [1944]). *The Geography of the Peace.* s.l., Archon Books.

Spykman, N. (1942). *America's Strategy in World Politics. The United States and the Balance of Power.* New York, Harcourt Brace.

Stavridis, J. (2017). *Seapower. The History and Geopolitics of the World's Oceans.* New York: Pengiun Books.

Sumida, J. (1999). Alfred Thayer Mahan, Geopolitician, In: G. Sloan & C. S. Gray, *Geopolitics, Geography and Strategy.* London: Frank Cass: 39–62.

Tabeta, S. (2021). 'China tightens rare-earth regulations, policing entire supply chain. Stricter export controls give Beijing leverage amid US tensions', *Asia Nikkei*, 16.01.2021, https://asia.nikkei.com/Business/Markets/Commodities/China-tightens-rare-earth-regulations-policing-entire-supply-chain , accessed: 7 March 2021.

Turner, R. (1943). Technology and Geopolitics, *Military Affairs*, 7(Spring): 5–15.

Yergin, D. (1992). *The Prize. The Epic Quest for Oil, Money and Power.* New York: Free Press.

Yergin, D. (2020). *The New Map. Energy, Climate, and the Clash of Civilizations.* New York: Penguin Books.

Vander Straeten, P. (2018). *An Overture to Geofinance: Global Finance, Geopolitics, and the Wielding of Power: Theory and Praxis.* s.l.: Value4risk LLC.

Vander Straeten, P. (2020). *Treatise on China's Clandestine Financial Warfare: China's Intelligence Community and the Communist Party As Key Players in Geofinance in the 21st Century.* s.l.: Value4risk LLC.

White House, (2021) *Executive Order on America's Supply Lines*, Retrieved from: https://www.whitehouse.gov/briefing-room/presidential-actions/2021/02/24/executive-order-on-americas-supply-chains/, accessed: 7 March 2021.

PART 2

Theoretical Approaches to Territorially Embedded Factors and IR

CHAPTER 3

Geopolitical Schools of Thought: A Concise Overview from 1890 till 2020, and beyond

David Criekemans

In this chapter, a concise overview is offered into geopolitical schools of thought. Geopolitics has again re-surfaced during the 1990s. Today, in the early 21st century, one can say that the geopolitical analysis of international relations is studied once again in a growing number of countries, both by political geographers, by specialists in international relations, and by historians. Geopolitics, in its essence, draws attention to the question what role 'territoriality' still plays in international politics, or in the foreign policy of a political entity. From the 1990s onwards, some scholars and writers believed that in the 'age of globalisation' the world was becoming "flat" (Friedman, 2015). Hence 'territoriality' would increasingly retreat as an explanatory factor. Its specific neoliberal nature also had profound geopolitical consequences, whereby the hope was expressed to incorporate countries such as Russia and China into international economic bodies and 'to spread democracy' (Dodds, 2007, p. 69). One could state that the early 21st century, to a certain extent, represents a 'counterpoint' to the beliefs of mainstream thinkers during the 1990s. The terrorist attacks on 11 September 2001 in New York and Washington, D.C., heralded the return of the geostrategic perspective to international relations, and caused a debate on the effect, if any, of these events on the course of international politics. This also brought up again one of the central questions in international politics; *what is power?* The growth of economies such as China, India and Brazil from 2003 onwards reminded observers of international politics that 'history had not ended' (Hirst, 2019). A scramble over energy resources and shifting spheres of influence gradually also changed the fabric of international relations itself. Scholars became increasingly concerned about growing global resource and energy competition (LeBillon, 2001; Klare, 2001; Klare, 2012; Yergin, 1992; Yergin, 2020). This process is even aggravated in an age of energy transition (Criekemans, 2018). The societal debate on 'climate change' heralded a return of 'ecology' as a factor to seriously be taken into account in the study in international politics. The new age of the Anthropocene had already begun during the Industrial Revolution (O'Lear, 2018), and provoked

 | DOI:10.1163/9789004432086_005

questions on how to deal with the intimate relationship between humanity and (the care for) its environment (Johnson & Morehouse, 2014). Through all the societal and global changes of the last decade, one can state that geopolitics again seems to be relevant and highly useful as a specific perspective to study what is happening in the world, how nations' foreign policies prioritise, how they try to give meaning to what happens, and how they try to 'shape' events. Recent years have seen rising turmoil on the geopolitical stage with regional and global power competition as a recurring theme. Northern Africa and the Middle East destabilised in the wake of the 'Arab Spring' with wars in Syria, Yemen and Libya. This heightened a regional power struggle between Saudi Arabia, Iran and Turkey. Tensions are also deepening between a 'Western' & 'Eastern' sphere of influence resulting in a war in the Eastern Ukraine, an enduring Belarus crisis and a looming security fear over the Baltics and, potentially, Balkans. The US and China seem to be locked in a power struggle with geo-economic, technological and geopolitical dimensions, with additional danger that the European countries themselves would be split right in the middle. In the wake of a global pandemic, questions remain over its geo-economic and geopolitical consequences, in which inequality within and amongst nations could strain global and regional relations. Geopolitics seems to have 'trumped' health in the global coronacrisis. At the same time, the recent years show a world in which revisionist powers take 'revenge' on the liberal world order. As Walter Russel Mead already underlined in 2014, the US and EU find such trends disturbing: *"Both would rather move past geopolitical questions of territory and military power and focus instead on ones of world order and global governance: trade liberalization, nuclear proliferation, human rights, the rule of law, climate change, and so on."* (Mead, 2014). As the world seems to be undergoing a more fundamental 'transformation', the words 'geopolitics' and 'geopolitical' are back in full vogue in the mainstream public debate. A similar development is slowly taking shape in International Relations, which is gradually rediscovering its own geopolitical roots and engaging anew with the rich and sometimes not fully known or appreciated body of geopolitical scholarship.

In order to understand Geopolitics as a body of knowledge, it is necessary to look into the past, to try to understand these different schools of thought. When and why did they come into being? Upon what specific aspect did they focus? To what extent did the geopolitical scholars working in these different research traditions affect the course of international politics? By formulating an answer to these questions, it is possible to gradually increase our own understanding of geopolitics itself. This chapter, although introductory and barely scratching the surface of the rich geopolitical scholarship since 1899, aims to make a contribution to that endeavour. In the final analysis, it will hence also become possible to formulate both the assets and limits of the geopolitical approach to international relations. What are its strengths and weaknesses, and how do various geopolitical schools of thought help us to better understand world politics?

1 Geopolitics as a 'Joint Project' of Political Geography and International Relations

To a certain degree, geopolitics experiences an 'identity problem'. Geopolitics is being confronted by an **implosion of explicit and implicit academic conventions about the subject of its research field** and hence also about its concepts and theoretically embedded approaches, or as the Dutch political geographer Virginie Mamadouh stated: *"geopolitics in the 1990s: one flag, many meanings!"* (Mamadouh, 1998). Sometimes, the utilised definitions of geopolitics are in contradiction to one another, which causes acute problems for the research field itself. The American Cold War-Specialist Robert Harkavy signalled this crucial problem already in 1982, in his book *'Great Power Competition for Overseas Bases: The Geopolitics of Access Diplomacy'* (Harkavy, 1982, p. 271): "[…] *the term "geopolitics" has come to be used in such a variety of contexts that it is no longer clear what it just means* […] *it has come to mean almost everything, and therefore perhaps nothing, at least for someone searching for empirically based definitions."* When reading the literature, it is often difficult to pinpoint how a certain author views the relation between geopolitics and political geography or between geopolitics and international relations. The division that is often stated between these fields of study is to a certain degree an artificial one. One could also defend the thesis that Geopolitics in fact constitutes a *joint project* or *common field* of study between Political Geography on the one hand, and International Relations on the other.

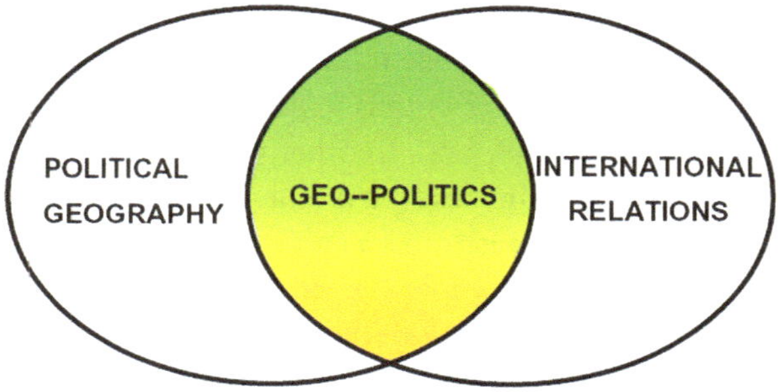

FIGURE 3.1
Geopolitics as a 'joint project' of both Political Geography (PG) and International Relations (IR)

In his pivotal article *'The origin and evolution of geopolitics'*, the IR-specialist Ladis D. Kristof already defended this point of view (Kristof, 1960, p. 20): *"Geopolitics should cover all the field parallel to, and intermedial between, political science and political geography, and, indeed, there have been a few such studies."*. But why does Geopolitics have such difficulties in presenting itself as a joint project of both PG and IR? The main explanation should be sought in the way in which scientists within PG and IR are organised (inter)nationally. Each (both having at their disposal their own academic structures, journals and means of finances) could create a tendency to "shut oneself" in one's own field of study, without being too much aware of the relevant developments within the complementary subfields of other scientific fields of study. When one embraces the idea of 'Geopolitics' as a 'joint project' of both PG and IR, one could define it as follows (Criekemans, 2007):

> Geopolitics is the scientific field of study belonging to both Political Geography and International Relations, which investigates the interaction between politically acting (wo)men and their surrounding territoriality (in its three dimensions; physical-geographical, human-geographical and spatial).

What categories of geopolitical studies exist? A number of different ways of representation are possible to develop an overview of and insight into the geopolitical literature. One possible way to establish such an overview is to develop an inventory of the literature based upon the different kinds of groups which 'reason geopolitically'. In 1998, Ó Tuathail made a distinction within the literature based upon the different 'production sites' where geopolitical discourses arise (Ó Tuathail & Dalby, 1998, p. 5) (see figure 3.2). Each of these institutions treat 'territorial-political variables' differently; each one also represents another form of geopolitics which draws attention to other kinds of societal and scientific problems. Ó Tuathail initially distinguished a *'formal'*, a *'practical'* and a *'popular geopolitics'*:

Central in this three-part typology stood the idea that Geopolitics does not have a uniform, singular meaning, but rather entails a *'plurality of representational practices'* (Ó Tuathail & Dalby, 1998, p. 4). In other words, geopolitics is not a phenomenon which merely remains restricted to a practice of political leaders and their advisors, but which constitutes a social and cultural phenomenon one can encounter in society as a whole. For this reason, Ó Tuathail makes a distinction between *'practical geopolitics'* (the practical geopolitical

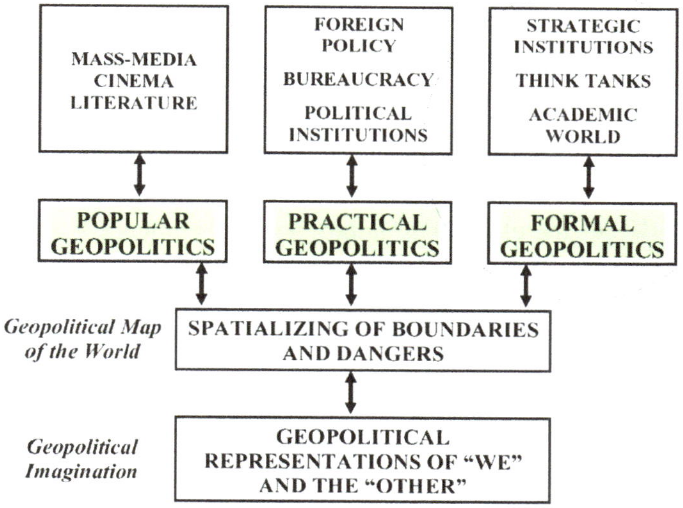

FIGURE 3.2 Geopolitics as a social-cultural phenomenon

reasoning and decisions of state leaders, foreign policy-bureaucracies & advisors), *'formal geopolitics'* (the development of geopolitical theories within strategically oriented institutions, think tanks and the academic world), and *'popular geopolitics'* (the geopolitical representations and convictions which one can detect within the broader popular culture, e.g. in literature, in magazines and newspapers from the mass media, in films & cartoons). Each of these variants of geopolitics is produced, distributed, and consumed at various sites. When one links every one of these to the other, then one would obtain an insight into the broader geopolitical culture of a certain region, state, or inter-state alliance. This chapter will only study *'formal geopolitical thinking'*; the basic geopolitical theories and 'research traditions' that have developed within the academic world and in think tanks around the globe. Hereafter, we will present a non-exhaustive yet insightful overview which focuses particularly on those theories and traditions that significantly contributed to new epistemological approaches in geopolitics. In many ways, all the geopolitical research traditions which came into being during the past century and earlier were influenced by the particular space (country) and time where and during which the individual scholars worked. Each geopolitical school of thought also focuses its attention to other aspects of the relation between 'territoriality' and 'politics'.

2 Geopolitics' Precursor before the 1890s: *Physiopolitics*

Geopolitical reasoning has been around from the very beginning of political thinking and civilisation. The earliest traces of geopolitical thinking can be discovered in the so-called *physiopolitics* of such classical thinkers as Aristotle, Thucydides, Lucretius, Strabo, Ibn Khaldûn, Jean Bodin, Montesquieu, etcetera. All of these authors searched for the 'laws of nature' (not the moral *jus naturale*, but the physical *jus naturae*) which influence human life in its natural setting (Kristof, 1960, p. 18). In their analysis, man is to a large extent influenced by the natural conditions. Within *physiopolitics*, the assembly of possible independent variables is limited to merely 'natural elements' (Deudney, 1997, p. 94). This constitutes a rather narrow interpretation of 'geography'. Moreover, one could state that *Physiopolitics* does not always succeed in clearly describing and explaining its proclaimed dependent variable, the 'political'. However, *Physiopolitics* did form a basis upon which Geopolitics as a research field would later be established at the end of the nineteenth century.

3 The Rise and Fall of 'Classical Geopolitics' between 1890 and 1945

The scientific field of study called Geopolitics came into being at the end of the nineteenth century. Its birth was not a coincidence. The period starting from 1890 onwards was in many ways unique. International politics was tainted by increasing strains between the (aspiring) big powers, the European (colonial) empires. These tensions were both geo-economic, geopolitical and geostrategic in nature. For the first time in history, they were also encompassing the whole globe. In 1890, German Kaiser Wilhelm II forced Bismarck into retirement. In 1897, Wilhelm proclaimed that Germany should be taken seriously. Henceforth a new *Weltpolitik* necessitated Berlin to possess its own colonies. This new policy was a conscious repudiation of Bismarck's continental policy and tried to give consistency to German diplomacy (Lowe, 1994, p. 141–165). But the *Reich* had a problem; almost all interesting and 'lucrative' parts in the south (in Africa, Asia) were already occupied by other European nations, in particular the British. As each year passed, the tensions between the big powers grew; the atmosphere became more competitive and ominous. This raised the question of how a confrontation could be avoided.

Parallel to these international-political developments, there were also some interesting evolutions in science. First, the scientific field of Geography had undergone quite an impressive rise during the last decades of the 19th century.

In almost every European country of stature, geographical institutions had been established. In many ways, one could argue that they constituted 'planning institutions' for the colonisation effort. Some advocated that Geography had done its bit for humanity; it had mapped the world in such detail that it had 'completed' its mission. For instance, the British geographer Halford John Mackinder claimed Geography's new mission would be to more actively develop comprehensive, 'holistic' analyses on the question how physical and human factors influence political relations. Second, the natural sciences had undergone an enormous revolution since Charles Darwin in 1859 had proposed his radical theory on the *'survival of the fittest'* and the evolution of species. In many ways, the human sciences at the end of the 19th century wanted to emulate that revolution. The theory of the *'survival of the fittest'* was seen by some as a conceptual and operational instrument to achieve a better insight into what was happening in international politics. Hence one of the basic assumptions of 'Classical Geopolitics' was born.

The earliest traces of the field of Geopolitics can be found within two families of scientific literature; on the one hand the work of the German founder of modern Political Geography, Friedrich Ratzel, which is permeated by the idea of 'state organicism' and on the other hand with the so-called 'geo-strategic thinking' of such authors as Alfred Thayer Mahan and Halford John Mackinder. In this way, 'Classical Geopolitics' combines its sensitiveness for the fate of the nation(al) state with a global dimension (in which the world is approached as a *'closed political system'*; see infra). Geopolitics was seen by its 'inventors', most notably by its creator the Swedish political scientist Rudolf Kjellén, as an analytical tool that could help nations' leaders to steer a 'safe course' in the increasingly gloomy and complex international environment of competition. It is therefore very unfortunate that today some scholars still only associate Geopolitics with war. One could state that actually the opposite is true; Geopolitics wanted to contribute to a safer international environment by analysing the geopolitical factors with which individual states were confronted, and offering the policy options and relevant scenarios to the leaders of states and to other interested individuals. Geopolitics officially came into being in 1899, exactly twenty years before in 1919 the first chair in IR came into being in Aberystwyth in Wales, Great Britain. Geopolitics is therefore much older than IR, and in many respects some IR schools of thought such as Realism have incorporated a good number of the ontological assumptions and analytical characteristics of 'Classical Geopolitics'.

Let us explore these elements step by step. Hereafter, we will briefly present some of the most important geopolitical scholars and the basic ideas they brought to the study of 'Geopolitics'.

Ratzel (1844-1904)

Friedrich Ratzel was a German geographer who is commonly seen as the father of modern Political Geography. He was also a romantic thinker in the sense that he saw the German agrarian life as an ideal; the farmer who lived in close connection to his own land, and who in fact constituted the forefront of the advancement of German *Kultur* and *Lebensraum* to the east. The latter concept would acquire an unintended life of its own some decades later in German national politics (Pierik, 1999). Ratzel had studied in detail Charles Darwin's analysis of the *'survival of the fittest'* between species, and tried to apply it to the behaviour of states. Hence, the term 'social Darwinism' could be used so as to grasp Ratzel's complex thinking (Lasserre, Gonon & Mottet, 2016, p. 156). A second concept intimately related to this is 'state organicism'. This entailed the idea that states are and act like individuals. Whereas before 1870 'state organicism' was used as a rather vague metaphor, it was 'solidified' between 1870 and 1890 via the inclusion of the naturalist theories of a presupposed *'survival of the fittest'* in the human sciences, and also in the study of the relations between states. For Ratzel, the *'struggle for existence'* in its essence constituted a *'struggle for space'* (*Kampf um Dasein = Kampf um Raum*). Every "nation-state" seemed to have a life of its own; *growth, development* (with 'differentiation' as a result; different components or 'organs' develop different functions), and finally *death*. The "vigorous strong states" where those that were growing steadily; when the people of a nation gradually occupied more and more land. The state later moves in. The strength of a state can be analysed according to Ratzel via focusing on two factors; *'Raum'* (space) & *'Lage'* (position). Furthermore, Ratzel developed some *"laws of nature"* for states (Zajec, 2016b, p. 32):

1. *The space of States grows with population expansion (e.g. 'Lebensraum' -- bio-geography);*
2. *The expansion of States follows other manifestations of the growth of peoples (e.g. demography, 'dollar diplomacy', traffic networks);*
3. *States grow by absorbing smaller, weaker rivals;*
4. *Territorial growth manifests itself at the periphery, by moving the border;*
5. *In their growth, States strive to absorbe geographically and politically valuable territory (e.g. access to the sea, energy resources, etc.);*
6. *The first stings to the territorial growth of primitive states come from outside;*
7. *The tendency to territorial annexation is transmitted among states & increases in intensity.*

In sum, ***international politics*** according to Ratzel entails a continuous struggle for survival, in which each state has to adapt itself to the environment; *it has to grow or die* (Sen, 1975, p. 188; Owens, 1999). Success in this existentialist struggle between national states was deemed more important than any other consideration; it was proclaimed by Ratzel and his followers as the only criterion on the basis of which a state should evaluate the effectiveness and morality of its international behaviour (Bassin, 1987, p. 477). International politics thus entails a struggle for space, a *zero sum-game* between national states which ultimately is tested during times of war. "War" was seen by Friedrich Ratzel as a 'natural phenomenon' in the political struggle to acquire as much 'power' as possible via territorial consolidation and expansion (Kost, 1989, p. 371). Ratzel must have seen the war of 1870–71, in which the German state was created and when the aspiration to become a *Weltmacht* firmly took root, as prove that Germany itself was a "vigorous strong state". Some look back at Ratzel and nuance his ideas (Stogiannos, 2019); he would have been conscious of the weaknesses embedded in his own analyses, but liked to generalise and could not have foreseen that others in his wake would interpret his 'romantic' ideas into a most dangerous (inter)national political direction (Muir, 1997, p. 72).

Mahan (1840-1914)

The American naval historian and Captain (later Rear Admiral) **Alfred Thayer Mahan** can be considered as one of the fathers of American geostrategic thinking. Having fought in the American civil war between 1861 and 1865 as a U.S. naval officer, he had experienced seapower first hand, especially when he participated in the U.S. blockade of the Mississippi river, which effectively had immobilised the Confederate's Navy. Later he would work mostly as a naval officer in the Pacific Ocean, and participated in a great tour from Asia to Europe, where he came into close contact with the British naval infrastructure at diverse 'choke points' along the UK-Asia route through the Strait of Malacca, the Strait of Hormuz and the Suez Canal. In 1885, Mahan became a Captain (Claval, 1996, pp. 38–39), and also an Associate Professor in 'Naval History and Tactics' at the newly created *'U.S. Naval War College'* in Newport, Rhode Island. Mahan's breakthrough as an author commenced with the publication of *'The influence of sea power upon history, 1660–1783'* (1890). In it, he described the struggle for the mastery at sea during the seventeenth and eighteenth century, with the United Kingdom, France, the Netherlands and Spain as main protagonists. This was a historical study, although he also wanted to illustrate the importance of sea power in the international relations of his own time. This was an important subject since the American maritime strength at this juncture (1890) was quasi inexistent. Similar to Ratzel was that **social Darwinism** constituted an inherent dimension in Mahan's thinking: he conceptualised international relations as a dynamic condition of a *continuing battle between nations in which acquiring 'sea power' is decisive* (Sloan, 1988, p. 90; Raffestin, Lopreno et al., 1995, p. 104, p. 107). Driven by social Darwinist thinking, Mahan believed (in comparable neo-Lamarckian terms as Ratzel) that a nation should expand territorially, or else be ruined (Sprout & Sprout, 1944 [1939], p. 214). Now that the Civil War was in the past, America should *"look outward"*; to foreign markets and territories in a broader endeavour for a richer and more prosperous existence. Mahan's philosophy combined in essence two elements: first a theory of national prosperity and destiny based upon a programme of mercantilist imperialism, secondly a theory of maritime strategy and defence. Formulated concisely, his reasoning went as follows. An expanding foreign trade was essential for (American) national prosperity and power in the world. In order to win the global struggle for markets, the US should have a strong trade fleet, secure harbours and transport routes at its disposal. This meant that Washington needed to get control over territory outside the traditional homeland and to develop a strong defensive fleet. Both elements would make that the nation would not only get a better grip upon its own destiny, but also upon international relations. The *States* would be able to assert its influence far beyond its own territory. In the era in which Mahan wrote, the US possessed neither. In the first chapter of his book in 1890, *'Discussion on the Elements of Sea Power'*, Mahan identified a number of factors which –according to his judgement– were decisive for the power of a nation at sea, and thus also for international relations. There where Ratzel had analysed 'state strength' only by looking at two factors –*'Raum'* (space) & *'Lage'* (position)–, Mahan stated that state strength was closely related to the sea power of a nation, which is determined by six factors:

1. geographical location vis-à-vis the sea;
2. natural aspects (e.g. the nature of the coastline);
3. territorial width & length of the coastline;
4. population (the *"numbers of people called by the sea"*);
5. national character (e.g. whether or not the people are trade oriented);
6. governmental policy.

It is not a surprise that the United Kingdom constituted Mahan's most favoured model. His analysis found that the rise of the British Empire had coincided with the development of Great Britain as a maritime (trade) power. Via this process, the most important global trade routes became *internal routes* of the

Empire (Dougherty & Pfaltzgraff, 1981, p. 61). If the United States of America wanted to play the international role to which its geographical position offered the possibility, then Washington should be inspired by the British example (Moreau Defarges, 1994, p. 45; Claval, 1996, p. 39).

The *States* could become a strong nation in international politics, but only if it possessed a powerful fleet and maritime bases spread across strategic locations. In no case whatsoever should the US make the mistakes that France had made during much of her history, by neglecting the importance of (the development of a) naval power (Sumida, 1999, p. 50). A big, modern fleet would allow the US to control the most important *"choke points"* of the international economic trade routes (the *'narrow seas'* or *'lines of movement between the force and its sources of supply'*), the key to acquiring power in an increasingly interdependent world (Sempa, 2002, p. 105). With regard to the bases and strategic routes, Mahan proposed that the *States* should annex the Hawaii islands, capture the control of the Caribbean, and take over the ill-fated French efforts to build a canal in Panama between the Atlantic and Pacific Ocean (Glassner & de Blij, 1989, p. 225; Dolman, 2002, p. 34). In his book *'The interest of America in sea power, present and future'* (1897), Mahan developed some policy advice for the near future: the US should associate itself with British naval power, at least until its own navy could be reinforced, but also afterwards. According to Mahan it was in the interest of the United States to oppose German ambitions to control the high seas, to remain vigilant vis-à-vis an expected Japanese expansion, and –finally– to collaborate with the European peoples in light of *'pressures emanating from the Asiatic peoples'* (Lorot & Thual, 1997, p. 28). In *'The Problem of Asia and Its Effect upon International Policies'* (1900), Mahan studied the way in which the Russians gradually tried to get access to a central area in Asia; the so called *'middle strip'*, which extended from the Middle East until the East China Sea – between the 30th and 40th degree north latitude. If Russia were to expand towards the 'middle strip', then it could also subdue parts of the Middle East and China, which could seriously destabilise the global balance of power in time (Deudney, 1989, p. 271). Mahan therefore stated in 1900 that the most important maritime nations –the United Kingdom, the United States of America, the German and Japanese empires– would feel themselves compelled by the circumstances to form an alliance against this Russian expansion (Harkavy, 1982, p. 284; Glassner & de Blij, 1989, p. 226; Lorot, 1995, pp. 37–38). Mahan became a close advisor to American president Theodore Roosevelt. His books were translated in many languages, including German and Japanese. To some extent, the seapower competition which increased in intensity during the first decade and a half of the twentieth century (e.g. between British & German fleets in the North Sea) were the direct result of his writings, and those of other so-called "blue water strategists". Mahan died before the First World War; he did not live to see the unintended consequences of his ideas and policy advice. Today, Mahan's work is again actively referred to in studies on some of the geopolitical maritime frontiers of potential clashes for the coming years; the South China Sea, the Indian Ocean, the Mediterranean, the Arctic Ocean and the Caribbean (Stavridis, 2017).

Mackinder (1861-1947)

In 1904, the British geographer **Halford John Mackinder** gave a noteworthy lecture called *'The Geographical Pivot of History'* at the Royal Geographical Society in London; the Columbian epoch, which had started officially in 1492 with the first voyages of discovery, would soon end. In its place, a post-Columbian epoch would henceforth come into being. In this era, the world itself would become a 'closed political system' (Blouet, 2005). What did Mackinder mean by this? This British geographer wanted to stress that in the past, local political problems (e.g. in Africa) did not affect the international politics in other parts of the world. However, now that the world had carefully been mapped by Geography, more and more areas also were incorporated within the 'spheres of influence' of (European) powers. In the post-Columbian epoch, local tensions would thus also affect the global balance of power. Mackinder warned that the 'closure' of the international system would entail far-reaching consequences for international relations. He was one of the first scholars to identify some of the political consequences of what we today call 'globalisation' and 'interdependence'. Mackinder stated that Geography's mission had been to a large extent completed; it had carefully mapped the world. In the post-Columbian epoch, Geography had to take one step closer in the direction of international politics; to advise politicians about the best course of action in their foreign policy. His *'New Geography'* wanted to offer a comprehensive framework to place human events in a broader perspective (Ó Tuathail, 1996, pp. 86–88), a conceptual bridge between the natural and social sciences (Heffernan, 1998, pp. 63–66) that tried to provide an answer to the problem that 'power' had become more difficult to measure in an industrialising world in which the 'natural seats of power' also were affected by the introduction of new technologies (the so-called *'geo-technical ensemble'*, as it is called by some scholars). Furthermore, Mackinder believed that in the post-Columbian epoch, the dominance of sea power (e.g. Great Britain) could come to an end as a result of a combination of new technologies (in particular railways) and demographic trends (to be more concrete, Russia's growing prominence). He predicted that the area which later would turn out to be the Soviet Union, constituted 'the geographical pivot of history', a potential new world power which could eventually force the other naval powers (especially Britain) out of their positions in e.g. Asia.

Later, in 1919, Mackinder would amend his theory by stating that the power which dominates Central Europe, would also dominate the 'World Island' (being Eurasia), and thus automatically also the world itself. Only via an active *'divide and rule'-policy* could the naval powers avert such an ominous prospect. In 1919, no British politician was willing to put into policy what Mackinder had advised so forcefully; a buffer zone of British (client-)states in Central Europe, and political & military aid to the 'white' Russian armies in their struggle against the communists. The British people were tired of war, and interventions abroad. Mackinder predicted in 1919 that, if his proposed policies were not pursued, it could take yet another world war before the geopolitical balance of power in Europe and the world would be restored… When in 1941 the Russians and Germans concluded a 'Non-Aggression Pact', Mackinder's work was re-discovered in the US and later also in the UK. In 1943, Mackinder wrote a third version of his 'heartland theory' in which he foresaw a post-war political and military cooperation between the USA and Europe in their continuing struggle to 'contain' heartland-Russia; his *'Midland Ocean'*-concept. A growing number of scholars argue that with these remarks, Mackinder single-handedly laid the foundations for the containment-policy that the American president Harry Truman would pioneer from March 1947 onwards, and during much of the Cold War. In many regards, some analysts even claim that aspects of the US containment policy as inspired by Mackinder continued after 1991 vis-à-vis Russia, for instance via the subsequent NATO enlargements (Kearns, 2009, pp. 223–228). Zbigniew Brzezinksi, a Polish-American geostrategic scholar and former US National Security Advisor under the Carter Administration, can act as an example. Brzezinski was a 'cold warrior' and architect of an American strategy against the Soviets post-1979. In several academic books, he would later actively refer to Mackinder in the context of the enduring US strategy to prevent any single power to control the combined resources of Eurasia (Brzezinksi 1986; Brzezinksi 1997a; Brzezinksi 1997b). Recently, researchers see a similar containment policy in the making by the 'West' against a rising China (Dale Walton, 2007). The 2006 US-India Cooperation Treaty (enacted under the Bush junior Administration in the US) entailed for instance both a nuclear and a naval component. It could also be seen as derived from Mackinder's original policy advice with regard to the question how Anglo-American powers could steer the 'global balance of power' in their favour. The efforts of the Biden Administration in the US to develop a "coalition of democracies" in the Indo-Pacific theatre can also be seen as indirectly inspired by Mackinder.

Rudolf Kjellén (1864-1922)

The Swede **Rudolf Kjellén** (speak:/*'tsjellén'*/) is the actual 'inventor' of the neologism 'geopolitics' and of the 'geopolitical approach' in political science. In 1891, he became a lecturer in the newly established political sciences course at the University of Göteborg. This teaching assignment obliged the holder of the Chair to also teach geography (Thermænius, 1938, p. 166). When Kjellén started to prepare for the second course, he became aware of the writings of Friedrich Ratzel and his book *'Politische Geographie'* (1897). The place and time in which Kjellén started to develop his own ideas is critical to understanding him as a scholar. Like some of the other early 'geopolitical scholars', Kjellén foresaw as early as 1897 the likelihood of a confrontation between the (European) powers. He feared for the security of Sweden, which would be confronted with Russian expansionism. Therefore, he thought only a 'vigorous strong state' such as Germany would be able to counter this danger; he thus proposed the creation of a Central-European bloc from Scandinavia and the Baltics to the Balkans, under the political leadership of Germany. In 1915, he described the First World War as a "battle between the ideas of 1789 and those of 1914"; against the Franco-British *'liberty, equality and fraternity'*, Germany placed *'order, justice and national solidarity'*. Kjellén thus was a protagonist of a strong Swedish state allied with an even stronger Germany so as to counter pan-Slavic expansionism. On the scientific front, Kjellén opposed the way in which the human sciences until then had conceptualised the State.

The early political sciences at the end of the nineteenth century were dominated by lawyers and legalists. They approached the State as a 'mere sum of (constitutional) legal articles', an 'institution which existed by and for the law'. In contrast, Kjellén made a plea for a 'modern' conceptualisation of the State which would lead political sciences to achieve its own academic place, separate from the Law faculties (Kristof 1960: 23). Inspired by Ratzel, he re-conceptualised the State as a 'complete, living organism', which operated organically both internally and externally. The *internal* organic behaviour of the state meant that *'the State could be considered as a body with a will bigger than the sum of the individuals belonging to the State'* (Lundén, 1986, p. 181; Holdar, 1992, p. 310; Heffernan, 2000, p. 45), and that the State had *'its own personality'* (Kristof 1960: 23). Gradually, a nation state would form which would aim for 'solidarity' amongst its initially diverse population. The *external* organic behaviour of the state was related to a second criticism of Kjellén vis-à-vis the contemporary conceptualisation of the State as a mere judicial phenomenon; it almost fully neglected the relations between States. As Edvard Thermaenius, one of Kjellén's followers, formulated it: *'In short, Kjellén began to conceive states not as legal bodies, but as Powers.'* (Thermænius, 1938, p. 166). Kjellén underlined that States as 'living organisms' in relation to one another spoke a wholly different language: the concept of **'power'** stood central in this. In their role as 'powers', national states should be understood as geographical entities (Thermænius, 1938, p. 166). Only by taking into account the territorial dimension in its analysis, could political sciences hope to achieve a better insight into the 'Great War' of that time, and better comprehend the interests at play among the states engaged in it (Parker, 1998, p. 13). How else could one explain (inter) national politics then as a recurring struggle for territory and spheres of interest? Everything thus started and ended according to Kjellén with the territory (Parker, 1994, p. 171), not with the (constitutional) legal articles or statements such as claimed by the (French) vision in 1789. In Kjellén's view, there existed a *'natural triad between population, territory and government'*. In this way he followed Friedrich Ratzel, who had suggested the existence of a kind of 'mathematical relationship' between the population expansion of cultural groups and the expansion of the state (Raffestin, Lopreno et al., 1995, p. 92). Kjellén went even further by suggesting that all peoples unconsciously develop a *'geopolitical instinct'* (Thermænius, 1938, p. 167). This was difficult to measure, but would nevertheless be active underlying. Moreover, this trinity reforged 'solidarity' into 'loyality' and 'nationality' (Thermænius, 1938, p. 169).

Kjellén's ideas above can be summarised into the following thesis—antithesis (see figure 3.3.):

The French & British empire **HAVE-nations**	**Germany, Sweden & *'Mitteleurope'*** **HAVE NOT-nations *('Habe-nichts')***
***'Ideas of 1789'*:** **liberty, equality & fraternity**	***'Ideas of 1914'*:** **order, justice & national solidarity**
No independent 'Political Sciences' existed at the end of the 19th century, only... ***'Staatswissenschaften'*** **dominated by judicial specialists**	**An independent 'Political Sciences'; the state = more than the mere sum of judicial articles** **Central thesis of Kjellén's 'Geopolitics':** ***the state = a 'power' thanks to/via its geographical embeddedness***
***"Bourgeois republicanism"*:** **the state as a (judicial) entity with an unclear relation to society**	**The state as an "organism"**
Limited attention devoted to the role that 'territoriality' plays in (inter)national politics	**Specific attention devoted to the role that 'territoriality' plays in (inter)national politics**

FIGURE 3.3 Kjellén's thesis – anti-thesis

Kjellén almost completely subscribed to **Ratzel's social Darwinist vision to state organicism.** The new element embedded within Kjellén's analysis (1914) in comparison to Ratzel was that he believed that the future would lie with those land powers that succeeded in achieving **autarky** within their own territory. The railways over land would considerably reinforce the *capacity for 'internal communication and power concentration'* (Holdar, 1992, p. 314; Herwig, 1999, p. 220, p. 226; Ó Tuathail, 2001, p. 21). Eventually, only a few world powers would remain (Dolman, 2002, p. 51). Kjellén suggested in 1897 that in the long run only three big continental political and economic zones would remain: a *pan-American system* under the leadership of the United States of America, a *Middle-European system* (possibly even a *Eurafrican system*) under the leadership of Germany and an *Eastern system* under the leadership of Japan (Holdar, 1992, p. 314). With these ideas, Kjellén did not make himself very popular with his countrymen. Next to this original conceptualisation of the *'state'* and *'Political Sciences'*, Kjellén was also unique in his perspective: he used the concept *'Ganzheit'* (*'the world as one functioning whole'*) and preferred a **'global perspective'** (Østerud, 1988, p. 192; Olson & Groom, 1991, p. 252; Parker, 1998, p. 15; Chauprade, 1999, p. 16).

Kjellén developed *'Geopolitik'* in 1899. It was part of a broader analytical framework; his so-called *'organic political sciences'*, a reaction to the then rather judicial *'Staatswissenschaften'*. As mentioned before, Kjellén believed the State was much more than a mere 'judicial skeleton'. Kjellén's *'Organic Political Sciences'* was composed of five subsystems;

1. *Geopolitik* ("the conditions and problems of the State, which find their origin in their geographical characteristics");
2. *Oekopolitik* ("the economic aspects which influence the position and power of the State");
3. *Demopolitik* ("the study of the ethnic composition of the State and of the problems which follow from this composition");
4. *Sociopolitik* ("the analysis of the societal groups and diverging 'classes' [elites] within the State, and the way in which they affect the unity of the State");
5. *Kratopolitik* ("the constitutional legislation and the 'constitutional life' of the State, its institutions, organisations, political parties and interest groups").

In principle, each of these subsystems was equally important, although Kjellén did mention that the State is especially a 'power' thanks to or via its geographical 'foundations' and 'embeddedness'. In its classical meaning as conceptualised by Kjellén, *'Geopolitics'* comprised three components of 'specific science areas':

1. *'physiopolitik'* (the influence emanating from natural-physical environmental variables – compare with Ratzel's *Raum* or 'space');
2. *'topopolitik'* (the influence emanating from the [relative] location upon [the interstate relations of] the Empire – compare with Ratzel's *Lage* or 'position'); and
3. *'morphopolitik'* (the impact of such factors as territorial width & form upon the success or failure of states – Kjellén proposed the *'concentric form'* as an ideal to aim for).

Kjellén saw his own scientific work as a 'reason for hope'; by applying scientific methods, the general crisis in the 'measurement of power' could be suppressed, and a clearer, 'more realistic' road could be drawn for national and foreign policy (Parker, 1998, p. 16). This Swedish political scientist certainly pioneered an approach that combined attention for territoriality with a more holistic analysis. In the 1920s and '30s, *'Geopolitik'* first took root in a humiliated Germany after Versailles. It is however wrong to think that *'Geopolitik'* only was embraced by extreme-right or radical-conservative circles; it was also utilised as an instrument and a frame of reference by those on the left and in the middle of the German political spectrum. The vagueness of *'Geopolitik'* (its unclear mix of social Darwinism, geographical determinism, anti-urbanism, mysticism) constituted both its strength and weakness; everyone saw it as useful, but as a result of this the confusion of tongues was complete, both conceptually, analytically as well as concerning the search and application of *'geopolitical laws'*. *Geopolitik*'s nomothetical ambition proved to be an illusion...

Karl Haushofer (1869-1946)

It was in a post-Versailles defeated Germany that *Geopolitik* firmly took root. The ex-military officer **Karl Ernst Haushofer** saw it as an analytical instrument that was extremely useful for German politicians, academics and the interested public to try to better understand the unique position with which the country was faced; its *Mittellage* or central position in Europe. This very special geographical position had important consequences for the foreign relations of the country, something which had not been fully appreciated by German political leaders and the general public. Haushofer taught at the University of Munich. He was of the opinion that Germany as a result of 'Versailles' had been blocked in its development to the level of a *'verhinderte Grossmacht'*. This nevertheless still entailed some possibilities for the future (Bakker, 1967, p. 77). By this *'Diktat'*, the German people had been dispersed over fourteen countries. In addition, buffer states (the so-called

'Teufelsgürtel') were created without taking into account the *'natural borders'* in this area. The Versailles-principle that *'nations'* and *'states'* should coincide as much as possible, was not upheld for the losers of the Great War. Germany had been deprived of its *'geopolitical natural entitlement'* to space (*'Raumrecht'*) (Bakker, 1967, pp. 77–79), with as a result a geopolitical *'Verstümmelung'* and an economical *'Versklavung'* (Pierik 1999: 73). These were but a few of Haushofer's considerations. Via his former student in 'Geopolitics', Rudolf Hess, Haushofer would come into contact with Adolf Hitler. Some have even accused Haushofer of provoking the Second World War, since he supposedly *"introduced dangerous geopolitical ideas to the Führer"*. Historical research has however proven that Haushofer's influence upon Hitler was marginal at best (Criekemans, 2007).

Under the leadership of Karl Haushofer, the German geopolitical school introduced at least two distortions vis-à-vis Kjellén's original *Geopolitik*. First, it applied "geopolitics" to the totality of Kjellén's system of 'organic political sciences', and introduced even wider areas of application. It seemed almost as though Political Science equalled Geopolitics. Between 1918 and 1933, substantial amount of geopolitical literature was produced in Weimar-Germany (Murphy, 1997). Secondly however, a further distortion of the concept of 'geopolitics' took root from the moment when Adolf Hitler came to power in 1933. Haushofer's original conceptualisation of 'geopolitics' had been relatively free from racial elements, this would change from 1934 onwards; the 'ideological Nazi-vision' was gradually introduced via the newly set up *'Arbeitsgemeinschaft für Geopolitik'*. Not everyone within German *Geopolitik* agreed with these practices (e.g. Richard Hennig). In other words, the ethno-nationalistic variant of *'Geopolitik'*, which developed between 1934 and 1944, was 'unreal'; it had little or nothing to do with the study of the relationship between 'territoriality' and 'politics' (as Kjellén originally conceptualised it). Geopolitics was violated, it was instrumentalised by the Nazis.

Contrary to what many believe, Haushofer's original geopolitical vision was that Germany should not engage in war with Russia, but rather that Berlin should cooperate with Moscow and Tokyo and create an immense German-Russian-Japanese alliance against the Anglo-American sea powers. Karl Haushofer's vision dated back from his contribution to secret tripartite negotiations between Germany, the Soviet Union and Japan, following the Treaty of Rapallo (1923). This geopolitical construction which he tried to promote, was much more similar in line with the prudent balance of power policy which Bismarck had developed in the period 1871–1890. There are two major differences in the thinking of Haushofer versus that of Hitler:

1. *Their attitude vis-à-vis the Soviet Union*; Hitler really thought in terms of military provocation and annexation of Russia's most lucrative territo-

ries, especially in the oil-rich Caucasus and in the vast agrarian territory west of Moscow.

2. *Their appreciation of the factor 'race'*; for Hitler this constituted an immanent component of his world vision (in which the Aryans would ultimately dominate the world), whereas Karl Haushofer's wife was Jewish. These elements force us to a more adapted and nuanced understanding of Haushofer and his role in German foreign policy between 1933 and 1945. The popular idea that he was *'the true (geopolitical) mastermind behind Germany's expansionist policies from 1938 onwards'*, constitutes an exaggeration of major proportion. The German geopolitical school of thought during these years should be re-evaluated in a much more moderate and nuanced way.

What for instance is hardly covered in the current literature on the historiography of Geopolitics, is that Karl Haushofer and his son Albrecht –a German diplomat and also a geopolitical scholar of some standing– played an important role in trying to broker a peace deal between Germany and the United Kingdom not long after the war broke out. Already in December 1940, the *Führer* had decided to attack Russia, thus violating the Non-Aggression Pact of 23 August 1939. Both Haushofers knew this. There is historical proof that they used both their academic and political contacts in the UK to broker some kind of peace deal between London and Berlin (Allen, 2003; Picknett, Prince & Prior, 2001). Only in this way could a fatal two-front war be avoided, as had been the case during 1914 to 1918. In their geopolitical analyses, the Haushofers feared this would eventually lead to the destruction of 'Western civilisation', the collapse of the British Empire and a victory for 'bolshevism'. They tried to convince their old friend, the now leader of the Nazi party and Deputy-*Führer* Rudolf Hess. It was decided that Hess himself would fly to Scotland to meet the Duke of Hamilton, who was believed to be member of a 'peace fraction' close to King George VI. Hess' flight took off in May 1941, exactly one month before Hitler's Barbarossa-campaign to conquer more *Lebensraum* in the east. Hess however was captured by Churchill, who aborted the desired 'peace talks' (Criekemans, 2007).

One who studies Haushofer's geopolitical scholarship, is struck by the fact that he himself developed little original concepts. What he mostly did, was put together the 'usable' elements from the work of Ratzel, Mackinder and Kjellén into a total vision on the world-to-be-analysed (Pierik, 2006; Pierik, 2012). Only some isolated concepts or applications in his work can be considered as 'innovative', such as his idea that boundaries should not be considered as *'static'* but as *'dynamic'* (Herwig, 1999). After Hess' failed peace flight in May 1941, Albrecht Haushofer was jailed by the Nazis and executed by the SS during the last days of the Second World War. He knew too much. Karl Haushofer committed suicide in 1946. With this, the German geopolitical school almost symbolically ended. Especially its association with the Nazi-ideology became fatal, at that time a more nuanced analysis was not possible because the events that occurred had been too troublesome for people to analyse more objectively. By having been used so openly in legitimating certain political objectives (the national-socialist aggression), *'Geopolitik'* was discredited after 1945 as a *'paria'* in the academic world. As a result of all this, the study of the relationship between territoriality, power and politics degraded after 1945 into a true 'intellectual mine field'. Henceforth, the role of 'territoriality' was scarcely studied in political analyses (e.g. in the scientific study of nationalism).

4 Reactions to 'Classical Geopolitics': The French Interwar School of Possibilism & the Work of the Dutch-American Political Scientist Nicholas John Spykman

'Classical Geopolitics' offered itself as a clarifying guide to the "real" distributions of power in the world and so promised to simplify the complexities (Polelle, 1999: p. 13). This ontological vision of a world locked in a social darwinist power struggle and the epistemological view that an analysis of the changing 'power distribution' can help us to understand that world, is where 'Classical Geopolitics' connects with various forms of contemporary 'Neo-Realism' in IR, as it may also be seen as an early precursor to it. Yet at the same time, both approaches are also markedly different and themselves products of 'other worlds' and their own *Zeitgeist*. The research tradition of 'Classical Geopolitics' can be reconstructed via its ontological, epistemological and methodological components:

- ONTOLOGICALLY, one can speak of 'Classical Geopolitics' when the respective author underwrites several of the following assumptions about the international-political reality:
  1. state organicism (see supra; Friedrich Ratzel);
  2. *Erdgebundenheit'* or geographical determinism;
  3. social Darwinism;
  4. absence of legality and morality;
  5. autarky;
  6. expansionism provoked by 'macro-economic tendencies';
  7. a 'closed political system' and *'Ganzheit'*;
  8. boundaries as 'dynamic, temporary stops'.
- EPISTEMOLOGICALLY, it is characteristic for 'Classical Geopolitics' that it believed in the modernist idea of the possibility of universal scientific

knowledge. Therefore, it should be possible to 'identify' and 'apply' *'laws of nature'* which explain how the world works.

– METHODOLOGICALLY, 'classical' geopolitical scientists will often develop overview tables in which individual countries or areas are being compared on the basis of their 'primary geopolitical factors' such as location, territorial form and width, climate, population, natural resources & industrial capacity, as well as the political and social organisation of the territory. Such analyses could further be 'adorned' with ('suggestive') maps.

Two immediate reactions to 'Classical Geopolitics' can be identified; the French interwar school of Possibilism & the work of the political scientist Nicholas John Spykman.

The ontological, statist framework of analysis that the German geopolitical scientists used, was criticised by their contemporary French colleagues from Geography as a rather uni-dimensional and reductionist perspective. Paul Vidal de la Blache can be seen as the founder of the French school of Geography (Zajec, 2008, p. 38). According to **Vidal de la Blache** and his followers, there existed a true 'geopolitical diversity' of complex relations beyond the state level between geographically circumscribed areas and human activity. Those scholars who hoped to gain substantial insights into the relation territoriality—man/politics, should recognise this diversity (especially the basic level of the local *'pays'*).

According to these French geographers, a deterministic influence of the environment upon man did not exist. In **'Possibilist Geopolitics'** as developed and exercised by the French geographers during the interbellum period, the environment is approached as being both *'constraining'* and *'enabling'*, and man is considered to be able to make choices (Vidal de la Blache, 1898; Vidal de la Blache, 1926). The environment provides a number of parameters or limitations to the whole spectrum of foreign policy actions which can be undertaken by an entity ('constraining'), but the environment also provides a political entity with a number of important opportunities (Sprout, 1971 [1965], p. 83). 'Man' stood central in 'Possibilist Geopolitics' because in the end the political decision-makers try to maximise the opportunities, and to minimise the limitations with which they are confronted. Thus, nature only laid the foundation for human development; the actual cultural and political progress depended on 'man' himself. According to Vidal de la Blache, the geographer should resist the temptation to formulate abstract 'laws'; it would be better to invest time in studying and interpreting *'the interaction between variables, which produce unique situations'*. The French possibilists developed the concept of *'genre de vie'*; the idea that culture and geography over time had become closely intertwined as a result of man's choices. This resulted in descriptive portraits of the

French mini-regions. There where German geopolitics had seen the world in terms of national states poised for confrontation, the ontological vision of the possibilists stated that a geographical diversity existed which actually 'invited' peoples across borders, rivers, in the Baltic and the Mediterranean Sea to cooperate with one another.

The Dutch-American political scientist **Nicholas John Spykman** is an important figure which played a crucial role in 'integrating' a number of basic principles from Geopolitics into the field of IR (Zajec, 2016a, pp. 497–530). Nicholas Spykman can indeed be viewed as another 'father of American Geopolitics', next to Mahan. According to the IR-specialist Spykman, geopolitics may be applied to the planning of the security policy of a country in terms of its 'geographic factors'. It recognises that the problem of peace inevitably involves the territorial relations of states in a geographical sense. Its method of analysis may thus be compared to the kind of thought which precedes the formulation and execution of policy in any field of action involving a choice of location and an awareness of the quality of space relations. The specific field of geopolitics is, however, the field of foreign policy, and its particular type of analysis uses geographical factors to help in the formulation of adequate policies for the achievement of certain justifiable ends (Spykman & Nicholl, 1969 [1944], pp. 5–6). For Nicholas John Spykman, Geopolitics constituted a policy-oriented *'method of analysis'* (see also: Furniss, 1952, p. 386), with special attention for the way in which *'territoriality'* had a continuing impact upon the security dilemma with which a nation was confronted.

Spykman subscribed to five of the eight ontological 'basic components' of Classical Geopolitics: (1) social Darwinism, (2) a moderated *'Erdgebundenheit'* or geographic determinism, (3) absence of legality and morality in international relations (only the realisation of 'collective security' and norms via a real, flexible 'balance' between powers), (4) a closed global political system, and (5) boundaries as 'flexible, temporary stops'. Only statist organicism and the German-Swedish ideas of autarky and 'expansionism provoked by macroeconomical tendencies' do not explicitly appear in his thinking. Spykman's approach to place the concept of 'power' central in his analysis, can be considered revolutionary for the (Anglo-American) field of international relations, which at that time during the 1930s was still dominated by idealists. The flight of the German-Swiss scholar Arnold Wolfers away from the Nazis to America brought Spykman in direct contact with the continental-European ideas about Geopolitics. Gradually, his thinking developed from a Wilsonian idealist world view towards a more pragmatic analysis of international relations 'based upon hard facts'. Spykman started his analyses from the 'geographical constellation', and linked this to such 'classical-geopolitical variables' as the (relative) population numbers & the available resources. Spykman's interpretation of 'power' was thus directly imported from the 'classical geopolitical scientists'; in his vision 'power' derived directly from the geographical constellation (next to economical and military factors). Spykman is most widely known for his alternative vision to international relations; he was inspired by Mackinder's *Heartland*-thesis to suggest an alternative adage, the so-called '*Rimland*-thesis'. Spykman proposed that instead of the 'heartland', rather the area equalling the belt between the sea & the heartland (today's enlarged European Union, the Middle East, parts of India and China), was a crucial territory: *"Who controls the rimland controls Eurasia; who rules Eurasia controls the destinies of the world."* (Spykman & Nicholl, 1969 [1944], p. 43). Spykman used 'Geopolitics' as an instrument to advocate an interventionist strategy for the United States of America to actively create a new 'balance of power'. In 1942, when the US was still fighting both Germany and Japan, he dared to state that Washington should develop close military and political ties with both countries after the war. The idea was that the US should build up individual links with many of the countries in the Rimland, so as to prevent a new hegemon from ever arising. There are a number of indications that Spykman's ideas were used behind closed doors after 1945 by practitioners of American foreign and strategic policy. The concepts which he helped to develop and spread (*'Rimland', 'balance of power'*) (un)consciously remained part of the collective memory and 'common frame of reference' of these American foreign policy and strategic elites. However, one can debate whether they interpreted Spykman's ideas in the way in which he originally meant them. From Kennedy over Johnson, Nixon, Carter and Reagan; almost all American presidencies referred to concepts originally developed by Spykman.

5 1945 to the 1970s: Geopolitics Goes 'Underground'

The term 'geopolitics' disappeared right after the Second World War from the jargon of international relations. Nevertheless, one could defend the position that the 'intellectual-military complex' in the United States of America after 1945 effectively developed its own 'geopolitical analyses'. These internal studies tried to better inform the intelligence, military and diplomatic elites in Washington D.C. of all available options/strategies so as to 'consolidate' the newly-attained superpower-role. In other words; geopolitics went 'underground'. The term 'geopolitics' between 1945–1976 is almost untraceable in publications accessible to the broader public, aspects of the 'geopolitical analysis' were nevertheless used within circles of defence and foreign policy. However, this does not reflect the complete picture. Stimulated by the forced emigration of (mainly) German- and Austrian-Jewish scientists such as **Robert Strausz-Hupé** and **Hans Morgenthau**, also quite a number of *'geopolitical analytical categories and arguments'* started to trickle into the Anglo-American literature of the developing IR school of Realism (1948) (Strausz-Hupé, 1942; Strausz-Hupé, 1943; Strausz-Hupé, 1945; Strausz-Hupé, 1957; Morgenthau, 1973). Today, this is not always fully realised within the field of international relations. In other words, Classical Geopolitics constitutes a *'missing link'* behind the history of the development of one of the most important IR-paradigms up until today; Realism and its offshoots (Criekemans, 2007).

After the Second World War, the field of Political Geography had a lot of trouble using the term 'geopolitics' in its analyses. Many (American) political geographers in this period tried to firmly distinguish their "objective and neutral" Political Geography from the so-called "subjective and dangerous" Geopolitics. But in many ways these same scholars sometimes tried to assimilate as inconspicuously as possible certain 'geopolitical perspectives' within Political Geography, which was deemed "more academic and objective". At a time when Geography had the inclination to turn in on itself and when it was rather isolated vis-à-vis (the formulation of theories within) other social sciences, such an attitude resulted in attempts to strip existing (geopolitical) concepts of their political dimension and to avoid public and political debates. Most of the publications written by political geographers in the years after 1945 had these characteristics. As a result of their a-political nature, one could therefore catalogue these under the denominator of *'Non-prescriptive' or 'Neutralised Geopolitics'*.

One exception to this trend within Political Geography to avoid "politically-laden subjects", was the work of the American scholar **Saul B. Cohen**. He was among the first political geographers to reintroduce the term 'geopolitics' as a means to interpret international relations. From 1963 onwards, he reintroduced "thinking on a world scale" within Political Geography, by explicitly developing new geopolitical perspectives. In his book *'Geography and Politics in a World Divided'*, Cohen also linked prescriptive policy analyses to his grand geopolitical thinking. The work of Cohen constitutes an interesting contribution to the 'geopolitical approach'. Its surplus value lies with his search for trends and dynamics in global international relations. During the past four decades, Cohen basically utilised the same 'world system' analytical framework. As time evolved, his 'model' was gradually adapted, but in its essence it remained quite stable. From this, Cohen time and again deduced lessons for American foreign policy. The question remains, however, how Cohen makes his jump to policy recommendations, and whether these are transposable to the foreign policy of another country or entity. In our opinion, the added value of Cohen's approach for IR lies rather at the conceptual level; more precisely with such concepts as *'gateways'* and *'shatterbelts'*, which he relaunched in the academic debate. These are quite useful to gain insight into certain regional developments via descriptive analyses. Cohen frequently adapted his global analyses to the new circumstances on the ground, for instance in his voluminous book *'Geopolitics of the World System'* (Cohen, 2003).

6 A Forgotten, Yet Epistemologically Important Geopolitical School of Thought: 'Cognitive Geopolitics' as Developed by Harold and Margaret Sprout

The vast majority of overviews of the geopolitical literature jumps directly from 'Classical Geopolitics' to 'Critical Geopolitics'. This way of representing the literature is in our opinion flawed and incomplete. After all, during the 1950s and '60s yet another reaction to 'Classical Geopolitics' was developed. We refer here to a variant which we ourselves label as *'Cognitive Geopolitics'*. In 1956, the American IR scholars **Harold and Margaret Sprout** developed a new, revolutionary epistemological approach; 'cognitive behavioralism'. It was the result of a fundamental reflection which the Sprouts started about the relation between 'territoriality' and 'politics'. The Sprout's conceptual work and their particular philosophy of science formed the real starting point of the cognitive-behavioralist approaches within IR and the foundation of the IR subfield of 'comparative foreign policy'. These aspects constitute strong indicators that (the debate on) 'geopolitics' which the Sprouts initiated can be considered as a kind of 'missing link' which helps us to better understand the development of IR during the 1950s and '60s (see also Chapter 4).

Harold and Margaret Sprout stated in their central hypothesis that environmental variables can only influence human activities in two ways. First, such factors can be perceived by individuals, who take these into account in their foreign policy decisions and responses. Only in such cases can one speak of 'influence' of human preferences & decisions by the environment, *'mediated'* by perception. Secondly, environmental variables can be approached as a kind of 'matrix' which possibly limits the results of foreign policy decisions ('foreign policy outcomes'), even if these environmental variables are not perceived. According to the Sprouts there are therefore two usable explanatory frameworks; the **'psychological milieu'** or **'psycho-milieu'** (*'the environment as perceived by the decisionmaker & upon which he/she bases his/her reaction'*) on the one hand, and the **'operational environment'** (*'the true environment in* *which the chosen policy is executed'*) on the other hand. The conceptual distinction between 'psycho-milieu' and the 'operational environment' in fact means a fundamental break with the realist school, which (still) believed that foreign policy decision makers can perceive their environment in a 'correct' way. This 'amendment' of the Sprouts had important consequences for the IR scholar. In case a researcher is trying to explain why certain decisions are taken in foreign policy, then one should try to analyse the 'psychological environment' of the decision maker. However, in case the analyst is more interested in the 'operational results' of a specific decision, then the 'operational (or geographical) environment' should be used as an explanatory framework (see figure 3.4.). The explanatory power which analysts attribute to the 'milieu', largely depends on the way in which their proposed *man-milieu-hypotheses* are embedded in a certain epistemology about the feasibility of scientific knowledge about the relationship territoriality–politics. Each geopolitical formulation of a theory rests on such initial assumptions.

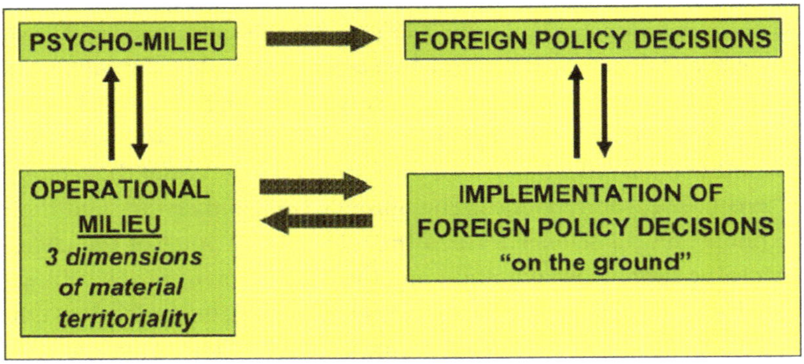

FIGURE 3.4 The conceptual revolution of Harold and Margaret Sprout: cognitive behavioralism and foreign policy analysis

In their book *'The Ecological Perspective on Human Relations with Special Reference to International Politics'* (1965, 1971), Harold and Margaret Sprout stated that in essence a researcher can choose from five possible epistemological ways of appreciating the relationship between environmental variables & (foreign) policy: *'geographical determinism'* (cf. Haushofer), *'free will environmentalism'* (cf. Spykman), *'environmental possibilism'* (cf. Vidal de la Blache), *'environmental probabilism'* and the approach developed by the Sprouts themselves: *'cognitive behavioralism'*. The latter one, cognitive behavioralism, starts from the following assumption: a central political decisionmaker (who conducts a foreign policy on behalf of a political entity) consciously responds to his/her milieu (environment) as he/she apperceives & interprets it in light of past experiences (Sprout, 1971 [1965], pp. 117–118).

The Sprouts considered classical-geopolitical theories as 'one-dimensional' since they often have the inclination to start from one specific group of unevenly spread, 'geographically embedded' variables in order to develop (far-reaching) explanations or predictions about the (power relations in) international politics. The Sprouts repudiated such 'one-dimensional' geopolitical theories in favour of a broader 'ecological perspective'. This approach constituted the development of a more integrated, holistic vision on the international environment; one which took both physical and non-physical elements into account. In short, the environment or 'milieu' was approached as a multidimensional system, in which both the perceptions about the environment by decisionmakers (the *'psycho-milieu'*) as the 'objective' conditions themselves, constituted the object of study. Their analytical framework emphasised the mutual interdependence between geography, demography, technology and resources. Both perceptual variables as quantitative factors such as population and territorial width were considered relevant. The complexity of the interdependence within and between national societies and the increasing irrelevance of the distinction between 'domestic' and 'foreign' questions, form central points of interest within the 'ecological perspective' to international relations. Each 'geopolitical theory' also makes assumptions with regard to the technology the concerned societies have at their disposal (Sprout, 1963).

According to the Sprouts, the 'ecological perspective' also offers a philosophical perspective from which one can observe current events in a critical and society-relevant fashion. The 'victory' of man upon nature, and the development of elaborate techniques for the manipulation of human behaviour, suggest that it is possible to twist the Earth around one's finger. New technologies may perhaps 'free' man from his 'natural environment', but could at the same time as a result of their 'perfection' also structurally undermine the liveability of the Earth. How one should handle these increasing capacities so as to change the human condition, thus forms the 'ultimate question' in international politics according to the Sprouts. The 'ecological paradigm' does not offer any ready-made solutions for this, but can help to identify the most important questions and decisions.

The Sprouts made an important distinction between analysing 'power' (or better: 'political potential') 'in terms of foreign policy-analyses' *versus* 'in terms of capacity analyses'. **Foreign policy analyses** are aimed at explaining or predicting policy decisions. Conversely, **capacity analyses** are aimed at explaining or predicting the operational results of decisions; the calculation of the opportunities and limitations which are implicitly embodied in the environment of a certain state. These exact elements will affect the 'operational results' of that which is undertaken, irrespective whether such factors are known by the decision makers. In both types of analyses, environmental variables play a role, but the relevant frames of reference and the applied explanatory hypotheses or theories are always different. Only foreign policy analyses focus on the way in which environmental variables are 'perceived'. In capacity analyses, 'perception' as such does not play a real role; as an analyst one rather develops an independent evaluation of the question what opportunities and limitations are implicitly embedded in the environment of the concerned state, and how these may affect the 'political potential' of a nation (in comparison to other countries and in function of certain previously postulated long or short term policy objectives).

Researchers such as Strausz-Hupé and Morgenthau had been focussed on measuring 'power' in terms of *capacity analyses*; they tried to fill in 'power' in a non-normative fashion in which they still believed that 'geography' and other 'territorially embedded' power factors were guiding the content of foreign policy. Scholars such as Strausz-Hupé did not analyse foreign policy as such, but rather made an 'inventory' of the material power sources (geographical location, size of the state, available resources, developed industries, demography, etcetera) of states (sometimes even without explicitly drawing attention to the necessary framework of reference of 'national policy objectives'). In fact, what really was studied was the virtual 'capacity' of states to influence international politics, instead of examining whether and to what extent such environmental variables effectively generate an impact upon daily foreign policy. The latter was a step which the Sprouts clearly did make.

What is striking is the way in which the Sprouts mainly concentrated their efforts upon the study of the possible impact of the 'environment' upon politics, though spending little to no attention to the question to what extent also a reverse influence of 'politics' on the 'milieu' exists. In that sense their work is similar to 'Classical Geopolitics'. They either had attention for the influence of the 'psycho-milieu' upon 'foreign policy decisions', or for the influence of the real, operational milieu upon the results of these political decisions (*'foreign policy outcomes'*). Their analytical framework was, however, at best appreciative of the *possibility* that 'politics' as such changed the structure of the ecological 'milieu', but much less for the possibility in which the milieu is being assigned a different 'meaning' starting from a political or social-societal discourse (read part 8. on 'Critical Geopolitics').

The research tradition of 'Cognitive Geopolitics' can be reconstructed on the basis of its ontological, epistemological and methodological components;

a. ONTOLOGICALLY, the following assumptions are at work within 'Cognitive Geopolitics':
    1. The idea that states are the most important political entities, which do not function as organisms – 'state action' entails "those deeds performed by those who act on behalf of the state".

2. The idea that *'Erdgebundenheit'* does not exist – the relationship between 'territoriality' and 'politics' is active from an 'ecological triad' (environment, environed entities and their mutual relationship). Moreover, there exists both an 'operational' and a 'psycho'-environment.

In addition to the principles formulated above, one could also mention some other elements as possible 'ontological principles' of 'Cognitive Geopolitics', although one does not always see these aspects in the interpretations of other cognitive-behavioralists:

3. "There exists an uneven distribution of physical and human 'resources' (cf. climate patterns, topology, available resources, human societies, etc.). This unequal distribution influences in significant ways all human enterprise, interactions, relations and interstate relations".
4. "Change and transformation are inherent to international relations. As technology develops further, also global interdependence increases".

b. FROM AN EPISTEMOLOGICAL POINT OF VIEW, it is characteristic of 'Cognitive Geopolitics' that one refused to subscribe to the implicit assumption of 'Classical Geopolitics' that it would be possible to explain or predict the (power relations within) international politics as a system based upon "objective laws of nature". In practice, 'Cognitive Geopolitics' looks at a lower level of analysis; that of the decision maker. There where 'Classical Geopolitics' departed from the assumption that the environment had a mere objective nature, 'Cognitive Geopolitics' states that *the decision-making is influenced by the environment as a subjective given.* The perception of central (foreign policy) decision makers is central in this. Consequently, the first task of the geopolitical scholar is not so much to make an inventory of the physical- and social-geographical environmental variables but rather to penetrate as far as the 'ideal factors'; the way in which a decision maker attributes a certain value to his/her environment. As regards the results of the (foreign-)policy decisions, one does have attention for the objective or operational environment. In short, 'Cognitive Geopolitics' starts from a certain tension between the 'objective' and the 'subjective' environment. However, the IR scholar is considered to be capable of making a distinction between both.

c. METHODOLOGICALLY, 'Cognitive Geopolitics' tries to fathom the actions of individual decision makers via examining their "beliefs" on the external environment. A clear 'methodology' for such studies was never really developed. However, one can discover within the cognitive-behavioralist literature of the 1960s and '70s some approaches which could be potentially useful; 'belief systems' (O. Holsti), 'operational belief code system' (A. George), 'mental maps' (P. Gould, R. White, A. Henrikson), 'sketch maps' (T. Saarinen), etcetera. Since 'Cognitive Geopolitics' was 'encapsulated' within the IR subfield of Comparative Foreign Policy, the methodology in fact was not 'crystallised out'. Today one can however from time to time find publications within *'Environmental Psychology'* which more or less build further upon this tradition.

The fundamental reflection of the Sprouts mentioned earlier about the "five possible epistemological ways of appreciating the relationship between environmental variables & (foreign) policy", caused a new research tradition to develop within IR, in 1991; the so-called *'New Geopolitics'* school of **Harvey Starr**. This focused especially on the study of the role of geographical factors in the coming into being and the spread of wars. Also, it developed its own *'environmental model'* for the study of the impact of geographical factors in foreign policy. However, this research tradition remains rather isolated within IR; always the same circle of researchers seems to be active in it, and there is a relatively limited resonance vis-à-vis other groups of IR scholars. Some names which often return in this research tradition; Harvey Starr, Benjamin Most, Michael D. Ward, Randolph M. Siverson, Gary Goertz and Paul F. Diehl (see: Most & Starr, 1980; Siverson & Starr, 1992; Goertz, 1994). It is nevertheless a fact that the concepts of (external) *'opportunity'* and (domestic) *'willingness'* as developed by Harvey Starr in 1978 (and built upon the scholarship of the Sprouts and others in 'Geopolitics') have over the decades developed into central tools in the study of international conflicts. Attention is for instance given to the role of geographical factors or so-called 'context variables' in the coming into being and spread of wars (see for instance: Most & Starr, 1980), in *the creation of alliances* (see: Starr, 1990), also in the *spread of democracy* (see: Starr, 1991). Starr more or less equated 'opportunity' with *'environmental possibilism'*, whereas 'willingness' is equated with the epistemological positions of *'environmental probabilism'* and *'cognitive behavioralism'*. In short, Starr's approach pretends to be more comprehensive. For instance, before policy makers take a decision to 'go to war', both 'opportunity' and 'willingness' need to be present, though these are not sufficient conditions. 'Geography' constitutes but one influencing factor. Moreover, *'opportunity'* and *'willingness'* are linked to one another; in case the 'opportunity' to 'go to war' is substantial, then there perhaps exists among decision makers more 'willingness' to do so (Diehl, 1991, p. 15). The *opportunity-willingness*-framework which grew out of the geopolitical literature therefore provides a usable analytical framework, although according to some the disadvantage is that it offers only limited opportunities for theory building (Mouritzen, 1998: p. 24). As an agent-structure model, Starr's opportunity/willingness echoes the Sprout's triad of entity, environment and the entity-environment-relationship (Starr, 2013, p. 155). *'New Geopolitics'* hence tries to analyse patterns of conflict and cooperation.

7 The Return of Geopolitics from the 1970s Onwards: The US and France

As mentioned earlier, the number of publications that openly used the term 'geopolitics' after 1945 was rather scarce. 'Geopolitics' was popularised anew in the Anglo-American public discourse and IR literature during the 1970s, first by Henry Kissinger and not much later by Colin S. Gray and Zbigniew Brzezinski. However, their concrete elaboration of the 'geopolitical approach' differed. Brzezinski leaned most closely to the (German) Classical *'Geopolitik'*, both in style as well as content. His work can be catalogued under the label of *'Neo-classical Global Geopolitics'* with a 'narrow', material interpretation of 'territoriality'. Henry Kissinger deviates most from Classical *'Geopolitik'*; although he introduced the term 'geopolitics' again in the US, the references to 'material' territoriality in his work are rather implicit – conversely, he devotes most attention to the 'balance of power'. Kissinger can therefore be catalogued under the label of *'Realpolitical Geopolitics'*, a very slim interpretation of Geopolitics which can today often be found amongst the work of American IR scholars. Gray's approach leans quite closely to the classical-geopolitical research tradition, although at the same time he incoporated the conceptual and epistemological 'progress' in the thinking on the relationship territoriality—politics after 1945 (cf. Harold and Margaret Sprout) in his application of the 'geopolitical approach' to American foreign policy. Seen from this perspective, Gray's approach deserves positive reassessment. Gray remained loyal to the original foundations of 'Geopolitics', from an adapted and more sophisticated epistemological position. His work can be catalogued under the label of 'Neo-classical Global Geopolitics' with a 'broader' –material as well as ideational– interpretation of 'territoriality').

In Europe, the French were among the first who actively tried to study the relationship between 'territoriality' and 'politics' after the inglorious demise of 'Geopolitics' in 1945. This movement started to gain momentum during the 1970s. It was Yves Lacoste who was one of the first within French Geography to break through the taboo surrounding "questions with a 'political' dimension". In his journal *'Hérodote'*, he developed a critical reflection on the relation territoriality–politics and with this laid the foundations for a new French geopolitical school of thought. Lacoste wanted to 'liberate geopolitics' out of the arms of military staff-elites, which were until then the only ones that 'practised' geopolitics. He also believed that next to the familiar imperialistic forms of geopolitical discourse, also other versions existed –for instance: 'the anti-imperialistic body of thought which tries to support the independence, the autonomy of the free speech'. In 1993, Lacoste defined 'Geopolitics' as *'the scientific study of territorial power rivalries and their repercussions in/for the public opinion'*. Following the French possibilists of the interwar period, Lacoste believes that more than one form of geopolitics exists aside from the one at the state level. There also exist *'d'autres géopolitiques'* (e.g. regionalisation). This *"Hérodote-school"* has a lot of attention for the geographical/geopolitical reasoning at different spatial levels of analysis (e.g. local, regional, national, macro-regional, global). The most important contribution of the group around Lacoste exactly lies in "bringing in" the notion of 'representation' into geopolitical analyses (this means; the way in which 'territoriality' is represented).

Epistemologically, the first contributions in the original version of the French journal *'Hérodote'* were still mostly inspired by the *'environmental possibilism'* of Vidal de la Blache. The group-*Hérodote* posed itself the question to what extent it is possible from an epistemological point of view to be 'objective' in geopolitical research. The geographer always has to control his/her a priori ideological position as much as possible, and to remain open to other views. Critics believe that around 1986 the epistemological debate as it was started by the group-Lacoste in 1976, missed some continuity. This task seemed to be 'labelled' as 'accomplished'; the main mission was now to 'apply'. According to some, the French *Hérodote*-school left the epistemological 'infrastructure' of [Classical] 'Geopolitics' largely intact, in this sense that it kept believing in the possibility of 'objective knowledge' and in approaching the world from a 'panopticonist' perspective. This is correct, however – from 1982 onwards, the journal *'Hérodote'* developed a critical-interpretative approach, with a certain onset to insights into the 'social-constructivist nature' of the way in which 'territoriality' is given 'meaning' via a (power)discourse (especially via the 'media').

Lacoste's vision with regard to the 'situated' nature of geographical knowledge is important to bear in mind because it asks attention for the complexity of the relation territoriality–politics. In *'Hérodote'*, the societal 'situatedness' (via the media) of geography, always lurks around the corner. Moreover, the group of scholars around Yves Lacoste had a lot of attention for important research subjects such as the 'nation', an often neglected and ignored (geopolitical) theme within the field of International Relations. Somewhat detrimental is that the group-*Hérodote* never really developed a clear 'methodology'; the 'geopolitical' analyst should in his/her empirical studies take into account a number of basic rules, but apart from that it is hard to speak of a tight analytical model or framework. This somewhat entails a danger for analyses which are 'incoherent' or 'free of obligations', as a result of which the direct usefulness of this approach to IR is less easy to pinpoint exactly.

But today, the French academic and popular debates are much more diverse. Next to the *Hérodote*-school, there are many different individual scholars and institutions in France which study 'Geopolitics'. Noteworthy in this regard is for instance the work of Aymeric Chauprade, who pioneered a detailed descriptive and analytical geopolitical analysis based upon facts. In this regard for instance his book *'Introduction à l'analyse géopolitique'* (1999) deserves to be mentioned. Somewhat similar in approach is the work of François Thual, e.g. in his book *'Méthodes de la Géopolitique. Apprendre à déchiffer l'actualité'* (1996). Thual also wrote a concise but stimulating book *'La géopolitique'* together with Pascal Lorot (1997). Lorot on his part wrote an interesting booklet on the history of geopolitics, called *'Histoire de la Géopolitique'*. At the same time, Lorot can also be considered as one of the pioneers in the study of geo-economics. The book that laid the foundations for this approach from an ontological and epistemological point of view was *'Introduction à la géoéconomie'* (1999). A French author which has made some interesting contributions to the study of the history of geopolitics, and the link with 'geostrategy' is Paul Claval, who originally comes from the perspective of Geography. For instance, his book *'Géopolitique et Géostrategie. La pensée politique, l'espace et le territoire au XXe siècle'* certainly had some impact. A French author who uses international relations as his departing point for analysis, is Philippe Moreau Defarges. In 1994 he wrote a concise booklet *'Introduction à l'analyse géopolitique'* which was quite influential; a new revised edition was published in 2005. More recently, Moreau Defarges wrote *'La Géopolitique pour les nuls. Déchiffrez les règles du jeu planétaire'* (2008). A French geopolitical author who appears less in overview articles, but who in our opinion can be considered to be a quite creative thinker both ontologically and epistemologically, is Gérard Dussouy. Especially his book *'Quelle géopolitique au XXIème siècle?'* (2001) can be considered as quite comprehensive. In many ways this monograph tries to bring geopolitical factors and perspectives together into an inclusive framework of analysis. There are many other interesting and important French geopolitical authors which we forget to mention here. The message is however clear; France can be considered one of the first European countries which again fully embraced Geopolitics; its literature has become vast. One crucial point of criticism to the French geopolitical literature is however that some authors seem to define *'Géopolitique'* in such a broad way that the division vis-à-vis *'Relations Internationales'* becomes paper-thin. This lack of conceptual precision can be considered as a danger for Geopolitics to further develop academically; Geopolitics' core business has been and always will be the focus on 'territoriality' in all its manifestations.

8 A New Approach: The Development of 'Critical Geopolitics' (1988–92)

The French geopolitical *Hérodote*-school did not mean the end of the epistemological debate with regard to the relation between 'territoriality' and 'politics'. Starting from the end of the 1980s, a number of Anglo-American political geographers developed a new approach; 'Critical Geopolitics'. In the meantime, this relatively new geopolitical school of thought has taken up a more than dominant position in the relevant literature amongst current political geographers. At the same time, it is still relatively unknown amongst the vast majority of IR scholars. The ontological and epistemological 'mission' of this new research tradition was developed between 1988 and 1996. Especially the book *'Critical Geopolitics'* of the Irish-American political-geographer Gearóid Ó Tuathail (pronounced: Gerald Otoal) takes up a special position in this endeavour. Between 1996 and 1998, further refinements were made to the formulation of an unequivocal scientific research agenda. The 'critical geopolitical scholars' were inspired by much of the same literature as the French *Hérodote*-school. However, since the French literature at that time was barely 'unlocked' towards the English scientific literature, one can see 'Critical Geopolitics' to a large extent as an independent geopolitical school of thought.

One who studies the early 'fundamental texts' which formed and positioned the Anglo-American school of 'Critical Geopolitics' as a scientific prism to international relations in 1988 to 1996, will notice that the authors in these days referred to an amalgam of diverging theoretical roots as 'sources of inspiration' for their new 'geopolitical research tradition'. One can count the following texts to the earliest *roots* of the critical perspective to 'Geopolitics':

1. the English translation in 1985 of a German article from Karl Wittfogel in 1929; *'Geopolitics, geographical materialism and Marxism'*;
2. the 1985 article *'The social origins of environmental determinism'* of Richard Peet; and
3. the English translation in 1987 of some of the foundational articles from Lacoste's review *'Hérodote'* (Girot & Kofman).

However, these constituted a mere first occasion to think critically about geopolitics. More important is that such analyses were further deepened and 'sharpened' by making use of the ideas of a number of dissidents within the theory of international relations, in particular the remarks in 1987 of Richard K. Ashley in *'The geopolitics of geopolitical space: towards a critical social theory of international politics'*, and also by further leaning on a number of developments in 'discourse analysis'. With regard to the latter, two sources of influence can be discerned throughout the *'Critical Geopolitics'*-literature; Michel

Foucault's approach to 'discourse' as a form of knowledge/power & his notion of history as a 'genealogy', and the theories of Jacques Derrida on 'textual deconstruction'. The influence of Derrida on Ó Tuathail's work is, however, less important than that of Foucault. In addition to these elements, other theoretical developments from the 1980s can be identified as sources of inspiration of 'Critical Geopolitics', such as post-positivism and postmodernism (Wolkersdorfer, 2000).

The rise of the research tradition of 'Critical Geopolitics' constituted a joint intellectual enterprise of a number of political geographers in the Anglo-American scientific world. A limited group of researchers played a leading and crucial role in this endeavour. In this regard, special mention is deserved for Gearóid Ó Tuathail, author of the book *'Critical Geopolitics'* (1996), based upon this doctoral dissertation from 1988. Together with the American political geographer John Agnew, he wrote a foundational article on the subject of 'practical geopolitical reasoning' (Ó Tuathail & Agnew, 1992). A person who also deserves a mentioning in this regard is Simon Dalby, currently Professor of Geography and Environmental Studies at Wilfrid Laurier University in Canada. Dalby articulated a number of theoretical foundations of the new research tradition of 'Critical Geopolitics' (1990, 1991). Finally, also the British geographer Klaus Dodds can be designated as one of the first who explicitly linked 'Critical Geopolitics' to the study of foreign policy (1993, 1994). There are many other authors who we here omit.

'Critical Geopolitics' starts from the assumption that 'geography' does not constitute an innocent product of nature. On the contrary, it is the result of the history of the battle between competing authorities about the power to organise, occupy and manage space. For Ó Tuathail, 'geographical knowledge' can be associated with the Foucauldian concept *'governmentality'* – the ways in which the government tries to normalise the activity and practice of 'knowing', both as the system for the organisation and conceptualisation of the management of the 'population', the 'economy', 'security', the 'environment', etcetera. It is precisely this mutual interwovenness between *'governmentality'* and geographical knowledge that creates a *'geo-power'*, the central object of study of Ó Tuathail's 'Critical Geopolitics'. In human language, one could also express it as follows; in their battle for 'power' politicians will apply aspects of geography and transform them in order to promote their own domestic and foreign agenda. Or to go even one step further, geographical elements are considered by 'critical geopolitical scholars' as crucial means in this process for the development of a *'governmentality'*. According to Ó Tuathail, 'Geopolitics' constitutes a historically grown form of *'geo-power'*, which was crucial in the development of *'governmentality'* in the twentieth century (Ó Tuathail, 1996, pp. 10–20; Antonsich, 2000, p. 202). The **scientific mission of 'Critical Geopolitics'** can thus be described as follows: *"to 'document and deconstruct' the 'forms of these new congealments of geo-power' and to 'problematize how global space is incessantly reimagined and rewritten by centers of power and authority'."* (Ó Tuathail, 1996, p. 249; Smith, 2000, pp. 365–366). In addition, the 'renaissance' or 'return' of formal and practical Geopolitics itself, especially in European countries, was questioned (Guzzini, 2013; Josten, 2004).

Especially **via discourse analysis**, 'Critical Geopolitics' tries to achieve insight into the way in which foreign policy-elites of territorial entities think about the relation of this entity vis-à-vis the "external environment". These elites try to spread such self created visions in society as a whole. As in the work of Michel Foucault and Edward W. Said 'discourse' is approached by Ó Tuathail as a *"matrix of argumentation"*, an *"ensemble of ideas and concepts"* or a *"truth regime"* which functions as a knowledge/power system which composes, presents and interprets the external world. The *'geopolitical discourse'* constitutes thus much more than mere rhetoric regarding international relations (Ó Tuathail, 2000, p. 126). In 'Critical Geopolitics', a 'discourse' is approached as a 'power structure', a rhetorical strategy and representational techniques sponsored by certain institutions and political forces which compete amongst one another in the public arena. Their final goal is to achieve 'rhetorical dominance'; the 'only truth' to perceive certain processes, crises and actors in global politics. Also, the 'geopolitical discourse' forms a system for 'historical reconstruction' and 'personal rehabilitation'; assertive power deeds which compete among one another in order to represent and 'stabilise' the past, present and future. Following Derrida's textual deconstruction, Ó Tuathail believes that 'meaning' has an unstable and a continuously changing core which politicians try to "stabilise" via e.g. 'binary oppositions' in their discourse (Ó Tuathail, 1994, p. 526; Antonsich, 2000, p. 203). Ó Tuathail distinguished three broad categories of research questions in 'Critical Geopolitics':

1. *the critical study of the geopolitical tradition* ('researching the geopolitical literature, thinkers & doctrines and the way in which their ideas and acts shaped international relations');
2. *the study of practical geopolitical reasoning in foreign policy* ('trying to gain an insight in the way in which geographical/geopolitical reasoning pervades and conditions the practice of international relations'); and
3. *global geopolitical changes in the risk society* ('the broader story of global geopolitical and geo-economic shifts; the big transformations of our time which may affect the world map of tomorrow – globalisation, nationalism, postmodernism, the influence of the media, informatisation, de-territorialisation and the so-called 'risk society' (Ó Tuathail, 2001).

On the topic of the relation between 'Critical Geopolitics' and the study of 'foreign policy', Agnew and Ó Tuathail developed four important theses (Ó Tuathail, 1998 [1992], pp. 81–82):

1. Geopolitics is reconceptualised as a discursive process not limited to a small group of "wise" men and women. Geopolitical reasoning starts at a simple level and pervades the daily practice of international politics;
2. the study of geopolitical reasoning refers to both the elaborated study of 'statesmanship' as a 'set of social practices';
3. the study of "geopolitical reasoning" requires studying the 'production' of geographical knowledge with a certain state and through the modern world system;
4. the focus lies with analysing the foreign policy elites of certain hegemonic states.

One can formulate a number of objections with regard to the fourth condition or thesis. In their aspiration to achieve insight into *'the bigger picture'*, Agnew and Ó Tuathail state that the focus of 'Critical Geopolitics' is aimed at analysing the foreign policy-elites of certain 'hegemonic states'. This conception is understandable since the 'great powers' such as the US, Russia, China and perhaps even the EU indeed influence and 'shape' the 'geopolitical landscape' and the resulting power relations via their 'discursive interventions'. Agnew and Ó Tuathail were inspired in this vision by Antonio Gramsci's concept of *'hegemony'*. A hegemonic power such as the US is by definition also a *"rule writer"* of the world community, as a result of which it also plays a central role in structuring the international space in which the 'drama' of international politics unfolds (Ó Tuathail, 1996, p. 61). Agnew and Ó Tuathail do have a point when they state that 'hegemonic states' have more capacities to give *meaning* to the international. Nevertheless, in our opinion their fourth and final thesis should not be read as a compelling condition in order to talk about 'Critical Geopolitics'. In other words, the study of the contribution of smaller political entities such as e.g. Belgium in the global debate about an alleged *'international war against terrorism'* could also constitute an interesting critical-geopolitical study (Belgium opposed this notion, together with others). In other words, also small states can develop a 'practical-geopolitical reasoning' which can gradually try to gain support within the international community without requiring that its 'messenger' should have to be a 'hegemonic state'.

'Critical Geopolitics' sees the 'practical geopolitical reasoning' in foreign policy as a dynamic process, a form of *'place (w)rit-ing'* (Ó Tuathail, 1994, p. 537). In short, 'geopolitical reasoning' works as a 'hegemonic discursive practice'; by suppressing the complex geographical reality of places in favour of 'controllable geopolitical abstractions' (Ó Tuathail & Agnew, 1992, p. 195). The big irony of 'geopolitical reasoning' is that *"it suppresses real geographical knowledge about the diversity and complexity of places via dominant discursive practices"*. 'Geopolitical reasoning' simplifies the world to a substantial degree to a sort of caricature which stands 'at the service' of the dominant political class. One of the main objectives of 'Critical Geopolitics' thus lies with exposing these dynamics. In foreign policy analysis, 'Critical Geopolitics' asks the following question; *what are the (political-) strategical objectives behind this simplified 'construction' of space, and what manipulative effect do they create?* This can for instance be applied to the study of the ways in which both the Anglo-American powers and the Russian Federation have each depicted the world and international politics since the attacks of 11 September 2001 as a "war against terrorism", in different ways. If you succeed in convincing the public that indeed such a war is raging, then you as a policy-maker may have already succeeded half-way in pushing through your own international policy-prescriptions. That is the process which 'Critical Geopolitics' wants to uncover and expose.

The research tradition of 'Critical Geopolitics' can be reconstructed on the basis of its ontological, epistemological and methodological components;

- ONTOLOGICALLY, 'Critical Geopolitics' approaches the world *not* as a manifest and relatively easily decipherable (material) reality (as 'Classical Geopolitics' did), *nor* as a reality which can be perceived by individual decision makers (cf. 'Cognitive Geopolitics'). Conversely, **'Critical Geopolitics' has attention for the role which social, cultural and political processes play in the 'giving of meaning' and 'construction' of the international-political reality.** The external world is seen as a reality which is difficult to "grasp" as a result of complex "processes of de- *and* re-territorialisation" (Newman, 2000). 'Critical Geopolitics' underlines the plurality of *'space'* and the multiformity of possible political constructions of space. Central in its approach is the idea that the image about the "external world" in first instance is being formed / constructed within broader society" (Ó Tuathail). 'Critical Geopolitics' can be described as *"a problematising theoretical enterprise which questions the existing power and knowledge structures"*. 'Critical Geopolitics' shuns the illustrious past of its classical predecessor; therefore, it will not be seduced easily in giving so-called 'advice to the prince'. Conversely, it criticises the 'superficial' and 'interested' way in which (Neo-) Classical Geopolitics studies the world map by projecting its own cultural and political assumptions upon its research object. The practice of each foreign policy is inherently geopolitical since it continually entails the *'construction'* of 'meaning', 'the importance of space', and of 'place'. Instead of asking the question how the external environment influences foreign policy (as 'Classical', but also 'Cognitive' Geopolitics did), 'Critical Geopolitics' rather tries to work out how certain geographical representations [in foreign policy] are constructed, and –moreover– how certain geographical representations in their turn structure the perceived reality of these places. Within 'Critical Geopolitics', geography is considered and treated as the 'crucial element' in the construction of 'words', instead of being the mere stage or background upon which these events occur. Another ontological element of 'Critical Geopolitics' concerns its **attitude vis-à-vis central actors in international politics.** According to some, 'Critical Geopolitics' places **question marks with the 'state-centric' and 'social-Darwinist' points of departure of classical-geopolitical literature.** 'Geopolitical reasoning' and 'acting' therefore does not limit itself to the state level, although the way in which these ideas are used by acting people and institutional structures will be dependent upon their logic and objectives. There where 'Classical Geopolitics' had a *state centric* vision upon the world and thus also upon international relations, 'Critical Geopolitics' treats the state no longer as unchangeable, detached of the context, or without being subject to pressures from beneath and above. 'Critical Geopolitics' rejects the vision of a territorially bounded *"us"* versus a territorially bounded *"them"* in favour of a more complex vision to international politics. In it, the state is no longer represented as an organism which requires more (strategic) resources in order to grow, a way of reasoning which according to 'Critical Geopolitics' perpetuates the competitive territorial expansion amongst states.

– EPISTEMOLOGICALLY, 'Critical Geopolitics' unfortunately reflects too little about the background which brought about its own existence. The same can be said about the special categories of social and political experiences which are "labelled valuable enough" to be identified by 'Critical Geopolitics' under the marker 'geopolitics'. Somewhat provocatively one could ask the question whether 'critical geopolitical scholars' are fully conscious of the epistemological context which gave rise to the research tradition of 'Critical Geopolitics' in the first place? In contrast to 'Classical Geopolitics' (and thus also to Realism), critical-geopolitical scholars are of the opinion that the assumption of an unbiased scientist who perceives the external environment as an 'objective whole', is deceptive. Critical approaches to world politics state that academic analyses risk legitimating existing power practices when the vested structures and power relations are not 'challenged' and 'questioned'. Moreover, the 'external environment' constitutes more than that which is *perceived* by foreign policy elites. In contrast to 'Cognitive Geopolitics', language is no longer considered a transparent medium via which *'meanings'* are smoothly passed without changes with respect to content. **According to**

'Critical Geopolitics', there does not exist anything like a 'direct' or 'pre-discursive' perception; each perception is embedded in and influenced by a complex process of **inter-subjective 'giving of meaning'**. One of the most important sources of 'Critical Geopolitics' which we did not mention until now is **(social) Constructivism.** This approach states that the researcher must realise that the world is a social construction. **Constructivism** states that this 'social reality' is constructed when individuals get into contact with one another and interact. Constructivists state that the social world can be understood if one departs from 'shared' knowledge and understanding among people. The social-constructivist interpretation rather emphasises the *meaning* which is assigned to international relations by certain 'hegemonic players' (e.g. the reformulation of international politics after 11 September, 2001 by the US and Russia as a so-called *"global war against terrorism"*, in which far-away countries and areas are assigned another meaning relating to this new 'supposed' central theme in international relations). In embryonic form, such 'geopolitical ideas' or appreciations originate in society as a whole, yet the politicians are those who manage these ideas creatively, and who reinforce certain appreciations until they are supported by the 'main stream' in society. In other words, the environment does not have an objective nature such as is the case in 'Classical Geopolitics', nor has one attention for the subjective perception by decisionmakers such as in 'Cognitive Geopolitics'. In 'Critical Geopolitics', the **environment is approached as an inter-subjective reality**, which gets its decisive form via 'discursive interventions'. According to the IR specialist Forsberg, one should be especially interested in **the way in which normative and symbolic elements suppress the direct material effects of geography** (Forsberg, 2003). From a scientific point of view, such a position is much more useful than the all too often recurring conclusion *"told you so; you thought this was a 'natural' phenomenon, but in reality it was constructed"*. In other words, the question which 'Critical Geopolitics' poses, is **not so much how or to what extent territoriality influences human agency, but rather: how does human agency "construct" territoriality?**.

– METHODOLOGICALLY, 'Critical Geopolitics' often utilises variants of *discourse analysis* since it is interested in the question of how the meaning of 'places' and 'geopolitical space' is *constructed* in (foreign) policy. The 'unit of analysis' of 'Critical Geopolitics' in the context of 'foreign policy' concerns the **meso-level**; the study of the geopolitical discourse about foreign policy which transcends the individual. The analysis of the 'geopolitical discourse' (about foreign policy) hence constitutes also an *inter-discursive field of research*, which touches upon all domains of public life of a nation;

geostrategic discourse, security, economy, ecology, culture, etcetera. Ó Tuathail developed a framework to analyse *'practical geopolitical reasoning'*. 'Geopolitical discourse' is a problem solving discourse with regulating aspirations, of which policy makers make use. The 'grammar of geopolitics' does not just construct 'visions of the world'. It forms a practically-oriented and problem-solving discourse which stands in dialogue with other positions, but which tries to safeguard and push through a certain 'normative order' (Ó Tuathail, 2002, pp. 621–622). In essence, politicians determine the content of a *'geopolitical script'*, and use this as an instrument in four consecutive phases of the foreign policy process, namely:

1. *the definition of a foreign policy-problem* (what relevance for the nation?);
2. *the determination of a 'geopolitical strategy'*;
3. *focussing and 'refinement' of this strategy* (*'geopolitical accommodation'*);
4. *'closure' of the problem*; identification, development and advancement of an alleged solution for the formulated problem.

With regard to the study of foreign policy, the first task of the 'critical geopolitical' scholar, is to subject the **utilised foreign policy discourse to a critical reflection**; *how do policy-makers make use of 'territoriality' to legitimate or 'push through' their opinion to the rest of the world?* In the abovementioned process, policy-makers make use of (geopolitical) *'scripts'* as a silent whole of standard-ways on the basis of which they can respond in speeches, but also how they can articulate certain foreign policy-challenges or problems. *'Scripts'* are defined as *"a set of representational practices, a collection of descriptions, attributions and scenarios which are deemed necessary in order to define a place'* (Dodds, 1993, p. 72). The *representations of places and people* as "foreign" constitutes a crucial element in the carrying out of a foreign policy. Dodds considers experts, foreign policy elites and the mass media as "privileged story-tellers" which develop and re-write *'scripts'* which simplify the world in more manageable forms. They try to legitimate the foreign policy; their perceptions of 'we' (*'self'*) versus 'others' (*'otherness'* or *'foreignness'*) will influence both policy and attitudes. A critical geopolitical analysis is interested in the way in which global space is being *scripted* by intellectuals (*'formal geopolitics'*) or by decisionmakers (*'practical geopolitics'*) (Ó Tuathail, 1996, pp. 66–67). In this framework, two concepts are used; **'geopolitical codes'** (Gaddis, 1982) and **'geopolitical visions'** (Dijkink, 1996). A **geopolitical code** can be defined as assumptions about the interest [of a geopolitical actor, e.g. a state] in the world, the potential dangers which affect these interests, and feasible responses (Gaddis, 1982, p. ix).

> A **geopolitical vision** can be defined as any idea concerning the relation between one's own and other places, involving feelings of (in)security or (dis)advantage (and/or) invoking ideas about a collective mission or foreign policy strategy. Whether an analysis of geopolitical visions can be separated from a thorough treatment of national identity is a more difficult question. As the inventor of the concept of 'geopolitical vision', the Dutch political geographer Gertjan Dijkink states: 'To outline the ideal type of a geopolitical vision requires outlining the structure of an account of the nation in its relations with the external world.' (Dijkink, 1996, p. 11). In its analysis of 'foreign policy', 'Critical Geopolitics' is also interested in the *'boundary-producing practices'* which characterise the 'daily life of states'.

One of the best overviews of the work conducted in the school of thought of 'Critical Geopolitics' was brought together in *'Ashgate Research Companion to Critical Geopolitics'* (Dodds, Kuus & Sharp, 2013). What criticism could one develop vis-à-vis 'Critical Geopolitics'? The following elements offer a concise list (see also: Criekemans, 2008):

1. the amorphous nature or the absence of a clear position on what 'Critical Geopolitics' actually means or entails;
2. is 'Critical Geopolitics' possible or desirable?;
3. is 'Critical Geopolitics' also applicable to non-hegemonic states or international-political actors?;
4. the relevance of 'globalisation', 'computerisation' and the 'risk society' & the question whether the dichotomy modern–postmodern Geopolitics is superfluous;
5. lack of attention to subjectivity and 'agency' in Ó Tuathail's conception of 'Critical Geopolitics';
6. no distinction between 'foreign policy decisions' and the 'operational results' of these decisions (as 'Cognitive Geopolitics' did);
7. less attention for *material* environmental variables (as 'Classical Geopolitics' did) ; and
8. unclear conceptualisation of the concept of 'politics' within 'Critical Geopolitics' (Criekemans, 2007).

In addition, there is the feeling coming from some other geopolitical schools of thought that, whilst 'Critical Geopolitics' instilled critical and innovative thinking, it sometimes shied away from engaging with actual questions of practical geopolitics and created a divide around the "naturalisation" of geography itself. Scholars in 'Critical Geopolitics' problematize the very way in which factors of geography are 'instrumentalised' to fit a specific (policy) agenda. But that in itself may cloud its actual useability in analysing current world problems of geo-economy, geopolitics and geostrategy. The French historian and geopolitical author Florian Louis is most critical and perhaps even harsh for this specific geopolitical school of thought. He is of the opinion that 'Critical Geopolitics' itself is *"a construction in service of "progressive" and "non-conservative" representations, at the service of interests which it tries to unveil"* (Louis, 2014, p. 190).

In chapter 5 of this book, Antonios Nestoras will further engage with the current entrenchment in a Classical/Critical divide within the field of Geopolitics. Based upon this analysis, he proposes an *'Analytic Geopolitics'*. 'Critical Geopolitics' meanwhile is further developing, for instance with recent calls to further develop its societal role, inspired by the Frankfurt School of critical theory (Bachmann & Moisio, 2020).

9 Non-Geopolitics: Neo-Classical, Ethno-Nationalistic Geopolitics

During the 1990s, a number of publications were circulated which did not always focus on the study of the relationship between 'territoriality' and 'politics'. Some of these even incorporated elements and considerations about the factor 'race'... A few examples can be found within Serbia under the regime of Slobodan Milosevic, the publications of the leader of the Russian extreme-right Liberal-Democratic Party Vladimir Zhirinovsky, or some –though not all– work of the 'new-right' ideologue Alexander Dugin. Such writings can be labelled under the denominator of the (*spurious*) *'neo-classical, ethno-nationalist geopolitics'*. They rather *undermine* geopolitics instead of focussing the debate on the relation between 'territoriality' and 'politics'. That is why they also can be seen as "non-Geopolitics".

10 Reconsidering the 'Geopolitical Schools of Thought' and Their Approaches to the Study of the Relationship between Territoriality and International Politics

This chapter has tried to offer a concise yet an as comprehensive as possible overview of the most important 'geopolitical schools of thought'. We focussed our synopsis on those schools which according to our analysis have contributed important insights from an epistemological point of view with regard to the relation between 'territoriality' and 'politics'. In order to get a more visual representation of these different schools of thought, and the different periods in which they were mostly developed and active, we offer an overview in figure 3.5.:

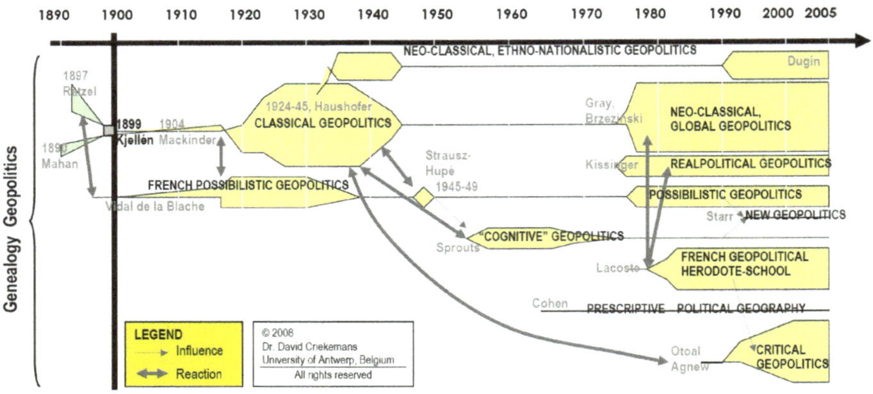

FIGURE 3.5 A genealogy of the Geopolitical Schools of Thought, seen from their epistemological contribution to the relation territoriality—(international) politics

It is indeed true that we did not talk about the interesting current geopolitical schools of thought in such countries as for instance Italy, or for that matter about the very rich debate on this topic in South America. However, this is only partly true. Most of the geopolitical schools of thought which today thrive in many countries in the world are intellectually tributary to one or more of the original schools of thought which we analysed in this overview.

If one takes a "long view" at the different geopolitical schools of thought, it is striking that many different schools approach 'territoriality' in quite different ways. Below, we offer a concise overview:

	TERRITORIALITY is considered as being …
I. Classical Geopolitics (1890-1933)	*Objective / material*
II. Cognitive Geopolitics (°1956)	*Subjective / cognitive*
III. - Realpolitical Geopolitics (°1970s) (Kissinger)	*Not that important; what counts is the 'balance of power'*
- Neo-classical Global Geopolitics (°1980s & 1990s) (Gray)	*Combination material & cognitive elements*
IV. - French geopolitical Hérodote-school (°1982) - Critical Geopolitics (°1988-92)	*Inter-subjective*

FIGURE 3.6 The very diverse interpretation of 'geo' or 'territoriality' by different Geopolitical Schools of Thought

For those engaged in geopolitical analysis, it is important to take into account that many geopolitical schools of thought focus on other aspects of the relation between 'territoriality' and 'politics'. In our opinion, there are possibilities to integrate a number of these schools of thought into a more integrated, holistic framework of analysis (Criekemans, 2007, Criekemans, 2008). Finally, it is also interesting to specify the 'assets' and 'limits' of the "geopolitical approach to international relations", independently of specific geopolitical schools of thought. In our opinion, the following aspects deserve to be mentioned;

ASSETS:

- ***attention for 'territorially embedded' explanatory factors****, that are all to often ignored within IR*
- ***'holistic' character****; an attempt to develop an insight in 'the bigger picture' of international-political issues*
- ***a certain 'timeless' character****; the relationship between 'territoriality' and 'politics' remains relevant in a globalising world*

LIMITS:

- ***not the only 'true' approach*** *to the study of questions of international politics*
- ***not an 'exact' science****, and it will never become one*
- *the danger for* ***geopolitical abstractions of the diversity on the ground***
- *the geopolitical schools* ***each originated in their own, quite specific 'Zeitgeist'***
- *some (have mis)use(d) 'Geopolitics' as an* ***instrument to expand their own power or to legitimize their decisions, as a result of which Geopolitics becomes politicized***

FIGURE 3.7 The 'assets' and 'limits' of the "geopolitical approach to international relations", independently of specific Geopolitical Schools of Thought

11 Is a 'Best of Both Worlds' Possible?

For those engaged in geopolitical analysis, it is important to take into account that many geopolitical schools of thought focus on other aspects of the relation between 'territoriality' and 'politics'. There are nevertheless possibilities to integrate a number of these schools of thought into a more integrated, holistic framework of analysis (Criekemans, 2007; Criekemans, 2008). When one compares 'Classical', 'Cognitive' and 'Critical Geopolitics', one comes to the conclusion that each of these three 'geopolitical schools of thought' merely examine some partial aspects of the relationship between 'territoriality' and 'politics'. Or, to put it more strongly; no one geopolitical research tradition seems to be able to really study the complex, vice versa interaction between 'geo' and 'politics'. Inspired by the Sprouts, but taking into account some advances developed by 'Critical Geopolitics', one could develop a dynamic overview of the potential relations of influence between 'geo' & 'politics', and vice versa:

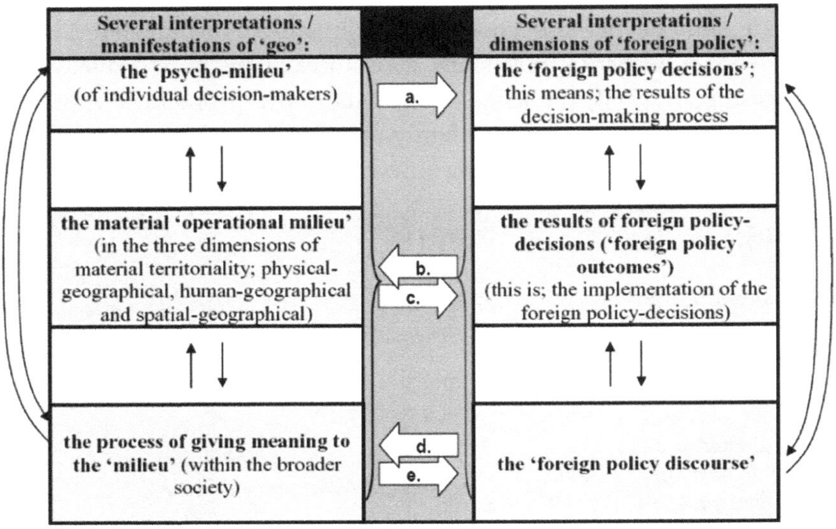

FIGURE 3.8 The components of a more holistic and dynamic framework of analysis?

According to science philosopher Larry Laudan, there exist two ways in which different research traditions can be integrated. *First,* in some cases a research tradition can be grafted upon another, without it being necessary to strongly re-adjust the basic assumptions. *Second,* it is possible that the fusion of two or more research traditions necessitate the rejection of a number of basic assumptions within each of the original research traditions. Most 'scientific revolutions' take place, not so much by the articulation of a research tradition whose *'ingredients'* are new and revolutionary, but rather by the development of a new research tradition whose old *'ingredients'* are combined in a new way (Laudan, 1978, p. 103–104). According to Laudan, one can talk about *'scientific progress'* in the event a research tradition succeeds in realizing a better 'problem solution', while at the same time limiting the number of anomalies and conceptual problems (Laudan, 1978, p. 124–125). However, the formulation of a *new geopolitical research tradition* constitutes a highly ambitious undertaking. What does become clear from our analysis, is how much a number of geopolitical research traditions are *complementary* to one another. The road towards a 'more comprehensive' geopolitical model or framework of analysis could therefore be one which entails *several aspects of the interaction between 'territoriality' and 'politics'.* A 'more comprehensive' geopolitical model (or framework) of analysis for foreign policy, could therefore consist of several phases:

The analyst *first* has to develop an inventory of the territorial, material power basis of a political entity. It involves a classical-geopolitical analysis like in the work of Strausz-Hupé and Morgenthau, in other words one which is based upon a possibilistic epistemology. One develops a so-called virtual 'capacity analysis' of the (future) relative power position of a region in relation to the predetermined objectives in the foreign policy. In short, one develops an initial inventory of the territorially embedded, material (power)factors which offer the foreign policy of an "actor of geopolitics" –a country, region, city or macro-region– certain opportunities and/or restrictions. In many ways, such a possibilist analysis is similar to 'Classical Geopolitics', though it has much less "to suffer" under the "heavy" ontological and epistemological assumptions of this last tradition. Who develops such a 'geopolitical inventory', can build up a sound and advanced insight into the material basis in which central political decision makers operate. This approach forms one of the most 'tried and tested' geopolitical methods of analysis. For example, one can find a guide for such descriptive geopolitical analyses of regions in the book *'Introduction à l'analyse géopolitique'* of the French scientist Chauprade (1999). The next question which then announces itself is this one; *how do central foreign policy-decision makers deal with this 'given' material world in their 'foreign policy'?* Or to put it differently; *what relationship between the different manifestations of 'geo' and the dimensions of 'foreign policy', and vice versa?*

Although classical-possibilistic geopolitical analyses generate interesting insights, they offer in our opinion insufficient possibilities to obtain an insight into the *conducted* foreign policy. Methodologically, such analyses do not succeed in *linking* (geopolitical) environmental variables and the actual foreign policy (decisions/implementation of these decisions/rhetoric), and vice versa. In order to achieve this from an analytical point of view, the deployment of other approaches is necessary. 'Cognitive' and 'Critical Geopolitics' are to a large extent complementary to one another (to be sure, only if one makes abstraction of those of their respective ontological & epistemological assumptions which *'conflict'* with one another). *First,* both study a *fundamentally different level of analysis, in which their insights do not necessarily have to exclude one another, but can also work to reinforce each other mutually.* 'Cognitive Geopolitics' conducts an analysis of foreign policy at the micro-level of the decision maker, whereas 'Critical Geopolitics' tries to analyze the meso-level of the (territorial and environmental assumptions) within the foreign policy discourse. *Second,* between both there exists a *difference in the way in which they have attention for the relation between 'geo' on the one hand and 'politics' on the other hand.* 'Cognitive Geopolitics' especially has attention for the way in which 'geo-factors' influence (the ideas of) the decision maker. 'Critical Geopolitics' rather has attention for the way in which 'politics', via a discourse, tries to ascribe a certain meaning to 'geo-variables'; the 'construction' of a 'meaning' to the territorial environment, and this with certain political objectives in mind.

From a *purely meta-theoretical perspective*, one should recognize that the perception of individual decision makers cannot do without the 'giving of meaning' within the broader society, and vice versa. Possibly, the geopolitical 'giving of meaning' about certain 'far away' territories via the mass media, influences the perception of decision makers (as 'Critical Geopolitics' asserts). In our opinion, both the 'environmental perception' of individual (or homogeneous groups of) decision maker(s) *and* the attention to the 'geopolitical' giving of meaning, can have a place within a geopolitical analysis. In view of our plea for a definition of Geopolitics which devotes attention to the interaction between 'geo' and 'politics', it seems useful to combine elements of 'Cognitive' and 'Critical Geopolitics'. Legrand made in 1999 a similar, yet by the literature undetected plea for a kind of *'Reflexive-Cognitive Geopolitics'* (which he called 'reflexive cognitive behavioralism') (Legrand, 1999). Nevertheless, there is a need for more research to further explore this idea. Irrespective of whether a real "fusion" of these approaches would be desirable or possible, the researcher can always keep in mind that both approaches are *complementary*; they each study different dynamics between the dimensions of territoriality and politics, and vice versa.

One should not forget that there also exists a *material, 'operational' reality*. Fundamental changes within it irrevocably generate (in the medium to long term) certain consequences for both the *'individual perception of policy-makers'* as for *'the geopolitical giving of meaning of certain distant areas within the broader society, via the mass media'*. One can find ample examples of such processes in today's international relations. Based upon our analysis, we can draw two conclusions: (1) in geopolitical analyses, one should never lose sight of the material territoriality; after all, this forms the 'basis' from which each practical-geopolitical analysis should start; (2) combining 'Cognitive' and 'Critical Geopolitics' could potentially contribute to a more comprehensive assessment of the interaction between (the components of) 'geo' & 'politics'. The 'more comprehensive' geopolitical model or framework of analysis which we here suggest, thus argues for a more pragmatic & sequential combination of the most important 'geopolitical research traditions':

A geopolitical analysis should not always have to comprise *each* of these approaches. In first instance, the approach of a practical-geopolitical analysis will be influenced by the *phrasing of the research question* of the researcher involved. An analysis can thus also perfectly be 'geopolitical' if/when it only examines parts of the full relation between 'geo' and 'politics'. Yet, if one aims

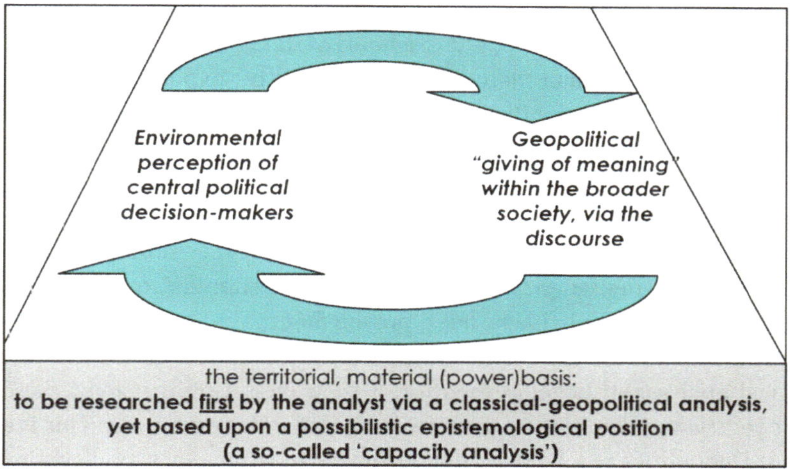

FIGURE 3.9 'Rosetta Stone'? Combining Classical, Cognitive & Critical Geopolitics

to develop the *most complete overview of the interaction between 'geo' and 'politics'*, then the framework suggested above can offer a potential route.

12 What Future for the Geopolitical Schools of Thought?

The final question which can be posed is what future development one can expect for the Geopolitical Schools of Thought. *First*, geopolitics has always been closely intertwined with the international problems with which countries, regions and localities are faced around the world. Current global politics has and will see a substantial rise of so-called 'new' security threats such as energy, climate, and water issues. It is very likely that these will move up substantially in the geopolitical literature in the years to come, and also influence theoretical approaches. *Second*, in the current Anglo-American geopolitical literature, it seems as though 'Critical Geopolitics' has taken a very central role, at least in one section of that literature. However, as was shown in this chapter, this specific school of thought focuses on very particular aspects of the relation between 'territoriality' and 'politics'. The relationship between both is actually much more nuanced and diverse. To formulate our remark differently; *there's more to geopolitics than Critical Geopolitics*. Elsewhere, we see a revival of Geopolitics in a more Realist sense. In order for Geopolitics to move forward as a scientific field of study, it would be interesting to see researchers more actively 'intermingle'; creatively developing research designs in which they study geopolitical problems via different methods of analyses emanating from diverse schools of thought. In this way, the ontological and epistemological assumptions of different geopolitical schools of thought could be 'weighed' against one another in light of their respective descriptive, exploratory, explanatory or even predictive capacities. A more active confrontation of the insights of diverse schools of thought could also possibly bare fruit to new geopolitical approaches, and more nuanced insights into the very complex, ever changing relationship between 'territoriality' and 'politics'. *Third*, as a body of literature, Geopolitics still is much too confined to the 'Western world'; most of the geopolitical thinkers being taught in class rooms are "Westerners", to use a 'geopolitical label'. It is not only likely, but a proven fact that in many other parts of the world (the Middle East, China, India, etcetera), many scholars conduct geopolitical analyses or develop theories of their own. Unfortunately, these have not yet *trickled down* to the international academic community. This is a pity, since Geopolitics as a field should become a 'meeting place' of diverging perspectives and insights. Only then will it be able to further grow and develop into a truly global field of science.

One thing is certain however; where people try to live together in harmony, and develop strategies so as to maximise their own potential in relation to their environment, there 'geopolitics' continues to play an important role – in its *'formal'*, *'practical'* and *'popular'* variants. As technologies and societies will change the coming decades, so will geopolitical schools of thought continue to adapt so as to try to grasp the ever more complex international relations on planet Earth. Geopolitics already has a new sister-science called *'Astropolitics'*, in which a fourth dimension of territoriality is studied; the control of the space surrounding the Earth (e.g. the deployment of satellites, the positioning of space bases on the most desired location on the Moon) (Dolman, 2002). Some of these thinkers follow the syllogistic format employed by Mackinder. They postulate that *whoever controls X space* (*the ocean, the heartland, the atmosphere, or orbital space*) *controls the world*. As Deudney points out, if such a region exists and can be effectively controlled by one actor, the system will tend towards hegemony or empire. Conversely, if the actors in a system are able to neutralize the axial region by effectively taking it out the reach of any one actor to control, then the system shifts from anarchy to one ordered by mutual restraint (Deudney, 2020, p. 283). The book *'Dark Skies. Space Expansionism, Planetary Geopolitics & the Ends of Humanity'* constitutes one of the most fascinating contributions on how space technology and human societies could evolve geopolitically (Deudney, 2020). As long as the finality of such analyses investigates the consequences of this positioning for the *balance of power* on Earth (e.g. a new space race between the US and China), such analyses can still be seen as part of Geopolitics (Spagnulo, 2021). When, however, in the farther future human communities start living on the Moon or even Mars, one may no longer speak of 'Geopolitics'. After all, such new realities may bare fruit to new 'extra-territorial' & 'anthropo-local' political realities, independent from Earth politics. These will need to be analysed on their own other merits, in their own contexts. Such a *Star Trek*-universe is however still some lightyears away for humanity. For the time being however, the Earth is where humanity makes its existential and political stand. Increasing demands on planet Earth regarding basic necessities as energy, food and water, will make Geopolitics highly relevant.

Geopolitical schools of thought may differ amongst each other with regard to how they conceptualise and operationalise the role which 'territoriality' plays in matters of foreign policy and international relations. Nevertheless, they all share in some fashion the analysis that spatiality remains at the core of problems with which humanity is being confronted. Factors of physical and human geography, location, changing spheres of influence, geopolitical representations and history, the geo-economic business model of entities and the geostrategic power shifts as a result of a combination of geographical, demographical and technological factors, each have their role to play. It is especially in moments of global and regional power shifts, or technological changes, that the world is in need of frameworks to better understand and give meaning to them. As globalisation grew further in the 1990s, mainstream International Relations as a field of study had somewhat 'forgotten' or 'ignored' the role of territorially embedded factors. The gradual *'revenge of geography'* has forced policy makers, observers and scholars of international relations to reflect upon the complex interrelationship of geopolitical factors (Kaplan, 2013). Some authors even try to build forecasting models based upon these geopolitical analyses (Friedman, 2009; Friedman, 2011), around which further work will have to be done in the coming years. The holistic nature of geopolitical analysis remains its strength but also its potential weakness. Nevertheless its unique selling proposition states that, to ignore territorially embedded factors, means to limit our potential in understanding and explaining international problems. A rich debate within and amongst different geopolitical schools of thought and relevant IR schools can help us to better grasp the essence of international relations today. Hence 'grounding' world politics anew and creating synergies & interconnections in the scholarship between IR and Geopolitics could prove very enriching in the decades to come.

Bibliography

Allen, M. (2003) *Het Hitler-Hess Bedrog. Het best bewaarde geheim van WO II.* Amsterdam & Leuven: Uitgeverij Balans & Uitgeverij Van Halewyck.

Antonsich, M. (2000). Dis-placing or re-placing hegemonic geopolitical discourse? Reading/writing Gearóid Ó Tuathail's 'critical geopolitics'. *Geo-Italy 4. Geographies of diversity. Italian Perspectives.* B. Cori, G. C. Pellegrini, G. Cortesiet al. Roma, Italian Committee for the International Geographical Union, Società Geografica Italiana. 4: 201–224.

Ashley, R. K. (1987). "The geopolitics of geopolitical space: towards a critical social theory of international politics." *Alternatives* 12(4): 403–434.

Bakker, G. (1967). *Duitse Geopolitiek, 1919–1945. Een imperialistische ideologie.* Assem, Van Gorcum & Comp.

Bachmann, V., & Moisio, S. (2020). Towards a constructive critical geopolitics – Inspirations from the Frankfurt School of critical theory. *Environment and Planning C: Politics and Space*, 38(2), 251–268. https://doi.org/10.1177/2399654419869016

Bassin, M. (1987). "Imperialism and the nation-state in Friedrich Ratzel's political geography." *Progress in Human Geography. An international review of geographic work in the social sciences and humanities*, 11(4): 473–495.

Blouet, B. W. (Ed.) *Global Geostrategy. Mackinder and the Defence of the West.* Abingdon: Frank Cass.

Brzezinski, Z. (1986). *Game Plan: The Geostrategic Framework for the Conduct of the US-Soviet Contest.* Boston, Massachusetts: Atlantic Monthly Press.

Brzezinski, Z. (1997a). A Geostrategy for Eurasia. *Foreign Affairs.* 76(5): 50–64.

Brzezinski, Z. (1997b). *The Grand Chessboard: American Primacy and its Geostrategic Imperatives.* New York: Perseus Books.

Chauprade, A. (1999). *Introduction à l'analyse géopolitique.* Paris, Ellipses.

Claval, P. (1996). *Géopolitique et Géostrategie. La pensée politique, l'espace et le territoire au XXe siècle.* Paris, Nathan.

Cohen, S. B. (1963). *Geography and politics in a World Divided.* New York, Random House.

Cohen, S. B. (2003). *Geopolitics of the World System.* Lanham - Boulder - New York - Oxford, Rowman & Littlefield Publishers, Inc.

Criekemans, D. (2007). *Geopolitiek. 'Geografisch geweten' van de buitenlandse politiek?* Antwerpen: Garant.

Criekemans, D. (2008). "Is a "best of both worlds"-approach possible? How traditional, cognitive and critical geopolitics could complement one another in the study of (the role of "territoriality" in) foreign policy and international politics", *ECPR Joint Sessions Rennes, Workshop 8 "The New Geopolitics and Changing Territorialities: Between International Studies and Political Geography"*, Rennes (France), 11–16 April 2008: 37 p.

Criekemans, D. (2018). Geopolitics of the Renewable Energy Game and Its Potential Impact upon Global Power Relations, In Scholten, D. (Ed.) *The Geopolitics of Renewables.* Cham: Springer.

Dalby, S. (1988). "Geopolitical Discourse: The Soviet Union as Other." *Alternatives* 13: 415–442.

Dalby, S. (1991). "Critical geopolitics: discourse, difference and dissent." *Environment and Planning D: Society and Space* 9: 261–283.

Dalby, S., Tuathail, G. Ó (1996). "The Critical Geopolitics Constellation: Problematizing Fusions of Geographical Knowledge and Power." *Political Geography* 15: 451–456.

Dalby (1998). Crossing Disciplinary Boundaries: Political geography and International Relations after the Cold War. *Globalization. Theory and Practice.* E. Kofman and G. Youngs. London, Pinter: 29–42.

Dale Walton, C. (2007). *Geopolitics and the Great Powers in the Twenty-first Century. Multipolarity and the revolution in strategic perspective.* Abingdon: Routledge.

Deudney, D. H. (1989). *Global Geopolitics: A Reconstruction, Interpretation, and Evaluation of Materialist World Order Theories of the Late Nineteenth and Twentieth Centuries.* Princeton: Princeton University Press (unpublished Ph D.-manuscript).

Deudney, D. H. (1997). Geopolitics and Change. *New Thinking in International Relations Theory.* M. W. Doyle and G. J. Ikenberry. Boulder, Colorado, Westview Press: 91–123.

Deudney, D. H. (2020). Dark Skies. Space Expansionism, Planetary Geopolitics & the Ends of Humanity. Oxford: Oxford University Press.

Diehl, P. F. (1991). "Geography and War: A Review and Assessment of the Empirical Literature." *International Interactions. Empirical and Theoretical Research in International Relations,* 17(1): 11–28.

Dijkink, G. (1996). *National Identity and Geopolitical Visions. Maps of Pride and Pain.* London, Routledge.

Dodds, K. (1993). "Geopolitics, experts and the making of foreign policy." *Area* 25(1): 70–74.

Dodds, K. (1994). "Geopolitics and foreign policy: recent developments in Anglo-American political geography and international relations." *Progress in Human Geography. An international review of geographic work in the social sciences and the humanities,* 18(2): 186–208.

Dodds, K. (2007) *Geopolitics. A Very Short Introduction.* Oxford: Oxford University Press.

Dodds, K., Kuus, M. & J. Sharp (Eds.), (2013). *The Ashgate Research Companion to Critical Geopolitics.* Farnham, UK & Burlington, USA: Ashgate.

Dolman, E. C. (2002). *Astropolitik. Classical Geopolitics in the Space Age.* London & Portland, Oregon: Frank Cass.

Dougherty, J. E., Pfaltzgraff, R. L. J. (1981). Environmental Theories. In: *Contending Theories of International Relations. A Comprehensive Survey.* New York: Harper Collins Publishers: 54–83.

Dussouy, G. (2001). *Quelle géopolitique au XXIe siècle?* Bruxelles : Editions Complexe.

Forsberg, T. (2003). "The Ground Without Foundation? Territory as a Social Construct." *Geopolitics* 8(2): 7–24.

Furniss, E. S. (1952). "The Contribution of Nicholas John Spykman to the Study of International Politics." *World Politics* IV(April): 382–401.

Friedman, G. (2009). *The Next 100 Years. A Forecast for the 21st Century.* New York: Random House.

Friedman, G. (2011). *The Next Decade. Where We've Been … and Where We're Going.* New York: Random House.

Friedman, T. (2015) Geopolitics and the Flat World, In Friedman, T., *The World is Flat. A Brief History of the Globalized World in the 21st Century.* London: Penguin Books.

Gaddis, J. L. (1982). *Strategies of Containment. A Critical Appraisal of Postwar American National Security Policy.* Oxford, Oxford University Press.

Girot, P., Kofman, E. (eds.) (1987). *International Geopolitical Analysis. A Selection from Hérodote.* London, Croom Helm.

Glassner, M. I. and H. J. de Blij (1989). Chapter 17: Development through World War II. *Systematic Political Geography.* M. I. Glassner and H. J. de Blij. New York, John Wiley & Sons: 223–230.

Goertz, G. (1994). *Contexts of International Politics.* Cambridge, Cambridge University Press.

Gray, C. S. (2004). "In Defence of the Heartland: Sir Halford Mackinder and His Critics a Hundred Years On." *Comparative Strategy* 23(1): 9–25.

Guzzini, S. (Ed.) *The Return of Geopolitics in Europa? Social Mechanisms and Foreign Policy Identity Crises.* Cambridge University Press.

Harkavy, R. E. (1982). *Great Power Competition for Overseas Bases. The Geopolitics of Access Diplomacy.* New York, Pergamon Press, Inc.: 363 p.

Haushofer, K. (1928). Politische Geographie und Geopolitik. Bausteine zur Geopolitik, In K. Haushofer, H. Lautensach, O. Maull & E. Obst (Eds.). Berlin, Kurt Vowinckel Verlag: 49–77.

Heffernan, M. (1998). *The Meaning of Europe. Geography and Geopolitics.* London: Arnold.

Herwig, H. H. (1999). Geopolitik: Haushofer, Hitler and Lebensraum, In C. S. Gray and G. Sloan (Eds.) *Geopolitics, Geography and Strategy.*. London: Frank Cass: 218–241.

Hirst, P. (2019) Endism: why 1989 was not the 'end of history'. Retrieved from: https://www.opendemocracy.net/en/endism/

Holdar, S. (1992). Political geographers of the past. The ideal state and the power of eography. The life-work of Rudolf Kjellén. *Political Geography,* 11(3): 307–323.

Johnson, E. & Morehouse, H. (Eds.) (2014). After the Anthropocene: Politics and Geographic Inquiry for a New Epoch, *Progress in Human Geography,* 38(1): 439–456.

Josten, D. (2004). *Gibt es eine Renaissance der Geopolitik?* München & Ravensburg: GRIN Verlag.

Kaplan, R. D. (2013). *The Revenge of Geography: What the Map Tells Us About Coming Conflicts and the Battle Against Fate.* New York: Random House.

Kearns, G. (2009). *Geopolitics and Empire. The Legacy of Halford Mackinder.* Oxford: Oxford University Press.

Kjellén, R. (1924). *Der Staat als Lebensform.* Berlin-Grunewald: Kurt Vowinckel Verlag.

Kjellén, R. (1944 [1924]). Autarchy, In A. Dorpalen (Ed.). *The World of General Haushofer. Geopolitics in Action..* Port Washington, N. Y., Kennikat Press, Inc.: 241–248.

Klare, M. (2001). *Resource Wars. The New Landscape of Global Conflict.* New York: Henry Holt and Company.

Klare, M. (2012). *The Race for What's Left. The Global Scramble for the World's Last Resources.* New York: Picador.

Kost, K. (1989). "The conception of politics in political geography and geopolitics in Germany until 1945." *Political Geography Quarterly*, 8(4): 369–385.

Kristof, L. K. D. (1960). The origin and evolution of geopolitics. *Journal of Conflict Resolution*, 4(1): 15–51.

Lacoste, Y. (1976). *Geographie, ça sert, d'abord, à faire la guerre.* Paris: Maspero.

Lacoste, Y. (1982). Editorial. D'autres géopolitiques. *Hérodote. Revue de Géographie et de Géopolitique* (25): 3–9.

Lacoste, Y. (1984). Geography and Foreign Policy. *SAIS Review* (4): 213–227.

Lacoste, Y. (1987). The Geographical and the Geopolitical, In P. Girot & Kofman, E., *International Geopolitical Analysis. A Selection from Hérodote.* London, Croom Helm: 10–25.

Lacoste, Y., (Ed.) (1993). *Dictionnaire de Géopolitique.* Paris, Flammarion.

Lacoste, Y. (2000). "Rivalries for Territory." *Geopolitics* 5(2): 120–158.

Lacoste, Y. (2014). *Geographie, ça sert, d'abord, à faire la guerre. Edition augmentée.* Paris: La Découverte.

Lasserre, F., Gonon, E. & Mottet, E. (2016). *Manuel de Géopolitique. Enjeux de pouvoir sur des territoires.* Paris: Armand Collin.

Laudan, L. (1978). *Progress and Its Problems: Towards a Theory of Scientific Growth.* Berkeley: University of California Press.

Le Billon, P. (2001) The Political Ecology of War: Natural Resources and Armed Conflicts, *Political Geography*, 20(5): 561–584.

Legrand, V. (1999). Foreign policy decision-making theories: some steps towards a more reflexive cognitive behavioralism, *Studia Diplomatica*, 52(1–2): 65–86.

Lorot, P. (1995). *Histoire de la Géopolitique.* Paris, Economica.

Lorot, P., & Thual F. (1997). *La géopolitique.* Paris, Montchrestien.

Lorot, P. (1999). *Introduction à la géoéconomie.* Paris, Economica.

Louis, F. (2014). *Les Grands Théoriciens de la Géopolitique.* Paris: Presses Universitaires de France.

Lowe, J. (1994). *The Great Powers, Imperialism and the German Problem, 1865–1925.* London: Routledge.

Lundén, T. (1986). Political geography around the World VI - Swedish contributions to political geography. *Political Geography Quarterly*, 5(2): 181–186.
Mackinder, H. J. (1919). *Democratic Ideals and Reality: A Study in the politics of Reconstruction*. London, Constable and Company, Ltd.
Mackinder, H. J. (1943). The Round World and the Winning of the Peace. *Foreign Affairs*, 21(4): 595–605.
Mackinder, H. J. (1994 [1904]). The Geographical Pivot of History from Geographical Journal (1904), In: G. Ó Tuathail, S. Dalby & P. Routlegde. *The Geopolitics Reader*. London, Routledge: 27–31.
Mahan, A. T. (1890). The United States Looking Outward. *Atlantic Monthly*, LXVI(December): 816–824.
Mahan, A. T. (1897). *The Interest of America in Sea-Power, Present and Future*. London, Sampson, Low and Marston.
Mahan, A. T. (1900). *The Problem of Asia and Its Effect upon International Policies*. London, Sampson, Loe and Marston.
Mahan, A. T. (1957 [1890]). *The influence of sea power upon history, 1660–1783*. Boston, Little, Brown.
Mamadouh, V. (1998). Geopolitics in the nineties: one flag, many meanings. *GeoJournal. An International Journal on Human Geography and Environmental Sciences*, 46(4): 237–253.
Mead, W. R. (2014). The Return of Geopolitics. The Revenge of the Revisionist Powers. *Foreign Affairs*, 93, 3(May/June), 69–79.
Moreau Defarges, P. (1994). *Introduction à la géopolitique*. Paris, Editions du Seuil.
Moreau Defarges, P. (2008). *La Géopolitique pour les nuls. Déchiffrez les règles du jeu planétaire'*. Paris, Editions First.
Morgenthau, H. J. (1973). *Politics Among Nations. The Struggle for Power and Peace*. New York., Afred A. Knopf.
Most, B. A., Starr, H. (1980). Diffusion, Reinforcement, Geopolitics, and the Spread of War. *American Political Science Review*, 74,(4 (December)): 932–946.
Mouritzen, H. (1998). *Theory and Reality of International Politics*. Aldershot, Ashgate.
Muir, R. (1997). *Political Geography. A New Introduction*. London, Macmillan Press, Ltd.
Murphy, D. T. (1997). *The Heroic Earth. Geopolitical Thought in Weimar Germany, 1918–1933*. Kent, Ohio: The Kent State University Press.
Newman, D. (2000). *Boundaries as Spatial and Social Constructs in a Reterritorialised World*, International Workshop on the Changing World Political Map: Geopolitics at the End of the Twentieth Century, Department of Politics and International Relations, Ben Gurion University of the Negev, Israel.
Olson, W. C., Groom, A. J. R. (1991). *International Relations Then & Now. Origins and Trends in Interpretation*. London, Harper Collins Academic.
Owens, M. T. (1999). In Defense of Classical Geopolitics. *Naval War College Review*, 52(Autumn): 59–76.

Østerud, Ø. (1988). The Uses and Abuses of Geopolitics. *Journal of Peace Research*, 25(2): 191–199.

Ó Tuathail, G., & Agnew, J. (1992). Geopolitics and Discourse. Practical geopolitical reasoning in American foreign policy. *Political Geography*, 11(2): 190–204.

Ó Tuathail, G. (1994). (Dis)placing geopolitics: writing on the map of global politics. *Environment and Planning D: Society and Space*, 12: 525–546.

Ó Tuathail, G. (1996). *Critical Geopolitics*. London, Routledge.

Ó Tuathail, G., Dalby, S. (1998). *Rethinking Geopolitics*. London, Routledge.

Ó Tuathail, G. (1998 [1992]). Geopolitics and Discourse. Practical geopolitical reasoning in American foreign policy, In: G. Ó Tuathail, S. Dalby & P. Routledge, *The Geopolitics Reader*. Londen: Routledge: 78–91.

Ó Tuathail, G. (2000). Geopolitical Discourses: A New Geopolitical Series. *Geopolitics*, 5(1): 125–128.

Ó Tuathail, G. (2001). Geopolitik - zur Entstehungsgeschichte einer Disziplin, In R. Zeilinger, C. Rammer, E. Binder, G. Menschik & P. Oberdammer, *Geopolitik. Zur Ideologiekritik politischer Raumkonzepte*. Wien, Österreich, Promedia Druck- und Verlagsgesellschaft: 9–28.

Ó Tuathail, G. (2002). Theorizing practical geopolitical reasoning: the case of the United States' response to the war in Bosnia. *Political Geography*, 21(5): 601–628.

Parker, G. (1994). Political geography and geopolitics, In: A. J. R. Groom & M. Light, *Contemporary International Relations: A Guide to Theory*. London, United Kingdom, Pinter Publishers Ltd.: 170–181.

Parker, G. (1998). *Geopolitics. Past, Present and Future*. London, Pinter.

Peet, R. (1985). The social origins of environmental determinism. *Annals of the Association of American Geographers*, 75: 309–333.

Picknett, L., Prince,C., & S. Prior, (2001). *Hess. Het dubbelleven van de man achter Hitler.* Antwerpen: Uitgeverij Manteau.

Pierik, P. (1999). *Hitlers Lebensraum. De Geestelijke Wortels van de Veroveringsveldtocht naar het Oosten*. Soesterberg, Nederland: Uitgeverij Aspekt.

Pierik, P. (2006). *Karl Haushofer en het Nationaal-Socialisme. Tijd, werk en invloed.* Soesterberg: Uitgeverij Aspekt.

Pierik, P. (2012). *De Geopolitiek van het Derde Rijk. De geestelijke wortels van de veroveringsveldtocht naar het Oosten*. Soesterberg: Uitgeverij Aspekt.

Polelle, M. (1999). *Raising Cartographic Consciousness. The Social and Foreign Policy Viison of Geopolitics in the Twentieth Century.* New York : Lexington Books.

Raffestin, C., Lopreno, D., et al. (1995). *Géopolitique et Histoire*. Lausanne, Editions Payot.

Ratzel, F. (1897). *Politische Geographie*. München/Leipzig: Verlag von R. Oldenbourg.

Sempa, F. P. (2002). *Geopolitics. From the Cold War to the 21st Century.* New Brunswick (U.S.A.) & London (U.K.): Transaction Publishers.

Sen, D. (1975). *Basic Principles of Geopolitics and History. Theoretical Aspects of International Relations*. Delhi: Concept Publishing Company.

Siverson, R. M., Starr, H. (1992). Opportunity, Willingness and the Diffusion of War, In: M. D. Ward, *The New Geopolitics*. Philadelphia, Pennsylvania, Gordon and Breach Science Publishers: 159–182.

Sloan, G. R. (1988). *Geopolitics in United States Strategic Policy, 1890–1987*. Brighton, Sussex (U.K.), Wheatsheaf Books Ltd. (Simon & Schuster).

Smith, N. (2000). Is a critical geopolitics possible? Foucault, class and the vision thing. *Political Geography*, 19(3): 365–371.

Spagnulo, M. (2021). *The Geopolitics of Space Exploration*. Cham: Springer.

Sprout, H. H., Sprout, M. T. (1944 [1939]). *The Rise of American Naval Power, 1776–1918*. Princeton, USA: Princeton University Press.

Sprout, H. H. (1963). Geopolitical hypotheses in technological perspective. *World Politics*, XV: 187–212.

Sprout, H. H., Sprout, M. T. (1971 [1965]). *The Ecological Perspective on Human Relations with Special Reference to International Politics*. Westport, Connecticut: Greenwood Press, Publishers.

Spykman, N., & Nicholl, H. R. (1969 [1944]). *The Geography of the Peace*. s.l., Archon Books.

Spykman, N. (1938). Geography and Foreign Policy, I. *The American Political Science Review*, 32(1): 28–50.

Spykman, N. (1938). Geography and Foreign Policy, II. *The American Political Science Review*, 32(2): 213–236.

Spykman, N., & Rollins, A. A. (1939). Geographic Objectives in Foreign Policy I. *American Political Science Review*, 33(June): 391–410.

Spykman, N., & Rollins, A. A. (1939). Geographic Objectives in Foreign Policy II. *American Political Science Review*, 33(August): 591–614.

Spykman, N. (1942). *America's Strategy in World Politics. The United States and the Balance of Power*. New York, Harcourt Brace.

Spykman, N., & Nicholl, H. R. (1969 [1944]). *The Geography of the Peace*. s.l., Archon Books.

Starr, H. (1978). "Opportunity" and "Willingness" as Ordering Concepts in the Study of War. *International Interactions. Empirical and Theoretical Research in International Relations*, 4(4): 363–387.

Starr, H. (1990). Alliances and geopolitics. *Political Geography Quarterly*, 9(3): 232–248.

Starr, H. (1991). Joining Political and Geographic Perspectives: Geopolitics and International Relations. *International Interactions. Empirical and Theoretical Research in International Relations*, 17(1): 1–10.

Starr, H. (2013). *On Geopolitics: Space, Place, and International Relations*. Boulder, Colorado & London: Paradigm Publishers.

Stavridis, J. (2017). *Seapower. The History and Geopolitics of the World's Oceans*. New York: Pengiun Books.

Stoggianos, A. *The Genesis of Geopolitics and Friedrich Ratzel. Dismissing the Myth of Ratzelian Geodeterminism.* Cham, Switzerland: Springer.

Strausz-Hupé, R. (1942). *Geopolitics. The Struggle for Space and Power.* New York: G. P. Putnam's sons.

Strausz-Hupé, R. (1943). It's smart to be geopolitical. *The Saturday Review of Literature.* 26: 4–5, 20–21.

Strausz-Hupé, R. (1945). *The Balance of Tomorrow. A Reappraisal of Basic Trends in World Politics.* Philadelphia, University of Pennsylvania.

Strausz-Hupé, R. (1957). The Balance of Tomorrow. *Orbis: a quarterly journal of world affairs,* 1(1): 10–27.

Sumida, J. (1999). Alfred Thayer Mahan, Geopolitician, In: G. Sloan & C. S. Gray, *Geopolitics, Geography and Strategy.* London: Frank Cass: 39–62.

Thermænius, E. (1938). Geopolitics and Political Geography. *Baltic and Scandinavian Countries,* IV: 165–177.

Thual, F. (1996). *Méthodes de la Géopolitique. Apprendre à déchiffer l'actualité.* Paris, Ellipses.

Vidal de la Blache, P. (1898). La géographie politique à propos des écrits de Mr. Frederic Ratzel. *Annales de Géographie,* 7(32): 97–101.

Vidal de la Blache, P. (1926). *Principles of Human Geography.* New York, Henry Holt and Company.

Wittfogel, K. A. (1929). Geopolitik, Geographischer Materialismus und Marxismus, I. *Unter dem Banner des Marxismus,* 3(1): 17–51.

Wittfogel, K. A. (1929). Geopolitik, Geographischer Materialismus und Marxismus, II. *Unter dem Banner des Marxismus,* 3(4): 485–522.

Wittfogel, K. A. (1929). Geopolitik, Geographischer Materialismus und Marxismus, III. *Unter dem Banner des Marxismus,* 3(5): 698–735.

Wittfogel, K. A. (1985). Geopolitics, geographical materialism and Marxism. *Antipode,* 17: 21–72.

Wolkersdorfer, G. (2000). *Politische Geographie und Geopolitik zwischen Moderne und Postmoderne.* Heidelberg: Universität Heidelberg.

Yergin, D. (1992). *The Prize. The Epic Quest for Oil, Money and Power.* New York: Free Press.

Yergin, D. (2020). *The New Map. Energy, Climate, and the Clash of Civilizations.* New York: Penguin Books.

Zajec, O. (2008). *Les secrets de la géopolitique.* Perpignan: Tempora.

Zajec, O. (2016a). *Nicholas John Spykman, l'invention de la géopolitique américaine. Un intinéraire intellectual aux origins paradoxales de la théorie realiste des relations internationals.* Paris: Presses de l'université Paris-Sorbonne.

Zajec, O. (2016b). *Introduction à l'analyse géopolitique. Histoire, outils, méthodes.* Monaco: Editions du Rocher.

CHAPTER 4

Where Geopolitics and Foreign Policy Analysis Once Met: The Work of Harold and Margaret Sprout and Its Continued Relevance Today

David Criekemans

1 Introduction

The relation between 'territoriality' and foreign/international politics has always interested students of both Geopolitics and Foreign Policy Analysis (FPA). These fields of study are much more interrelated than traditionally has been acknowledged. In this chapter, we study the important work of Harold and Margaret Sprout, who played a key role in introducing insights on 'geopolitics' into what later would become known as 'foreign policy analysis'.

In today's literature on Foreign Policy Analysis, the work of Harold and Margaret Sprout is being considered as *"one of the three paradigmatic works/origins of Foreign Policy Analysis"* (read: Hudson, 2008, p. 12). Valerie M. Hudson refers in particular to the article of Harold and Margaret Sprout *"Man-Milieu Relationship Hypotheses in the Context of International Politics"* which first was developed as an essay in 1956, and which was later revised into an article in 1957. On the basis of this article, Harold and Margaret Sprout developed a book in 1965 titled *"The Ecological Perspective on Human Relations with Special Reference to International Politics".* Unique in the Sprouts' contribution was their statement that, to explain undertakings of foreign policy actors, one should look at the "psycho milieu" of the individuals and groups making the foreign policy decision. The psycho-milieu is the international and operational environment or context as it is perceived and interpreted by these decision makers. As Hudson rightly stresses, incongruities between the perceived and the real operational environment can occur, leading to less than satisfactory choices in foreign policy (Hudson, 2008, p. 15).

For those scholars who want to further study the contribution of Harold and Margaret Sprout, the available literature is rather scarce. Apart from some references in key introductory texts on foreign policy analysis (e.g. Dougherty, 1981), little in depth literature seems to exist which introduces the Sprouts' contribution to foreign policy analysis – let alone the roots upon which they based

 | DOI:10.1163/9789004432086_006

their ideas. This chapter tries to make a modest contribution to the existing lacuna in the literature. Interesting is indeed that the sources of the Sprouts' thinking can be found in their earlier academic work on Geopolitics, and the criticisms they developed upon that literature.

After an introduction into the life and academic work of Harold and Margaret Sprout (1.), we will try to gain a better insight into the ideas of the Sprouts (2.). What did their suggested 'ecological triad' entail? What are the consequences of the distinction between the 'operational' and the 'psychological' milieu for the study of foreign policy? How is 'cognitive behavioralism' related to other possible epistemological appreciations regarding the relationship between 'territoriality' and 'foreign policy'? What does the distinction mean between 'foreign policy analyses' and 'capacity analyses'? Next, we will identify three ways in which Harold and Margaret Sprout influenced IR and FPA (3.). Afterwards, we will reconstruct the ontological, epistemological and methodological assumptions and traits of 'Cognitive Geopolitics' (4.). Finally, we will formulate some critiques on 'Cognitive Geopolitics', while at the same time developing some ideas on the continued relevance today of the work of Harold and Margaret Sprout (5.).

2 Introduction into the Life and Academic Work of Harold and Margaret Sprout

According to IR scholar William Fox, Harold and Margaret Sprout can be seen as some of the American political scientists who –throughout their career– showed a continued interest in & influence upon geopolitical thinking, in the period between the 1930s and the 1970s (Fox, 1985, p. 27). The American political scientists **Harold Hance Sprout** and **Margaret Tuttle Sprout** developed an interest in the study of international relations and foreign policy only after having gained academic experience in other fields of study. They met as bachelor students in Oberlin College (USA), and married in 1924. Afterwards, they studied at the University of Wisconsin (Madison, USA), where Harold started a Master in Law. After a short-lived stint at the law firm of Margaret's father, both returned to Madison in the fall of 1927 (Rosenau, Davis et al., 1972, p. 2). In 1929, Harold defended his Ph.D. titled '*The Status of Customary International Public Law in the Federal Courts of the United States*.' Margaret finalised her '*Masters in Political Science and Geography*'. Until 1931, Harold Sprout had a teaching assignment at the University of Stanford and also briefly at the University of Miami (Ohio) (Sprout & Sprout, 1971). Later on, he would move to the University of Princeton, where he would stay for the remainder of his career until

Harold en Margaret Sprout
SOURCE: © PRINCETON UNIVERSITY LIBRARY. PRINCETON UNIVERSITY ARCHIVES, DEPARTMENT OF RARE BOOKS AND SPECIAL COLLECTIONS, PRINCETON UNIVERSITY LIBRARY

1969 (Rosenau, Davis et al., 1972, p. 2). In the 1930s, Harold Sprout started to develop an interest into Political Geography, in particular on its insights for the study of foreign policy and international relations. Possibly his interest was provoked by Margaret's earlier MA studies in political science *and* geography. In 1929–1930, Harold Sprout organised a course 'Political Geography' for students in Political Science at the University of Stanford (Sprout, 1931, p. 440). In 1930–1931, this course was extended and offered to a broader group of BA- and MA-students. Moreover, an *'advanced seminar'* on the theme of the 'Pacific Ocean' was created (Sprout, 1931, p. 442). At the end of the 1930's, Harold Sprout created together with Edward Mead Earle the *'Institute for Advanced Study'* at Princeton, one of the very first strategic *"think tanks"* in the United States of America (Coogan, 1991, pp. 63–64). As so many scholars, Harold Sprout worked for the US Government during the Second World War. In 1943, he was a *consultant*, both for the US *'Office of War Information'* and for the *'War Department'* (Sprout & Sprout, 1971); he helped to develop "propaganda-material" aimed against the 'hostile powers' (Mason, 1978). In 1944, Harold was *consultant* and *'desk officer'* with the State Department. From 1944 tot 1947, he also advised the *'Navy Department'*, where he was involved in the development of the *'Navy V-12*-course' on Geopolitics, together with Robert Strausz-Hupé and Edward Mead Earle. Harold Sprout was President of the Department of Political Sciences in Princeton from 1949 until 1952. From 1952 until 1969, he was *'Henry G. Bryant Professor of Geography and International Relations'* (Sprout & Sprout, 1971). This assignment further built upon his earlier work on 'Geopolitics' starting in the 1930s. During their long career, Harold and Margaret Sprout worked together on the research for their books. For years, Margaret was a 'silent partner' and researcher in the academic work of her husband (Hersh, 2003). Together, they wrote nine books in total, and a great number of articles.

The life and academic work of the Sprouts is interesting in many ways; (1°) the role they played during the 1930s and '40s to introduce the future American political, diplomatic and military elite into 'power analyses' via the literature on 'Geopolitics', (2°) the fact that this geopolitical literature produced a fundamental epistemological reflection by the Sprouts on the relation between 'environmental variables' and 'politics', and the feasibility of scientific knowledge about this relationship (cf. *'cognitive behavioralism'*, see infra), and (3°) the process via which this fundamental reflection caused the Sprouts to contribute to an 'ecological paradigm' in the study of international relations, long before these themes became common in scientific and societal realms.[1] Current specialists in International Relations, such as for instance the British scholar John Groom, confirm that the Sprouts placed 'ecology' on the agenda of the field of International Relations (Groom, 2003, p. 8). Harold Sprout died in 1980, Margaret Sprout only in 2004 at a high age.

3 Towards a Better Insight into the Academic Work of Harold and Margaret Sprout

3.1 *The 'Geopolitical Foundations' of the Sprouts' Later Work on Foreign Policy Analyses: The Period between 1931 and 1948*

In 1931, Harold Sprout pleaded to make Political Geography *"part of the curriculum in Political Sciences"*. Between 1939 and 1948, he further built upon this idea together with his wife Margaret. They both wrote several books on 'geopolitical' thinkers and questions. In this way, they played a rather important role in introducing in a more systematic way the teachings of continental-European 'Geopolitics' into the still quite young (Anglo-American) field of International Relations:

- Interesting is that the Sprouts' first book (1939) dealt with a 'classic' geopolitical theme; the importance of *sea power* in the international-political (power) position of a country. Fifty years after the first publications of Alfred Thayer Mahan, the Sprouts published *'The Rise of American Naval Power: 1776–1918'* (Sprout & Sprout, 1944 [1939]). Mahan had been the scholar who had developed, between 1890 and 1914, a *ratio* for the development of an American sea power as a means to 'gather' international-political power. The work of Mahan made the Sprouts more sensitive to the question of the relation between *'man'* and the *'environmental variables'* which affect his policy-options and choices. A number of concepts and approaches that the Sprouts

1 Moreover, there also exists a scientific prize named after Harold and Margaret Sprout, which is annually awarded by the *'International Studies Association'*. This award, which was launched in 1972, recognizes scientific publications on *"international-ecological questions which have contributed to the study of international environmental policy, or related questions of (domestic) politics"* (Hersh, 2003).

developed in this book, would later inspire their work during the 1950s and '60s. According to Rosenau, Davis and East, the book *'The Rise of American Naval Power'* contained a number of important impulses to make International Relations and the study of foreign policy more 'scientific' (Rosenau, Davis et al., 1972, p. 2). The key or *'missing link'* the Sprouts proposed, is the 'level of analysis' of the individual decision maker in foreign policy. In an early precursor to *"linkage politics"* the Sprouts exchanged the old, discredited concept of the *'national character' and its influence upon foreign policy* for a more operationally accessible and empirically more researchable approach; the *'styles of statemanship'* of national actors that enter into the international arena (Rosenau, Davis et al., 1972, p. 2). Via researching the foreign policy behaviour of central policymakers, the Sprouts tried to make the foreign policy-behaviour of states scientifically more tangible. In other words, they "exchanged" the abstract level of analysis of the state for a more concrete, and empirically more tangible level of analysis.

- In their second book, *'Toward a New Order of Sea Power: American Naval Policy and the World Scene, 1918–1922'*, (1940) the Sprouts 'fused' together their attention for national actors with the context of the international system. This book described the Conference of Washington (1921–22) on the limitation of maritime armament (Rosenau, Davis et al., 1972, p. 3). In it, the Sprouts recognized the modest, yet tangible impact of 'non-state actors'.
- Based upon his involvement in the *'Navy V-12*-course' on Geopolitics, Harold Sprout developed –together with Margaret– in 1945 a third monography. This was an extensive *reader*, titled *'Foundations of National Power. Readings on World Politics and American Security'*, which was compiled for the training of American officers and diplomats (Sprout & Sprout, 1945).[2] For years, this book was used in the education of maritime officers, but also in other

---

2 In the introduction of this book, the Sprouts formulated their aims (Sprout & Sprout, 1945, pp. vii–viii): *"The first step –for the ordinary citizen as for the statesman, staff officer, or foreign-office official– is to* ***achieve a clear and realistic view of the current world situation****, and of the major trends in sight. We want answers to such questions as: How has the war altered the international position of Great Britain and the British outlook on the world? Can France recover her former standing and influence among the nations? Can the German people play a constructive role in a new world order or must they be subjected indefinitely to international controls? What changes are taking place in eastern and southeastern Europe, in the Mediterranean, and in the Near and Middle East? Will China be rent by civil war or will the Chinese emerge from their long struggle with Japan politically united and prepared to play a large role in world affairs? Can a disarmed and demilitarized Japan still be a menace to security in the Pacific? How strong is the Soviet Union? What do the Russians want in Europe, in the Middle East, in the Far East?* ***Do Soviet aims conflict seriously with our own?*** *What is the measure of American strength?* ***How has the war affected our national position in the world?"***.

circles. Soon, it became one of the first, most widely distributed texts on international relations after 1945. (American) 'national security' was central in this publication, in contrast to the emphasis that publications before 1940 placed upon 'collective security' (Sprout, 1963, p. 29; Olson and Groom 1991, p. 105). According to Rosenau, Davis en East, one of the new aspects of this publication was that the Sprouts developed multiple analytical categories and concepts in order to better understand the 'behaviour' of national states within the context of the complex international system, with special attention for the 'conditioning environment'. Just like Strausz-Hupé's book in 1945 *"The Balance of Tomorrow: Power and Foreign Policy in the United States"* had been an attempt to study the concept of 'power' in a more scientific way, so did this book of the Sprouts attempt to approach 'power' not in normative terms, but in terms of ***'capacity analysis'***. According to Rosenau, Davis and East, the surplus value of this book was to be found with the concepts and categories to 'capture' the conduct of national states within the complex global system. The Sprouts situated this within a conditioning *environment*, which was composed of both human and non-human elements (Rosenau, Davis et al., 1972, 4). In many of these texts, a clear 'geopolitical component' was present[3] (Rosenau, Davis et al., 1972, pp. 3–4).

From the 1950s onwards, the Sprouts would further build upon their 'geopolitical' work from the years 1939–1948. Increasingly, their attention turned to the level of analysis of the individual decision maker in foreign policy.

3.2 *The Sprouts' Work in the 1950s and '60s: Distancing Themselves from the 'National Power'-Approach in Favour of the More Tangible Level of Analysis of the Individual Decision Maker*

From the 1950s onwards, Harold and Margaret Sprout distanced themselves from the 'national power'-approach in favour of the more tangible level of analysis of the individual decision maker. With this position, they can be regarded as among the first IR-specialists to make a plea for a "more balanced" approach to international relations, in which they wanted to spend more attention to the 'relative weight' of the 'different categories of potential explanatory variables in international politics' (Baldwin, 2002, p. 179). Moreover, their 'unit of analysis' changed from the rather abstract 'national interest' in the direction of the more tangible level of the political decision maker. One of the main reasons for

3 A multiple number of book chapters by Spykman and Mackinder were reproduced in this *reader*. A few other American 'geopolitical' authors' work was reproduced in this *reader*; Robert Strausz-Hupé, Arnold Wolfers, Walter Lippmann, William T. R. Fox, Enemy Brooks, Derwent Whittlesey, etc.

this reversal seems to lie with the more nuanced appreciation that the Sprouts developed on the relation between 'geopolitical' environmental variables *on the one hand* and foreign policy *on the other hand*. In this context, the crucial book *'The Ecological Perspective on Human Relations with Special Reference to International Politics'* deserves some special attention (Sprout & Sprout, 1971 [1965]).[4] In the 1950s and '60s, the Sprouts also published a host of important scientific articles in the most prestigious American IR journals. Among these, the following publications can be mentioned: *'Environmental Factors in the Study of International Politics'* (Sprout & Sprout, 1957), *'Geopolitical hypotheses in technological perspective'* (Sprout, 1963) & *'Geography and International Politics in an Era of Revolutionary Change'* (Sprout & Sprout, 1964). Further building upon this work, the Sprouts published in 1968 the pioneering *'An Ecological Paradigm for the Study of International Politics'* (Sprout & Sprout, 1968). Most of their academic research was financed by both the *'Center for International Studies'* at the University of Princeton, and by the *Rockefeller Foundation*. The Sprouts mentioned IR specialist Kenneth Thompson in particular. Thompson was a scientific advisor with the *Rockefeller Foundation*, a person who encouraged them as already as the 1950s to develop an ecological perspective to international politics (Sprout & Sprout 1968, p. iii). This financial and moral support from the *Rockefeller Foundation* is perfectly in line with earlier efforts by this foundation during the 1930s to introduce the teachings and analyses of 'Geopolitics' in the American field of International Relations (read: Criekemans, 2007).

The work of the Sprouts during the 1950s and '60s was characterized by fruitful interactions with their colleagues, both inside and outside the University of Princeton (Rosenau, Davis et al., 1972, p. 5). A leitmotiv in the work of Harold and Margaret Sprout lies in their *disappointment* with the persistent trend via which researchers describe the impact of *'environmental variables'* in a *'determinist' reasoning*. In contrast, the Sprouts proposed the development of a more 'sensitive' appreciation of the 'operational relation' between environmental factors and human behaviour. The Sprouts believed that *man* is a fundamental actor in all social systems, also in national states. In this way, Harold and Margaret Sprout became more and more interested in the human thought

4 In 1962, the Sprouts also published *'Foundations of International Politics'*. Chapter 1 consists of an analysis of the field of International Relations. The next three chapters contain an overview of the components of the 'international system', in which new visions were developed based upon such terms as 'power', 'power potential' and 'capacities'. The rest of this book contained a revision of material from their earlier book *'Foundations of National Power'* (Sprout & Sprout, 1967 [1962]).

processes and their consequences for policy-making in the external affairs of states. From this reasoning, they developed an adapted epistemological vision on the question of the *feasibility of scientific knowledge with regard to the relation environment–man/politics.*

3.3 *The Sprouts' Conceptual Breakthrough of 1956: The 'Ecological Triad' and the Distinction between the 'Operational' & 'Psychological' Milieu*

The Sprouts did not like the term 'environment'. Especially in the US, there existed a tendency to interpret 'environmental variables' too much in non-human, or –to put it differently– in restrictive physical-geographical terms (Sprout & Sprout 1957, p. 311; Sprout & Sprout 1968, p. 17). This is the reason why the Sprouts used the French concept of *'milieu'* (Rosenau, Davis et al. 1972, p. 6), because the link with the 'social' is more clear (Sprout & Sprout, 1968, 17).[5] 'Milieu' thus entail the whole spectrum of environmental factors; both human and non-human, tangible and non-tangible (Sprout & Sprout, 1971 [1965], p. 27).

3.3.1 The 'Ecological Triad'

The contribution of the Sprouts in 1956 brought a new vitality in the debate on the relation between 'geography' and 'politics', which was gradually becoming rather banal and repetitive (Muir, 1997, p. 185). The first 'breakthrough' the Sprouts made, was at first instance a conceptual one, but also had far-reaching ontological, epistemological and methodological consequences. This first step of the Sprouts was the introduction of their concept of the **'ecological triad'**. This triad consists of: (1°) *an* ***entity*** *('environed unit')*, (2°) *his/her* ***environment****, and* (3°) *the* ***relation*** *between the entity & his/her environment.* The relation between an 'entity' and his/her environment always entails a combination of the **properties of the entity** with the **surrounding conditions.** If there is a change in one of both, then also a different relationship develops. From this, the Sprouts deduced the proposition that *change and transformation are typical for the ecological perspective* (*to international relations*) (Sprout & Sprout, 1968, pp. 17–18). In other words, the stress lies with the interdependence, which even seems to increase as a result of technological development, population growth and the increase of the urban nature of human societies. Just like the

5 The Sprouts formulated it as follows (Sprout & Sprout, 1968: p. 17): *"So used, milieu includes social as well as nonhuman phenomena to which human activities may be relatable. Since the French language contains no adjectival form of milieu, we shall continue to use the English adjective environmental."*

'classical' geopolitical scientists of the 1930s and '40s, the Sprouts stress that there exists a fundamental problem; on earth, there exists an unequal distribution of these physical and human *'resources'* (cf. climate patterns, topology, available resources, human communities, etc.). From this, the Sprouts postulated the proposition that *this unequal distribution influences in a significant way all human enterprise, interactions, relations and inter-state relations* (Sprout & Sprout, 1968, p. 21). The concept of the *'ecological triad'* states that the attention of the IR scholar, or of the FPA analyst, should focus on the study of a three-part whole; (1°) **the processes of policy choices within an entity**, (2°) **(the nature of the) environment**, and (3°) **the interaction between the entity & the environment** (Sprout & Sprout, 1968, pp. 11–21; Starr, 1992, p. 3). The next step the Sprouts took, was the further refinement of the concept 'environment' or 'milieu'.

3.3.2 The Distinction between the 'Operational' & 'Psychological' Milieu

Harold and Margaret Sprout stated in their central hypothesis that environmental variables can only influence human activities in two ways. First, such factors can be perceived by individuals, who take these into account in their 'foreign policy decisions' and responses. Only in such cases can one speak of a form of 'influence' of human preferences & decisions by the environment, *'mediated'* by perception. Second, environmental variables can be approached as a kind of 'matrix' that possibly limits the results of foreign policy decisions ('foreign policy outcomes'), even if these environmental variables are not perceived. According to the Sprouts two usable explanatory frameworks could be distinguished; the **'psychological milieu'** or **'psycho-milieu'** (*'the environment as perceived by the decision maker & upon which he/she bases his/her reaction'*) on the one hand, and the **'operational environment'** (*'the true environment in which the chosen policy is executed'*) on the other hand. The Sprouts formulated it as follows (Sprout & Sprout, 1968, pp. 33–34):

> We desire to make this distinction between psycho-milieu and operational milieu as explicit as possible, since failure to do so has been the source of endless confused and muddy thinking. Psycho-milieu denotes a human individual's perceived image of a situation, an image that may or may not correspond to reality. Operational milieu denotes that the situation as it actually exists and affects the achievements and capabilities of the entity in question (whether a single individual, group or community as a whole).

The conceptual distinction between *'psycho-milieu'* and the *'operational environment'* in fact means a fundamental break with the Realist school, which (still) believed that decisionmakers in foreign policy can perceive their environment in a 'correct' way. This 'amendment' by the Sprouts had important consequences *for the FPA scholar* and *for the decision maker in foreign policy*:

- First, the consequences for the **FPA scholar**. In case a researcher is trying to explain why certain decisions are taken in foreign policy, then one should try to analyse the 'psychological environment' of the decision maker. However, in case the analyst is more interested in the 'operational results' of a specific decision, then the 'operational (or geographical) environment' should be used as an explanatory framework (see figure 4.1). Especially the *first of these two analyses* is certainly not easy for the FPA analyst. He/she then should try to work out how the involved (group of) decision maker(s) perceived the world, and which opportunities or limitations they saw for themselves. For the researcher, this task entails many obstacles; one has to develop a reconstruction based upon 'second hand'-material (what the decision maker said and did). Even the most 'neutral' analyst is not free of introducing his/her own linguistic or ideologically biased ideas. Moreover, one has to work with incomplete and sometimes even openly contradictory information (Sprout & Sprout, 1957, pp. 319–320). In the *second kind of 'analyses'*, the researcher tries to illustrate how the 'reality on the ground' changes as a result of decisions which were taken earlier, and how the 'characteristic properties' of the environment 'enforce' possible limitations on the 'operational results' of foreign policy decisions which were taken earlier.

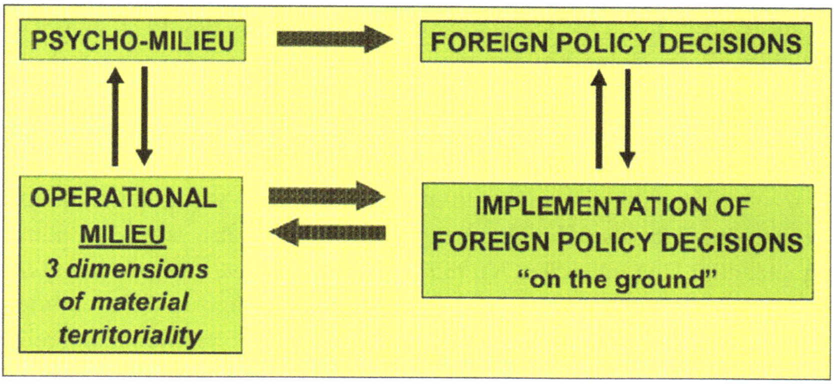

FIGURE 4.1 The conceptual revolution of Harold and Margaret Sprout

- Second, the consequences for the **decision maker in foreign policy**. The decision maker **should try to keep the gap between the 'objective' and the 'perceived' environment as small as possible** (Dougherty and Pfaltzgraff, 1981, p. 67). One could state that too big a gap between both is 'lethal' for foreign policy, and in some extreme cases even for the very existence of the nation. Many examples exist, some are also mentioned by the Sprouts; (1°) the Japanese attack on Pearl Harbor in December 1941 could only take place because the American military and political elite did not (want to) realize that a Japanese *'task force'* so far from home could be used in an offensive operation (Sprout & Sprout, 1957, p. 318; Sprout & Sprout 1971 [1965], p. 12), (2°) the American Monroe-doctrine was proclaimed in 1823 by president James Monroe at a time when the danger for a large-scale invasion by sea in the 'Western Hemisphere' had subsided, (3°) a more recent example from 2003 could go as follows; in the "mental map" of the American president George W. Bush, Saddam Hussein's Iraq was labelled an 'imminent threat' because he had been playing 'cat and mouse' for a number of years with the international community on the issue of whether his regime still had weapons of mass destruction. By his own words, Bush junior felt that in such an unclear situation, he had to act, certainly in the 'world after 9/11'. However, on 6 October 2004, the American *'Iraqi Survey Group'*, a group of weapons inspectors and specialists, stated that Iraq had not possessed WMD (thus indirectly stating that the basic legitimation by the US to topple Saddam's regime had been flawed). Apart from that, this case also forms an excellent illustration of another remark the Sprouts made about heads of state and government; *"The higher one moves in the hierarchy of a great power's government, the more one is impressed by the remoteness of executives from the operational environment in which their decisions are executed"* (Sprout & Sprout, 1957, p. 321). Bush lived in his own world (*'psycho-milieu'*), which in itself perhaps had a logic of its own, but which in practice did not always correspond with the reality of the ground (*'operational milieu'*). Often, decision makers take refuge in a form of thinking in analogies, in which one refers to history in order to make the case for a certain policy choice in foreign policy. However, the same conditions never really repeat themselves because the meaning of geography and technology changes through time (see also: Houghton, 1996). The Sprouts also asked the following question: *"To what extent is a top-level executive a virtual prisoner of the civil and military officials who provide data for him?"* (Sprout & Sprout 1957, p. 321). The civil and military officials provide the decision makers in foreign policy with data on the 'operational environment', but these data are often prepared in a way "in which the official thinks the president would like to see the world" (cf. *'psycho-milieu'*). This forms one of the most important difficulties with which intelligence agencies struggle. The gap between the *'operational'* and the *'psychological'* environment forms a powerful conceptual tool in order to approach the subtle interaction between environment & politics in a more nuanced way.

From this framework of reference, Harold and Margaret Sprout developed in 1957 seven theses, which they tried to defend in this publication (Sprout & Sprout, 1957, p. 310):

1. Environmental factors become related to the attitudes and decisions which, in the aggregate, comprise a state's foreign policy *only* by being apperceived and taken into account by those who participate in the policy-forming process.
2. Conclusions as to the manner in which apperceived environmental factors are dealt with in foreign policy making depend on the theory or theories of decision making which the analyst brings to bear on the case under consideration.
3. Hypotheses as to the manner in which apperceived environmental factors enter into the decision making process can provide fruitful linkages between ecological and behavioural approaches to the study of international politics.
4. Environmental factors can be significantly related to the operational results of policy decisions, even though such factors are not apperceived and taken into account in the policy making process.
5. What is called analysis of state power or international power relations or (preferably, in our view) analysis of state capabilities consists essentially of calculating opportunities and limitations latent, or implicit, in the milieu of the state under consideration.
6. Capability calculations or estimates are always carried out within some framework of assumptions regarding the policy objectives, operational strategy, and political relations of the state under consideration.
7. Conclusions as to the opportunities and limitations which are implicit in a state's milieu and which may affect the operational results of its policy decisions depend on the ecological theory and the topical explanatory premises which the analyst brings to bear in the specific case under consideration.

The explanatory power that analysts attribute to the 'milieu', largely depends on the way in which their proposed *man-milieu-hypotheses* are embedded in a certain epistemology with regards to the feasibility of scientific knowledge about the relationship territoriality–politics. Each geopolitical formulation of a theory rests on such initial assumptions.

3.4 *The Sprouts' Continuum: A Synthesized Perspective on the Relation Territoriality—Politics*

In their book *'The Ecological Perspective on Human Relations with Special Reference to International Politics'* (1965, 1971), Harold and Margaret Sprout stated that in essence a researcher can choose between five possible epistemological ways of appreciating the relationship between environmental variables & (foreign) policy: *'geographical determinism'* (cf. Haushofer), *'free will environmentalism'* (cf. Spykman), *'environmental possibilism'* (cf. Vidal de la Blache), *'environmental probabilism'* and the approach developed by the Sprouts themselves: *'cognitive behavioralism'*. The latter one, cognitive behavioralism, starts from the following assumption: a central political decision maker (who conducts a foreign policy on behalf of a political entity) consciously responds to his/her milieu (environment) as he/she apperceives & interpretes it in light of past experiences (Sprout, 1971 [1965], pp. 117–118).

We call the whole of the possible postures, the *"Sprouts-continuum"* (see figure 4.2.). It is a continuum since every step towards the right entails an epistemological attitude which offers man more freedom in the relation territoriality–politics, whereas every step towards the left of the figure below allocates a more determinist, dominating role to 'geography'.

More freedom for man

1.	2.	3.	4.	5.
"environmental determinism"	*"free-will environmentalism"*	*"environmental possibilism"*	*"environmental probabilism"*	*"cognitive behavioralism"*

Increasing determinist influence of 'geography'

FIGURE 4.2 The "Sprouts-continuum": different attitudes with regard to the feasibility of scientific knowledge on the relation territoriality–politics

These five postures towards the man-milieu-relationship issue are not very rigid categories. They are neither conceptually parallel nor quite mutually exclusive. But these labels do identify recognized postures towards man-milieu relationships. The Sprouts critically analysed each of these postures. Their attention was aimed at the question to what extent these postures are useable in explaining or predicting a foreign policy. They also asked the question whether it was possible to establish a generally consistent, logically tenable, and more fruitful mode of thinking about man-milieu relationships (Sprout & Sprout, 1971 [1965], p. 47).

First, the Sprouts identified four already existing philosophical postures;

- ***'Geographical determinism'*** generally refers to the thesis that some set of environmental factors, less than the total milieu, is sufficient to account for, or to provide a firm basis for predicting, both the psychological behavior of human beings and the empirical outcomes of their undertakings. Applied rigourously, this philosophical posture envisages man as a sort of chip in the stream of history. He is borne along by a current which he is incapable of resisting, within a channel from which he cannot escape. Man has no capacity for choice. This posture can be detected in the traditional German geopolitical literature of the 1930s (Sprout & Sprout, 1957, p. 312; Sprout & Sprout, 1971 [1965], p. 48).

- ***'Free will environmentalism'*** is a 'watered' down version of *'geographical determinism'*. In this posture, man is assumed to have a free will. Nature gives him instructions, but he is capable of choosing, however unwisely, to disregard them. This posture can be detected in the writings of such American geopolitical thinkers as Alfred Thayer Mahan and Nicholas John Spykman (Sprout & Sprout, 1957, p. 312; Sprout & Sprout, 1971 [1965], p. 71).
- ***'Possibilism'*** forms a reaction (of the French so-called *'possibilists'*) against the alleged 'geographical determinism' of German geopolitical authors. In this posture, the *initiative lies with man*, not with the milieu that 'surrounds' him. The environment does not force man into anything, it is merely present (Sprout & Sprout, 1971 [1965], p. 83). The milieu is thus conceived as a set of opportunities and limitations. The environment is conceived as a "kind of matrix which influences the operational results of what is undertaken". The environment is both **'enabling' & 'constraining'**; (1°) it provides a number of parameters or limitations to the whole spectrum of foreign policy actions which can be undertaken by an entity ('constraining'), (2°) the environment provides a political entity also with a number of important opportunities. This posture presupposes that both these limitations and opportunities can be *discovered*. The methodology via which this should happen, often remains unclear. One may assume that a hypothetical omniscient observer can identify and delineate *all* the interrelations between milieu and the environed unit. But, of course, no observer is omniscient. The most one can do is to frame hypotheses as to what environmental factors are significantly relevant for the action under consideration and how these set limits to the operational results thereof. There is no certainty that any two observers will formulate identical explanatory hypotheses (Sprout & Sprout, 1957, p. 313). Thus, environmental possibilism is the frame of reference within which the capabilities of states are calculated. But possibilism provides no basis for analyzing environmental factors in the context of policy formation (Sprout & Sprout, 1957, p. 314). In the possibilist frame of reference, decisions and undertakings are taken as 'given', not as behaviour to be analyzed and explained or predicted (Sprout & Sprout, 1971 [1965], p. 96). A possibilistic analysis yields either an *explanation* or a *prediction* of the *outcome* of a 'given' undertaking, actual or postulated (Sprout & Sprout, 1971 [1965], p. 203).

- *'Environmental probabilism'* is based on the assumption that **specific (foreign policy) choices or actions are more probable given a certain 'environmental matrix' than others.** The reason for this probability lies in the (supposed) predictability of human (and thus also of state) conduct. The specific character of a particular environment offers man already certain 'keys' or 'hints' regarding what is 'possible' & what political choices are 'obvious'. The environment not only makes an entity attentive *of what is possible*, but also *of which (political) choices are most desirable /appropriate* taking into account the specific circumstances. Discussions of foreign policy and of foreign policy-making very commonly exhibit the characteristics which can be described as "common-sense probabilism". Underlying assumptions are often obscured in environmentalistic rhetoric. *"But"*, so argue the Sprouts, *"scratch the surface* [...] *of almost any discussion of foreign policy or the conduct of foreign relations, and one is apt to discover the familiar premises that men are predominantly acquisitive, adequately knowledgeable, and generally rational"* (Sprout & Sprout, 1971 [1965], p. 111). From this, hypotheses can be developed with regard to the *probability* that certain (foreign) policy choices will be taken, taking into account the environment (and the specific context in which a decision maker in foreign policy finds himself). The disadvantage of *'environmental probabilism'* is that such models will never succeed in transcending the assumptions on which they are based. The Sprouts stated in 1965 that there was *"an ever-present need for more factual data both to fashion better models, and to describe and explain the specific behaviour of particular decision makers in specified settings"* (Sprout & Sprout, 1971 [1965], p. 117).

3.5 *A 'New' Epistemological Attitude on the Feasibility of Knowledge about the Relation Territoriality—Politics; 'Cognitive Behavioralism'*

Harold and Margaret Sprout developed their own approach, in which they linked 'ecological' and 'behavioralistic' perspectives to Political Science (Muir, 1975, p. 68), and to the study of foreign policy. Their epistemological position goes one step further in granting influence to the individual with respect to the relationship territoriality–politics; ***'cognitive behavioralism'***. It starts from the following assumption; *a central political decision maker (who conducts a foreign policy on behalf of a political entity) consciously responds to his/her milieu (environment) as he/she* ***apperceives*** *& interpretes it in light of past experiences.*

What does this approach entail, and what are its consequences for the study of foreign policy? 'Cognitive behavioralism' states that there exists a difference between the *'objective milieu'* as it is in reality and the *'psychological milieu'* (the environment as perceived by the decision-maker). How people perceive their environment (the content of their image about this environment) forms a central and crucial element in the selection process of a certain political policy (e.g. in the foreign policy which one conducts vis-à-vis a certain environment) (Holsti, 1989, p. 41). A person's values and other psychological predispositions direct his attention selectively to certain features of his milieu, and he interprets what he selectively perceives in the light of conscious memories and subconscious stored experience. Instead of basing certain assumptions on how people would probably respond (see supra; *'environmental probabilism'*), cognitive behavioralists will try to investigate as accurately as possible how (foreign policy) decision makers perceive the world, and respond to it (Sprout & Sprout, 1971 [1965], p. 118). With regard to moods, attitudes, preferences, choices, decisions and undertakings, erroneous ideas of the milieu may be just as influential as ideas that conform to the "realities" of the milieu (Sprout & Sprout, 1971 [1965], p. 122). In first instance, the 'real world' is thus irrelevant (Sprout & Sprout, 1971 [1965], p. 119). The 'operational environment' only plays a role starting from the moment of the implementation of (foreign) policy decisions on the terrain, namely in the possibility that it can *limit* the results of these decisions.

What are the disadvantages of 'cognitive behavioralism' as developed by Harold and Margaret Sprout as an analytical perspective to foreign policy decision making? The American political scientist Hyam Gold developed some critical remarks in an article called *"Foreign Policy Decision-Making and the Environment: The Claims of Snyder, Brecher and the Sprouts"*, published in 1978 in International Studies Quarterly;

– A *first disadvantage of the model of the Sprouts* is that 'cognitive behavioralism' *does not take into account the possible impact of non-perceived environmental variables on foreign policy decisions*. As Gold appropriately observes, it is possible that decision makers are influenced by certain environmental variables without them being actively aware of this (Gold, 1978, p. 582). This point of criticism indicates that the question of the 'influence' of environmental variables upon 'politics' can be more complex and subtle than anticipated by the Sprouts.[6] It is possible that the perception of *other* decision makers *mediates* between the 'unperceived influences emanating from the environment' & the decisions which form the object of this analysis. One could accept that in the model of the Sprouts the *'non-perceived environmental factors'* do not influence political decisions directly, but rather have an impact upon the way in which decision makers interpret other environmental factors differently (Gold, 1978, p. 583).

6 In the book *'The Analysis of International Politics. Essays in Honor of Harold and Margaret Sprout'*, Rosenau remarks that the *'external environment'* forms an interdependent whole of factors. He utilizes the analytical concept *'change'* as an interesting way to make a link with the foreign policy behaviour (Rosenau, 1972, p. 153).

- A *second disadvantage of the model of the Sprouts* is that their approach too little takes into account the *possibility that different participants in the group of 'foreign policy decision makers' have conflicting perceptions about the environment.* In case a certain process of 'bureaucratic decision making' precedes, the model of the Sprouts has little to offer according to Gold.[7] The Sprouts' approach is, however, useable in two cases: (1°) when there exists, within a dominant subgroup of decision makers, a quasi-unanimity about the way in which the environment should be perceived [8], *and* (2°) when the decision making process itself is the reason for a fundamental reflection about the environmental perception, and this quasi unanimously within the decision making cell (Gold, 1978, p. 584).[9]

The abovementioned 'corrections' by Hyam Gold offer a somewhat sobering, yet necessary criticism to the Sprouts' 'cognitive behavioralism'. However, this does not harm the characteristic traits and surplus value of *this* geopolitical approach to the study of foreign policy, but rather places *'cognitive behavioralism'* in the right context. All too often, geopolitical models of analysis 'suggest' a *"deus ex machina"* explanation of foreign policy on the basis of some environmental variables without taking *'bureaucratic politics'* into account. However, it cannot be said that *every* decision making process is complex. In many countries, there often exists a 'consensus' about the main components of its national foreign policy vis-à-vis a third country. Sometimes there is no real internal debate at all. If this is the case, the Minister of Foreign Affairs and/or the Head of Government play a central and dominant role in the formulation of foreign policy decisions. *Their* environmental perception can thus often mean the necessary boost for a certain foreign policy vis-à-vis a third country of area. Keeping this in mind, the application of a 'Cognitive Geopolitics' in a foreign policy analysis seems justified and illuminating, at least as long as it can be demonstrated that the decision-maker-to-be-analysed plays/played a

7 Gold however remarks that the Sprouts would not fully agree with this (Gold, 1978, p. 585): *"what [the Sprouts] would find harder to accept, however, would be the rather limited decisional significance, in such situations, of the environmental perceptions of the individual decision makers engaged in intense bureaucratic-political games".*

8 A more recent example could be; the 'perception of the environment' by the group of 'neo-conservatives' within the American government of President George W. Bush.

9 The terrorist attacks of 11 September 2001 can be seen as one of the most recent examples of a dramatic turn which caused a change in the 'analysis of the environment' by the foreign policy elites of the United States of America. The events of that day changed policy almost overnight; from that day onwards, every regime which offered shelter and/or support to terrorists, was put under severe diplomatic and military pressure by the US and its allies. The 'war on terrorism' suddenly became one of the central themes in foreign policy, at least during the first months after the terrorist attacks.

role of significance in the articulation of the foreign policy. Yet, as with every perspective to international relations, the researcher should always bear in mind that this approach entails a very specific 'lens' to international politics and foreign policy.

3.6 *A More 'Holistic' Vision on the Role of 'Environmental Factors' & the Difference of Their Operation in 'Foreign Policy Analyses' and 'Capacity Analyses'*

The Sprouts considered classical-geopolitical theories as 'one-dimensional' since they often have the inclination to start from one specific group of unevenly spread, 'geographically embedded' variables in order to develop (far-reaching) explanations or predictions about the (power relations in) international politics. The Sprouts repudiated such 'one-dimensional' geopolitical theories in favour of a broader 'ecological perspective'. This approach constituted the development of a more integrated, holistic vision on the international environment; one which took both physical and non-physical elements into account. In short, the environment or 'milieu' was approached as a multi-dimensional system, in which both the perceptions about the environment by decision makers (the *'psycho-milieu'*) as the 'objective' conditions themselves, constituted the object of study. Their analytical framework emphasized the mutual interdependence between geography, demography, technology and resources. Both perceptual variables as quantitative factors such as population and territorial width were considered relevant. The complexity of the interdependence within and between national societies and the increasing irrelevance of the distinction between 'domestic' and 'foreign' questions, form central points of interest within the *'ecological perspective'* to international relations. According to the Sprouts, one cannot forget the fact that each 'geopolitical theory' also makes assumptions regarding the technology that societies have at their disposal.

According to the Sprouts, the 'ecological perspective' also offers a philosophical perspective from which one can observe current events in a critical and society-relevant fashion. The 'victory' of man upon nature, and the development of elaborated techniques for the manipulation of human behaviour, suggest that it is possible to wrap the Earth around one's finger. New technologies may perhaps 'free' man from his 'natural environment', but could at the same time as a result of their 'perfection' also structurally undermine the liveability of the Earth. How one should handle these increasing capacities so as to change the human condition, thus forms the 'ultimate question' in international politics according to the Sprouts. The 'ecological paradigm' does not offer any ready-made solutions for this, but can help to identify the most important questions and decisions.

The Sprouts made an important distinction between analysing 'power' (or better: 'political potential') 'in terms of foreign policy analyses' *versus* 'in terms of capacity analyses'. **Foreign policy analyses** are aimed at explaining or predicting policy decisions. Conversely, **capacity analyses** are aimed at explaining or predicting the operational results of decisions; the calculation of the opportunities and limitations that are implicitly embodied in the environment of a certain state. It is exactly these elements that will affect the 'operational results' of that which is undertaken, irrespective of whether such factors are known by the decision makers. In both types of analyses, environmental variables play a role, but the relevant frames of reference and the applied explanatory hypotheses or theories are always different. Only foreign policy analyses focus on the way in which environmental variables are 'perceived'. In capacity analyses, 'perception' as such does not play a real role; as an analyst one rather develops an independent evaluation of the question what opportunities and limitations are implicitly embedded in the environment of the concerned state, and how these may affect the 'political potential' of a nation (in comparison to other countries & in function of certain previously postulated long or short term policy objectives). An overview:

TABLE 4.1 The role of environmental variables' in 'foreign policy analyses' and in 'capacity analyses'

What aspect of the relation between 'environment' and 'politics'?	*Nature of the analysis*	*Nature of the predictive and / or explanatory hypotheses*
"Influence" of the 'environment' upon *'foreign policy decisions'*, mediated via the perception (*"psycho-milieu"*)	Foreign policy analyses with special attention for the question of the influence of the 'environment' on 'politics'	Explanations or predictions with regard to the environmental perception in foreign policy decisions, past or future
"Influence" of the *operational milieu* on the results of foreign policy-decisions – *'foreign policy outcomes'*	Capacity analyses with special attention for the question of the influence of the 'environment' on 'politics'	Explanations or predictions with regard to the operational results of foreign policy decisions, past or future

Before the Sprouts, researchers such as Strausz-Hupé and Morgenthau had been focussing upon measuring 'power' in terms of *capacity analyses*; they tried to fill in 'power' in a non-normative fashion in which they still believed that 'geography' and other 'territorially embedded' power factors were guiding the content of foreign policy. Scholars such as Strausz-Hupé did not analyse foreign policy as such, but rather made an 'inventory' of the material power sources (geographical location, size of the state, available resources, developed industries, demography, etcetera) of states (sometimes even without explicitly drawing attention to the necessary framework of reference of 'national policy objectives'). In fact, what really was studied was the virtual 'capacity' of states to influence international politics, instead of examining whether and to what extent such environmental variables effectively generate an impact upon daily foreign policy. The latter was a connection that the Sprouts did make.

What is striking is the way in which the Sprouts mainly concentrated their efforts upon the study of the possible impact of the 'environment' upon politics, though paying little to no attention to the question to what extent there also exists a reverse influence of 'politics' on the 'milieu'. In that sense their work is similar to 'Classical Geopolitics'. They either paid attention to the influence of the 'psycho-milieu' upon 'foreign policy decisions', or for the influence of the real, operational milieu upon the results of these political decisions (*'foreign policy outcomes'*). Their analytical framework, however, was at best appreciative of the *possibility* that 'politics' as such changed the structure of the ecological 'milieu', but much less of the possibility in which the milieu is being assigned a different 'meaning' starting from a political or social-societal discourse.

4 Three Ways in Which Harold and Margaret Sprout Influenced IR and FPA

In what way did Harold and Margaret Sprout influence IR and FPA? Three important aspects can be discerned: (1°) their contribution to one of the foundations of 'Foreign Policy Analysis', (2°) their contribution as a motor behind *'cognitive behavioralism'* in IR – the way in which such cognitive-behavioralist IR concepts as *'perception'* & *'misperception'* (Jervis) and *'mental maps'* (Henrikson) came about, and (3°) the Sprouts as 'agenda-setters' of researching environmental issues within IR.

4.1 *The Work of the Sprouts as one of the Most Important Fundaments for the Coming into Being of the IR Field of 'Comparative Foreign Policy' (Later: Foreign Policy Analysis)*

The conceptual and 'operational' breakthrough by the Sprouts impacted the literature quite rapidly. In 1954, the Princeton scholars Richard C. Snyder, Henry Bruck and Burton Sapin published the book *'Decision-making as an Approach to the Study of International Politics'* (Snyder, Bruck et al., 1962). This constitutes one of the first important attempts at that time to develop an approach to analyse foreign policy decision making (Smith 1986, p. 14; Gerner 1995, p. 19). States were not approached as abstract entities, but as bodies which are represented by decision makers. The actions of the state can therefore be analysed via devoting more attention to the *actions of those who represent the state* (Geeraerts, 2003). Snyder and his colleagues approached 'foreign policy decision making' as a process of *input-output interaction* of variables; they postulated that *the way in which decision makers define a situation* forms a key factor to a better understanding of foreign policy behaviour (Itoh, 1995). The *"Snyder-Bruck-Sapin-model"* operationalised the process whereby decision makers defined the situation by identifying three sources of 'stimuli': (1°) *the decision making process itself* (influence from within the governmental organisations which 'produce' the decision), the *'internal setting'* (influence emanating from non-governmental aspects of the society within which the decisions are taken), and *last but not least* the *'external setting'* (influences emanating from outside society). The *"Snyder-Bruck-Sapin-model"* is relevant in at least two ways. First, it offered a comparable operational model to study the *organisational, domestic,* and *'external'* variables[10] as possible sources of the foreign policy-decision-making process (Itoh, 1995). *Second,* as one of the first, it paid attention to *perceptions* and the role of non-governmental, domestic factors in foreign policy decision making (Geeraerts, 2003).[11] In the *"Snyder-Bruck-Sapin-model"*, 'geopolitical variables' became part of a broader category of 'external'

---

10 In the *"Snyder-Bruck-Sapin-model"*, these last two groups of variables are granted a place under the denominator *'setting'*, which is being defined as *"a set of categories of potentially relevant factors and conditions which may affect the action of any state".* Snyder and his colleagues hereby make a difference between the *'internal'* and the *'external setting'* (Snyder, Bruck et al., 1962, pp. 66–67). The *'internal setting'* of the decision-making consists of: the non-human environment, the society and human environmental variables such as population and culture (Snyder, Bruck et al., 1962: p. 72). The *'external setting'* refers to *"such factors and conditions beyond the territorial boundaries of the state – the actions and reactions of other states (their decision-makers), the societies for which they act, and the physical world* [...] *It should be noted that our conception of setting does not exclude certain so-called environmental limitations such as the state of technology, morbidity ratio, and so on, which may limit the achievement of objectives or which may otherwise become part of the conditions of actions irrespective of whether and how the decision-makers perceive them."*. According to Snyder and his colleagues, the 'external setting' changes continuously, and exists in its essence of those components *which decision-makers find important* (Snyder, Bruck et al., 1962, pp. 66–67).

11 By way of criticism, one could state that this *"Snyder-Bruck-Sapin-model"* did not entail more than an inventory of the possible influences upon foreign policy-decision-making (see: Geeraerts, 2003).

variables. Through *perception*, these played an important role in the way in which a foreign policy decision maker defines the situation in which he finds himself.[12] According to Rosenau, Davis and East, there exist clear parallels between the ideas of the Sprouts and those of Snyder, Bruck an Sapin. From this, it can be concluded that Harold and Margaret exerted 'behind the scenes' influence upon their colleagues at Princeton University (Rosenau, Davis et al., 1972, p. 5), and not vice versa.[13] According to this view, the Sprouts were among the first scholars to 'break up' the national state into a more accessible 'unit of analysis'; the foreign policy decision makers. This was only possible thanks to and via their earlier fundamental reflection on the relation territoriality–politics.

According to Hudson, the added value of the Sprouts' work for *'Foreign Policy Analysis'* lies in the *extra* dimension they offered by placing foreign policy in its right *context*. In order to place the foreign policy actions of policy makers in their right context, the Sprouts thought it was necessary to acquire an insight into the *'psycho-milieu'* of decision makers. If inconsistencies existed between the international *objective* environment and the way in which it is *perceived*, this led to a 'suboptimal' foreign policy (Hudson, Sims et al., 1993, pp. 213–214). The mission of the 'cognitive behavioralist' researcher therefore is to find out how certain decision makers perceived the 'environment', and how they responded to it in a certain way (Sprout & Sprout, 1971 [1965], p. 118). The incorporation of *'external variables'* via the filter of *perception* constitutes an idea which was developed by Snyder and his colleagues, but which was in fact highly influenced by the work of the Sprouts, although Harold and Margaret Sprout had not committed these thoughts to paper in 1954. Reading Rosenau, it nevertheless becomes clear that Snyder and his colleagues at the Department of Political Sciences of the University of Princeton were highly influenced by their *senior* colleagues Harold and Margaret Sprout (Rosenau, Davis et al., 1972, p. 5). The most important analytical goal of Snyder, Bruck and Sapin

---

12 Snyder and his colleagues wrote (Snyder, Bruck et al.,1962: p. 65, p. 67): "[...] *the key to the explanation of why the state behaves in the way it does lies in the way its decision-makers as actors define their situation* [...] *Relevance of particular factors and conditions in general and in particular situations will depend on the attitudes, perceptions, judgements, and purposes of state X's decision-makers, that is, on how they react to various stimuli."*

13 This opinion is shared by the political scientist Mayumi Itoh (Itoh, 1995): *"Richard Snyder and Michael Brecher, among others, developed conceptual models of foreign policy decision-making process. These existing models inherit the pioneering work on the "man-milieu relationships" postulated by Harold and Margaret Sprout.* [...] *Built upon Sprouts' conceptualization of the man-milieu relationship, Richard Snyder and his colleagues developed a model of foreign policy decision-making."*

was indeed to be found in the *reconstruction of the world view of the decision maker(s)* (Geeraerts, 2003). Wholly in line with the logic of the Sprouts, Snyder, Bruck and Sapin thought this offered the only possibility to explain foreign policy behaviour. When current FPA analysts devote attention to the *'definition of the situation'* by decision makers, they will often deem the 'perceived environment' more important than the 'objective reality'. In other words, today most of these researchers accept this fundamental difference between the *'psycho-milieu'* and the *'operational environment'* (Gold, 1978; Dougherty & Pfaltzgraff, 1981, p. 470).

4.2 The Work of the Sprouts as Immediate Cause for the Development, within IR, of Cognitive-Behavioralist Notions as 'Perception' & 'Misperception' (Jervis) & 'Mental Maps' (Henrikson)

In his book *'Belgium and its foreign policy'*, the Belgian IR specialist Rik Coolsaet pertinently remarks that new notions such as ***'perception'*** and ***'misperception'*** were developed based upon the work of Snyder and his colleagues (Coolsaet, 1998, pp. 518–519). Coolsaet refers indirectly to the work of the American IR scholar Robert Jervis; *'Perception and Misperception in International Politics'.* In the introduction of this book, Jervis explicitly states he built his work on the conceptual distinction by Harold and Margaret Sprout between the 'operational' and the 'subjective' milieu, and implicitly also on the epistemological position of 'cognitive behavioralism' (see: Jervis, 1976, p. 13). Jervis' thesis stated (also based upon the *'consistency principle'* from Cognitive Psychology) that decision makers will always try to *perceive their environment as consistently as possible, and to avoid contradictions.* They will even be inclined to ignore incoming information which does not fit "into their picture", or even adapt their subjective formation of an image to reality. One could then speak of a *misperception*, a process which according to Jervis *consciously* takes place with the foreign policy-decision maker (Soetendorp, 1994, p. 48). Jervis applied this dynamic also to the perception of the 'external environment', under the title *'Impact of Constant Factors'*. He wrote that if the environment of an actor offers him/her certain problems or opportunities, the actor will be inclined to fit them into earlier 'patterns'. Jervis also wrote that the physical isolation of the United States of America and the United Kingdom resulted in a situation whereby these countries were not capable of gaining a deeper insight into the way in which other (e.g. continental European) countries responded so intensely to uncertain security dilemmas. When the technological developments resulted in a situation whereby their physical isolation was no longer guaranteed, it took a long time before the British and later American minds adapted themselves to conduct an active foreign policy, fully engaged in world affairs (Jervis, 1976, pp. 271–273). The above reasoning forms a logical extension of the consequences emanating from the distinction that the Sprouts had made between the *'operational'* and *'psychological' milieu*.[14]

Apart from the abovementioned 'impact' of the Sprouts upon IR literature, a number of other 'embranchements' to their thinking can be mentioned. In 1973, the geographer Peter Gould launched the concept ***'mental maps'***,[15] in a contribution to the book *'Image and Environment'* by Downs and Stea (Gould, 1973).[16] In 1974, Gould worked with Rodney White to further develop his ideas in the book *'Mental Maps'* (Gould and White, 1985 [1974]). A *'mental map'* is the same as a *'cognitive map'* (Henrikson, 1980, p. 498; Saarinen, 1995, p. 107).[17] A 'mental map' can be seen as part of a *'belief system'* of a person; a more or less integrated whole of convictions which one has *about one's physical and social environment.* Following the American IR specialists Keohane and Goldstein, one could postulate that such 'mental maps' can –just like other 'ideas'– function as *'road*

14 Jervis for that matter also recognized that, within the political elites of countries, differences may exist with regard to their perception of the external environment (Muir, 1997, p. 183).

15 The term *'mental maps'*, however, was not new. The writer J. B. Priestly used this term in one of his works of fiction during the 1920s. In the early 1960s, the concept *'mental maps'* was applied as a general term to refer to the cartographical representations of collective images of people about 'where they would like to live' (*'residential desirability'*). It is this kind of research which indicated to researchers in Geography that there existed an impact of language, culture, age & political and religious convictions upon the formation of such 'common images' of the environment. It appeared that a certain rudimentary 'filtering process' was part of this. It was concluded that collective forms of human behaviour could often be predicted by certain 'mental maps', for instance in the migration of young adults (within the US) and in the estimation by individuals of distances. From the 1970s onwards, the term *'mental maps'* began to cover a more broader meaning (Gould, 1973; Gould, 1991).

16 The book *'Image and Environment'* of Downs and Stea further built upon a research tradition on the topic of *'environmental perception'*, which originated during the 1960s. In it, special attention was given to dangers emanating from the environment, and for the way these were evaluated by people when they had to make choices of where to live or work (Gould, 1991). Also Kenneth E. Boulding's book *'The Image'* can be seen as a basis upon which this reader of Downs en Stea further built upon; Boulding was also asked to write the preface in this book (see: Boulding, 1973).

17 The 'cognitive map' is a term which dates from the 1970s, an attempt to study the convictions of policy makers in a more specific and more rigorous way. A 'cognitive map' refers to a specific set of convictions of a policy maker, and to their interconnection as they exist in the mind of a decision-maker with regard to a certain aspect of the environment (Rosati, 1995, pp. 56–57). Downs and Stea define *'cognitive mapping'* rather as a process (Downs and Stea, 1973: p. 9): *"a process composed of a series of psychological transformations by which an individual acquires, codes, stores, recalls, and decodes information about the relative locations and attributes of phenomena in his everyday spatial environment."*

maps'; ideas which help people bring their uncertainty about the world to an acceptable level, so that they are better capable of figuring out through which decisions they can best strive for their interests (see: Goldstein & Keohane 1995). In their book *'Mental Maps'*, Gould and White suggested that 'mental maps' could be very important in order to better understand the behaviour of political and military decision-makers (see: Gould and White, 1985 [1974], pp. 140–144).[18] It is the American diplomatic historian and political scientist Alan K. Henrikson who tried in 1980 to further 'operationalise' the concept of *'mental maps'* in foreign policy analysis. In an interesting article published in the *'International Political Science Review'*, titled *'The Geographical "Mental Maps" of American Foreign Policy Makers'*, Henrikson developed his vision. For that matter, he started his reasoning with a neo-Sproutian proposition: *"Statesmen respond to the world as they perceive and imagine it – which may not be the way the world really is"* (Henrikson, 1980, p. 495), and he also paid homage[19] to the contribution of the Sprouts. Henrikson defined *'mental maps'* in the following way (Henrikson, 1980, p. 498):

> mental map means an ordered but continually adapting structure of the mind –alternatively conceivable as a process– by reference to which a person acquires, codes, stores, recalls, reorganizes, and applies, in thought or action, information about his or her large-scale geographical environment, in part or in its entirety.

Henrikson had the ambition to analyse American foreign policy via *'mental maps'*.[20] After all, foreign policy planners and military strategists base their

---

18 In their work, Gould and White based some of their ideas on an unpublished PhD-thesis (promoted by Gould) by Richard Eaton in 1985; *'Geopolitical mental maps: a search for synthesis'* (University Park, Pennsylvania).

19 Henrikson explicitly referred to the work of the Sprouts as one of the foundations for his *'mental maps'* (Henrikson, p. 1980): *"The mental maps of persons involved in politics are, of course, not an entirely new subject of interest. One salutes, above all, the pioneering work of Harold and Margaret Sprout (1956), who were perhaps the first to apply the notion of a subjective environment to the study of international affairs."*

20 The political-geographer Richard Muir identified in his book *'Political Geography: A New Introduction'* yet another concept which closely leans upon the 'mental maps' of policy-makers. In 1962, Kenneth Boulding published the book *'Conflict and Defense: A General Theory'*. In it, he suggested the concept *'critical boundaries'*; imaginary lines on the earth which policy makers consider to be fundamental political and ideological borders which should *always* be defended and enforced (Muir, 1997, p. 183). Boulding's ideas were especially relevant for the politics of the US during the Cold War. Today, such *'critical boundaries'* at global level are much less easy to identify. In the 'war on terrorism' –according to

ideas upon 'unspoken mental maps' in order to be able to better form a picture of the external world, as a fundamental tool to consider what kind of a foreign policy one should conduct (Henrikson, 1980, p. 496). Henrikson was of the opinion that the 'mental maps' of (American) policy makers could be brought to the surface by analysts via two main ways; (1°) devoting attention to the question how these decision makers see their environment, and what they say about it, or (2°) by investigating what decision makers do in practice:

- A *first way* consists of *identifying the 'geographical spirit' or ideology of the decision maker* (Henrikson, 1980, p. 508). Here the method of intellectual history and 'content analysis' can be utilized. The aim of such an investigation consists of identifying the central geographical concepts and related images which policy makers use in order to develop and legitimize their foreign policy. This can be achieved via a scrupulous analysis of the language (both visual and verbal) which is used in public speeches, in diplomatic notes, in treaty texts, etc.[21] The used geographical concepts can be very explicit and will, generally speaking, form coherent patterns. Yet, it is not easy to discover them. The fact that spatial-geographical terms so often appear in foreign policy texts suggests, according to Henrikson, that the very structure of the spatial mind of the decision maker is often made concrete this way (Henrikson, 1980, pp. 508–509). When one wants to work out to what extent the 'geographical mind' of decision makers impacts their foreign policy planning, this can be done via studying the *'image plans'* of decision makers (Tuan, 1975, p. 209; Henrikson, 1980, p. 512). This approach assumes that the foreign policy of a country is based upon certain 'previously imagined spatial patterns of the world' and of the place that the nation takes on this broader 'chess board' (e.g. Brzezinski's *'Arc of Crisis'*-concept; a term which was used by the Carter Administration, in particular after the invasion of the Soviets in Afghanistan) (Henrikson, 1980, pp. 515–516).
- A *second way* consists of *literally drawing the geographical field in which a policy maker moves*. According to Henrikson, one of the most effective approaches to determine the 'psycho-milieu' of a policy maker, is to describe his/her foreign policy behaviour geographically. For instance, one could represent all the foreign voyages of a policy maker on a map, with an indication of the dates and duration of the stay. Such *'itinerary maps'*

some a new central theme in today's international relations–, the 'enemy' is of a non-territorial nature.

21 An alternative could be that one asks *policy makers to draw a 'map of the world'* (so-called *'sketch maps'*); how do they 'imagine' the world? (see also: Saarinen, 1985 [1974]; Pinheiro, 1998).

are of course in themselves no mental maps, but rather hasty 'sketches' (Henrikson, 1980, pp. 510–511). Henrikson labels such 'spaces generated by activities' as *'behaviour-spaces'* (Henrikson, 1980, pp. 517–518). A note of criticism could however be; to what extent do such maps and itinerary summaries[22] offer the researcher any valuable data? At the most, one can distil some general trends, yet it remains fairly difficult to draw any far-reaching conclusions from this. Moreover, one could also defend the thesis that official foreign visits no longer carry the same weight and meaning in an era of direct communication via phone, fax and e-mail. Such overviews of official foreign visits are often studied only in a quantitative way, and thus risk to have little attention for the political weight that is attributed by leaders to certain partner countries. Each official foreign visit is analytically viewed at a similar level. In other words, the researcher has –via this 'method'– little or at least limited attention for the relative political weight that should be attributed to each of these official foreign policy visits.

In short, there exist two types of approaches to study the 'mental maps' of decision makers, and two types of corresponding 'evidence'. This first approach concentrates on what people see and say, as can be detected in the visual and verbal language. The second has attention for what decision makers in foreign policy do in practice, as can be detected through their travels (Henrikson, 1980, p. 512). Critics such as the political-geographer Klaus-John Dodds appropriately state that Henrikson does not seem to recognize that the analyst can 'affect' these 'observations'. Henrikson seems to ignore that it is rather problematic to assume that it would be possible to (re)present the activities of others (Dodds, 1994, p. 197). In the school of 'Critical Geopolitics', which originated at the end of the 1980s, these concerns are given much more attention. Alan K. Henrikson continued work on *'mental maps'*.[23] For instance, in 2002 he published an interesting article on the relation between *distance* and *foreign policy* (see: Henrikson, 2002). In response to the argument of some that distance is an 'illusion', Henrikson responds that it is still a *meaningful* illusion. Henrikson identifies three variations in which 'distance' still is relevant as a 'mental map'

---

22 In 2001, the Russian political-geographers Kolossov and Turovksy developed in their article *'Russian Geopolitics at the Fin-de-siecle'* a similar overview of the 'geographical distribution' of the visits of Russian political leaders with each of the countries of the 'Near Abroad' (period 1991–2000) (see: Kolossov and Turovsky, 2001, pp. 152–153).

23 The Canadian IR specialist John D. Young appropriately stresses that with the introduction of the idea of a *'mental representation'* or *'cognitive cartography'*, a form of *'bounded rationality'* was built in (Young, 1994, p. 272).

that influences foreign policy-decision-making (Henrikson, 2002, p. 437, pp. 460–462):

1. ***'Gravitational theory'*** is built upon the old idea that distant objects are more difficult to control than ones that are nearby. It also suggests that there is "no escaping" the power of gravity, for it is pervasive—unaffected by intervening objects, or defenses. *"Because the effect of force is in inverse proportion to the distance from its source,"* observed the political geographer Nicholas J. Spykman in his book *'America's Strategy in World Politics'*, *"widely spaced regions can preserve a certain degree of autonomy but they cannot hope to live in isolation"* (Spykman, 1942, p. 165) (cf. the *'loss of strength gradient'* of Spykman and Boulding). Nevertheless, such theories recognize that this principle can partly be 'corrected' by the scale of a political entity (*example 1.* the idea of a French-German core-Europe; *example 2.* the vision by many decision makers that an enlarged European Union will exert a force of attraction to its external environment);
2. ***'Topological space'*** is a generalization of Euclidean space in which the idea of closeness, or limits, is defined in terms of configurations of points, or point sets. A question is for instance whether it is better for nations, most of which now have achieved full legal and political independence, to remain "apart," in topological spaces of their own, rather than to become integrated into, and perhaps somewhat subsumed within, larger, encompassing, and to some extent supranational entities, such as the European Union (Henrikson, 2002, pp. 456–457).
3. The decision to associate or not, and perhaps even how to do so, depends not only on geographical mass (gravity) or on location (topology) but also on non-geographical affinities, that is, on the *attributes* that countries do, or do not, share (Henrikson, 2002, p. 457). ***'Attributional distance'*** for instance can explain why there exists a certain alienation or feeling of solidarity among countries *as a result of the alleged different/similar values and political convictions* (e.g. those who are against a Turkish membership of the EU often refer to negative attributions with respect to values and norms; they claim that there exists a value-gap between the current EU-members and Turkey).

'Mental maps' offer the analyst a useful picture of the way in which decision makers attribute a subjective meaning or 'value' to their environment. They constitute one of the few ways to deeper penetrate the world of the subjective perception and appreciation of 'environmental variables' by decision makers. This 'Cognitive Geopolitics' has however not yet fully been 'crystallized out' on a methodological level; only a limited number of researchers applied the broader concept of *'mental maps'* to questions of foreign policy[24], although some IR scholars did refer to 'mental maps' in their work.[25]

4.3 *The Sprouts as Agenda-Setters within IR/FPA on 'Ecological Questions'*

Concerning the impact of the work of the Sprouts on IR and FPA, one last aspect can be mentioned. As regards content, Harold and Margaret Sprout can be considered to be researchers who early on during the 1970's demanded more attention for ecological questions. IR specialists such as John Groom recognize the 'ecological paradigm' as developed by the Sprouts as a very important contribution (Groom, 2003, p. 8): *"Harold and Margaret Sprout deserve our thanks for keeping the ecological aspects of human affairs on the agenda."*

4.4 *Conclusion*

The examples just mentioned offer an overview of the far-reaching impact that the Sprouts have had on IR and FPA. A number of behavioralist IR analytical frameworks, in particular the first analytical research-models of 'foreign policy', could only take shape after the more fundamental theoretical-philosophical reflection on the relation between 'territoriality' and 'politics' of Harold and Margaret Sprout. Especially their conceptual work and philosophy of science could be considered to be one of the first impulses to cognitive-behavioralist approaches within IR and to the foundation of 'Foreign Policy Analysis'. All these elements moreover form strong indicators that 'Geopolitics' also formed an important body of literature that helped scholars in the 1950s and '60s to devise new analytical frameworks.

---

24 In the historical study *'Variable geography: America's mental maps of a Greater Europe'*, the IR-specialist Martin Walker tries to develop an insight into the way in which subsequent American policy-makers saw Europe, based upon studying officially published American documents on foreign policy (see: Walker, 2000). Outside of IR, one can also find approaches which are quite similar to Henrikson's mental maps. An example of this is the study by three Russian psychologists, called *'Russian Citizens' Representations of the Country's Position in the Geopolitical Space of the Commonwealth of Independent States, Europe, and the World'* (see: Petrenko, Mitina et al., 2003). The aim of this study was to reconstruct the 'geopolitical' categories via which the Russians perceive the CIS, Europa and the world.

25 Kenneth E. Boulding for instance explicitly referred in 1991 to Peter Gould's book *'Mental Maps'* in a chapter called *'The Nature and Causes of National and Military Self-Images in Relation to War and Peace'*, in the reader *'The Political Geography of Conflict and Peace'* (Boulding, 1991, p. 145).

5 The Ontological, Epistemological and Methodological Assumptions and Traits of 'Cognitive Geopolitics'

The research tradition of 'Cognitive Geopolitics' can be reconstructed on the basis of its ontological, epistemological and methodological components;

a. ONTOLOGICALLY, the following assumptions are at work within 'Cognitive Geopolitics':
    1. The idea that states are the most important political entities. They do not function as organisms – 'state action' entails "those deeds performed by those who act on behalf of the state".
    2. The idea that *'Erdgebundenheit'* (environmental determinism) does not exist. The relationship between 'territoriality' and 'politics' operates within an 'ecological triad' (environment, environed entities and their mutual relationship). Moreover, there exists an 'operational' and a 'psycho'-milieu.

       Besides the principles formulated above, one could also mention some other elements as possible 'ontological principles' of 'Cognitive Geopolitics', although one does not always see these aspects in the interpretations of other cognitive-behavioralists:
    3. "There exists an uneven distribution of physical and human 'resources' (cf. climate patterns, topology, available resources, human societies, etc.). This unequal distribution influences in significant ways all human enterprise, interactions, relations and inter-state relations".
    4. "Change and transformation are inherent to international relations. As technology develops further, so increases global interdependence".

b. FROM AN EPISTEMOLOGICAL POINT OF VIEW, it is characteristic of 'Cognitive Geopolitics' that it refuses to subscribe to the implicit assumption of 'Classical Geopolitics' that it would be possible to explain or predict the (power relations within) international politics as a system based upon "objective laws of nature". In practice, 'Cognitive Geopolitics' looks at a lower level of analysis; that of the decision maker. There where 'Classical Geopolitics' departed from the assumption that the environment had a mere objective nature, 'Cognitive Geopolitics' states that *the decision making is influenced by the environment as a subjective given*. The perception of central (foreign policy) decision makers is central in this. Consequently, the first task of the geopolitical scholar is not so much to take inventory of the physical- and social-geographical environmental variables. Rather one should devote attention to the way in which a decision maker attributes a certain value to his/her environment. As regards the results of the (foreign-)policy decisions, one does have attention for the objective or operational environment. In short, 'Cognitive Geopolitics' starts from a certain tension between the 'objective' and the 'subjective' environment. However, the scholar is considered to be capable of making a distinction between both.

c. METHODOLOGICALLY, 'Cognitive Geopolitics' tries to fathom the actions of individual decision makers by examining their "beliefs" on the external environment. A clear 'methodology' for such studies was never really developed. However, one can discover within the cognitive-behavioralist literature of the 1960s and '70s some approaches that could be potentially useful; 'belief systems' (O. Holsti), 'operational belief code system' (A. George), 'mental maps' (P. Gould, R. White, A. Henrikson), 'sketch maps' (T. Saarinen), etcetera. Since 'Cognitive Geopolitics' was 'encapsulated' within the IR-subfield of Comparative Foreign Policy, the methodology in fact was not 'crystallised out'. Today one can, however, from time to time find publications within *'Environmental Psychology'* that more or less build upon this tradition.[26]

---

26 The fundamental reflection of the Sprouts also caused a new research tradition to develop within IR, in 1991; the so-called *'New Geopolitics'*-school of Harvey Starr. This focuses especially on the study of the role of geographical factors in the coming into being and the spread of wars. It developed its own *'environmental model'* for the study of the impact of geographical factors in foreign policy. The names which are often mentioned in this research tradition, are; Harvey Starr, Benjamin Most, Michael D. Ward, Randolph M. Siverson, Gary Goertz and Paul F. Diehl (see: Most and Starr, 1980; Siverson and Starr, 1992; Goertz, 1994). It is nevertheless a fact that the concepts of (external) *'opportunity'* and (domestic) *'willingness'* as developed by Harvey Starr in 1978 (and built upon the scholarship of the Sprouts and others in 'Geopolitics') have over the decades developed into central tools in the study of international conflicts. Attention is for instance given to the role of geographical factors or so-called 'context variables' in the coming into being and spread of wars (see for instance: Most & Starr 1980), in *the creation of alliances* (see: Starr, 1990), also in the *spread of democracy* (see: Starr, 1991). Starr more or less equated 'opportunity' with *'environmental possibilism'*, whereas 'willingness' is equated with the epistemological positions of *'environmental probabilism'* and *'cognitive behavioralism'*. In short, Starr's approach pretends to be more comprehensive. For instance, before policy-makers take a decision to 'go to war', both 'opportunity' and 'willingness' need to be present, though these are not sufficient conditions. 'Geography' constitutes but one influencing factor. Moreover, *'opportunity'* and *'willingness'* are linked to one another; in case the 'opportunity' to 'go to war' is substantial, then there perhaps exists among decision-makers more 'willingness' to do so (Diehl, 1991, p. 15). The *opportunity-willingness*-framework which grew out of the geopolitical literature therefore provides a usable analytical framework, although according to some the disadvantage is that it offers only limited opportunities for theory building (see: Mouritzen, 1998, p. 24).

6 Some Critiques on 'Cognitive Geopolitics' & Some Ideas on the Continued Relevance Today of the Work of Harold and Margaret Sprout

What criticism can be formulated against 'Cognitive Geopolitics'? Since this approach was 'encapsulated' in *'Foreign Policy Analysis'*, some standard criticism on the behavioralist literature of *'psychological factors'* in foreign policy analysis can be reiterated.

6.1 *Criticism 1: A Blind Belief in Positivism (The Inclination to Approach 'Beliefs' in a (Solely) Quantitative Way)*

'Cognitive Geopolitics', encapsulated with Foreign Policy Analysis (cf. the *"Snyder-Bruck-Sapin-model"*), has an inclination to approach beliefs in a solely quantitative way. Some researchers question whether it is possible to gather enough useful information through these quantitative models (Larsen, 1997, pp. 7–9), and whether or not such analyses should be complemented with other approaches.

6.2 *Criticism 2: The a-Historical Nature of Cognitive Behavioralism*

A second criticism focuses on the lower 'unit of analysis' of cognitive behavioralism. The political-geographers John O'Loughlin and Herman van der Wusten refer to the fact that the behavioralist school, because of its focus upon the concrete behaviour of decision makers, *devoted little attention to theory-building*, and also has a rather *a-historical attitude* (O'Loughlin and van der Wusten, 1986, p. 485). Opposed to this, there is the position of 'Classical Geopolitics' that, because of its highly generalizing nature, assumes that the geographical conditions of countries do not change, and thus that in the past, similar 'geopolitical patterns' "dictated" the foreign policy of a nation into a certain direction. Such a position is hard to defend within a cognitive-behavioralist approach. After all, cognitive-behavioralists assume that throughout history, the *perception* of each decision maker about the environment which surrounds him was and is *unique*. Certain conclusions on the 'world view' of a decision maker are thus much less easy to generalize upon. This brings us to a third point of criticism…

6.3 *Criticism 3: "Methodological Individualism" or the Tendency to Concentrate Research on the Level of the Individual Decision Maker*

Partly thanks to the work of the Sprouts a school within IR was created that tries to understand foreign policy starting from the level of the individual decision maker as 'unit of analysis'. According to IR specialist Henrik Larsen the existing literature about (individual) *'belief systems'* suffers from the problem that the relation between the beliefs of the individual and the more 'general line' of the foreign policy never becomes totally clear (Larsen, 1997, p. 4). On the other hand, the IR specialist Kenneth Boulding approaches the *'image'* of the environment as a 'broad social concept' (Boulding, 1969 [1959]). Yet, according to Larsen, Boulding is quite unclear about the question whether this 'image' finds its origin with the individual or within a broader social context. Some researchers will rather expand their perspective to include the vision of certain elites, in which this group becomes 'individualised' (Larsen, 1997, pp. 4–5). In short, the literature of *'Foreign Policy Analysis'* to a certain extent seems to suffer under what some have called the **'problem of methodological individualism'**. Some approaches within FPA offer only a limited description and explanation of the way in which material interests, ideas and institutions interact with one another (Lee, 1995, p. 146). The reason why the focus of FPA researchers so often is concentrated on individuals (or central political decision makers) lies in the fact that this is easier from a methodological point of view. This is for that matter a result of the often positivist approach within *'Foreign Policy Analysis'* to try to read *'beliefs'* as accurately as possible, preferably by even quantifying them to some extent. The question is whether individual decision makers always play a decisive role in the foreign policy process. Earlier in this chapter the criticism of Hyam Gold was identified, who stated that when there are a lot of bureaucratic decision-making-processes within a foreign policy, then the 'cognitive behavioralist' approach will not always be useable. According to Larsen, the impact of individual decision makers in 'normal' decisions is less decisive, while individuals may have much more impact in crisis situations. This also explains why in Robert Jervis' book *'Perception and Misperception in International Politics'* so many examples are mentioned of crisis situations; central decision makers do play a role of some meaning in them (and will have more opportunities to push through their own visions of the world during a crisis situation). Jervis' conclusions are thus not immediately transposable to 'normal' decision making processes on foreign policy (Larsen, 1997, p. 5).

6.4 *Criticism 4: The Assumption That 'Language' forms a Transparant Medium, without Its Own Dynamics (The Inadequate Attention for 'Inter-Subjectivity')*

In conclusion, the traditional literature assumes that language can be approached as a 'transparant medium', which passes on *'meanings'* easily without any changes as regards content (Larsen, 1997, p. 9). Alan K. Henrikson for instance proposes to compose and analyse the 'mental maps' of central decision makers via studying the foreign policy discourse of decision makers. However, he does not mention the possibility that the utilized discourse itself could perhaps even 'dictate' certain meanings to reality. In other words, cognitive-behavioralists believe in a 'direct perception' of the environment, which manifests itself via the utilized language (Jimenez, 1997, p. 55). In the 1990s, the school of 'Critical Geopolitics' developed an 'amendment' to this; contrary to 'Cognitive Geopolitics' it believed that the perception of a spatial environment takes place within a broader societal and political context – it is constructed via discourse as a "power structure". From this point of view, one could state that 'cognitive behavioralists' devote much less attention to the role that is played by language in the creation of meanings (cf. limited attention to a possible 'inter-subjectivity'). The Sprouts recognized that both the practice of foreign policy and the IR field itself were permeated by geopolitical reasonings and assumptions.[27] Their more nuanced, holistic framework of analysis (the *'ecological paradigm'*) forms one of the most important and original contributions from inside IR on the relationship 'territoriality' & foreign policy/ international politics.

6.5 *The Continued Relevance Today of the Work of Harold and Margaret Sprout*

This chapter has shown that the work of Harold and Margaret Sprout on cognitive behavioralism, and on the tensions between the 'psychological' and the 'operational' milieu, has had a fundamental impact upon Foreign Policy Analysis. In many ways, it is thus fitting to view their work as 'paradigmatic'; today's FPA scholars are in many ways intellectually tributary to the "revolution" that was started by Harold and Margaret Sprout. Moreover, they illustrated the continuing relevance of 'geopolitical factors' in foreign policy, although perhaps in more subtle ways compared to the period before 1945.

In chapter 8 of this book, Luis da Vinha further builds upon the work by Harold and Margaret Sprout to conduct an applied analysis of geographic mental maps and the Emergence of the Carter Doctrine.

27 See: *"Those who practice statecraft, as well as those who study and write about it, seem generally to take for granted that the phenomenon called 'international politics' is meaningfully related to the setting or environment or milieu in which political decisions are taken and executed."* (Sprout & Sprout 1957: 309). In *'The Ecological Perspective on Human Relations with Special Reference to International Politics'* added (Sprout & Sprout 1971 [1965]: 6–7): *"[those who interpret and theorize about international politics] seldom exhibit much awareness of the connotations of [environmental terms]. They exhibit even less concern with the instrumental mechanisms of man-environment relationships which, as a general rule, they simply take uncritically for granted."*

Bibliography

Baldwin, D. A. (2002). Power and International Relations. In W. Carlsnaes, & Risse, T., Simmons B. (Eds.). *Handbook of International Relations*. London: SAGE Publications: 177–191.

Boulding, K. E. (1969 [1959]). National Images and International Systems. In R. E. Kasperson, & Minghi, J. V. (Eds.). *The Structure of Political Geography*. Chicago: Aldine Publishing Company: 341–349.

Boulding, K. E. (1973). Foreword. In R. M. Downs & Stea, D. (Eds.). *Image and Environment. Cognitive Mapping and Spatial Behavior.* Chicago: Aldine Publishing Company: vii-xi.

Boulding, K. E. (1991). The Nature and Causes of National and Military Self-Images in Relation to War and Peace. In N. Kliot, & Waterman, S. (Eds.). *The Political Geography of Conflict and Peace*. London, Belhaven Press: 142–152.

Coogan, P. (1991). *Geopolitics and the Intellectual Origins of Containment*, Chapel Hill: University of Carolina at Chapel Hill.

Coolsaet, R. (1998). *België en zijn buitenlandse politiek*. Leuven: Uitgeverij Van Halewyck.

Criekemans, D. (2007). *Geopolitiek: 'geografisch geweten' van de buitenlandse politiek?* Antwerpen: Garant.

Diehl, P. F. (1991). Geography and War: A Review and Assessment of the Empirical Literature. *International Interactions. Empirical and Theoretical Research in International Relations.*, 17(1): 11–28.

Dodds, K. (1994). Geopolitics and foreign policy: recent developments in Anglo-American political geography and international relations. *Progress in Human Geography. An international review of geographic work in the social sciences and the humanities*, 18(2): 186–208.

Dougherty, J., & Pfaltzgraff, R. (1981). Environmental Theories. In *Contending Theories of International Relations. A Comprehensive Survey*. New York: Harper Collins Publishers: 54–83.

Downs, R., & Stea, D. (Eds.). (1973). *Image and Environment. Cognitive Mapping and Spatial Behavior*. Chicago: Aldine Publishing Company.

Fox, W. (1985). Geopolitics and International Relations. In Zoppo, C., Zorgbibe, C., *On Geopolitics: Classical and Nuclear*. Dordrecht: Martinus Nijhoff Publishers: 15–44.

Geeraerts, G. (2003). Theorie van de Internationale Betrekkingen - Transparanten: 4.2. Buitenlandse politieke besluitvorming. Brussel: Vrije Universiteit Brussel.

Goertz, G. (1994). *Contexts of International Politics*. Cambridge: Cambridge University Press.

Gold, H. (1978). Foreign Policy Decision-Making and the Environment: The Claims of Snyder, Brecher and the Sprouts. *International Studies Quarterly*, 22 (December): 569–586.

Goldstein, J., & Keohane R. O. (Eds). (1995). *Ideas & Foreign Policy. Beliefs, Institutions and Political Change.* London: Cornell University Press.

Gould, P. (1973). On Mental Maps. In R. M. Downs, & Stea, D. (Eds.). *Image and Environment. Cognitive Mapping and Spatial Behavior.* Chicago: Aldine Publishing Company: 182–220.

Gould, P. & White R. (1985 [1974]). *Mental Maps.* Winchester, USA: Allen & Unwin Inc.

Gould, P. (1991). Mental Maps. In Dunbar, G. S., *Modern Geography. An Encyclopedic Survey.* Chicago & London: St. James Press: p. 113.

Groom, A. J. R. (2003). *International Relations: Never just an American Social Science.* European Political Science Network 2003 Annual Conference Proceedings.

Henrikson, A. K. (1980). The Geographical "Mental Maps" of American Foreign Policy Makers. *International Political Science Review*, 1(4), 495–530.

Henrikson, A. K. (2002). Distance and Foreign Policy: A Political Geography Approach. *International Political Science Review/ Revue internationale de science politique*, 23(4 (October)), 437–466.

Hersh, M. (2003). Township Activist Celebrates Centennial Birthday. *Town Topics - Princeton's Weekly Community Newspaper since 1946.* Princeton, New Jersey. LVII.

Holsti, O. R. (1989). Models of International Relations and Foreign Policy. *Diplomatic History* (Winter), 15–43.

Houghton, D. P. (1996). The Role of Analogical Reasoning in Novel Foreign-Policy Situations. *British Journal of Political Science*, 26, 523–552.

Hudson, V. M., & Sims, S. M. (et al). (1993). The Domestic Political Context of Foreign Policy-Making: explicating a Theoretical Construct. In D. Skidmore, & Hudson, V. (Eds.) *The Limits of State Autonomy. Societal Groups and Foreign Policy Formulation.* Boulder, Colorado: Westview Press: 25–48.

Hudson, V. M. (2008). The history and evolution of foreign policy analysis. In S. Smith, & Hadfield, A., Dunne, T. (Eds.). *Foreign Policy: Theories, Actors and Cases.* Oxford: Oxford University Press: 11–29.

Itoh, M. (1995). *Japan-Southeast Asia Relations: Perception Gaps, Legacy of World War II, and Economic Diplomacy.* Asian Studies on the Pacific Coast (ASPAC) Conference,, Pacific University, Forest Grove, Oregon.

Jervis, R. (1976). *Perception and Misperception in International Politics.* Princeton, New Jersey: Princeton University Press.

Jimenez, M. (1997). *La psychologie de la perception.* s.l.: Flammarion.

Kolossov, V., & Turovsky R., (2001). Russian Geopolitics at the Fin-de-siecle. *Geopolitics*, 6(1), 141–164.

Larsen, H., (1997). *Foreign Policy and Discourse Analysis. France, Britain and Europe.* London, Routledge/London School of Economics.

Lee, K. (1995). A neo-Gramscian approach to international organization: an expanded analysis of current reforms to UN development activities. In J. Macmillan, & Linklater, A. (Eds.). *Boundaries in Question. New Directories in International Relations.* London, Pinter Publishers: 144–162.

Mason, A. (1978). *The Department of Politics. A Princeton Companion.* A. Leitch: Princeton University Press.

Morgenthau, H. J. (1978). *Politics Among Nations. The Struggle for Power and Peace.* New York.: Afred A. Knopf.

Most, B. A., & Starr, H., (1980). Diffusion, Reinforcement, Geopolitics, and the Spread of War. *American Political Science Review*, 74 (4 (December)): 932–946.

Mouritzen, H. (1998). *Theory and Reality of International Politics.* Aldershot: Ashgate.

Muir, R. (1997). *Political Geography. A New Introduction.* London: Macmillan Press, Ltd.

Olson, W. C., & Groom, A. J. R. (1991). *International Relations Then & Now. Origins and Trends in Interpretation.* London: Harper Collins Academic.

O'Loughlin, J., van der Wusten, H., (1986). Geography, war and peace: notes for a contribution to a revived political geography. *Progress in Human Geography. An international review of geographic work in the social sciences and the humanities*, 10(4): 484–510.

Petrenko, V. F., & Mitina O. V., et al. (2003). Russian Citizens' Representations of the Country's Position in the Geopolitical Space of the Commonwealth of Independent States, Europe, and the World. *European Psychologist*, 8(4 (December)), 238–251.

Pinheiro, J. Q. (1998). Determinants of cognitive maps of the world as expressed in sketch maps.*Journal of Environmental Psychology*, 18, 321–339.

Rosati, J. A. (1995). A Cognitive Approach to the Study of Foreign Policy. In Neack L., Hey, , Haney, P. *Foreign Policy Analysis. Continuity and Change in Its Second Generation.* Engelwood Cliffs, New Jersey, Prentice Hall: 49–70.

Rosenau, J., & Davis V., et al. (1972). *The Analysis of International Politics. Essays in Honor of Harold and Margaret Sprout.* New York: The Free Press.

Saarinen, T. F. (1985 [1974]). Students Views of the World. In P. Gould, & White, R. (Eds.). *Mental Maps.* Winchester, USA: Allen & Unwin Inc.: 148–161.

Siverson, R. M., & Starr, H., (1992). Opportunity, Willingness and the Diffusion of War. In Ward, M. D. (Ed.) *The New Geopolitics.* Philadelphia, Pennsylvania, Gordon and Breach Science Publishers: 159–182.

Soetendorp, R. (1994). Analyse van buitenlands beleid. In K. Koch, & Soetendorp, R., van Staden, A. (Eds.), *Internationale Betrekkingen. Theorieën en Benaderingen.* Utrecht, NL, Uitgeverij Het Spectrum: 40–66.

Smith, S. (1986). Theories of foreign policy: an historical overview. *Review of International Studies*, 12: 13–29.

Snyder, R. C., & Bruck, H. W., et al. (1962). Decision-Making as an Approach to the Study of International Politics. In R. C. Snyder, & Bruck H. W., Sapin B. M. (Eds.), *Foreign Policy Decision Making. An Approach to the Study of International Politics.* New York, The Free Press of Glencoe (The Macmillan Company): 14–185.

Sprout, H. (1931). Political Geography as a Political Science Field, *American Political Science Review*, 25, 439–442.

Sprout, H., & Sprout, M. (1944 [1939]). *The Rise of American Naval Power, 1776–1918*. Princeton, USA, Princeton University Press.

Sprout, H., & Sprout, M. (1945). *Foundations of National Power. Readings on World Politics and American Security*. New York: D. Van Nostrand Company, Inc.

Sprout, H., & Sprout, M. (1957). Environmental Factors in the Study of International Politics, *The Journal of Conflict Resolution*, 1, 309–328.

Sprout, H. (1963). Geopolitical hypotheses in technological perspective, *World Politics*, XV, 187–212.

Sprout, H., & Sprout, M. (1964). Geography and International Politics in an Era of Revolutionary Change. In W. A. Douglas Jackson (Ed.). *Politics and Geographic Relationships. Reading on the Nature of Political Geography*. London: Prentice-Hall International, Inc.: 34–52.

Sprout, H., & Sprout, M. (1967 [1962]). *Foundations of International Politics*. Princeton (New Jersey), Van Nostrand.

Sprout, H., & Sprout, M. (1968). *An Ecological Paradigm for the Study of International Politics*. Princeton: Center for International Studies, Woodrow Wilson School of Public and International Affairs, Princeton University.

Sprout, H., & Sprout, M. (1971 [1965]). *The Ecological Perspective on Human Relations with Special Reference to International Politics*. Westport, Connecticut: Greenwood Press, Publishers.

Spykman, N. (1942). *America's Strategy in World Politics. The United States and the Balance of Power*. New York, Harcourt Brace.

Starr, H. (1990). Alliances and geopolitics. *Political Geography Quarterly*, 9(3), 232–248.

Starr, H. (1991). Joining Political and Geographic Perspectives: Geopolitics and International Relations. *International Interactions. Empirical and Theoretical Research in International Relations.*, 17(1), 1–10.

Starr, H. (1992). Joining Political and Geographic Perspectives: Geopolitics and International Relations. In Ward, M. D. (Ed.) *The New Geopolitics*. Philadelphia, Pennsylvania: Gordon and Breach Science Publishers: 1–10.

Strausz-Hupé, R. (1945). *The Balance of Tomorrow. A Reappraisal of Basic Trends in World Politics*. Philadelphia, University of Pennsylvania.

Tuan, Y.-F. (1975). Images and mental maps. *Annals of the Association of American Geographers*, 65(June), 205–213.

Walker, M. (2000). Variable geography: America's mental maps of a Greater Europe. *International Affairs*, 76(3), 459–474.

Young, J. D. (1994). Approches et développements de la géopolitique française. In Montifroy, G. A., *Géopolitiques Internationales*. Paris: Editions Frison-Roche: 267–292.

CHAPTER 5

Analysing Geopolitical Myths: Towards a Method for Analytic Geopolitics

Antonios Nestoras

1 Introduction

Mirroring the postmodern trends that have been sweeping the discipline of IR and other major academic disciplines in the past three decades, geopolitics has also seen a fundamental shift of philosophical assumptions that underline theoretical approaches in the field. What was essentially conceived at the turn of the twentieth century as a reflection on how geography affects (or should affect) the power and by extent the grand strategy of states, in the end of the same century geopolitics was criticised as a textual, linguistic and ideological practice of statecraft. Instead of scientific treatises, geopolitical theories came to be understood as instruments of power and reflections of the socio-political agendas of hierarchies, interest groups and state bureaucracies.

In the course of the twentieth century, this shift from Classical Geopolitics to Critical Geopolitics was largely ontological and epistemological in nature and it replicated the standard dualisms previously introduced in the discipline of IR with the advent of the postmodern condition. In ontological terms, the scientific materialism of Classical Geopolitics (i.e. the belief that there is a material reality that has essential properties) was overturned by the social constructivism of Critical Geopolitics (i.e. reality has no essential properties, only relative, socially constructed properties). In epistemological terms, the positivism of Classical Geopolitics (i.e. through geographical survey and philosophical reflection we can know the essential properties of the material reality) was substituted by the interpretivist stance of Critical Geopolitics (i.e. without fixed essential properties, reality is relative to the ideological interpretation of the observer).

These dualisms – materialism vs. idealism and positivism vs. interpretivism – outline a Classical/Critical divide in geopolitics, which diverts scholarly attention from important research questions, puts the field in an unfavourable position, and reduces its potential to understand and explain patterns of behaviour in IR that may be grounded in geography.

 | DOI:10.1163/9789004432086_007

This chapter reviews the philosophical assumptions that underline geopolitics through the prisms of New Materialism and Critical Realism and, drawing from the growing literature on political myth, attempts to initiate a discussion on possible new research directions for geopolitics. The proposed approach, called *Analytic Geopolitics*, as a structural analysis of geopolitical myths into their constitutive elements, their historical emergence and their effect on patterns of state behaviour, it offers a new grounding of the discipline of IR, not only on geography, but also on history, culture and politics.

2 Beyond the Classical/Critical Divide

Geopolitics has a troubled past and a puzzling present as a distinct inquiry into domestic and international politics, but it also seems to hold great potential in explaining behavioural patterns of the modern, territorial state. The relationship between politics and geography may seem at times so obvious that it is beyond demonstration; what is more uncertain and contentious, enigmatic even, is the socio-political processes that mediate this relationship.

Looking back at the course of scholarship spanning the twentieth century, one can discern a lineage of Classical geopolitical thinkers who acknowledged space as a material container of politics and purported to study the impact of physical geography on politics (Mackinder, 1904; Spykman, 1944; Cohen, 1963; Gray, 1991; Cohen, 2003; Gray, 2005). In Classical Geopolitics, physical geography and other related material factors (e.g. mineral resources) are independent variables that influence the power, the strategic culture and the behaviour of a state.

More recently, in the 1990s, drawing from a critique of Classical Geopolitics, there emerged the so-called Critical Geopolitics, a postmodern approach understanding geography as a social construction subjected to power relationships and political or ideological agendas. From this angle, geography is what people make of it, and geopolitical theories are discourses forged by privileged, powerful elites, such as state bureaucracies, politicians and the media, academics and think tanks (Dalby, 1990; Agnew and Corbridge, 1995; Tuathail, 1996; Tuathail and Dalby, 1998; Agnew, 1998). In turn, these loaded representations of geography enchain individuals and the state apparatus to an undesirable way of thinking, speaking and acting; and therefore the stated aim of Critical Geopolitics is to deconstruct geopolitical texts, to expose their artificiality and neutralise their political function as instruments of power and control.

The boundary between these diametrically opposite viewpoints marks out an irreconcilable Classical/critical divide in the field of geopolitics. Acutely different ontological and epistemological assumptions about geography underline this divide. On the one hand, Classical Geopolitics assumes that geography is an external reality with essential properties that we can know; in this sense, geography is inescapable, immutable and imposes discernible limitations or opportunities on states. On the other hand, Critical Geopolitics assumes that we cannot know any essential properties of geography, only its various meanings that are socially constructed by political actors in existing power structures.

The problem with the Classical/Critical divide is that it is somewhat debilitating for both approaches. For one, considering how difficult it is to determine the 'true value' of physical geography independently of a given socio-political context, it is relatively easy to criticise Classical Geopolitics as a pseudo-science, or an academic inquiry loaded with ideological biases and instrumental abuses of geography. At the same time, however, there is a good deal of warranted criticism directed at Critical Geopolitics as well.

First, the issue with textual deconstruction in Critical Geopolitics is that it 'can only take place through reapplying the very form of meaning-construction that is deconstructed' (Müller, 2013, p. 51). In turn, this alternative construction of meaning appears as an interpretation of superior insight and perception, which contains its own 'will to power' and claims to truth (Sharp, 2000, pp. 361–362; see also Sparke, 2000).

Second, these double standards are absorbed by a correspondence of Critical Geopolitics with critical theory, applying scientific knowledge for socio-political critique and emancipatory aims (Kelly, 2006). In this context, criticism becomes a sort of political activism, or a responsibility to help society break free from the political restrictions imposed by the powerful.

Last but not least, the excessive focus on the text and the motives of the authors also implies a complete detachment from material conditions (such as economic modes of production and technology) that may affect mental representations. This disproportionate focus on socially constructed meaning has been criticised even from prominent post-modernists in the field of political geography (Harvey, 1990).

Overall, the impression one gets from theoretical inconsistencies and the general moralization in Critical Geopolitics in particular, but also in critical approaches in general is that this kind of criticism is running 'out of steam' (Latour, 2004) and losing touch with political and social realities.

For Critical Geopolitics there is no objective material reality worth speaking of, there are only social representations subjected to ideological agendas. However, even if we were to accept that there are no objective facts in geopolitical theories (or anywhere else for that matter), even if we were to accept that our view of the world, our maps, our borders, our strategy, like most of our intellectual artefacts were pure social constructs (they are, after all, produced by human beings), then these artificial constructs may take on a life of their own, sometimes irrespective of the intentions and the agendas of their creators, and leave a material footprint on the political process.

Under what circumstances a social construct as a geopolitical theory can become so embedded in public discourse that is accepted as common sense? Where does the power of socially constructed concepts of geography come from? What is the deep structure of a geopolitical theory that allows it to generate legitimacy for specific decisions and policies? This is just a small fraction of the significant and consequential questions that are left unanswered in the current entrenchment of the field in a Classical/Critical divide, which impedes our ability to understand the role of geography in domestic and international politics and our insight into the spatial dimension of international relations.

There is no going back to the simplistic conceptions of the world in Classical Geopolitics, but there is also little space for novelty in front of us in the form of criticism and deconstruction. Geopolitics would do well to consider how to move beyond the caveats of the Classical/Critical divide and towards new modes of inquiry; how to take stock of a number of philosophical 'turns' in social science and, in this way, to re-think its place in the study of international relations and conceptualise an inquiry that builds some distance from both Classical and Critical Geopolitics.

First, geopolitics could engage with the literature on New Materialism and work with the assumption that material conditions and mental representations are co-constructing the social world (Coole and Frost, 2010; see also Barad, 2007; Latour, 2005; Bennet, 2004). In this sense, social constructs should not be considered as completely detached from material circumstances. In contrast, within the context of certain socio-political processes, material objects (like geographical features, in the case of geopolitics) can become active elements in the production of social constructs. In this sense, geopolitics could be concerned not with studying what geography is, but with what it does (Fox and Alldred, 2017). This is a shift from ontology to agency, which involves a revision of the critical agenda of geopolitics, in line with a more pragmatist approach as in the Latourian idea of moving from 'matters of facts to matters of concern' (Latour, 2004, p. 231).

Second, and in order to avoid an essentialist and deterministic slide, geopolitics could also engage with the philosophical or meta-theoretical stance of critical realism. A philosophy of science, critical realism posits that the world we study in social sciences – the social world – may be based on the natural world, but it is not reducible to facts and objects, in the same way that the biological organisms are dependent on chemical reactions but are not reducible to them (Collier, 1994, pp. 107–136; see also Bhaskar, 1975; 1979; Archer, 1995; Stenmetz, 1998; Sayer, 2000; Vandenberghe, 2015; Price and Martin, 2018) Geography may not be easily verifiable and quantifiable; nevertheless, knowledge of the geopolitical condition of the world is still possible. Not in the form of models, theories or other law-like forms with deterministic cause/effect explanations, but in probabilistic forms, or in other words, a reasonable expectation based on observable patterns of state behaviour.

A range of IR scholars have recently drawn from this critical realist mix in order to: clarify the philosophical underpinnings of IR and open up new paths of inquiry (Jackson, 2016); problematize and re-conceptualize centrepiece IR notions such as state power (Jessop, 2007); re-think core ontological elements of IR investigations such as agency, structure and causation (Kurki, 2008; Wight, 2008); or to examine the sociological implications of IR study objects such as international organizations (Joseph, 2014). It seems like in IR, critical realism has been helpful in lessening the tension between post-positivists (e.g. neorealism-neoliberalism) and post-modern interpretivists (e.g. constructivism). However, in geopolitics we are yet to see such philosophical re-alignments. Still, in the context of the material/ideational and positivist/interpretivist divides, critical realism seems to offer a novel way forward.

Third, in line with yet another 'turn' in social science that deals with narratives as 'basic forms of social life' (Czarniawska, 2005, pp. 1–3), geopolitics could also engage with the growing literature on political myth and move from deconstructing texts and discourses, to taking up the concept of political myth as the object of its study. A myth is a dramatic narrative that specifies a desirable action, performance or pattern of social behaviour (Malinowski, 2011; Eliade, 2009; Lévi-Strauss, 1979). By the same token, a political myth is a narrative that encodes a model of political behaviour and identity, or explains the origins and purpose of a political community and increases cohesion and unity (Tudor, 1973; Meyer and Rowan, 1977; Friedrich, 1963; Smith, 2009; Schopflin and Hosking, 2014; Nancy and Connor, 2012; Bell, 2003).

The use of myth in IR has seen a large range of applications, which, by and large, fall under the broad categories of post-modern and, more specifically, post-structuralist approaches. From their critical standpoint, the discipline of IR itself is based on political interpretations of history (Buffet and Heuser, 1998); and the IR theories are almost always a collection of myths that serve as axiomatic truths (Weber, 2014). For example the concept of myth has been used in attempts to expose the artificiality of fundamental concepts, such as those of sovereignty contained in the Westphalia Treaties, as the 'mythical' origins of the modern international system (Teschke, 2003; Osiander, 2001);

attempts to expose the mythical status of the end of the First World War for the First Great Debate in IR (Carvalho, Leira and Hobson, 2015; Wilson, 1998); to reveal the artificiality and mythical function of the concept of the balance of power in the thought of Classical IR scholars (Little, 2009); or to uncover the Eurocentric mythology of IR (Hobson, 2012). In general, myth in IR has been understood as false history serving as a 'powerful paradigmatic narrative or a deeply engrained commonly held belief' (Bliesemann, 2016, p. 1). For the most part, the application of the concept of myth on IR has been 'mostly reduced to a 'myth-busting' or 'uncovering' role of sorts'.

The approach of myth as inherently false and the attempt to expose this falseness bears a resemblance to the deconstruction of geopolitical theories and texts from critical approaches. This is a view of myth as something detached from a material reality, an artificial construct that needs to be exposed and uncovered. There is also, however, another path that leads to a usefulness of the concept of myth in IR and geopolitics, which however rests upon a different understanding of myth. This understanding points to a reflective, philosophical function of myth that interacts with core psychological processes of human beings and eschews the casual pejorative definitions, and the binary distinctions of myth versus reason, fiction versus reality, and truth versus falsehood.

From this angle, political myths may instead be vital for people, societies and nation-states because they are associated with people's profound psychological 'need for significance' (Blumenberg, 2010; Bottici, 2010; Bottici and Challand, 2012; 2014). Significance does not refer to a design or purpose, neither an ultimate meaning in religious terms; what significance means essentially is to have a rightful place in a vast and indifferent world. In this regard, significance seems to be a function of psychosomatic processes like emotions, feelings and identity. To the extent that identity is the consciousness of the feeling, experiencing self, it is not an abstract and entirely immaterial thing, but a result of psychosomatic reactions to external phenomena (Damasio, 2018; 2006). This psychological dimension – this need for significance, meaning and purpose in the world – speaks also to the concept of ontological security.

A psychoanalytic term, ontological security refers to a mental state that entails a sense of completeness, order and temporal continuity of the individual (Laing, 2010, pp. 41–42); but a relatively recent body of IR literature also views ontological security as something that complements physical security (e.g. sovereignty and territorial integrity) and explains state behaviour also in terms of perceptions and identity (Huysmans, 1998; Mitzen, 2006a; 2006b; Chernobrov, 2016; Steele, 2014; Rumelili, 2016). As Della Sala (2016) notes, this search for completeness and temporal continuity may be also associated with the significance of political myths for individuals and societies; the point being that political myths provide a chronological narrative that orders time in a meaningful way for individuals and for political communities, and, in this way, myths contribute to their ontological security.

The overall argument here is that the possibility that myths engrain beliefs and attitudes, the view that myths preserve and perpetuate patterns of thought and social behaviour (and, thus, play a role in the political process), is grounded in profound psychological needs of people and their political communities. In this sense, myths are not a cultural product of primitive societies, but a 'feature of advanced societies' (Tudor, 1973, 14). And, to some degree, it is 'the mark of a modern mind to be able to explicitly create a "myth" as a way of influencing others' (Sabine and Thorson, 1973, p. 14); or that a myth is a universal and 'socially significant product of humanity's irrepressible urge to construct meaning' (von Handy, 2002, p. 333).

Moreover, the process of creating meaning that is encoded in a myth – the mythmaking process – is not an entirely mental process, but necessarily operates on data or information from the external world. This means that myths can be conceptualized as 'lenses' through which people look at the world (Bennet, 1980); but also as an 'organizing and filtering procedure for the reception of new information, be it the combination of sights and sounds into images of physical objects or the complex perception of social situations'(Flood, 2002, p. 81). Hence, myths are not pure fantasies or social constructs that are completely detached from material reality.

In Della Sala's words, political myths 'have some grain of truth in them'; they are 'born in facts, but then they take on a life of their own in the hands of storytellers and listeners' (2010, p. 5). And so, myths are not by default dangerous political falsehoods, but structured information about the external world that may be linked to facts or be based on reality (Archard, 1995). In any case however, the degree of correspondence of myth to an external reality is not a matter of concern. Instead, what should concern us is 'whether the story serves to connect the storyteller and the listener to a broader construction of a political community and its forms of political power. A myth that survives over time is one that continues to transmit a message that captures and shapes the normative and cognitive frames of a political community' (Della Sala, 2016, p. 530).

In a new materialist framework, a myth can be viewed as a discursive surface that forms a boundary between matter (i.e. information about the external world) and meaning (i.e. our mental representations thereof). Inside this surface, inside a myth, material conditions operate jointly with mental representations, in order to co-construct a story, a narrative, an image of the world in a specific situation, which specifies a pattern of action for a political community.

Conceivably, we could think of the concept of *geopolitical myth* as a story or a narrative with distinct geographical terms or connotations, which captures and communicates a pattern of geopolitical behaviour and, in this way, it is also linked to a wide array of territorial state practices (such as strategy and foreign policy). Geographical terms or connotations refer for example to myths that describe the relative position or direction of the state on the world map; designate allies and enemies relative to the points of a compass or other specified spaces; create a sense of locational awareness or a sense of belonging by specifying a location as the property of the state; cite the state as a member of a particular group or organization, or as having an affinity for a special group of states or a region, or as being rightly placed in a specified position.

Following the same logic as before, the concept of geopolitical myth combines the physical experiences associated with specific geographic conditions (matter) and the socio-psychological processing of these experiences into a coherent story or narrative (meaning). In this sense, the concept of geopolitical myth as the object of study for geopolitics could complement the new materialist and critical realist turns to open up a new path of inquiry for geopolitics.

This novel approach, termed as *Analytic Geopolitics,* instead of deconstructing texts and discourses, could be analysing the internal logic and deep structure of geopolitical myths, which give them their operating power: their constitutive elements (i.e. narratives and stories), the stages of their historical emergence and their effect on domestic and international behaviour of states. Instead of revealing their artificiality as social constructs, and challenging the ideological agendas or motives of individuals, groups and foreign policy establishments, Analytic Geopolitics could take on the notion of myth as a neutral object of study and examine it in the frame of geographic and other material conditions, in conjunction with the social processes that facilitated their emergence and their power to produce meaning.

In the context of Analytic Geopolitics, geopolitical myths should be understood as products of historical and political processes, not as concrete, immovable objects sculptured in time, inside a text. Simply put, the real power of geopolitical myths does not lie with the author and the text that use them at a moment in time; it lies hidden under layers of repetitions through texts and speeches, images and stories of different authors and creators. For sure, every political myth has an ultimate purpose as they are rarely if ever used for their aesthetic value, but this purpose should not 'detain us long', because a myth 'may well be used for one purpose at one time and for a different purpose on another [...] both can be real, and this is because the purpose of a myth depends entirely on the circumstances in which it is told and the intention of the man who tells it' (Tudor, 1973, pp. 37–39). Hence, a geopolitical myth cannot be subjected to a textual deconstruction associated with Critical Geopolitics.

By the same token, a geopolitical myth differs from the concept of discourse as it has been used in Critical Geopolitics. For Analytic Geopolitics, myths are connected series of geopolitical narratives and stories that relate to a geographic condition. The study of a geopolitical myth does not assume the existence of a discourse as a great unity of statements and concepts that reflect an existing power structure, or define a distinctive theory of identity, nor a singular source of influence (such as the existence of an ideological or political agenda). A myth is an ensemble of narratives and stories that show a regular appearance in public discourse and may or may not have an impact on domestic and foreign policies.

Therefore, instead of deconstructing texts and discourses, Analytic Geopolitics is decomposing myths into their constitutive geopolitical narratives and stories. Instead of merely exposing their social construction and artificiality, Analytic Geopolitics is investigating the internal logic and deep structure of geopolitical myths that gives them their operating power. Instead of displacing the motives of individuals, groups and foreign policy establishments, Analytic Geopolitics takes on the notion of myth as a neutral object of study – which does not imply that there are no hidden intentions, agendas and ideologies but that these are difficult to isolate and examine independently from the geographic conditions and the psychological processes that framed them in the first place.

So, after all, irrespective of the intentions and the agendas of their users, or their correspondence to an external reality, myths might be leaving a significant (but so far largely understudied) footprint on our political processes. Myths seem to be present in all activities in which people need to agree about the meaning of the external world and work jointly towards the same goal in a way that is appropriate to the particular circumstances. And, even if we were to agree that 'myths exist only in people's collective imagination' they still give people the 'unprecedented ability to cooperate flexibly in large numbers' (Harari, 2015, p. 27, pp. 30–31). This means that myths are here to stay for as long as people create, control and cooperate in political communities. After all is said and done, myths might be an indispensable feature in the social architecture of our world.

Deconstructing and exposing myths as pure fantasies or immoral instruments of power politics, does not mean that they are no longer active components in the everyday life of a society, in the territorial practices of the modern state and the macro-dynamics of the international system that it has created. And perhaps, no amount of criticism, fact-checking and textual deconstruction might be able to eradicate myths, at least not without undermining the foundations of the social world or our ability to understand it.

3 A Structural-Historical Analysis

3.1 *Constitutive Elements of Geopolitical Myths*

In the context of political competition, people express both their interests and their perceived identity with stories in narrative form. Security concerns are justified using simple or complex stories, the interests of the great powers are reported as variations or in reference to a story, national identity is articulated in narrative form with stories about the past, the reflection of power relations penetrate a country's own intellectual production and its social fabric as macro-historical narratives. And although it is difficult to separate a national interest independently from the person who articulates it - as much as it is difficult to isolate a national identity from the norms that do or do not constitute it - it is quite possible in comparison to locate and single out the stories that people tell in order to express both their interests and their identities.

Similarly, people and political communities narrate their relation to a specific territory; tell stories that connect them to the landscape and the geographical features of their environment; more often than not, people articulate their sense of place and physical experiences of geography as a series of events that took place in a topographical space of their definition. In this sense the geopolitical myth becomes an interface for geography and our representations of geography, it becomes a point where material reality and our perceptions intersect to produce a structural, material order of things.

This order of geopolitical myths is separate, autonomous and irreducible to its parts (reality and perception), but most importantly, it also has the additional analytic benefit of being measurable and commensurable – something that its parts are lacking. A geopolitical myth is not an exact depiction of external reality in as much as it is not entirely a product of an ideological imagination. Rather, it is a device that fuses them to make them both meaningful and suitable for political use – this is the essential property of myth that raises its analytical value for geopolitics and for politics in general.

At the core of the co-constructing process that generates geopolitical meaning inside a myth, there is a relational series of narratives and stories being told and retold, printed and reprinted, used and reused in public discourse. This means that a geopolitical myth does not hold a sublime or autonomous meaning in itself, but rather depends on specific narratives and stories, and in particular on the relationship between them. In other words, myths by themselves could be nothing more than clichés or an incomprehensible gathering of innuendos; it is narratives and stories within them that organize information from the outside world and create meaning. In this respect, a geopolitical myth is a structural object; it is structural because it is an assembly of constitutive elements (namely narratives and stories) that make up a complex whole; and it is an object in as far as it is a materializing thing that can be read in printed texts, seen in maps and spoken or listened to in speeches.

A story is an account of past events in the life of individuals or communities or a report of contemporary developments. A geopolitical narrative is a sequence or a collection of stories or events that show a particular locational awareness of a political community. This sequence of stories may define the temporal but also the spatial organization of the narrative, the cause-and-effect logic (i.e. the plot) and ultimately the overarching geopolitical consequences for the political community that it refers to. Stories are the fundamental building blocks of a myth, whereas the narrative is the order and manner in which these stories are presented to the reader. Within the narrative, collections of stories and reported events are organized in such a way as to reveal the geopolitical condition of the political community.

Narratology, the examination of how narratives produce and distribute meaning, makes up a whole subfield of inquiry in literary and popular culture studies (Bal, 2017). A common theme of narratology is that the narrative form plays a key role in in ordering time and space and in this way giving meaning to historical representations (White, 1987). Consequently, geopolitical myths and myths in general as a narrative form par excellence, they may also set up a an ordering of time and space and in this way reveal a geopolitical knowledge that gives a sense of place. The structural analysis of geopolitical myths is an examination of the way in which their constitutive elements, i.e. the narratives and stories structure a geopolitical understanding of a political community's place in the world.

3.2 *Narrative Qualities of Geopolitical Myths*

If a geopolitical myth is a set of narratives that in turn refer to a time-series of stories with regular repetition, then this structural line of inquiry necessarily needs to be also historical. Instead of focusing exclusively on a text or a limited series of texts, Analytic Geopolitics tries to trace regularities in the repetition of geopolitical narratives and stories that perhaps frame a particular pattern of behavior with contemporary relevance, but also continuity in time.

In this respect, a historical approach is necessary and in line with recent developments in the study of international politics, that is the historical turn in IR, which contents that the study of history is indispensable to the study of international politics (Suganami 2015, p. 257). History and international relations have a long symbiotic relationship (Hobson and Lawson, 2008, p. 415). IR scholars of all approaches and on all levels of analysis have employed history in their research, albeit with many methodological question marks (Lawson, 2012, pp. 203–226).

The most pertinent of these question marks is the post-modern ontological divide that permeates all social science, and which in history could be summed up as: is there a history or is it many histories? Is it possible to have an objective view of the past or is the past almost completely lost to us and open to innumerable interpretations? This "problem of history" dividing historians, is also transferred in IR to limit history from being employed as a methodological approach (Vaughan-Williams, 2015, pp. 215–233). Therefore, questions ridding the use of a macro-historical approach in combination with geopolitics and political myth might be also considered as a limitation of Analytic Geopolitics.

However, the aim of Analytic Geopolitics is not to provide a complete history of a geopolitical myth. Yet, the long view, even if selective at times, it is strictly necessary and appropriate in an effort to trace patterns of statements in a very specific topic, that is to say geopolitical mythmaking. On the contrary, the focus on a few critical periods as 'snapshots' or 'still images' of history is a much better use of resources. This way one can compare these images in order to spot differences or similarities, to identify patterns and to describe a system of formation of geopolitical myths.

If a geopolitical myth is constituted in narratives and stories and their relationship or arrangement in texts and in time, then the structural-historical method of Analytic Geopolitics is necessary and predicated on evaluating first, its historical existence (continuity), second its marginal variations that allowed it to adapt to different contexts (adaptability) and, third, its appearance in different texts, mediums and formats (intertextuality).

Continuity is understood here as being present throughout the history of the political community in question or for a significant part thereof and especially at those critical junctions that defined its geopolitical behaviour. Continuity can be evaluated based on the usage of a myth by political actors including intellectuals, politicians, bureaucracies and the media in their debates concerning strategic policies and decisions. If substantiated by a historical investigation into the development and evolution of a geopolitical myth, it can account for the myth's capacity to deliver a 'timeless message'. A myth's marginal variation or adaptability also works in the same way, by elevating the geopolitical myth above and beyond specific intellectual, ideological and socio-political contexts. Finally, intertextuality should be understood as a property that increases the credibility of the myth – hence increases its truthiness and acceptability. Similarly to how academic research builds authority by citing previous publications, a geopolitical myth gain credibility by referring to previous myth versions, but also on past reiterations of its constitutive narratives and stories.

Continuity and intertextuality of the belonging myth, confer with what Bouchard calls 'piggybacking', a quality of an efficient myth to, *"build on old, well established myths and symbols so as to partake of their authority. (...) To this end, the new myth is presented as a simple extension or a corollary of the latter. The strategy is particularly useful when proponents of radical changes seek to make them more palatable to dissenters by wrapping them in a veil of continuity"* (2016, p. 361).

More importantly, however, it is necessary to notice the weighted significance and consequence of adaptability. Bouchard defines adaptability, as the "capacity to live on through changing settings and challenges, thanks to a process of constant redefinition and renegotiation". He also enumerates two more qualities of myths, namely polysemy, i.e. the capacity of having several meanings or ambiguous enough to harness consent from disparate social groups and audiences; and relevance, i.e. the capacity to retain meaning regardless of a change in setting (*ibid*).

3.3 *Historical Emergence and Effect*

Geopolitical myths may provide a sense of temporal and spatial continuity, an emotional attachment to a place, a sense of belonging, direction and purpose in the world. But it seems like the legitimizing effect of myth – the idea that it has the potential to legitimize and frame specific policies and decisions – is the most interesting and at the same time the least developed concept in the literature.

Indeed, the understanding of myth as a source of legitimacy and mobilization for the public spans the literature from Sorel and Cassirer all the way to Bottici and Della Sala. Sorel saw myths not merely as 'descriptions of things' but as expressions of a determination to act': in his mind, the myth of the general strike was 'the only idea that could have value as a motivating force' (2009, p. 32). In the *Myth of the State*, Cassirer (2013) singles out the myth of the Aryan race as the key idea that legitimized Nazi brutality.

More recently, Lincoln (1989) argued that myths lend credibility and authority when used in politics and therefore are extremely useful tools for politicians. Similarly, Hosking and Schöpflin (2013) regarded myths as political instruments that justify the authority of the government and the legitimacy of its action. Myth provides in simple, legible form all those 'symbolic values within which people share an idea of origin, continuity, historical memories, collective remembrance, common heritage and tradition, as well as a common destiny' (Obradovic, 1996, p. 196) – this is rather like legitimacy in pill-form. And it is seems like, as an artificial construction any political community needs these kind of stimulants in order to legitimize the use of power and authority, on a variety of issues, including the economy (Jones, 2010). The very existence and sovereignty of a state or the reason for being of an international institution may hinge on the acceptance of a myth that legitimizes the form and function of the governing body (Smith, 1999; Della Sala, 2016). All in all, 'one of the central purposes of political myth, then, is to generate legitimacy for political rule' (Della Sala 2010, p. 5).

The legitimacy effect of myth in a common place between scholars. However, why and how does that legitimization take place? How come a myth becomes so embedded in public consciousness that is accepted as an absolute truth? Most importantly where does its truthiness and acceptability come from? In asking those questions, we ask what makes a myth effective enough to become successfully imprinted on the public mind.

In this regard, Strath (2005), Ricoeur (2010), Bottici and Challand (2013), they all link somehow the success of a myth with the qualities of its narrative form, for example their wide recognition and intelligibility, how comprehensible they are to the audience.

In this sense, the three properties of myth that concern Analytic Geopolitics (continuity, adaptability and intertextuality) can also serve as key indicators of the myth's historical emergence and its effect on the behaviour of the political community, i.e. the legitimacy it may have generated with regards to policy or political action. In other words, these properties are conditions of its historically contingent truthiness: not its veracity or true correspondence with an external reality, but the historical process by which a myth becomes widely accepted as an apparent truth.

Gérard Bouchard (2013; 2014; 2016) describes a complete theory of the historical emergence of myth that can be applied in the similar form in Analytic Geopolitics. According to Bouchard, the mythmaking process begins with the initial spreading of the myth to the wider public (*diffusion*), continues with a series of political actions that are modelled on the myths narrative core (*ritualization*) and ends with the myth becoming a thing of mysterious and sacred significance (*sacralisation*). Bouchard's three-stage mythmaking process that makes a successful myth is a wonderful concept that makes mythmaking more familiar to the outsider; it demystifies the packed concept of myth and its role in the political process. It is also very helpful in conceptualizing how a myth becomes widely accepted.

Nevertheless, we could envisage the introduction of one or two intermediate stage of *opposition/adaptation*, in order to open the door to politics into the mythmaking process, as a dynamic contestation of a myth's diffusion by rival myths, but also as an explanation for the adaptive quality of the myth. Mythmaking does not happen in a straight line, without any political friction, and competition from rival geopolitical narratives and myths, might actually spur an evolutionary adaptation that may actually contribute to the wide acceptability of a geopolitical myth.

Bouchard talks also about specific conditions that a successful myth should meet in order to become accepted, i.e. in terms of content, a definition of community and its territory, the invention of threats and adversaries etc. and in terms of its qualities, symbolic power, adaptability and a reference to previous myths. Consequently, the legitimacy and mobilization effect of myth depends on its acceptability. In turn, acceptability is dependent on wide recognition and intelligibility, and how comprehensible the myth is to the public.

Acceptability in terms of recognition, intelligibility and comprehension refers to an implicit quality of myth that we could term *truthiness*. Recall here that myth is a neutral term – neither true, nor false; neither fact, nor fiction; neither fantasy, nor reality. By truthiness, we do not refer to the veracity of the myth, neither to its correspondence to an external reality, but to its potential to appear as truth, its quality of being felt to be true even if it is probably impossible to verify. This understanding on truthiness seems to be of utmost importance for the success or acceptability of myth and in consequence for its potential for legitimizing political authority, policies and decisions. It is crucial therefore to analyse those properties of myth that cause its truthiness in their historical dimension.

If geopolitical narratives and supporting stories are disseminated effectively, if they prove to be resistant in time, malleable into different means and formats, and adjustable to changing contexts, then we may consider that they form a myth that has an objective and material reality. If they manage to overcome the unavoidable opposition that follows their diffusion, adapt and form a ritual, then we may consider that they gave rise to a dominant geopolitical myth that appears as a common sense or an apparent truth.

Therefore, in continuity, adaptability and intertextuality, we are also looking at a set of qualities that contribute to the historical evolution and effectiveness of the geopolitical myth, from its original diffusion to its making of a 'sacred' myth, i.e. rooted so deeply in what people consider to be common sense that it is beyond scrutiny and dispute; because any doubts about its truthiness is enough to shake the foundations of the political community or the policy to which it serves as the basis of its legitimacy (Bell 2003). These qualities – the continuity that manifests as a timeless message of almost mystical origins, the adaptability that transcends historical, political or ideological contexts, and a frame of reference between many different texts – is what define the historical existence of a geopolitical myth and what makes it a source of legitimacy for the political community.

A historical analysis of myth is not a historical record, neither a direct causal interpretation of the origins and the emergence of a myth, nor a linear account of their reiterations in the order of their appearance. Certainly, an analysis of the historical development and evolution of myths is crucial in highlighting their contingency and artificiality; however, it is far more important to use the historical approach in order to reveal the variations of myths and analyse them to their constituent parts. The point here is to chronicle the repetitions of myths, their various versions and usage in politics, but also their interaction or opposition with alternative or rival myths, where applicable. In this way we should be looking to substantiate both their 'high degree of constancy' and their 'marginal variation' that Blumenberg (2010, p. 34) speaks of, and gauge their adaptability – which gives them a sense of timelessness and continuity (see also Bottici, 2010, p. 187).

4 New Directions for Research in Geopolitics

Using an Analytic Geopolitics framework, research could branch out in two directions. First, the vertical in-depth analysis of several country-specific cases that may illuminate the form and deep internal structure of geopolitical myths (i.e. their meaning as it emerges from the constitutive narratives), the stages of their historical emergence or their current level of acceptance and status (e.g. is it still active? Do political actors, no matter how marginal, still represent it?), and the degree of their efficiency or potential for legitimacy and mobilization in the political process.

A quick scan of the world and the available literature will show that many geopolitical myths frame historical patterns of behaviour, setting out the ground parameters for geopolitical competition, both nationally and internationally. The majority of those geopolitical myths and narratives are well documented in the literature, but, as discussed in the beginning of the dissertation, they have been approached as fantasies of the past, or as pure products of the imagination that still need to be dispelled. Although this endeavour has been quite successful and extremely enlightening, we are running the risk of believing that these myths have stopped having an impact on society and politics just because they have been exposed and dispelled.

To start with, American history is full of symbolism and myth, as well as narratives of national missions that many times assumed a religious and millenarian guise (Smith, 2009; Cherry, 2015; Tuveson, 1980; Burns, 1973). For example there is the well-documented American myth of 'Manifest Destiny' as a set of stories that accompanied an expansionist project to civilize and remake the West in the model of the United States, justified with a narrative of superiority of American culture (Weinberg, 1999; Merk, 1970). Manifest Destiny may also be a case in point for the role of geopolitical myths in identity and national interest formation in relation to foreign policy (Hietala, 2003). Manifest Destiny can be considered as a precursor to United States foreign policy in the twentieth century, to the extent that, as David Campbell (2008, pp. 153–154) writes, the 'overseas adventures' of the United States in Cuba, Hawaii, Puerto Rico, Guam and the Philippines, among others, and up to the Cold War, 'were justified in the same terms that had rationalized the oppression of Indians and others at home'.

Then, there is also the American frontier myth of the West as a wide-open land of opportunity at the edge of civilization (Slotkin, 1998; 2006; 2008). It would be interesting to examine not only the geopolitical components of these myths, but also to trace a possible lineage that connects them with contemporary myths and geopolitical patterns of behaviour in the United States.

From this angle, Russia shares similar religious geopolitical visions with the United States that still inform national identity, strategy and foreign policy and can be traced back to the Enlightenment and Russia's uneasy relationship with European modernity. For example, Russian self-awareness as the defender of the Orthodox faith – that cites Moscow as the Third Rome – manifests around religious history and messianic narratives that still inform the geopolitical vision of the country and Moscow's sense of place and mission in the world, especially in relation to Europe and the West (Sidorov, 2006; Engström, 2014; Suslov, 2015; 2018).

In contrast, colonialism and imperialism used to define Great Britain's place and 'civilizing' mission in the world; but, what is more fascinating about the case of Britain is a rich history of narratives and stories that may constitute a myth of the island, which expresses opposite feelings of isolation and insularity (Kincaid, 2007). If there is indeed a dual narrative tradition between 'global empire' and 'island' in British strategy and foreign policy, this would make a fantastic case in point for a mythmaking process that revolves around the opposition between rival myths and narratives (especially if traces of this duality or opposition can be found in the context of Brexit).

Germany also exhibits a historical emergence of a geopolitical mission, although it moves in the opposite direction from the United States, looking eastward; there, "a varied cast of German writers, artists, philosophers, diplomats, political leaders, generals, and Nazi racial fanatics have imagined (often in very different ways) a special German mission in the East, forging a frontier myth that paralleled the American myths of the 'Wild West' and 'Manifest Destiny'" (Liulevicius, 2011; Kakel, 2014). Moreover, the Germans developed an affinity narrative and a sense of Europeaness or Westerness in comparison to the Eastern position of – and a perceived threat from – Russia (Gassner, 2011).

Finally, a narrative of centrality and dilemma between East and West, seems to follow a general pattern in Europe, which Wolff (2010) traces back to the invention of Eastern Europe by the European Enlightenment. Consequently, we see a plethora of states on the 'periphery' of Europe, developing narratives of centrality between East and West (and affinity with Europe): Poland, like Germany, used Russia to counter-define her affinity narrative with Europe; Greece and Finland developed geopolitical narratives that were torn between centrality and marginality in the East, the West and the North; Belarus was also undecided 'in between'; even Turkey, interestingly enough, developed the centrality narrative of a 'bridge' between East and West that was followed by a EC membership bid and a Westernization debate that mirrored the Greek one in time, but also in character and intensity (see relevant chapters in Maxwell, 2011).

In a second research direction, these vertical insights should accumulate enough comparative data in order, for example, to create type collections of geopolitical myths, and expand the research agenda to more general, horizontal questions. Collections of myths should allow us to develop taxonomical criteria, understand cross-country variation and perhaps yield meaningful comparative insights about the structure and use of myths when we are talking about geopolitics and patterns of state behaviour. If the historical analysis of a geopolitical myth in a country is a vertical analysis of its internal structure, constituent narratives and the relationship between them, then collections are a horizontal analysis that allows us to make comparisons of various myths from different countries.

Looking forward to such classification of geopolitical myths and narratives, it is already possible to describe a few categories according to their meaning and the locational awareness they prescribe to states, e.g. myths and narratives that steer the state towards a direction or provide a directional sense (north/south, east/west), myths that locate the state in the centre or the margins of a region; myths that speak about the continuity of a state on a territory or describe a territorial loss as a discontinuity in the nations' history; myths that narrate the interests of a global empire or myths that account for isolationist or "island" stories; myths of belonging and of alienation or affinity and aversion towards a region; myths that connect/disconnect or open/close a state or a region with a topographical space; and conceivably many more. In this regard, what kind of general patterns of behaviour, if any, such geopolitical myths that emerge under similar geographic conditions create?

Geopolitical myths may belong or combine several types and content from the above categories. Considering however that myths about the state also involve an emotional attachment to a place and that the state is necessarily a territorial unit, then all myths about the state also include a significant geopolitical element. They tie the state to a territory, they naturalize the national borders or in other terms they legitimate the state sovereignty over a particular geographical area. The point of collecting, classifying and chronicling geopolitical myths would also be to understand how these myths use different combinations of types and contents to enhance their legitimizing effect and create patterns of political action.

These were only the opening philosophical propositions and general research suggestions of Analytic Geopolitics as a study of geopolitical myths that could help the field move beyond the Classical/Critical divide and the artificial dualism of material/ideational components of geopolitics.

Classic thinkers take a positivist stance in saying that geography is inescapable and immutable, because its parameters and features can be measured and be compared; and therefore, it is valid to look for regularities, cause/effect variables, and law-like forms. On the contrary, critical scholars adopt the exact opposite, interpretive stance that claims that geography is only what people make of it and nothing– at least not anything meaningful – exists independent of their thinking. Everything would have been so much easier if we could tell where the material world (i.e. physical geography) 'ends' and where the observer's ideas (i.e. geographical imagination) 'begins'.

Working around this difficulty, Analytic Geopolitics draws attention instead to the point where matter and ideas 'meet' and interact with each other, on the surface of the myths, the narratives and the stories that people and political communities tell in order to make sense of the world. This approach can complement in various interesting way our understanding of the social fabric of the modern territorial states and their patterns of geopolitical behaviour in international relations.

Bibliography

Agnew, J. A. (1998). *Geopolitics : Re-visioning World Politics.* London: Routledge.

Agnew, J., & Corbridge, S. (1995). Mastering Space. London: Routledge

Archard, D. (1995). Myths, Lies and Historical Truth: A Defence of Nationalism. Political Studies, 43, 3, 472

Archer, M. (1995). *Realist Social Theory.* Cambridge: Cambridge University Press

Baeten, E. M. (1996). The magic mirror: Myth's abiding power. Albany: State University of New York Press

Bal, M. (2017). *Narratology: Introduction to the theory of narrative.* Toronto: University of Toronto Press

Barad, K. (2007). *Meeting the Universe Halfway.* Durham, NC: Duke University Press

Bell, D. S. A. (2003). Mythscapes: memory, mythology, and national identity. *British Journal of Sociology, 54,* 63–82

Bennett, J. (2004). "The Force of Things." *Political Theory* 32 (3): 347–372.

Bennett, W. L. (1980). Myth, Ritual, and Political Control. Journal of Communication, 30, 4, 166–179

Bhaskar, R. (1975). *A Realist Theory of Science.* London: Verso

Bhaskar, R. (1979). *The Possibility of Naturalism.* Atlantic Highlands, NJ: Humanities Press.

Bliesemann, . G. B. (2016). Myth and narrative in international politics: Interpretive approaches to the study of IR. London: Palgrave Macmillan.

Blumenberg, H. (2010). Work on myth. Cambridge, Mass: MIT Press

Bottici, C. (2010). A philosophy of political myth. Cambridge [et al.: Cambridge University Press

Bottici, C. and Challand, B. 2013. *Imagining Europe: Myth, Memory, and Identity.* Cambridge: Cambridge University Press.

Bottici, C., & Challand, B. (2012). The myth of the clash of civilizations. Abingdon, Oxon England: Routledge

Bottici, C., & Challand, B. (2014). *Imagining Europe: Myth, memory, and identity.* Cambridge: Cambridge University Press

Bouchard, G. (2013). 'National myths: an overview' in G. Bouchard (ed.), National Myths: Constructed Pasts, Contested Presents. London: Routledge.;

Bouchard, G. (2014) Raison et Dèraison du Mythe: Au Coeur des Imaginaires Collectifs. Montreal: Boréal.

Bouchard, G. (2016). Social Myths: A New Approach. *Philosophy Study.* Vol. 6, No. 6. 356–366. p. 361

Buffet, C., & Heuser, B. (1998). Haunted by history: Myths in international relations. Providence, R.I: Berghahn

Burns, E. M. N. (1973). The American idea of mission: Concepts of national purpose and destiny. Westport, Conn: Greenwood Press;

Campbell, D. (2008). *Writing security: United States foreign policy and the politics of identity.* Minneapolis, Minn: University of Minnesota Press

Carvalho, B. ., Leira, H., & Hobson, J. M. (January 01, 2015). The Big Bangs of IR: the Myths that Your Teachers Still Tell you about 1648 and 1919. Historical International Relations, 2, 321–346;

Cassirer, E. (2013). The myth of the state. New Haven: Yale University Press

Chernobrov, D. (October 01, 2016). Ontological Security and Public (Mis)Recognition of International Crises: Uncertainty, Political Imagining, and the Self. *Political Psychology, 37,* 5, 581–596

Cherry, C. (2015). God's New Israel: Religious Interpretations of American Destiny. Chapel Hill: The University of North Carolina Press.

Cohen, S. B. (1963). Geography and Politics in a World Divided. New York: Random House.

Cohen, S. B. (2003). Geopolitics of the World System. Lanham: Rowman & Littlefield.

Collier, A. (1994). *Critical realism: An introduction to Roy Bhaskar's philosophy*. London u.a: Verso.

Coole, D, and Frost, S. (2010) "Introducing the New Materialisms." In Coole, D, and Frost, S. (eds). *New Materialisms: Ontology, Agency, and Politics*. Durham, NC: Duke University Press, 1–43.

Czarniawska, B. (2005). *Narratives in social science research: Introducing Qualitative Methods*. London: Sage publications ltd. pp. 1–3

Dalby, S. (1990). American security discourse: the persistence of geopolitics. *Political Geography Quarterly*, 9(2), 171–188;

Dalby, S. (1998). Rethinking geopolitics. New York: Routledge

Damasio, A. (2018). *Strange Order of Things : The Biological Roots of Culture*. Knopf Doubleday Publishing Group

Damasio, A. R. (2006). Descartes' error: Emotion, reason and the human brain. London: Vintage Books

Della Sala, V. (2010). Political Myth, Mythology and the European Union. Journal of Common Market Studies, 48, 1, 1–19

Della, Sala. V. (2016). Europe's odyssey? Political Myth and the European Union. *Nations and Nationalism, 22*, 3, 524–541

Eliade, M. (2009). Myth and reality. Long Grove, Ill: Waveland Press;

Engström, M. (December 01, 2014). Contemporary Russian Messianism and New Russian Foreign Policy. Contemporary Security Policy, 35, 3, 356–379;

Flood, C. (2002). Political myth. New York: Routledge.

Fox, N. J., and P. Alldred. 2017. *Sociology and the New Materialism: Theory, Research, Action*. London: Sage. pp. 151–175.

Friedrich, C. J. (1963). Man and his government: An empirical theory of politics. New York: McGraw-Hill. p. 97;

Gassner, F. (2011) Becoming a Western Nation: German National Identity and the Image of Russia. In Maxwell, A. (ed). The East-West discourse: Symbolic geography and its consequences. Oxford: Peter Lang

Gray, C. S. (1991). Geography and Grand Strategy. Comparative Strategy, Vol. 10, No. 4, 311–329;

Gray, C. S. (2005). Inescapable Geography. In C. S. Gray, & G. R. Sloan, Geopolitics, Geography and Strategy (pp. 161–177). New York: Routledge;

Harari, Y. N. (2015). *Sapiens: A brief history of mankind*. London : Vintage Books. pp. 27, 30–1

Harvey, D. (1990). Between Space and time: Reflections on the Geographical imagination. *Annals of the Association of American Geographers, 80*(3), 418–434

Hietala, T. R. (2003). Manifest design: American exceptionalism and empire. Ithaca, N.Y: Cornell University Press

Hobson, J. M. (2012). The Eurocentric conception of world politics: Western international theory, 1760–2010. New York: Cambridge University Press

Hobson, J. M., & Lawson, G. (2008). What is History in International Relations? *Millennium, 37*(2), 415–435.

Huysmans, J. (January 01, 1998). Security! What do you mean? From concept to thick signifier. *Security! What Do You Mean? from Concept to Thick Signifier.*

Jackson, P. T. (2016). The Conduct of Inquiry in International Relations: Philosophy of Science and Its Implications for the Study of World Politics. Florence: Taylor and Francis

Jessop, B. (2007). State power: A strategic-relational approach. Cambridge: Polity

Jones, E. (2010). The Economic Mythology of European Integration. *Jcms: Journal of Common Market Studies, 48*, 1, 89–109

Joseph, J. (2014). The social in the global: Social theory, governmentality and global politics. Cambridge: Cambridge University Press

Kakel, C. P. (2014). The American West and the Nazi East: A comparative and interpretive perspective. New York: Palgrave Macmillan.

Kelly, P. (2006). A critique of Critical Geopolitics. *Geopolitics, 11*(1), 24–53.

Kincaid, P. (January 01, 2007). Islomania? Insularity? The Myth of the Island in British Science Fiction. *Extrapolation, 48*, 3, 462–471

Kurki, M. (2008). Causation in international relations: Reclaiming causal analysis. Cambridge: Cambridge University Press;

Laing, R. D. (2010). *The divided self: An existential study in sanity and madness*. London: Penguin

Latour, B. (2004). Why has critique run out of steam? From matters of fact to matters of concern. *Critical inquiry, 30*(2), 225–248

Latour, B. (2005). *Reassembling the Social: An Introduction to Actor-network-theory.* Oxford: Oxford University Press. p. 54

Lawson, G. (June 01, 2012). The eternal divide? History and International Relations. *European Journal of International Relations*, 18, 2, 203–226

Lévi-Strauss, C. (1979), The Structural Study of Myth, in Sebeok, T. A. Myth: A symposium. Bloomington: Indiana Univ. Press

Lincoln, B. (1989). Discourse and the Construction of Society: Comparative Studies of Myth, Ritual, and Classification. Oxford: Oxford University Press.

Little, R. (2009). The balance of power in international relations: Metaphors, myths, and models. Cambridge: Cambridge Univ. Press

Liulevicius, V. G. (2011). *The German Myth of the East: 1800 to the Present.* New York: Oxford University Press.

Mackinder, H. J. (1904). The Geographical Pivot of History. *The Geographical Journal* vol. 23, 419–441;

Malinowski, B. (2011). Myth in primitive psychology. New York: W.W. Norton & Company, Inc;

Maxwell, A. (2011). ed. The East-West discourse: Symbolic geography and its consequences. Oxford: Peter Lang

Merk, F. (1970). Manifest Destiny and mission in American history. New York: Alfred A. Knopf.

Meyer, J. W., & Rowan, B. (1977). Institutionalized Organizations: Formal Structure as Myth and Ceremony. *American Journal of Sociology, 83*, 2, 340–363

Mitzen, J. (2006a). Ontological Security in World Politics: State Identity and the Security Dilemma. *European Journal of International Relations, 12*, 3, 341–370

Mitzen, J. (2006b). Anchoring Europe's civilizing identity: habits, capabilities and ontological security. *Journal of European Public Policy, 13*, 2, 270–285

Müller, M. (2013). Text, discourse, affect and things. In Dodds, K., Kuus, M., & Sharp, J. P. (eds). The Ashgate research companion to Critical Geopolitics. London: Routledge (pp. 49–68).

Nancy, J.-L., & Connor, P. (2012). *The inoperative community*. Minneapolis, Minn: University of Minnesota Press

Obradovic, D. (1996) 'Policy Legitimacy and the European Union'. *Journal of Common Market Studies* , Vol. 34, No. 2, pp. 191–221

Osiander, A. (April 01, 2001). Sovereignty, International Relations, and the Westphalian Myth. *International Organization, 55*, 2, 251–287

Price, L., & Martin, L. (March 15, 2018). Introduction to the special issue: applied critical realism in the social sciences. *Journal of Critical Realism, 17*, 2, 89–96. p. 89

Ricoeur, P. 2010. *Time and Narrative*, Vol. 3. Chicago: University of Chicago Press.;

Rumelili, B. (2016). *Conflict resolution and ontological security: Peace anxieties*. London: Routledge.

Sabine, G. H., & Thorson, T. L. (1973). A History of political theory. Hinsdale, Ill: Dryden Pr

Sayer, A. (2000). *Realism and Social Science*. London: SAGE; Vandenberghe, F. (2015). *What's Critical about Critical Realism?* London: Routledge.

Schopflin, G., & Hosking, G. (2013). *Myths and Nationhood*. Florence: Taylor and Francis;

Sharp, J. P. (2000). Remasculinising geo-politics? Comments on Gearoid O'Tuathail's Critical Geopolitics. Political Geography, 19(3), 361–364. pp. 361–362.

Sidorov, D. (July 01, 2006). Post-Imperial Third Romes: Resurrections of a Russian Orthodox Geopolitical Metaphor. *Geopolitics, 11*, 2, 317–347.

Slotkin, R. (1998). The fatal environment: The myth of the frontier in the age of industrialization: 1800–1890. Norman: University of Oklahoma Press.

Slotkin, R. (2008). Gunfighter nation: The myth of the frontier in twentieth-century America. Norman, Okla: Univ. of Oklahoma Press.

Slotkin, R., (2006). Regeneration through violence: The mythology of the American frontier, 1600–1860. Norman: University of Oklahoma Press.

Smith, A. D. (1999). Myths and the Memories of the Nation. Oxford: Oxford University Press.

Smith, A. D. (2009). Myths and memories of the nation. Oxford: Oxford University Press.

Smith, H. N. (2009). Virgin land: The American West as symbol and myth. Cambridge, Mass: Harvard Univ. Press.

Sorel, G., (2009). Reflections on violence. Cambridge: Cambridge University Press.

Sparke, M. (2000). Graphing the geo in geo-political: Critical Geopolitics and the re-visioning of responsibility. *Political Geography, 19*(3), 373–380.

Spykman, N. J. (1944). The Geography of the Peace. New York: Harcourt, Brace.

Steele, B. J. (2014). *Ontological security in international relations: Self-identity and the IR state*. Routledge.

Strath, B. 2005. 'Methodological and substantive remarks on myth, memory and history in the construction of a European community', *German Law Journal* 6, 2: 255–71.

Suganami, H. (January 01, 2015). Narrative Explanation and International Relations: Back to Basics. *Historical International Relations*, 1, 257–284. p 257.

Suslov, M. (January 01, 2018). "Russian World" Concept: Post-Soviet Geopolitical Ideology and the Logic of "Spheres of Influence". *Geopolitics, 23*, 2, 330–353.

Suslov, M. D. (January 01, 2015). "Holy Rus": The Geopolitical Imagination in the Contemporary Russian Orthodox Church. *Russian Social Science Review, 56*, 3, 43–62.

Teschke, B. (2003). The myth of 1648: Class, geopolitics, and the making of modern international relations. London: Verso.

Tismaneanu, Vladimir. (2009). *Fantasies of Salvation: Democracy, Nationalism, & Myth in Post-communist Europe*. Princeton Univ Press.

Tuathail, G. Ó. (1996) Critical Geopolitics: the politics of writing global space. *London and New York: Routledge.*

Tuathail, G. Ó. & Dalby, S. (1998). *Rethinking Geopolitics*. London: Routledge.

Tudor, H. (1973). Political myth. London: Macmillan

Tuveson, E. L. (1980). Redeemer nation: The idea of America's millennial role. Chicago: The University of Chicago Press.

Vaughan-Williams, N. (January 01, 2015). International Relations and the Problem of History. *Historical International Relations*, 1, 215–233.

von Handy. A. (2002). The modern construction of myth. Bloomington, Ind: Indiana Univ. Press

Weber, C. (2014). International relations theory: A critical introduction. London: Routledge

Weinberg, A. K. (1999). Manifest destiny: A study of nationalist expansionism in american history. Chicago: Quadrangle books

White, H. (1987). *The Content of the Form: Narrative Discourse and Historical Representation*. Baltimore: Johns Hopkins UP

Wight, C. (2008). Agents, structures and international relations: Politics as ontology. Cambridge, UK: Cambridge University Press

Wilson, P. (1998). The Myth of the 'First Great Debate'. *Review of International Studies, 24*, 1–16

Wolff, L. (2010). Inventing Eastern Europe: The map of civilization on the mind of the enlightenment. Stanford CA: Stanford University Press

PART 3

Empirical Studies: The Enduring Relevance of Territorially Embedded Factors in IR

CHAPTER 6

Post-Cold War NATO Enlargement and the Geopolitical Instrumentalization of 'Liberal Peace': Lessons from George Kennan

Alexandre Lambert

1 Introduction

This chapter elaborates on a basic concept of Classical Geopolitics, containment. It seeks to connect relevant scholarship in International Relations to the literature of Geopolitics. In the context of the nascent Cold War in Europe after the Second World War, the establishment of the North Atlantic Treaty Organisation (NATO) in 1949 was essentially to contain the former Soviet Union. Similarly, in the contemporary European politics of the post-Cold War era, NATO's eastward enlargement could be read as a "neo-containment" of post-Soviet Russia. Notably, the subsequent post-Cold War enlargement waves[1] of the Transatlantic Alliance have provided for an extended sphere of influence and territorial control by the US. It also has strengthened pro-Atlantic voices within Europe to some degree. This includes the Central-Eastern European zone of countries situated in-between Germany and Russia, stretching from the Baltics all the way down to the Black Sea. NATO's eastern boundaries now lay right at the Russian territorial borders (consider for instance the challenging geostrategic position of the Baltic states). The European Union's own enlargement process almost exactly followed track with the territorial extension of NATO

1 NATO enlargement occurred in several waves. On 3 October 1990, East- and West-Germany were reunited as part of a deal between Gorbachov and the American president Bush senior. Instigated by the American president Bill Clinton, a first enlargement wave was consolidated on 12 March 1999 when the Czech Republic, Hungary and Poland joined the Alliance. The American president Bush junior promoted a second wave which was executed on 29 March 2004 when Bulgaria, Estonia, Latvia, Lithuania, Romania, Slovakia and Slovenia joined. On 1 April 2009, Albania and Croatia followed. On 5 June 2017, Montenegro joined. Still in the 'waiting chamber' are such countries as North Macedonia (accession protocol signed in February 2019), Bosnia and Herzegovina (part of the Membership Action Plan since December 2018), Georgia (Intensified Dialogue since September 2006) and Ukraine (Intensified Dialogue since April 2005).

 | DOI:10.1163/9789004432086_008

eastward. Hence, the new politico-economic space of what is now generally referred to as the 'Euro-Atlantic area', has substantially transformed both the geopolitical and geo-economic realities in Europe. This chapter further delves into this process, and its consequences for geostrategy.

The main problem with this process is the potential overestimation of the capacity of NATO (and to a lesser extent of the EU) to spread liberal democracy to the newly independent post-communist and post-soviet countries in Central-Eastern Europe. This problem of appreciation is present in both the Euro-Atlantic policy-community as well as in the wider diplomatic world. With the geopolitical label of 'East-Central Europe', we refer to the countries laying within the boundaries of Central Europe and which formerly belonged to the 'Eastern Bloc' of communist countries. While there is no commonly shared definition of 'Central Europe'[2]. For the purpose of this article, 'East-Central Europe' includes the Baltics (Estonia, Latvia, Lithuania), the 'Visegrad' group of countries (Czech Republic, Hungary, Poland, Slovakia), as well as South-Eastern Europe or the Balkans (Albania, Bosnia and Herzegovina, Bulgaria, Northern Macedonia, Romania, Slovenia and Serbia). This demarcation of 'East-Central' (or Central-Eastern-) Europe also coincides with the geographic zone on which both NATO- and EU-enlargement processes have been focusing since the collapse of the Warsaw Pact in 1991.

This chapter therefore contrasts the perceived benefits of especially NATO enlargement for the spread of 'liberal peace'. This very enlargement process de facto created new geopolitical realities; the extension of the 'sphere of influence' of Atlantic seapowers. The author argues and defends the position that this may very well be at the detriment of continental power politics in Europe. With this, we mean that the eastward expansion of the Transatlantic Alliance (traditionally led by the two Atlantic Sea Powers; the United Kingdom and the United States of America), may push back the strategic interests of the two main continental powers in Europe; Germany and Russia. As a result, this may very well contribute to the effective containment of Berlin and Moscow, and could ultimately prevent their potential strategic collaboration.

Overall, this chapter aims at responding to the question as to what extent a more assertive NATO enlargement process may actually fuel a new type of Cold War situation in Europe. Consider for instance the situation as recently felt

2 Since the Middle Ages, Central Europe was split among the Eastern- (Byzantine) and Western- (Rome) Christian communities and catholic and orthodox countries correspondingly. In modern history, it was very much shaped by the Austro-Hungarian Empire or more generally referred to as the geographic area laying in-between Germany and Russia, or what would be called in German 'Mittel- or Zwischen-Europa'.

over the question of whether countries like Georgia or even Ukraine should be invited to become NATO members. This situation may not only have alienated post-Soviet Russia from European integration, but also from productive and mutually beneficial relations with the West overall. It may also produce a dangerous security dilemma for continental Europe itself.

This chapter is organised in the following way. *First*, it historically reviews the strategy of containment of the former Soviet Union according to its policy advocate, George Kennan. However, in contrast to wide-spread perception that containment was essentially a military strategy, we argue that Kennan actually proposed a non-military approach. *Second*, drawing some parallels between the situation in Europe after the end of the First World War and after the end of the Cold War, this chapter examines the question of NATO enlargement in the context of the talks between the US and the former Soviet Union after the fall of the Berlin Wall. More specifically, we devote attention to the alleged American pledge not to expand NATO in exchange for a reunified Germany which itself could nevertheless become a NATO member. *Third*, the conception of 'liberal peace' will be critically analysed against the background of the perception that NATO enlargement may spread democracy. *Fourth*, this leads to the assertion that NATO's post-Cold War eastward enlargement did in fact trigger a kind of 'Cold War II' scenario in Europe. The author argues that, in order to spread liberal democracy and free market economics, the countries in East-Central Europe should rather rely on the Council of Europe, the Organisation for Security and Co-operation in Europe (OSCE), and the European Union (EU). *Fifth*, this chapter deconstructs the liberal peace thesis, defending the position that considerable tensions remain - not only among capitalist societies themselves. More often than not, liberal peace tends to be overshadowed in the literature and public debate by the idea that *"democracies only tend to end up in a military conflict with non-democracies"*. *Finally*, based upon a recent initiative within the German *Bundestag*, this chapter questions the need for further NATO enlargement. It rather argues that Europe's stability and prosperity would benefit from an *inclusive, Pan-European Security arrangement* based on the normative principles set forth by the OSCE.

2 George Kennan and the Cold War Heritage of Containment

George Kennan can be considered one of the most distinguished personalities in the history of US foreign policy. As a diplomat working for the *US State Department* between 1927 and 1953, and from 1956 as a scholar at the *Institute for Advanced Study* at Princeton University, he dealt with practically every important foreign policy issue with which the United States was confronted from the period of Franklin Roosevelt to that of Ronald Reagan. According to Henry Kissinger, *"George Kennan came as close to authoring the diplomatic doctrine of his era as any diplomat in our history"* (Rojansky, 2016).

More specifically, George F. Kennan is known as the father of the *containment strategy* over the Soviet Union that would largely guide US foreign policy throughout the Cold War and that would also be referred to as the *Truman Doctrine.*[3] First it was formulated in a secret *'Long Telegram'* in 1946 that Kennan dispatched from the US Embassy in Moscow to Washington (Kennan, 1946). At that time he acted as diplomatic deputy head in the Soviet capital. Kennan would later reprise his analysis and proposed strategy under the pseudonym *'Mr. X'* in an article titled *'The Sources of Soviet Conduct'* published in *Foreign Affairs* in July 1947. That same year, Kennan became the Director of the *State Department Policy Planning Staff* in Washington D.C.. Arguably, not only had George Kennan been one of the most influential Foreign Service officers in the United States history (Leffler, 2006, p. 1), he was also one of the most authoritative expert and observer of US-Russian relations until the post-Cold War period. At that time, NATO started to expand eastward into the post-Soviet space. This distinguished observer and shaper of East-West relations died as a centenarian in 2005. That means he did also witness at a high age how those relations again took a turn for the worse after 1999.

Mainstream international relations theory largely focused on military interpretations of containment. Herewith many of these publications largely overlooked the fact that its founder, George Kennan, would essentially prescribe a *non-military strategy.* Not only would he stand firm against a militaristic approach to containment, he was also an *"outspoken, articulate opponent of the nuclear arms race"* (Rojansky, 2016). As Leffler underscores:

> During the very first meetings of the Policy Planning Staff in May 1947, Kennan stated that the problems facing the United States were **political**, not military and that the political problems needed to be addressed through **economic policies.** He championed the allocation of economic aid and played a **key role in formulating the Marshall Plan.** The focus of attention, he insisted, must not be on the communist threat, but on restoring the health and vigour of European society. Moreover, occupation policies in Germany and Austria needed to be configured so that their resources could make a maximum contribution to overall European

3 The Truman Doctrine was a US foreign policy whose purpose was to counter Soviet geopolitical expansion during the Cold War.

> recovery. The place to begin, Kennan advised, was the **coal-producing areas of the Rhine River Valley** (referred to in German as the 'Ruhr Gebiet'). Coal production, in Kennan's view, was the key to reviving production in Western Europe, overcoming the dollar gap, generating hope, and undercutting the appeal of indigenous communists (emphasis added). (Leffler, 2006, p. 6)

Kennan also anticipated the creation of the European Union whose original institutions would provide for a *"multi-national administration of those coal-producing areas of the Rhine River"*. From a strategic point of view, containment was ultimately inspired by Anglo-American geopolitical representations of continental Europe and Eurasia itself, the world's largest continental landmass. While Kennan would become the 'policy-father' of containment, the strategy's 'intellectual founder' was Yale's political science professor Nicholas Spykman who belongs to the US's most influential geopolitical thinkers of the twentieth century (Csurgai, 2019, p. 30). Spykman's *'Rimland' theory* was inspired by the British scholar Halford Mackinder[4] and his *'Heartland' theory*.[5] These two geopolitical authors reflected also on the two *Atlantic sea powers* that dominated world affairs throughout the past two hundred years. Just like the British Empire of the nineteenth century, so was the United States of America in the twentieth century primarily concerned with the control over the vast *Eurasian landmass*. The two main *European continental powers*, Germany and Russia, had to be contained if the Anglo-American powers would ever hope to be able to preserve their respective hegemonies in world

4 As Sloan underlines, there were no *explicit* references to any geopolitical concepts in Kennan's writing (Sloan, 2017, p. 160). Mayers nevertheless believes Kennan had studied the work of Halford John Mackinder. Another influence appears to have been Walter Lippman, more specifically on the questions what constitutes power and how foreign centres of power related to US security. Kennan agreed with Lippman that 'vital' and 'peripheral' interests had to be distinguished, but he rejected formulas as being too rigid and simple (Mayers, 1988, p. 130). In addition, Sloan believes that in 1951, Kennan articulated a geopolitical framework that closely resembled the third version of Mackinder's Heartland Theory of 1943: "[...] *no single continental land power should come to dominate the entire Eurasia landmass. Our interest has lain rather in the maintenance of some sort of stable balance among the powers of the interior, in order that none of them should effect the subjugation of the others, conquer the seafaring fringes of the land mass, become a great sea power as well as land power, shatter the position of England, and enter – as in these circumstances it certainly would – on a overseas expansion hostile to ourselves and supported by the immense resources of Europe and Asia."* (Kennan, 1951, p. 5).

5 For more on the thinking of the geopolitical scholars Halford John Mackinder and Nicholas John Spykman, read chapter 3 of this book.

affairs. Arguably, both the Cold War containment strategy and post-Cold War NATO enlargement have been serving this purpose. This is also exemplified in the writings of the Polish-American geopolitical author and former US National Security Advisor Zbigniew Brzezinski's influential writing *'The Grand Chessboard'*. This article and later book under the same title were published two years before NATO implemented its first wave of post-Cold War enlargement into what was now called 'Central-Eastern Europe' (Brzezinski, 1997a; Brzezinski, 1997b).[6]

George Kennan was perfectly aware of the outstanding challenges that both Germany and Russia would pose to US pre-eminence, especially if they were to combine their continental might. Kennan's fear was a joining of Russian and German power (Leffler, 2006, p. 6). With reference to Kennan's article of April 1947, Leffler would herewith quote the arguably most serious challenge to Anglo-American geopolitics in Europe over the past two hundred years: *"The only really dangerous thing in my mind ... is the possibility that the technical skills of the Germans might be combined with the physical resources of Russia"* (Leffler, 2006, p. 6).[7]

3 German Reunification and Controversy over NATO's 'Non-Expansion Pledge'

There has been a controversy over the question of whether the US leadership had given assurances (so-called 'non-expansion pledge') to Soviet leaders. During the talks on German reunification in February 1990 between the then US Secretary of State James Baker III and Soviet Secretary General Michail Gorbachov, Baker allegedly gave American assurances that NATO would not to expand beyond a reunified Germany. Gorbachov still claims this while the

6 Zbigniew Brzezinski's academic writing follows the geopolitical tradition of Mackinder and Spykman in that he identifies and further elaborates on Eurasia as the core of his geostrategic vision. He would be one of the most influential national security advisors of consecutive US Administrations since the American president Jimmy Carter, in whose administration he served from 1977 till 1981. He would later become, amongst others, the co-founder of the Trilateral Commission with David Rockefeller. Up until a high age, Zbigniew Brzezinski remained an important geopolitical scholar and policy advisor in American policy-circles. He died in May 2017. For more on the geopolitical thinking of Zbigniew Brzezinski, read chapter 3 of this book.

7 One might add the stand-alone *territorial* extent of Russia and its strategic geographic position connecting Eastern Europe with East Asia. In addition, the Russian Federation has *demographic* strength, as it harbours Europe's largest population.

American side disagrees as to whether such an offer was ever made by the US. The point was that those negotiations did not take place among evenly powerful parties since the Soviet Union was about to collapse economically. Thus, as Itzkowitz correctly mentions, the US would not only be the dominant nation within NATO. It would effectively hold an *"outsized influence on the issue of German reunification"* (Leffler, 2006, p. 9). Consequently, a reunified Germany was to be integrated into NATO which would in turn safeguard that any future German-Russian cooperative arrangements in Europe were made technically impossible. In the context of post-Cold War NATO enlargement, a corresponding slogan about European integration states: *'Keep Germany in and keep Russia out'*. This is nothing but a corollary of what the first ever Secretary General of the Alliance, Hastings Ismay, stated about the very purpose of NATO, namely *'to keep the Russians out, the Americans in, and the Germans down'* (Hurowitz, 2018).

Whatever US diplomats may have *officially communicated* and even promised during those talks with Michail Gorbachov and his fellow Soviet leaders, their *de facto geopolitical perspective* was to look beyond Germany and to eventually expand NATO further into East-Central Europe. This happened at a time when both the Soviet Union and post-Soviet Russia were simply too weak (after the collapse of the Soviet Union and dissolution of the Warsaw Pact in 1991), especially economically, to halt the process. Moreover, by expanding NATO to Eastern Europe, the US would also make sure that no *intra-European* or *Pan-European* security system could emerge after the end of the Cold War. In the words of Itzkowitz:

> the available evidence suggests a sharp disjuncture between what the United States told the Soviet Union and what U.S. policymakers **privately intended** [...][namely] privately [...] U.S. policymakers sought to expand the United States' presence in Central-Eastern Europe; they discounted the importance of the **cooperative and pan-European security structures** presented to the Soviet Union, and they opposed arrangements that would foreclose future U.S. options in Europe (emphasis added). (Leffler, 2006, pp. 39–40)

The consequences of these geopolitical intentions and follow-up actions that would expand NATO right up to Russia's post-Soviet borders in the Baltics (Estonia, Latvia and Lithuania) were particularly felt within the OSCE. This institution was Europe's cooperative (sic!) and inclusive security structure from a Pan-European point of view. With the eastward enlargement of NATO, the security dialogue within the OSCE gradually degraded into some sort of 'finger-pointing club'. The overwhelming majority of participating States were *de facto* streamlined by a US-dominated NATO with the implicit objective to 'isolate' and 'exclude' the Russian Federation from post-Cold War European integration. As a matter of fact and geopolitical reality, over the past three decades, the OSCE tended to become a 'Russia-bashing'[8] (Gower & Timmins, 2013, p. 94) organisation. This situation culminated in two major crises between Russia and the West over Georgia (2008) and Ukraine (2014).

Russia's involvement in Georgia and Ukraine during the 2008 Russo-Georgian War and the secession of Crimea in 2014 were in part responses to the broken non-expansion agreement (Itzkowitz, 2016, pp. 7–44). Moreover, Leffler points out that *"Russia's actions may stem from feelings of insecurity and real worries that the West is an unreliable partner. Hard-line measures to deter Russian aggression such as troop deployments and sanctions will therefore only increase Russia's sense of isolation and betrayal"* (Leffler, 2006, pp. 9–10).

After all, as the Bush Junior Administration decided to invite Georgia and Ukraine into the NATO membership, the US would thereby cross a hard, red line of what was yet acceptable from a Russian national security perspective. Therefore, as Mearsheimer underscored with the situation in Ukraine in particular, President Putin had no other choice but to respond with *Realpolitik*. The Russian President perceived the so-called 'revolution' on the 'Euro-Maidan' in Ukraine's capital city of Kyiv as, in fact, *'a coup d'état fuelled by Western interference against a democratically elected President'*. In the West, Russian actions in Georgia and Ukraine were called 'acts of aggression'. From a Russian perspective, this constituted an aggressive (and unnecessary) NATO eastward expansion that was felt like it was an existential threat. To borrow a hypothetical analogy, Mearsheimer would rightly state: *"Imagine the outrage in Washington if China built an impressive military alliance and tried to include Canada and Mexico in it."* (Mearsheimer, 2014).

4 Revisiting the Liberal Perception that NATO May Spread Democracy

By the mid-1990s, NATO was preparing for the first post-Cold War enlargement round of NATO. The organisation invited three former Warsaw Pact countries for formal membership in the Alliance; the Czech Republic, Hungary, and Poland. By that time, Michael Mandelbaum, responded to an article issued by

8 Jean-Claude Juncker has called for an end to "Russia-bashing" in May 2018, two months after countless Moscow diplomats across the EU were expelled in response to the alleged use of a nerve agent in the UK (Skripal Case).

Richard Holbrook in *Foreign Affairs* that held the provocative title *'America, a European Power'*. He argued that this move was *"at best premature, at worst counterproductive"*. In any case, it was *"largely irrelevant to the problems confronting the countries situated between Germany and Russia"* (emphasis added) (Mandelbaum, 1995, pp. 9–13). Those who were in favour of the Alliance's eastward enlargement to post-communist Europe would refer to the liberal vision of 'democratic peace'. They argued that NATO enlargement would not only spread democracy but also free-market economics. Indeed, fairly optimistic about the peace dividend in Europe after the collapse of the Soviet Union and the dissolution of the Warsaw Pact back in 1991, academic and policy discourses on the post-Cold War era tended to be dominated by liberal theory. This ideological dominance within International Relations was further nurtured by Francis Fukuyama's notion of the *'end of history'*. It asserted that after the fall of communism, liberal democracy was the only possible solution to society. Less officially, some more hawkish policy-advisors in Washington would push the idea of 'neo-containing' (Wallander, 2005) post-Soviet Russia. The withdrawal of troops of the Warsaw Pact from East-Central Europe would leave a considerable security gap in this part of Europe. This entailed the risk that the Russian Federation could take advantage of this by re-extending her political and economic influence there.

However, Russia was far too preoccupied to cope with all sorts of post-Soviet legacies. Moscow was even put under a harsh structural adjustment program by the International Monetary Fund (IMF) during the 1990s. Thus, there were neither any plans nor any means to interfere in the internal affairs of, let alone to intervene militarily into former Warsaw Pact satellite countries in East-Central Europe. In short, post-Cold War Russia would not pose any tangible threat to the whole of Europe, and since *"the logic of extending the alliance for reasons of neo-containment is far from implausible"* (Mandelbaum, 2014, p. 11). Moreover, drawing some analogy with the Marshall Plan after the end of the Second World War, Mandelbaum reflected on Kennan's views. He pointed out that East-Central Europe's priorities were not political but *economic*. Accordingly, membership of the *European Union* was much better suited to their needs and preoccupations (this applied for instance to the Visegrad group of countries):

> In fact… NATO is not an effective instrument for promoting either free markets or democracy. In the second half of the 1940s, when the fate of democracy and free markets in Western Europe was the preeminent international issue, the principal response – and an extremely successful one – was the Marshall Plan. The plan provided capital, market access, and incentives for economic cooperation, all of which central Europe currently needs. The logical source for all three is not NATO; it is the

> European Union, membership in which is a matter of the **highest priority for each of the Visegrad countries** (emphasis added). (Mandelbaum, 2014, pp. 9–10)

Mandelbaum implicitly took up the idea of setting up economic development and cooperation incentives as a means of promoting stability. This entailed an idea that was already outlined in the 1940s by George Kennan, the main architect of the Marshall Plan. Mandelbaum implicitly referred to the context in which the EU de facto became the main vehicle for the promotion of *liberal economic development*. At the same time, his recommendations regarding the EU's role in promoting *liberal political values* remained less assertive. Indeed, just like NATO is not a 'humanitarian agency', the EU's core business has been regional free trade and the creation of a single market among member states. However, when it comes to the promotion of democracy, human rights, and the rule of law in Europe, this has been the core mission of the Council of Europe (CoE) based in Strasbourg. The CoE is a Pan-European Organization which also includes the Russian Federation among its member states.[9] In any event, it is elusive to think that a military alliance may effectively spread democracy. While NATO may contribute to the delivery of humanitarian aid, the military is among the least suitable institutions to promote democracy. The very same lesson would also have to be learned upon the invasion of Iraq in 2003 by a US-British military 'coalition of the willing'. The Bush Junior Administration was of the view that their action would thereby not only deter terrorism but actually "spread democracy" throughout the Middle East. This was, of course, complete nonsense. By any standard, democracy cannot be imposed from abroad, let alone 'enforced militarily', nor can it be exported like a commercial commodity; to work properly, it must be home-grown (Lambert, Wilson III, Foster, 2009, pp. 46–63).

Normative considerations apart, NATO post-Cold War enlargement would become a *geopolitical reality* informed by Anglo-American strategic goals in continental Europe. There, the US would seek to keep political, economic, and spatial control over Europe's post-Cold War integration process. This was done with the aim of controlling the geographic zone situated in-between Germany and Russia.

On 12 March 1999, the three Visegrad countries (the Czech Republic, Hungary, and Poland) joined the Alliance. By that time, NATO was already preparing

9 At the same time, the European Union is funding many human rights and democratization programs of non-governmental organizations in and beyond Europe and is one of the most important humanitarian and development donors in the world.

for a next round of eastward expansion. The plan was to invite more countries situated near Russia's national borders. This would include even some of the former member states of the Soviet Union (Estonia, Latvia and Lithuania), who joined by 29 March 2004. However, two years after the first enlargement round and three years before the second, Dan Reiter would draw some pessimistic lessons about NATO's capacity to spread democracy, taking into account the Alliance's Cold War records. Paraphrasing the former US Ambassador to the United Nations (UN), Jeane Kirkpatrick who was of the view that it was not international organisations but the spread of democracy that was the only reliable guarantee against aggression (e.g. potentially from Russia), Reiter would reject such views. Furthermore, his assessment would coincide with Mandelbaum's prior analysis in the mid-1990s:

> NATO membership **has not and will not advance democracy.** The empirical record during the Cold War is clear: Inclusion in NATO did not promote democracy among members. Further, enlargement did not contribute much do democratization in the three East European states admitted in 1999, and the promise of NATO membership is unlikely to speed democracy within any of the nine countries currently awaiting a decision on their requests for membership… Instead, the **West should rely on the European Union (EU) to spread democracy**, an approach that is more likely to foster democratization yet less likely to alienate Russia. (Reiter, 2001, pp. 41–67)

Mandelbaum and Reiter nevertheless slightly differ in that the latter expressed a more assertive recommendation that the West ought to rely on the EU to 'spread democracy'. While still omitting the circumstance institutionally, and as stated above, it is the essential business of the Pan-European CoE to defend democracy, the rule of law, and human rights, including in Russia! Anyway, they in turn coincided in their view that NATO was definitively not an appropriate vehicle to spread democracy. Precaution was needed in order to counterweigh against a 'militaristic' approach to US foreign policy in Europe. Mandelbaum and Reiter herewith resonate George Kennan's critique of a militaristic approach to containment during the Cold War and his public advocacy against the nuclear arms race. For this, he would receive special recognition in the early 1980s by the *Albert Einstein Peace Prize* and the *German Booksellers Association* (Rojansky, 2016).

In fact, by the early 1980s, Ronald Reagan launched the *Strategic Defence Initiative* (SDI), occasionally referred to as the 'Star Wars' program. Mainstream literature in the West still often identifies this initiative as the main policy proposal that contributed to the collapse of the Soviet Union and thus the end of the Cold War. However, as Richard Ullman warned in 1983, the massive increase of defence expenditures associated with SDI would symbolise a perversely militaristic foreign policy tendency in the US. In order to rebalance this tendency, Ullman suggested that the US should instead build on a more comprehensive security approach beyond the military (Ullman, 1983, pp. 25–32). Ullman's views would not only coincide with Kennan's advocacy for improved US-Soviet relations and appeasement. His precautions against a disproportionately militarised foreign policy posture would also reflect the theory of the 'rise and fall of great powers' developed by Yale historian Paul Kennedy. He had explained that the decline of great powers in history essentially occurred as a result of excessive military overspending. This constituted a theory that would actually predict the collapse of the Soviet Union. Moscow could no longer compete with Washington in terms of defence spending. Soviet military attempts to keep track with the strategic arms race could be maintained. The Americans were outspending the Soviets in all theatres, including now also a new additional strategic frontier: space. Moscow's attempts to keep up led to a crippling of their civilian economy. As a consequence, the Soviet communist model would implode (Kennedy, 1988).

However, largely neglected by policy elites in the West even today, Kennedy would also anticipate what may happen with the United States themselves. By the turn of the twenty-first century, the *States* themselves would spend half of the world's defence budget alone.[10] This massive budgetary expenditure is today spread over some thousand military bases of various size and in all corners of the world. The US would spend, measured in terms of public taxes and national budget, around forty times more on their military than on diplomacy (including development and humanitarian aid).[11]

In a rare criticism of US foreign policy, Charles Kupchan would around that time argue that his country had failed to deliver a new generation of well-trained foreign service officers. The 'American era' was about to end in face of re-emerging Asia and Europe. He associated their main strength with the emphasis that was put on economic development and regional cooperation (Kupchan, 2002). The Anglo-American coalition would invade Iraq two years later. Both France and Germany stood firm in their opposition to *Uncle Sam*.

10 According to the Stockholm International Institute for Peace (SIPRI).

11 After all, when the American president Donald Trump recently increased the US Defence budget by some sixty billion US dollars (while cutting in turn the budgets of some civilian departments), this almost amounts to the total of the Russian annual defence budget which is about $ 80 billion.

They advocated the need for a formal mandate by the United Nations Security Council (UNSC), and openly objected to this action against a sovereign state. In the opinion of both Paris and Berlin, the American actions in Iraq could be considered contrary to the most fundamental principles of international law. Significantly, not only are these two countries at the heart of the European integration process. They also form the central block within the EU. In addition, France and Germany function as the most important NATO allies on the Western part of the European peninsula. Largely omitted by the Western mainstream press and academic literature, the second post-Cold War enlargement process thus took shape at the heat of a major internal controversy, if not a genuine identity crisis within the Atlantic Alliance itself.

Moreover, two additional regional organizations beyond NATO and the EU have substantially contributed to regional stability in Europe and to overcoming the Cold War. This was completely overseen and neglected by many Western observers, especially in the United States.

First, as already referred to above, Western mainstream literature typically associates the EU as the main promotor of democracy and human rights in Europe. However, the continent's statutory regional and multilateral institution in charge of promoting and defending these values, including the rule of law, is the Council of Europe (CoE). Furthermore and most importantly, the Russian Federation is a member state of the CoE. This institution not only constitutes an indigenously Pan-European organization. The CoE, based in Strasbourg, provides for the world's most effective international human rights regime. Any individual originating from a member state may sue their government if their claim has been rejected by their national constitutional courts. This is something that would be impossible at the level of the EU, whose core institutions such as the European Commission are faced with a lack of tangible democratic legitimacy.[12] After all, since the CoE is an intergovernmental multilateral organization, it also counts Europe's neutral and non-allied countries among its statutory member states.

Second, Europe's Pan-European security organization is the *Organization for Security and Cooperation in Europe* (OSCE). The emphasis needs to be put here on 'cooperation'. In contrast to a defence alliance whose very identity remains antagonistic with an outside power or defence alliance of other states such

---

12 The most pronounced feature of the democratic deficit of the European Union lies largely in the fact that EU Commissioners are not appointed directly or without any involvement of the European Parliament. As the European Union's executive branch, this constitutes a lacuna. However, candidate-Commissioners do have to pass a hearing before relevant parliamentary committees in the EP.

as the Warsaw Pact during the Cold War, the OSCE provides an inclusive and comprehensive approach of 'cooperative security'. Moreover, the OSCE is not only the world's largest regional security organisation. It ranges from 'Vancouver to Vladivostok'. Herewith it encompasses not only the entire post-Soviet area but also both Canada and the US. Just like the CoE, the OSCE is based on the principles of multilateral diplomacy. It constitutes a statutory regional organization under the UN Charter. Moreover, based on its cooperative security conceptions, it *inter alea* provides for the world's most advanced regional Confidence and Security Building Measures (CSBMS) regime. Launched during the *détente* period of the Cold War period in the mid-1970s (then the CSCE), the CSCE/OSCE made a significant contribution to building trust between the formerly Western and Eastern blocs. It continues to prevent conflict in Europe to this very day. The organisation also played a crucial role in 2014 to de-escalate the conflict in Ukraine. Anglo-American academia and policy circles always tended to downplay the relevance of the OSCE for security and stability in Europe. Was this because, within the OSCE, the US would have to sit at the same table and at the same level as the former Soviet Union and now Russia?

The ultimate purpose and added value of both the CoE and the OSCE have been to forge political stability across Europe down to the Urals. In this way, an enhanced economic cooperation may take shape. However, this stands in the way of Anglo-American geopolitics whose eternal rationale has been to avoid any tangible, let alone territorial approach between Germany and Russia. Consequently, they have chosen to keep NATO alive after the end of the Cold War. With the Alliance's enlargement it was gradually promoted as the main security organisation in both Western and East-Central Europe. As NATO now stretches from the Baltic Sea down to the Black Sea, it has effectively been in a position to alienate Russia from European integration. Both the EU and NATO have their headquarters situated in the very same place in the capital city of Brussels. This has given Washington some advantage to more efficiently 'coordinate' policy in-between the Union and the Alliance, including when it comes to their joint foreign policy approaches towards Russia. The EU's *de facto* bandwagoning strategy with an 'Atlantist' geopolitical posture vis-à-vis Russia was gradually felt during the period in between the two conflicts of Russia with Georgia (2008) and Ukraine (2014). This coincided with the French strategy advocated by President Nicholas Sarkozy to reintegrate France into the military command structure of NATO. The EU remained silent over the Alliance's controversial intervention in Libya in 2011. France developed a tacit alliance with the US and Britain in their actions against the Syrian regime of Bashar al-Assad. The Russian Federation remained their most important strategic partner, and maintained an important naval port on the Syrian

Mediterranean coast, Tartus. This port, together with the Russian navel port at Sebastopol at the Crimean peninsula, became a key strategic asset for Moscow in its own fight against Islamic State in Syria. What is also worth noting is that the People's Republic of China had to repatriate tens of thousands of working migrants from Libya. For that purpose, it sent a small military presence through the Suez Canal. This did not go unnoticed. Later Beijing would also provide for some economic aid to Iraq and Syria for post-conflict reconstruction. Both Eurasian powers thus played their own role in the region, be it in very different leagues.

5 NATO Enlargement Would Trigger Cold War II in Europe

In an interview with Thomas Friedman in *The New York Times* in 1998, George Kennan considered NATO's first post-Cold War enlargement to East-Central Europe (1999) a "strategically fatal decision". In this rare critique of US foreign policy, Kennan identified this enlargement as a 'tragic mistake' which fueled another Cold War situation in Europe. In an earlier part of his career, Kennan had received professional training on the former Soviet Union and fluently spoke Russian. Hence he commented that the decision to expand NATO would reflect utter lack of imagination that characterised US foreign policy in the late 1990s:

> I think it (NATO Enlargement) is the beginning of a **new cold war** [...] [as] [...] the Russians will gradually react quite adversely and it will affect their policies ... (and that) [...] it is a **tragic mistake**. There was no reason for this whatsoever (for expanding NATO) [...] **No one was threatening anybody** [...] [and] [...] it [read: the decision to expand NATO] shows so little understanding of Russian history, of Soviet history ... **This expansion would make the Founding Fathers of this country (USA) turn over in their graves!** ... I was particularly bothered by the references to Russia as a country trying to attack Western Europe. Don't people understand? Our differences in the cold war were with the **Soviet Communist Regime**. And now **we are turning our backs on the very people who mounted the greatest bloodless revolution in history** [read: the peaceful dissolution of the Soviet Union and Warsaw Pact] to remove that Soviet regime. And **Russia's democracy is as far advanced, if not farther, as any of these countries we've just signed up (via NATO membership) to defend from Russia!** ... This has been my life, and it pains me to see it so screwed up in the end. (Kennan, in: Friedman, 1998)

The 1990s were also the time when NATO would intervene militarily in the Balkans. In the case of Kosovo and the corresponding bombing of Serbia in 1999, it would do so without authorisation of the United Nations Security Council. From a geopolitical perspective, it is important to note that the Russian Federation was strictly opposed to NATO's actions in Kosovo. This was due to the fact that Slavic and Christian-orthodox Serbia was her privileged ally in the Western Balkans. Fifteen years later, Russia would to some extent take revenge by annexing Crimea during the conflict over Ukraine. As Mearsheimer has pointed out, this conflict has been deliberately fuelled by the West. Mearsheimer also referred to the fact that through the *National Endowment of Democracy* (NED), the US allegedly had allocated some five billion dollars since the early 1990s (Mearsheimer, 2014). This money was used to bring Ukraine into Western European structures and thus out of the orbit of Russia's direct influence. Next to the 'regime change' in Kyiv, the US seems to have had plans for regime change in Moscow too – at least that is what policy makes in Moscow believed. What is also worth noting is that during NATO's military intervention against Serbia, it would *inter alia* bomb the Chinese embassy in Belgrade. Whether accidental or intended, China would respond with what the new leadership in Beijing has called the 'permanent modernization of the Chinese armed forces'. In any event, fatal decisions were made in Washington and arguably also in London (keep for instance the invasion of Iraq in March 2003 in mind). These policy choices would, by the turn to the twenty-first century, set the scene for a new geopolitical contestation that would range far beyond Europe. This would again technically paralyse the United Nations Security Council just like it was the case during the heat of the Cold War. However, Anglo-American strategic thinkers may have underestimated the 'Russian Bear' but also the 'Chinese Dragon'. Both giants would gradually start to enhance their bilateral strategic cooperation. This instigated a geopolitical process that would invert the Eurasian chessboard in a more fundamental way.

6 Shortfalls of Capitalism and the Need to Redevelop Expertise on Russia

In his famous *'Long Telegram'* which George Kennan wrote in 1946 at the heat of the escalating Cold War he made a remarkable comment about the shortcomings of capitalist societies:

> [the] capitalist world is beset with **internal conflicts, inherent in [the] nature of capitalist society**. These conflicts are insoluble [...] [using]

> [...] peaceful compromise. [...] [the] greatest of them is that between England and (the) US (!)[...] internal conflicts of capitalism inevitably generate wars. Wars thus generated may be of two kinds: intra-capitalist wars between two capitalist states, and wars of intervention against (the) socialist world... to speak of [the] possibility of intervention against USSR today, after elimination of Germany and Japan and after example of [the] recent war, is [the] sheerest nonsense. [...] (emphasis added). (Kennan, 1946)

Kennan's observations are remarkable for at least two reasons. First, he deconstructed the liberal 'democratic peace' thesis. Kennan argued that there remains high conflict potential among liberal societies themselves, let alone between the two closest Trans-Atlantic allies. Elaborating on the 'corollary' to the democratic peace thesis (*'liberal societies are likely to wage war on non-liberal societies'*), he points to the risk and precautions against waging war on the Soviet Union. Second, Kennan made an implicit distinction in his *Telegram* between an indigenously liberal society combining free-market politics with socio-democratic institutions on the one hand and pure 'capitalism' on the other. The latter's real face coincided with the neo-liberal market fundamentalism, as exemplified by deregulated and unchecked financial market flows. It only paid lip-service to redistributive justice.

Arguing that the contemporary US leadership would be well advised to follow Kennan's prescriptions, Matthew Rojanski pointed out that *"Kennan was horrified by ... militarized interpretations of containment"* and that post-WWII Europeans were not only *"tired and frightened by experiences of [the] past"*. But that they were also "less interested in *abstract freedom* than in security" (emphasis added) (Rojansky, 2016). Moreover, with further reference to Kennan, Rojansky draws some parallel to US-Russia relations today. Kennan would warn against any attempt to push regime change in Moscow. Not only America but the Western world as a whole should rather address its *structural challenges*. These essentially entailed the consequences of a free-lance capitalist system, combined with a militaristic foreign policy. As a result, a tendency had developed to divert vital funds for the protection of domestic public services aimed at providing basic human and civilian needs:

> The new U.S. administration's central challenge – and the challenge facing the West as a whole – is whether it can provide the positive vision that was integral to Kennan's containment strategy, especially in addressing persistent problems like **education, health care, infrastructure, and employment**. If Washington demonstrates vision and resolves to

> address its **pressing challenges**, Americans can have a far greater influence on developments in Russia… Indeed, the Cold War ended to a great degree because of Russians came to view the United States as a successful and prosperous society, whose model they hoped to emulate and whose partnership they desired to manage global challenges. By contrast, today's deterioration in relations has been deepened by American failures in Iraq and Afghanistan and the lingering consequences of the global financial crisis of 2008, which **shattered Russians' faith the American model for economic development** (emphasis added). (Rojansky, 2016)

Furthermore, Russia's contemporary insecurity perceptions do not only stem from Washington's plans of regime change in Moscow. Also 'NATO encirclement' of Russia and American 'meddling in Russia's post-soviet neighbourhood' played a role: *"Donald Trump is right to want to break with the policies of his predecessors that are in part responsible for the dismal state of relations (with Russia) today."* (Rojansky, 2016). That same year, Rojansky addressed the NATO Defence College in Rome. He recalled Kennan's essentially non-military strategy to contain the (former) Soviet Union. *Inter alia*, he suggested that the West should re-develop what he called a robust Western capacity to understand Russia – a capacity Kennan would judge to be sadly lacking today. In a similar fashion, the United States and Western Europe would be well advised not only to restore financial support for the development of *'robust Russian area expertise'*, but to actually set this as a *top national security imperative*. (emphasis added) (Rojansky, 2016).

7 Germany: Quo Vadis?

Early 2019, an initiative was taken by a group of German parliamentarians. Among them politicians were involved of the left-wing fraction (*'Linke Fraktion'*) in the German *Bundestag*. They had been criticizing the logic of NATO enlargement. In their opinion, NATO military manoeuvres in the Baltic region were a dangerous development. Furthermore, to preserve peace and arms control in Europe, the initiator's corresponding public report suggested to strengthen the OSCE anew. After all, this is Europe's cooperative and Pan-European security organization which also includes Russia. The authors *inter alia* regretted that the North Atlantic Treaty Organisation had strayed away from its original mission. From a *defence alliance* it had become what they coined *'an intervention alliance'* (Wagenknecht & Bartsch, 2019, p. 1).

Particular concern is expressed regarding Germany's distinct role in NATO's *'Enhanced Forward Presence'* in the Baltics. This means that Germany participates as a lead European country in substantial military manoeuvres some 150 kilometres from Saint Petersburg. For all those who have studied European history of the first half of the twentieth century, this should be an alarm bell. Moreover, emphasizing the OSCE's core normative principle of *indivisibility of security*, the report criticizes NATO's posture of direct confrontation with Russia over the past decade. This situation has culminated in the two crises over Georgia and Ukraine. The resulting geopolitical stalemate, threatens the OSCE's vision of 'inclusive security'. This is referred to as the *'Common European House'* (Wagenknecht & Bartsch, 2019, p. 1).

The German parliamentary report recommended that *"'European Security Cooperation' should return to 'equal security opportunities'"*. Especially the need is stressed to reinclude Russia into the 'Pan-European Security Dialogue'. Furthermore, it suggests that *"NATO shall not be further expanded"* (e.g. to Georgia, Ukraine, etc.). Finally, the Alliance's *'Very High Readiness Joint Tasks Force'* should be dissolved. In addition, Germany's participation in the NATO *'Enhanced Forward Presence'* in the Baltics immediately needed to be abolished. Correspondingly, the report recommended that the Russian Federation should, in turn, provide *new security guarantees and tangible new confidence building measures*. This is especially crucial with regard to the countries situated in 'East-Central Europe' (Wagenknecht & Bartsch, 2019, p. 3).

8 Conclusion: Towards an Indigenous Pan-European Security Architecture

Many experts of European Security may still remember the controversy when Russian President Dmitry Medvedev, on 5 June 2008, put forward an initiative to develop a new pan-European security treaty. The main idea of his statement was to *"create – in the context of military and political security in the Euro-Atlantic region – a common undivided space in order to finally do away with the Cold War legacy"* (President of Russia, 2009). However, few remember that already back in the early 1990s, France had tabled a similar proposal within the OSCE. That diplomatic initiative coming from Paris proposed to negotiate a 'new and Pan-European security treaty'. France at that time still pursued a 'Gaullist' foreign policy and *inter alia* advocated for a more independent European security and defence system. It was then no surprise that this French proposal was rejected by the United States. According to the late international relations professor and distinguished expert on the OSCE, Victor-Yves Ghébali, the main reason for US resistance to such a new and legally binding treaty was to keep NATO the main security organization in Europe. *Inter alia*, he explained that the *Code of Conduct on Politico-Military Aspects of Security*[13] would instead be adopted as the residue of the corresponding post-Cold War normative discourse on European security:

> The Code grew out of a French project concerning a pan-European security treaty which would have included the codification of the OSCE's existing security norms and spelt out additional security norms to cope with the needs of post-Communist Europe. **Mooted within NATO**, the idea was dismissed entirely by the United States and the overwhelming majority of allies, all equally motivated by the necessity of preserving the Alliance's future [...] ultimately, the idea was reformulated and downsized under the form of a French-German proposal for a politically binding Code. (Ghébali, 1996, pp. 5–13)

Contemporary architects of European security will have to face a historical opportunity choice. From a Russian perspective, the Cold War had definitively ended back in 1991. Moscow had hitherto not been posing any tangible security threat to Western Europe. Alienating Russia from collaboration with the West might prove to become a risky if not fatal strategic endeavour. Washington and Brussels imposed one-time joint economic sanctions on the Russian Federation in retaliation for its 'annexation' of Crimea in 2014. In addition, they excluded the Russian Federation from the G8. This has constrained Moscow. In response, it turned away from Europe and the West. Instead, it opted to pursue its own geopolitical 'Asian pivot' through an enhanced collaboration with the People's Republic of China. Earlier under President Obama in 2011, the US had engaged in its own geostrategic 'pivot to Asia'. In contrast to the later Russian 'Asian Pivot', American foreign policy in the Asia-Pacific increasingly turned 'anti-China'. This was also exemplified by Barack Obama's initiative for a *Trans-Pacific Partnership Agreement*. However, it had to be read geopolitically as including 'anybody but China'.

Ironically, Russia's Asia pivot reads 'pro-China'. China in addition launched its own *'One Belt, One Road' Initiative* (OBOR) in 2013, as well as the *Asia Infrastructure Investment Bank* (AIIB) in 2015. The BRICS-countries launched the *New Development Bank* (NDB) in 2014. Moscow unveiled the *Eurasian Economic Union* (EAEU) the same year. Both India and Pakistan joined the *Shanghai*

13 Organization for Security and Co-operation in Europe. Code of Conduct on Politico-Military Aspects of Security. https://www.osce.org/fsc/41355

Cooperation Organization (SCO) in 2017. As a result of this rapid succession of diplomatic initiatives, the geopolitical chessboard of Eurasia is about to completely transform. Meanwhile Western leaders continued to complain about Russia's actions in Ukraine. Some seem to be bent on trying to deter Russia or cause regime change in Moscow. The EU and US are increasingly driving themselves into internal political chaos and go through a serious identity crisis. Western geostrategic thinking appears to stay dormant vis-à-vis the profound transformation of world politics and the rise of the developing world, which increasingly opts for South-South cooperation and is no more reliant on aid by OECD countries. As a result, with two decades into the twenty-first century, the West faces a historical choice. In a first scenario, it opts for strategic partnership with the Russian Federation. This, in our opinion, would arguably be the ultimate 'trump card' in face of a fast-rising China. The power potential of Beijing may go far beyond the one of the former Soviet Union. Hence, there would be a common interest between the 'West' and Russia. In a second scenario, the West opts for continued exclusion and *de facto* containment of Russia. This will however run the risk that a colossal Beijing-Moscow alliance could emerge that may some day even incorporate Berlin, for instance via the new economic dynamics set in Eurasia by the *'One Belt, One Road' Initiative*. However, in geostrategic terms this would result in a 'checkmate' for the Anglo-American camp and Atlantic seapower politics for the first time in the last two hundred years.

Bibliography

Brzezinski, Z. (1997a). A Geostrategy for Eurasia. *Foreign Affairs*. 76(5): 50–64.

Brzezinski, Z. (1997b). *The Grand Chessboard: American Primacy and its Geostrategic Imperatives*. New York: Perseus Books.

Csurgai, G. (2019). *Geopolitical Analysis: A Multidimensional Approach to Analyze Power Rivalries in International Relations*. Rome: Aracne. http://www.aracneeditrice.it/aracneweb/index.php/pubblicazione.html?item=9788825529142 .

Friedman, T. (1998). [*Opinion*]. Now a word from X. *Foreign Affairs*. Retrieved from http://www.nytimes.com/1998/05/02/opinion/foreign-affairs-now-a-word-from-x.html

Ghébali, V.Y. (1996). Introducing the Code. In Gert, Nooy. (Eds.). *Cooperative Security, the OSCE, and its Code of Conduct* (Volume 24). The Netherlands. Martinus Nijhoff Publishers.

Gower, J., & Timmins, G. (Eds.). (2013). *The European Union, Russia and the shared neighbourhood* (1st Edition) (p. 94). London: Routledge.

Hurowitz, R. (2018). "What is NATO for"? *Washington Examiner*. July 25. Retrieved from: https://www.washingtonexaminer.com/weekly-standard/what-is-the-purpose-of-nato-keep-the-russians-out-the-americans-in-and-the-germans-down .

Itzkowitz, J. R. (2016). Deal or no deal? The end of the cold war and the u.s. offer to limit nato expansion. *International Security, Volume 40* (Issue 4), 7–44. Retrieved from https://www.mitpressjournals.org/doi/full/10.1162/isec_a_00236#fn1.

Kennan, G. (1946). *Long Telegram*. Retrieved from History and Public Policy Program Digital Archives and Records Administration. Department of State Records (Record Group 59). Central Decimal File, 1945–1949, 861.00/2–2246. reprinted in the US Department of State. Foreign Relations of the United States. (1946), Volume 6. Eastern Europe: The Soviet Union. Washington, DC: United States Government Printing Office. Retrieved from http://digitalarchive.wilsoncenter.org/document/116178.

Kennan, G. (1951). *American Diplomacy*. Chicago: University of Chicago Press.

Kennedy, P. (1988). *The Rise and Fall of Great Powers: Economic Change and Military Conflict from 1500 to 2000*. London / Sidney / Wellington: Unwin Hyman.

Kupchan, C. (2002). *The End of the American Era: U.S. Foreign Policy and the Geopolitics of the Twenty-first Century*. New York: Alfred Knopf.

Lambert, A. (2009). Democracy by Force. In Wilson III, I., & Foster, J.J.F. (Eds.). *Handbook of Defense Politics: International and Comparative Perspectives*. New York / London: Routledge.

Leffler, M. P. (2006). *Remembering George Kennan: Lessons for Today?* Special Report 180. United States Institute of Peace.

Mandelbaum, M. (1995). Preserving the New Peace: The Case Against NATO Expansion, *Foreign Affairs*, 74(3): 9–13, https://doi.org/10.2307/20047118

Mayers, D. (1988). *George Kennan and the Dilemmas of U.S. Foreign Policy*. New York: Oxford.

Mearsheimer, J. (2014). Why the Ukraine Crisis is the West's Fault: The Liberal Delusion that Provoked Putin. *Foreign Affairs*, 93(5): 77–89.

President of Russia. (2009). *The draft of the European Security Treaty*. Retrieved from http://en.kremlin.ru/events/president/news/6152.

Reiter, D. (2001). Why NATO Enlargement Does not Spread Democracy. *Quarterly Journal: International Security*, 25(4), Retrieved from https://www.belfercenter.org/publication/why-nato-enlargement-does-not-spread-democracy

Rojansky, M. (2016). *George Kennan is Still the Russia Expert America Needs: The Architect of Washington's Cold War Strategy Offers President Trump the Best Guide for Managing Moscow*. Retrieved from http://hdl.loc.gov/loc.pnp/ds.07025.

Rojansky, M. (2016). *George Kennan, Containment, and the West's Current Russia Problem*. Zürich: ETH Zurich Center for Security Studies.

Sloan, G. (2017). *Geopolitics, Geography and Strategic History*. Oxon, United Kingdom: Routledge.

Ullman, R. (1983) Redefining Security. *International Security*. In Lambert, A. & Young, N. (Eds.) (2010). *The Oxford International Encyclopedia of Peace, Volume 4*. Oxford / New York: Oxford University Press.

Wagenknecht, S., & Bartsch D. (2019). German Bundestag. The Organization for Security and Cooperation in Europe for Peace and strengthen disarmament. Retrieved from http://dip21.bundestag.de/dip21/btd/19/071/1907121.pdf.

Wallander, C. A. (2005). *Geopolitics and Neo-containment, as well as Common Security: Russian Views of Proliferation* (Policy Memo No. 371). Retrieved from http://www.ponarseurasia.org/memo/geopolitics-and-neo-containment-well-common-security-russian-views-proliferation.

CHAPTER 7

The Increasing Importance of Geoeconomics in Power Rivalries: From the Past to the Present

Gyula Csurgai

1 Introduction

The introduction of the term *geoeconomics* to a large audience has been mainly attributed to the US expert on strategy Edward Luttwak.[1] He argued at the end of the Cold War that ideological rivalries between Western liberal and communist collectivist models of societies would be replaced by a worldwide economic rivalry, in which trade, finance, and the mastering of important technologies often prevail over military power (Luttwak, 1990). Indeed, relations between states in the post-Cold War period have been shaped by an increased economic competition. This includes *Non-Market* factors such as intelligence sharing between state agencies and private businesses, successful economic diplomacy and different techniques to influence and manipulate non-governmental organisations to weaken an economic adversary, among other things. The considerable influence of these *Non-Market* factors illustrates the limits of the liberal economic theories that emphasise the dominant role of market forces and the rather limited role of the state in economics. Moreover, the 2008 financial crisis, the increasing use of financial means by China to gain geopolitical influences worldwide, the Russian strategy to use energy as an instrument in foreign policy, the use of extraterritorial jurisdiction by the United States as a tool of economic warfare, the state-capitalist models of economic development and the growing competition for scarce resources necessitate the re-evaluation of the role of the state in economic security and development. The main objectives of this chapter are the following: to examine the links between geopolitics and geoeconomics in the context of the growing importance of various economic means that are used as strategic instruments in contemporary power rivalries. In addition, this contribution seeks to discuss

1 This book chapter is an updated and extended version of the article 'The Increasing Importance of Geoeconomics in Power Rivalries in the Twenty-First Century', published previously in the journal *Geopolitics*, Vol. 23, Number 1 (2018).

 | DOI:10.1163/9789004432086_009

the role of the state in the organization of a national geoeconomic disposition. Some historical perspectives on the role of economic factors in power rivalries are integrated as well.

2 Geostrategy and Geoeconomics

The practical application of geopolitics is *geostrategy*, that is, the strategic management of geopolitical interests which can also be defined as the strategies of actors designed to achieve their geopolitical objectives. Although the classical perception on strategy has been state-centric and mainly concerned with the military aspect of the term, it can be stated that both state and non-state entities can use different strategies and apply both military and non-military means to achieve their aims.

According to a considerable number of experts, the use of the concept of geostrategy has been most often reserved for the military aspects of geopolitics: the use of spatial dimensions in the logic of armed conflict; and, the application of geographic reasoning in the conduct of war (Claval, 1994, p. 6) and in the organisation of the disposition of national defence (Foucher, 1991, p. 37). But, as mentioned above, the concept of strategy does not only concern the military sphere. Furthermore, all strategies – military or non-military – have spatial dimensions, and therefore, geostrategic relevance (Gray, 1999, p. 161).

As the US-led interventions in Iraq and Afghanistan have illustrated, military confrontation and direct control of a given geographic area by armed forces are often perceived as less advantageous than the use of non-military strategies in order to achieve the different geopolitical objectives of states. The growth of Chinese investments in resource-rich Africa, and the German economic strategy in Central Europe (which is a traditional sphere of influence of Germany), illustrate, among other examples, the growing importance of economic means to achieve geopolitical ends. Consequently, the use of these economic instruments to achieve various geopolitical objectives evidences the links between geoeconomics and geostrategy (Blackwill & Harris, 2016, p. 20). The term geoeconomics is explained by Edward Luttwak in 1990:

> Everyone, it appears, now agrees that the methods of commerce are displacing military methods – with disposable capital in lieu of firepower, civilian innovation in lieu of military-technical advancement, and market penetration in lieu of garrisons and bases. States, as spatial entities structured to jealously delimit their own territories, will not disappear but reorient themselves toward geoeconomics in order to compensate

> for their decaying geopolitical roles… …geoeconomics is the best term I can think of to describe the admixture of the logic of conflict with the methods of commerce. (Luttwak, 1990, p. 17)

Geoeconomics illustrates the strategic interactions between state agencies and various economic sectors for enhancing the power position of states in the contemporary international system. The French scholar, Pascal Lorot, director of the French Review, *Géoéconomie*, defines geoeconomics,

> as the analysis of economic strategies--notably commercial--, decided upon by states in a political setting aiming to protect their own economies or certain well-identified sectors of it, to help their national enterprises acquire technology or to capture certain segments of the world market relative to production or commercialization of a product. The possession or control of such a share confers to the entity--state or national enterprise--an element of power and international influence and helps to reinforce its economic and social potential. (Lorot, 1999, p.15)

Going beyond Luttwak's and Lorot's interpretations, geoeconomics can also be understood as economic power projections driving foreign policy outcomes. Such outcomes are not necessarily limited to the economic sphere. Indeed, geoeconomics can refer to the use of economic instruments to promote and defend national interests and achieve specific geopolitical goals (Blackwill & Harris, 2016, p. 20). States can often implement a geoeconomic strategy that simultaneously advances multiple interests: geopolitical, diplomatic, political and economic. The strategy of China towards Taiwan is rather interesting from a geoeconomic perspective and illustrates well how economic means can be used to achieve wider geopolitical objectives. In June 2010, an Economic Cooperation Framework Agreement (ECFA) was signed between China and Taiwan in order to liberalise important aspects of "Cross-Strait" economic relations. Subsequently, China became Taiwan's largest trading partner, with a cross-strait trade volume totalling around 150 billion dollars in 2018.[2] As a result, China has become Taiwan's largest export market and the most important market for Taiwanese investments as well. Furthermore, about 4 million Chinese tourists visit Taiwan each year. Parallel to this growing economic interdependence between China and Taiwan, Beijing uses its geoeconomic influence

---

2 Trade data obtained from the Bureau of Trade Statistics of Taiwan, Directorate General of Customs Administration, Ministry of Finance. Retrieved December 20, 2019, from: https://cus93.trade.gov.tw/FSCE030F/FSCE030F

to isolate Taiwan on a diplomatic level by providing aid, economic advantages and investments to countries that cut their diplomatic relations with Taiwan. Through such strategies, Beijing seeks to corner Taipei into political integration with the Chinese mainland. In Fall 2019, China offered economic aid and financial assistance to the Solomon Islands, a South Pacific archipelago, which influenced the decision of this small but strategically located state to end its diplomatic relations with Taiwan and establish diplomatic relations with China. Since 2016, the following countries opted for the switch of their diplomatic relations in the same way: Burkina Faso, the Dominican Republic, Sao Tome and Principe, Panama and El Salvador.

3 Economic Factors and Power Rivalries: From the Past to the Present

Although the concept of geoeconomics was first introduced to a larger public from the end of the Cold War, the interrelations between state power, economy and international trade had been taken into consideration throughout history. Controlling trade routes, gaining access to natural resources and conquering markets have been important factors in international economic relations. Venice became gradually a powerful geoeconomic actor from the 11th century. In spite of its small geographic configuration, this city state became a considerable trading power thanks to its strategy of alliance building combined with an efficient diplomacy, the mastering of advanced technologies in ship building, the use of economic espionage, and a well-developed financial sector, among others.

Strategic *economic means* for the purpose of weakening an adversary and influencing the outcome of geopolitical rivalries have been used throughout history.[3] Already, by the close of the Middle Ages, some kings were employing economic influence to support their military actions. For instance, in the war between the French King Louis XI and Charles I of Bourgogne, Louis commanded his fleet to block corn and herring supplies to Flanders (in the Kingdom of Bourgogne) and likewise convinced bankers to stop funding his rival. Moreover, Louis XI encouraged the hosting of fairs in Lyon in order to reduce the money flow to Geneva, which at the time was the main trade hub between Bourgogne, Germany, and Italy (Gagliano, 2018; Harbulot, 1992).

Mercantilism, closely associated with the rise of the nation state in Europe during the period spanning from the 15th to the 18th century, advocated state

3 On this subject one can read the following book: Laïdi, A. (2016). *Histoire Mondiale de la Guerre Economique*. Paris: Perrin.

intervention in the economy for the sake of the security of that state. Protectionist trade and monetary policies were used to achieve trade surplus that increased the wealth and power of the state. The German economist, Friedrich List (1789–1846), advocated economic nationalism to support state policies to help industrialization, and in general, to build domestic economic power in order to gain security and independence (List, 2013). List considered that the choice between an interventionist and a liberal economic policy is a strategic question dependent on the particular situation of a nation, its economic development, and political power (Bolsinger, 2004). Jean Baptiste Colbert (1619–1683), minister at the court of the French King Louis XIV, was a main figure of French mercantilism. Under Colbert, the French state financed road construction and provided tax exemptions and subsidies and imposed import tariffs, in order to support French exports. Colbert created a network of agents whose task was to identify and attract talent from Holland, Germany, Sweden, and Italy, in order to complement French industrial capabilities. Colbert's policies resulted in the rapid development of France's industrial output and its economy. However, Colbert was less successful in turning France into a major trading power. Britain and the Netherlands remained supreme in that field.

The *Navigation Act*, imposed by England in 1651, was an example of a mercantilist policy as concerns a sea power. This act was implemented to ensure that foreign vessels would not be able to engage in trade along the coast of England. England required exports from its colonies to first pass through British control before being redistributed throughout Europe. Governmental actions such as these protected Britain's commercial interests in a mercantile fashion and increased its wealth. Geopolitically dominant powers gained predominance in world trade by virtue of superior military power. The great powers, in different historical epochs, shaped and to some extent enforced the rules and norms for the international economy. This was the case with the Netherlands after the Thirty Years' War (1648), with Britain after the Napoleonic Wars (1815), and the United States after the Second World War (1945). For example, the international financial and economic institutions of the Bretton Woods system grew out of US predominance after the Second World War.

In peace and in war, *economic warfare* has been applied against countries in order to weaken them economically and thereby reduce their political and military power and/or to influence a given state to change its behaviour. Some instruments of economic warfare are trade embargoes, boycotts, sanctions, tariff discrimination, freezing of capital assets, suspension of aid, prohibition of investment and other capital flows, expropriation, and blocking of access to natural resources. Economic rivalries have often resulted in geopolitical competition and led to different types of conflicts, including military ones. In both the First and Second World Wars, economic warfare played a key role in weakening military adversaries. For example, before Japan's attack on Pearl Harbour, a US financial embargo had been implemented against Tokyo, in tandem with an oil embargo, in the immediate aftermath of the Japanese Empire's invasion of Southern Indochina in July 1941 (Miller, 2007).

The so-called "Democratic Peace" theory is one of the important constituents of the liberal paradigm to study international relations (Mello, 2017). This theory states that the form of domestic politics within democracies makes state mobilization for war difficult and leads to the empirical observation that democracies have not fought a war with each other (Elman, 2001). Although pre-World War One Germany, Great Britain, France and the United States could not be considered as full-fledged democracies by contemporary standards, these states were more or less based on a parliamentary system and were not dictatorships. These countries had intensive commercial ties with each other. Nonetheless, France, Great Britain, and the United States considered the rapid rise of German economic and military power as a major challenge. It is not the type of political regime but the perceptions of the changing balance of power by Great Britain, France and the US, due to the increasing international influence of Germany that influenced the transition from peace to war. Thenceforth, World War One broke out, in which Great Britain, France, and the United States had the objective of considerably reducing the power potential of Germany. This objective of the main victorious powers manifested itself as well by the imposition of the humiliating conditions of the Versailles Treaty on Germany after the end of that war. There is a limitation of the Democratic Peace theory to explain wars between contemporary democracies that are fought by non-military means for geoeconomic supremacy. In fact, geoeconomics can be considered as war by other means than the military ones, as Robert D. Blackwill and Jennfer M. Harris argue (Blackwill & Harris, 2016).

During the Cold War, there were some tensions related to diverging economic interests within the US led western bloc. However, the necessity to maintain the cohesion of the Western alliance vis-à-vis the Soviet bloc resulted in a situation in which these tensions were not supposed to challenge the unity of the West. Economic means were considered as an effective instrument to weaken the Communist bloc; this was illustrated by the US strategy in the 1980s that included the following among others: a) The implementation of the Strategic Defence Initiative (SDI) to use ground and space-based systems to protect the United States from attack by strategic nuclear ballistic missiles. The USSR could not cope with this initiative in the context of the logic of the Cold War arms race. b) In 1983, the US administration approved the National Security Decision Directive 75, which resulted in the implementation of a strict regime of sanctions to limit the foreign policy and military options of the Soviets. c) The US exercised its influence on Saudi Arabia in 1985 to drastically increase oil production to cause a sharp drop in oil prices that, in turn, impacted considerably Soviet revenues from oil exports that accounted for a significant part of Soviet hard-currency earnings.

After the end of the Cold War, the disintegration of the communist bloc followed by the erosion of the cohesion of the US-led western bloc. At present, western democracies occasionally wage economic wars on each other. Similarly, political and military allies can engage in fierce geoeconomic battles to conquer markets, control technologies, and maintain financial and monetary domination, as well as other matters. The nature of "Ally – Adversary" relations is manifested in Trans-Atlantic relations. Although European NATO member states are in a military alliance with the United States, commercial rivalries are part of the EU-US relations, such as the mutual accusations in the World Trade Organization related to subsidies given to Boeing and Airbus. A stronger example is the use of the ECHELON electronic surveillance system, managed by the United States in collaboration with other English-speaking Western countries, and PRISM, a clandestine surveillance program under which the United States National Security Agency (NSA) collects data of internet and phone communications. The information collected through ECHELON and PRISM and given to economic actors can be used to promote the economic interests of the US (Gaiser, 2016, pp. 177–186), illustrating the role of the state apparatus in the active support of US private corporations.

4 The Contemporary Global Power Shift

One of the most important megatrends that impacts contemporary geoeconomics is the global power shift. The current international system is characterised by a transition from a US-led Western hegemonic system to a multipolar system. The relative economic and political power is shifting away from the Euro-Atlantic zone most notably to Asia, but also to other world regions. This global power shift is due to the rapid rise of China in the first place, and secondly to the strong economic growth of India and Southeast Asia in the last few decades. The Asia – Pacific zone has become the centre of gravity of global geopolitics and geoeconomics. The current global power shift is mainly economic. The US remains the most important military power with the highest military spending in the world, reaching 649 billion US dollars in 2018 (SIPRI, 2019). The US military budget has remained by far the largest in the world almost as much in 2018 as the next eight largest-spending countries combined.

China, the second-largest spender in the world had its military expenditure at a level of $250 billion in 2018 (SIPRI, 2019). The US maintains nearly 800 military bases in more than 70 countries and territories abroad—from giant bases to small radar facilities. Britain, France and Russia, by contrast, have about 30 foreign bases combined.

Concerning the economic aspects of the global power shift, it is important to mention that comparing the GDP on a Purchasing Power Parity (PPP) basis, China has since 2014 already a bigger economy than the US (MGM Research, 2018). Projections for 2050 indicate the dominant share of Asian countries of the world economy: China will be the leading economic player, India the second, Indonesia the fourth and Japan will be in the fifth position. The US will be the third largest economy and none of the European countries will be in the five most important economies on a global scale (Davidson, 2019; PWC, 2017). The Forbes list of the world's biggest companies in 2018 indicate that the Asia-Pacific region leads with 792 names, 40 percent of the list.[4] Concerning the population factor it is important to mention the relative demographic decline of Europe and the United States. The population of Asia is already about four times bigger than the combined population of North America and Europe (UN DESA, 2019).

One of the most relevant examples of the global power shift is the Belt and Road Initiative (BRI) launched by China in 2013. The BRI is a monumental project includes a massive infrastructure development to link the Eurasian landmass, as well as Africa, both by land and sea, to China. The BRI will connect, through 6 trade corridors, more than 60 countries representing 69% of the world population and 51% of its GDP. The BRI provides a relevant example on how geoeconomic strategy may impact both economic development and geopolitics. Some of the main strategic benefits of the BRI include bolstering regional stability, improving China's energy security, developing export markets and re-reorienting trade. The BRI also favours the development of China's inland regions and can subsequently contribute to the enhancement of the geopolitical cohesion of China. The BRI will increase Chinese influence in East Asia, South East-Asia, Eurasia, Middle East, Africa, the Artic region and Latin America. In addition, more than half of the world economy will be taken out of the US dollar dominated trade and economic relations which can lead to the strengthening of the global role of RMB / yuan. Consequently, the BRI may

4 Data obtained from Forbes Global. The Forbes Global 2000 is a list of the world's largest corporations as measured by revenues, profits, assets and market value (Murphy, A., Ponciano, J., Hansen, S., Touryalai H. (2019, May). Global 2000, The World's Largest Public Companies. Retrieved from: https://www.forbes.com/global2000/#7161a2a9335d).

contribute to the emergence of new international financial order. This process could be accelerated in case of a new financial crisis that could start from the US and spread to other regions. The BRI places China in the centre of the *Eurasian Heartland*.[5] One of the main geopolitical significance of the BRI is to connect the major land powers of Eurasia: China, Russia and Germany. The collaboration of these three states and the Chinese land and maritime strategies to gain influence over the *Rimlands* of Eurasia can be considered as the strengthening of Eurasia and the weakening of the US led sea power strategy that seeks to prevail the emergence of peer competitors in Eurasia.[6] In case of a potential collaboration of India with the BRI, the gravity of the international system would be significantly altered and an Asian led globalisation cycle would impact significantly the norms, trade rules and the narratives about global governance (Khana, 2019, p. 321). The global power shift, represented by the gravitation of global power back to Asia from the Euro-Atlantic zone, should be perceived in the *longue durée* (*long duration*) perspective of historical cycles. As a matter of fact, China and India had been leading the world economy for many centuries (Lambert, 2019).

5 The *Strategic State* and Its Geoeconomic Disposition

From a geoeconomic perspective, it can be stated that there has been no diminution of the importance of the state, but a transformation of its strategic role in order to adapt to a new power reality of the 21st century in which commercial, financial, technological and cultural factors play an increasing role (Kirsch, 2008). The objective of this *Strategic State* is to create the conditions for establishing a successful geoeconomic disposition that can create synergy between the private and public sectors of the economy and government agencies. The tools used to create a national geoeconomic framework of cooperation include education and training, research and development, commercial strategy, economic diplomacy, and economic intelligence among others. Grouping together, each of these elements into a national geoeconomic

5 In this context it is interesting to observe the map made by Researcher Hao Xiaoguang and published in September, 2013, with the authorization of National Administration of Surveying, Mapping and Geoinformation of China (A New Version of World Map Published. *Institute of Geodesy and Geophysics*, Chinese Academy of Science. Retrieved December 20, 2019, from: http://english.whigg.cas.cn/ns/es/201312/t20131211_114311.html)

6 On the concept of the Rimland on can read the book of the Dutch American geopolitical thinker, Spykman, N. (1942). *America's Strategy in World Politics, The United States and the Balance of Power. New York:* Harcourt Brace and Co.

disposition may determine the influence of the state in the international system in the 21st century and impact considerably its socio-economic development. This process is influenced by cultural, historical, and geopolitical factors, and by a shared perception by various actors of public and private sectors, on the role of geoeconomics to enhance the economic security of the state. In this context, it is important to note the existence of different national approaches to develop and implement geoeconomic strategies.[7]

In the case of Japan, cultural, historical, and geopolitical factors have influenced this nation to develop its geoeconomic power. The relatively small size of Japanese territory, combined with high population density, the lack of natural resources, a consensus-based society, in which authority, discipline, and collectivism are important values, and the country's defeat in World War Two, all influenced Japanese strategic thinking after the conflict. The objective was to create a strong national geoeconomic disposition including an efficient system of Economic Intelligence. The Ministry of Economy, Trade and Industry (METI) played an important role in the strategic coordination between the public and the private sectors. Training, and other activities in fields related to the elaboration of geoeconomic strategies, were organized. Different networks between industrial groups and government agencies were created to develop a culture and practice of economic intelligence based on a systematic collection, analysis, and dissemination of information to actors in the economy (Harbulot, 1992, pp. 29–34). These coordinated geoeconomic activities played an important role in the successful market penetration of Japanese firms in the United States, in Europe, and in Latin America from the 1960s.

Cooperation between state agencies and companies runs counter to the tenets of neo-liberalism. The neo-liberal ideology advocates a high degree of deregulation, opening up rapidly the domestic economy to international exchanges and investments, privatization of most sectors of the economy, and limitation of the public sector. The neo-liberal model failed in several countries. One can mention the Argentinian economic depression taking place between 1998 and 2002, or the devastating consequences of the Russian "shock therapy" in the 1990s. Contrary to the rapid liberalization and deregulation of the economy, the East Asian states opted for a gradual opening of their economies combined with a long-term economic development approach in which the state played a strategic role (Vogel, 1993). One of the

7 On this subject, one can consult the following books by Christian Harbulot : Harbulot, C. (1992). *La Machine de Guerre Economique*. Paris: Economica; Harbulot, C. (2007) *La main invisible des puissances*. Paris: Ellipses; Harbulot, C. (2015) *Manuel d'intelligence économique*. Paris: PUF.

most obvious examples of this approach – also called State Capitalism – is the successful economic development of South Korea which was a rather poor country in the 1960s. However, it became gradually a developed and prosperous state with competitive export oriented economic sectors by the 1990s (Chung, 2007).

An important constituent of a national geoeconomic disposition is *Information Power* of a given state which depends, to a considerable extent, upon its capabilities of strategic management of information and which plays a key role in geoeconomics. The growing impact of information and communication technologies (ICT), and related issues such as big data, artificial intelligence, and cyber security among others, contributed to create a new complexity, as ICTs increase the speed of the impacts of changes that affect political, economic, security and military matters. One of the most important components of a successful geoeconomic strategy is Economic Intelligence (EI). EI can be defined as the research, analysis, and dissemination of information, useful to different actors of a given business entity or of a given state to support geoeconomic strategies of these entities (Csurgai, 2017). EI can be understood as the transformation of information into knowledge and the knowledge in operational choices (Jean & Savona, 2011, p. 21). To have an efficient geoeconomic disposition, strategic networks of EI should be established between the state level and business. Economic Intelligence is not limited to the research, analysis and dissemination of information. This intelligence is often applied in offensive and indirect strategies such as disinformation, perception management, lobbying and destabilisation of an adversary company. Business and state entities therefore have developed both defensive and offensive capacities of EI. Defensive strategies related to information protection are very important as an enterprise can become a potential target of information gathering by competitors to obtain information on financial situation, market penetration strategies, clients, potential clients and innovation among others (Harbulot, 2015). The 2015 takeover of the energy division of the French company Alstom by US company General Electric (GE) provides a relevant example on the importance of Economic Intelligence and geoeconomic analysis. Alstom energy division was targeted by a strategy of destabilisation that included among others: the arrest and imprisonment of one of its chief executives in the United States, the use of US extraterritorial jurisdiction, lobbying and the imposing of a huge fine, 772 million US $ by the US Department of Justice which aggravated the financial vulnerability of Alstom's energy divisions.[8]

8 A detailed description of this take-over can be found in the book: Pierucci, F. (2019). *Le piège américain*. Paris: Editions JC Lattès.

6 Conclusion

Geoeconomics can be considered as applied research and it can be understood as both an analysis and practice by states and businesses. In spite of its increasing role, geoeconomics does not substitute geopolitics. The two concepts are closely linked and therefore to examine contemporary power rivalries both geopolitical and geoeconomic analysis must be carried out. The strategic approach to international economic relations and the re-consideration of the role of the state in economic policies should be a priority for states. Indeed, defending states' economic interests in the 21st century requires a modified perception of their security needs in order to develop an efficient geoeconomic coordination between state agencies and private businesses. Moreover, states can use geoeconomics to achieve different foreign policy goals and promote their national interests. Study programs in geoeconomics and economic intelligence should be more integrated in professional training curriculum and university education to train current and future decision makers and analysts of both private and public sectors.

Bibliography

Blackwill, R. & Harris, J. (2016). *War by Other Means, Geoeconomics and Statecraft*. Cambridge: Harvard University Press, p. 20.

Bolsinger, E. (2004). *The Foundation of Mercantile Realism, Friedrich List and the Theory of International Political Economy*. Paper presented at the University of Lincoln.

Bureau of Trade Statistics of Taiwan, Directorate General of Customs Administration, Ministry of Finance. Retrieved December 20, 2019, from: https://cus93.trade.gov.tw/FSCE030F/FSCE030F

China vs United States – A GDP Comparison (2018, December). Retrieved from: https://mgmresearch.com/china-vs-united-states-a-gdp-comparison/

Chinese Academy of Science. *A New Version of World Map Published*. Institute of Geodesy and Geophysics. Retrieved December 20, 2019, from: http://english.whigg.cas.cn/ns/es/201312/t20131211_114311.html

Chung, Young-Iob. (2007). *South Korea in the Fast Lane: Economic Development and Capital Formation*. Oxford, New York: Oxford University Press.

Claval, P. (1994). *Géopolitique et Géostratégie*. Paris: Nathan, p. 6.

Csurgai, G. (2017). Geoeoconomic Strategies and Economic Intelligence. In Munoz, J.M. (Ed.), *Advances in Geoeconomics*. London, New York: Routledge.

Davidson, P. (2019, January). China, India close gap with U.S. as world's top economy. Retrieved from: https://eu.usatoday.com/story/money/2019/01/11/china-india-gain-us-worlds-top-economy/2551849002/

Elman, C. (2001). Introduction: History, Theory, and the Democratic Peace. *The International History Review, 23:4*. Retrieved from : http://dx.doi.org/10.1080/07075332.2001.9640946

Foucher, M. (1991). *Fronts et Frontières*. Paris : Fayard, p. 37.

Gagliano, G. (2018). Historical aspects of the economic warfare in the interpretation of Christian Harbulot. *Modern Diplomacy*. Retrieved from https://moderndiplomacy.eu/2018/01/31/historical-aspects-economic-warfare-interpretation-christian-harbulot/

Gaiser, L. (2016). *Economic Intelligence and World Governance, Reinventing States for a New World Order*. Citta di Castello: Il Cerchio, pp.177–186

Gray, C. (1999). Incapable Geography. In Gray, Colin S. & Sloan, Geoffrey (Eds), *Geopolitics, Geography and Strategy*. London: Frank CASS Publishers, p. 161.

Harbulot, C. (1992). *La Machine de Guerre Economique*. Paris: Economica.

Harbulot, C. (2007) *La main invisible des puissances*. Paris: Ellipses.

Harbulot, C. (2015) *Manuel d'intelligence économique*. Paris: PUF.

Jean, C. & Savona, P. (2011). *Intelligence Economica*. Soveria Mannelli: Rubettino, p. 21

Khana, P. (2019). *The Future is Asian, Global Order in the 21st Century*. London: Weidenfeld Nicolson, p. 321

Kirsch, H. (2008). (Ed.) *La France en guerre économique, Plaidoyer pour un Etat stratége*. Paris: Vuibert.

Laïdi, A. (2016). *Histoire Mondiale de la Guerre Economique*. Paris: Perrin.

Lambert, A. (2019). *China's Belt and Road Initiative in a New Era of Geoeconomic Rivalries*. Conference Paper, GIGS (Geneva Institute of Geopolitical Studies) Summer Course "Geopolitics".

List, F. (2013). *National System of Political Economy*. New York: Cosimo Classics

Lorot, P. (Ed). (1999). *Introduction à la géoéconomie*. Paris: Economica, p.15

Luttwak, E. (1990). From Geopolitics to Geoeconomics: Logic of Conflict, Grammar of Commerce. *The National Interest*, No. 20. 1990.

Mello, P. (2017). Democratic Peace Theory. In Joseph, P. (Ed.), *The SAGE Encyclopedia of War: Social Science Perspectives*. Sage Publications. Retrieved from: http://dx.doi.org/10.4135/9781483359878.n188

Miller, E. (2007). *Bankrupting the Enemy: The U.S. Financial Siege of Japan before Pearl Harbor*. Annapolis, MD: United States Naval Institute Press

Murphy, A., Ponciano, J., Hansen, S., Touryalai H. (2019, May). Global 2000, The World's Largest Public Companies. Retrieved from: https://www.forbes.com/global2000/#7161a2a9335d

Pierucci, F. (2019). *Le piège américain*. Paris: Editions JC Lattès

SIPRI Yearbook 2019: Armaments, Disarmamaent and International Security (2019). Stockholm International Peace Research Institute. Retreived from: https://www.sipri.org/yearbook

Spykman, N. (1942). *America's Strategy in World Politics, The United States and the Balance of Power. New York:* Harcourt Brace and Co.

The long View: How will the global economic order change by 2050? (2017, February). Retrieved from: https://www.pwc.com/gx/en/world-2050/assets/pwc-world-in-2050-summary-report-feb-2017.pdf

United Nations, Department of Economic and Social Affairs, Population Division (2019). World Population Prospects 2019 (ST/ESA/SER.A/424)

Vogel, E. (1993). *The Four Little Dragons: The Spread of Industrialization in East Asia.* Cambridge, MA: Harvard University Press

World military expenditure grows to $1.8 trillion in 2018. (2019, April). Retrieved from: https://www.sipri.org/media/press-release/2019/world-military-expenditure-grows-18-trillion-2018

CHAPTER 8

Dangers on the Edge of the Map: Geographic Mental Maps and the Emergence of the Carter Doctrine

Luis da Vinha

1 Introduction

The Carter Doctrine enunciated in President Jimmy Carter's 1980 *State of the Union Address* effectively coupled the security of the Persian Gulf region with American global security (Yetiv, 1990). While the region had always been important in US strategic considerations, it was the Carter administration that ultimately gave the Middle East its pivotal role in US foreign policy. In other words, the US transformed the Middle East, particularly the Persian Gulf, into a new "critical defense zone" by communicating to the Soviets "clearly and in advance, exactly which parts of the planet they deem indispensable to their own security and, hence, which expansive political or military changes initiated by or enuring to the benefit of an adversary will be unacceptable and likely to lead to war" (Reisman, 1982: 589). By attempting to articulate the purpose of American foreign policy, the Carter Doctrine represented a momentous shift in US geopolitical and geostrategic considerations, placing the Persian Gulf region as the second priority for resource allocation after Europe (Blidall, 2011; da Vinha, 2017; Kupchan, 1987; Michaels, 2011; Njølstad, 2004; Odom, 2006; Rosati, 1991).

Moreover, the Carter Doctrine purportedly dealt a fatal blow to détente (Freedman, 2009). By signaling a turn towards a more assertive military posture regarding the Soviet Union, particularly in the Middle East region, it overturned many of the administration's prior foreign policy initiatives, such as nuclear non-proliferation, demilitarization of strategic regions, curtailment of conventional arms transfers to Third World countries, and the promotion of human rights. In their place emerged a policy which emphasized a massive military build-up, increased military supply to Third World nations, and increased US global military presence (Brown, 1994; Garthoff, 1985). By repudiating the Nixon Doctrine's reliance on local forces to guarantee their own security, the Carter Doctrine presented itself as a major revision of US policy.

 | DOI:10.1163/9789004432086_010

From that moment on, the US committed itself to a renewed policy of containment involving:

> (1) a pledge of American resolve and commitment to stop any further Soviet advance in the Southwest Asia-Persian Gulf Area, buttressed by a series of political and military steps; (2) a more general diplomatic effort to confront Soviet power, including further play of the China card; and (3) a renewed stress on building American military power across the board – strategic forces and general purpose land, air, and seapower, as well as the Rapid Deployment Force. (Garthoff, 1985: 973)

Over the decades, authors have offered several explanations interpreting the rise of the Carter Doctrine. Some authors justify the change in the administration's foreign policy by highlighting domestic factors such as mounting political opposition and electoral concerns (see Quandt, 1986; Skidmore, 1996). However, most studies hold external actors and events accountable for the administration's wholesale foreign policy change. Scholars have acknowledged several different critical international events responsible for setting in motion a comprehensive change in the administration's foreign policy. The bulk of the research has emphasized a combination of crises arising in the Middle East in 1979, beginning with the fall of the Shah in Iran and culminating with the Iranian hostage crisis and the Soviet invasion of Afghanistan (Brown, 1994; Dobson & Marsh, 2001; Freedman, 2009; Gaddis, 2005; Hunt, 2007; Lebow & Stein, 1993; Palmer, 1999; Wittkopf et al., 2008; Yetiv, 2008).

This chapter challenges the conventional accounts of the development of the Carter Doctrine. It argues that the Carter administration's Middle East policy and the development of the Carter Doctrine was the result of the continuous re-construction of the foreign policy decision-makers' geographic mental maps since the early days of the Carter presidency. More precisely, developments in the Third World affected decision-makers' mental maps, leading the administration's regional policies to be continually re-evaluated and re-constructed. In particular, foreign policy crises in peripheral regions were increasingly integrated into the administration's broader strategic assessments of the Third World. As the administration's problem representations changed, so too did the policy recommendations perceived as best to deal with the challenges facing US security interests in the greater Middle East region.

The remainder of this chapter is organized as follows. First, a heuristic description of geographic mental maps is presented, as well as a brief account of their influence on foreign policy decision-making. The subsequent sections assess how the foreign policy crises in sub-Saharan Africa contributed to changing the Carter administration's mental maps regarding Soviet involvement in the Third World, particularly the threats the USSR posed to America's strategic interests in the greater Middle East. The conclusion provides a brief summary of this argument and some general considerations on the importance of employing mental maps as an analytical tool in foreign policy analysis.

2 Geographic Mental Maps and Foreign Policy Decision-Making

Research in foreign policy analysis (FPA) has long acknowledged that decision-makers act with regard to their perceived political environment, meaning that "what matters in the explanation of decisions and policies is how the actor imagined his environment to be, not how it actually was" (Sprout & Sprout, 1960: 147).[1] As a result, in accordance with their perceptions, political actors can respond differently to the same event in the international environment. Therefore, studying political decision-makers' geographic mental maps helps develop a better understanding of their policy choices and, ultimately, their impact on international politics.

Geographic mental maps are cognitive constructs "which encompass an individual or group's beliefs about the geographic character of a particular place or places and their relationship to other places or spatial phenomena" (da Vinha, 2019: 78). At the most basic level, these geographic beliefs act as filters through which individuals manage and interpret information about the political world and serve as relatively stable socialized templates which help select, organize, process, and understand the signals received from the international environment (da Vinha, 2015; Erforth, 2016). Mental maps are particularly relevant to decision-makers by affecting the way they define a "problem representation" and indirectly condition the options for subsequent action.[2]

Mental maps are dynamic because decision-makers are constantly reevaluating policy issues and reconstructing different places and spaces through social interaction. In particular, it is through communication that individuals create, maintain, and change their mental maps by creating and recreating shared meanings and beliefs. The more individuals interact, the greater the probability that new narratives, representations, and mental maps are generated, since opportunities for discussing new realities arise (Ford, 1999). In

1 For a similar argument, see the seminal work in FPA by Snyder, Bruck, and Sapin (2002 [1962]).

2 For a detailed account of how foreign policy problem representations influence policy choices and outcomes, see Sylvan (1998), Taber (1998), and Vertzberger (2002).

other words, communicative interactions transform existing assumptions and beliefs which then creates the need for new policies. Communicative interactions allow for decision-making groups to share their expectations and objectives in order to work out the course of action that potentially best satisfies their organizations' requirements.[3]

We can identify four different combinations of communicative acts, corresponding to four different types of communicative interactions, involved in the process of changing existing mental maps: 1) initiative communication, 2) communication for understanding, 3) communication for performance, and 4) communication for closure (da Vinha, 2017; Ford & Ford, 1995). Initiative communication is usually prompted by the recognition of an incongruity or problem and is critical to initiating the change process. In the communication for understanding phase, decision-makers discuss the need for transforming the situation and commence an interaction process in order to establish the actions necessary to solve the problem or incongruence detected. Ultimately, communication for understanding is the fundamental dynamic involved in (re)defining the problem representation. The definition of the problem is critical for future action since it has repercussions on "which kinds of evidence bear on the problem, which solutions are considered effective and feasible, who participates in the decision process, how policies are implemented, and by which criteria policies are assessed" (Weiss, 1989: 97–98).

However, understanding is not synonymous with action. Therefore, a catalyst is needed to move the change process forward. Communication for performance usually generates requests and promises that will produce the actions that will allegedly satisfy the desired policy objectives. As the discussions generate a new language for defining the problem, they correspondingly create a new language for action. In other words, because communicative interactions transform existing assumptions and beliefs, the need for new actions and policies is also created (Barret, Thomas, & Hocevar, 1995). Communicative interactions allow for decision-makers to share their expectations and objectives in order work out the course of action that potentially best satisfies the group's requirements.

Finally, the communication for closure stage involves placing the perceived events in perspective and completing the change process (Ford & Ford, 1995). However, as mentioned above, the interaction process is extremely dynamic. Therefore, closure is a temporary phenomenon at best. From this point of view individuals and groups are "conceived as webs of beliefs and habits of action

3 For a more detailed explanation of the causal factors underlying communicative interactions and foreign policy change, see da Vinha (2017).

that keep reweaving (and thus altering) as they try to coherently accommodate new experiences, which come from new interactions over time" (Sterman, 2001: 13). Moreover, if foreign policy-making is extended and connected throughout time, it is natural that most of the communication involved will also be extended and intertwined with multiple other communication processes. Therefore, rather than view this communicative interaction as a linear process, we should consider it as a cyclical model in which individuals and groups are constantly reviewing their existing mental maps.

Accordingly, in order to understand the development of the Carter Doctrine, the following sections highlight the communicative interactions involving the Carter administration's broader Middle East policy. More precisley, the analysis focuses on how changes in the administration's mental maps of peripheral regions influenced its understanding of the challenges and threats facing America's strategic interest in the Middle East.

3 The Carter Administration's Mental Maps of Africa and the Persian Gulf

The Carter administration arrived in Washington in the wake of several years of constructive engagement between the US and the USSR. Upon assuming the presidency, Carter did not deviate from this line of reasoning and sought to maintain a policy of détente whilst devaluing the traditional East-West focus on international relations. In particular, he intended to adjust US military commitments to the available resources and downplay the long-standing US-Soviet antagonism (Skidmore, 1996). For the Carter administration, détente was understood as a combination of cooperation and competition. Since each superpower had expanding global interests, managing US-Soviet relations was crucial to avoid a devastating military conflict between the two superpowers.

In a letter to Brezhnev in January 1977, Carter assured the Soviets that "it is my goal to improve relations with the Soviet Union on the basis of reciprocity, mutual respect and benefit" (cited in Brzezinski 1983: 151–152). Carter identified several areas in which the US and the Soviets could cooperate to reduce the risk of nuclear proliferation: 1) conclusion of the Strategic Arms Limitation Talks (SALT), 2) comprehensive ban on nuclear tests, and 3) renewed effort to move forward on the Mutual and Balanced Force Reductions (MBFR). In addition, the president informed Brezhnev that he believed the Soviets could contribute to promoting a peaceful settlement in the Third World disputes, such as those in the Middle East and Southern Africa. The faith in broadening the scope of cooperation was illustrated in the joint-US-Soviet statement, issued on 1 October 1977, calling for the convening of the Geneva Peace Conference to work out a just and lasting comprehensive settlement of the Arab-Israeli conflict (Vance to Carter, 1 October 1977).

However, while Carter was hopeful the US could forge a comprehensive peace settlement in the Middle East and strengthen its position in the region, progress seemed to elude the administration. In particular, events outside of the Middle East contributed to reinforce the conviction of many key officials regarding the need to assume a more assertive US policy in the region. The emerging crises in Africa were especially persuasive of the need for a more active policy towards the Middle East region, principally in the Persian Gulf.

3.1 *The Shaba Conflict and the Turn to Africa*

Signs of concern with growing communist assertiveness began in the early months of the Carter Presidency. In March 1977, approximately 2,000 men of the Front for the National Liberation of the Congo (FNLC) invaded Zaire's Shaba province from Angola setting off the Shaba I crisis. The source of crisis can be traced to the troubled decolonization process which resulted in Zaire's (i.e., Democratic Republic of the Congo) independence from Belgium in 30 June 1960 (Odom, 1992).[4] Conflict quickly erupted as the Belgian-sponsored Katangan forces tried to secede the mineral-rich province of Katanga (i.e., Shaba).[5] With the defeat of the secession initiative in 1963, the Katangan Gendarmerie was exiled in Angola. However, the country was ravaged with internal strife throughout the decade as Joseph Mobutu consolidated his power as head of the regime. As Mobutu strengthened his domestic power base, relations with Western countries, particularly Belgium, deteriorated when he nationalized several foreign-owned enterprises and the economy plummeted.

Mobutu also tried to influence the politics of recently independent Angola. Looking to deny power to the Popular Movement for the Liberation of Angola (MPLA) led by Agostinho Neto, in the summer of 1975 Mobutu sent his *Forces Armees Zairoise* (FAZ) into Angola to try to neutralize the MPLA. However, support from the former Katangan Gendarmerie – now FNLC – helped the MPLA hold off the Zairian offensive until the Cubans could bring in troops, armor, and aircraft and repel the FAZ. As a result, the MPLA was able to consolidate its power in Angola.

4 Zaire was formerly the Belgian Congo. After the country's independence in 1960 it became the Democratic Republic of the Congo until 1971 when it officially became known as the Republic of Zaire. Since 1997 the name of the country reverted again to Democratic Republic of the Congo.

5 Between 1971 and 1997 the Katanga province was officially known as the Shaba province.

After its successful rally round the MPLA, the FNLC mounted its own attack on Zaire in an attempt to retake the Shaba province (Odom, 1992).[6] FNLC forces were able to quickly seize their initial objectives, winning most military confrontations with the Zairian forces. FAZ forces revealed numerous difficulties in holding back the incursion until the arrival of 1,500 Moroccan troops supported by France and Belgium, helped push back the FNLC. In mid-April 1977, one month after the raid began, the FNLC retreated to Angola accompanied by about 50,000 to 70,000 Zairian refugees (Garthoff, 1985).

Throughout the conflict Mobutu tried to rouse international support by denouncing the incursion as a communist invasion, underlining Cuba's aid to the FNLC (Garthoff, 1985; Odom, 1992). After the Organization of African Unity (OAU) revealed itself unresponsive to this potential menace, Mobutu turned to the US for assistance.[7] Contrary to Mobutu's expectation, the Carter administration responded to the Zairian leader's request unenthusiastically. The administration cast the conflict within a regional framework which consequently required a regionally based solution. At the outset, Carter (1977) played down the conflict by claiming at a press conference that "Zaire was involved, I think at least indirectly, in the Angolan conflict, and there are some remaining hard feelings between Angola and Zaire on that part". As a result of this situation, Carter (Idem) argued that "Some of the Katangans who lived in the southern part of Zaire are now involved in trying to go back into the area where they formerly lived".

Congress endorsed the administration's strategy as it was equally wary of US involvement in another Third World conflict. American reluctance to further commitments to Zaire was also due to the fact that the administration was seeking to normalize relations with Angola.[8] The US did agree to expedite some non-lethal military supplies to Zaire. However, with the continuation of the conflict, Congress ultimately reduced credits for military assistance from $30 to $15 million (Odom, 1992). Ultimately, Carter and his advisers did not perceive the conflict as a threat significant enough to destabilize the security environment in the adjoining regions. Therefore, the administration was satisfied in backing America's European allies in their endeavors to prop the Mobutu

6 The FNLC counted on Agostinho Neto's support since Mobutu kept aiding Angolan opposition groups such as the National Union for the Total Independence of Angola (UNITA) and the Front for the Liberation of the Cabinda Enclave (FLEC).

7 Since the 1960s, the US had supported Mobutu's regime on numerous occasions, providing military aid and international diplomatic support.

8 In fact, before the Shaba crisis began, the US and Angola had agreed to meet in April to commence discussions (Vance, 1983). The talks between the two parties were eventually delayed due to the Shaba conflict.

regime. Despite America's reluctance, the Shaba I crisis did, however, spark a debate within the Carter administration on Cuban (and Soviet) involvement in Africa (Njølstad, 1995).

3.2 *The Ogaden War and the Remapping of the Administration's Regional Security Concerns*

The president's National Security Adviser, Zbigniew Brzezinski, sounded the alert to the growing nuisance of Cuban involvement in African politics in the early months of the presidency. In a memo submitted to the president on 11 March 1977, Brzezinski pointed out that "Cuban leaders intend to make Africa a major focus of Cuba's foreign policy, since they view that continent as a fertile field for revolutionary activity, unlike Latin America" (Brzezinski to Carter, 11/03/1977: 1).

Brzezinski's notice was preceded by an assortment of events which had stirred politics in the Horn of Africa since the beginning of the year. The first incident occurred in early-February when Lieutenant Colonel Mengistu Haile Mariam seized power in Ethiopia. Mengistu's ascension to power put an end to several years of internal struggle for power within the Dergue.[9] After seizing power, Mengistu imposed a sweeping reformulation of Ethiopia's international orientation by declaring it a Marxist-Leninist state (LeoGrande, 1980). The Carter administration's singling out of Ethiopia for human rights abuses and withdrawal of further military aid in February certainly did not improve the situation. In fact, Ethiopia had been America's main ally in the Horn of Africa. The two countries had a mutual defense agreement since 1953 and until 1973 Ethiopia had received half of all US military aid to Africa (Njølstad, 1995). Consequently, beleaguered by American pressure and enticed by Soviet overtures, Ethiopia accepted Soviet military aid and severed military relations with the US in April 1977 by expelling the American military mission (LeoGrande, 1980).[10]

Around the same time, Somali forces mounted a series of armed incursions into the Ogaden province in southern Ethiopia. Since its establishment in 1960, Somalia had repeatedly tried to wrest the Ogaden province from Ethiopia,

---

9 The Dergue was the name given to the Provisional Military Administrative Council set up in Ethiopia after the 1974 revolution which deposed Emperor Haile Selassie.

10 The eviction of the US military from the country was particularly significant due to the loss of the Asmara base, which was the largest strategic US international airbase. As Makinda (1982: 101) has recalled, the Asmara airbase was the "centre of all American air and space operations from the Korean war to the Vietnam war and Apollo flights, and everything went through the great air observation and tracking instruments of the 2,500 metre high site."

claiming that the area was culturally and ethnically Somali. This claim was part of a larger design for a Greater Somalia which would also include parts of Djibouti in northern Ethiopia and parts of Kenya. Economic interests may have equally fueled Somali expansionist ambitions, since the region also had some of the richest agricultural lands in the region. Regardless of the justification, Somalia had consistently trained and organized dissident groups within Ethiopia with the intent of promoting the liberation of the province.[11] Devoid of success hitherto, in 1976 Somalia supported a guerrilla war which had begun in northern and southern Ethiopia. By early-1977, the guerrillas had gained control of a large portion of the Ogaden (Tareke, 2000). Hostility between the rebels and the Ethiopian army continued throughout the following months, increasing the tension between the governments in Addis Ababa and Mogadishu.

Additionally, Cuba's Fidel Castro congratulated Mengistu for his rise to power and sponsored a summit between Ethiopia and Somalia in South Yemen in March 1977 to try to calm hostilities (Garthoff, 1985; LeoGrande, 1980). Castro proposed that the two countries cooperate in the creation of an anti-imperialist federation which would also include Yemen, autonomous Ogaden, and autonomous Eritrea. While Mengistu rejected the proposal on such terms, Fidel travelled to Moscow and reaffirmed Cuban commitment to aid southern African guerrillas (LeoGrande, 1980).

This succession of events led Carter to request a review of US policy towards the Horn of Africa on 17 March 1977. Although the Policy Review Memorandum (PRM-21) was undertaken with specific reference to Kenya and Sudan, it did request that numerous other regional issues be specifically addressed, such as:[12]

- Whether to continue, reduce, or suspend US military and economic aid programs in Ethiopia and the likely consequences of such actions;
- The implications of the independence of TFAI and steps that might be taken to avert a Somali-Ethiopian clash;[13]
- Prospects for loosening Somalia's ties with the Soviet Union.

11 President Barre was also aware that only by force could Somalia acquire its territorial ambitions since the 1964 Cairo Resolution passed by the OAU declared that the existing borders in Africa would be maintained and honoured (Jackson, 2007; 2010).

12 Presidential Review Memorandums (PRM) were used to direct the different departments and agencies to carry out policy reviews and analyses, namely by identifying the issues to be considered by the NSC, defining the problem, setting a deadline for the analysis, and assigning responsibility for it to one of the NSC committees.

13 TFAI refers to the French Territory of Afars and Issas which was the name given to present-day Djibouti between 1967 and 1977.

In addition, the review also called for a general assessment of "US interests in the whole Horn-Red Sea area, examining the impact of our actions in each country as they affect the others" (PRM-21: 2). Provisions were equally made for policy recommendations, namely those best suited for dealing with the Soviets in the Horn of Africa.

The resulting report was submitted on 1 April 1977 and stressed that, while the Soviets were trying to displace America as the dominant foreign power in Ethiopia, it also provided the US with an opportunity to promote American influence in the region as a whole by exploiting Soviet involvement (Njølstad, 1995). Overall, the study was optimistic in its appraisal of the recent events. Although in the immediate future there were few prospects for improved US-Ethiopian relations, the study anticipated that an eventual fall of Mengistu could bring a regime which would be more favorable to American interests. In effect, the report resulting from PRM-21 suggested that "any improvement in our relations with Somalia and Sudan should stop short of activities perceived as hostile towards Ethiopia as a nation" since it could potentially hurt America's ability to reestablish a cooperative relationship with a successor regime in Addis Ababa (cited in Njølstad, 1995: 169).

The Policy Review Committee (PRC) convened on 11 April 1977, to discuss the report and the situation in the Horn of Africa (PRC, 11/04/1977: 2).[14] The general conclusion was that the regime in Ethiopia was beleaguered by multiple problems, particularly due to insurrections and raids, but had the capacity to maintain power in the near future. The committee also shared the conviction that the US should not withdraw completely from Ethiopia on the grounds that it should be in a position to reassert its influence in case a new government ascended to power. Nevertheless, it concluded that additional support to the Mengistu government could no longer be justified and pending military aid (ordered and paid for) would be postponed.

PRC members also decided to instruct the US Ambassador in Mogadishu to talk with Somali president Siad Barre to ascertain his overall intentions and understand what he expected from the US if Somalia was to disengage from the Soviets. However, the discussion highlighted the risks of committing too quickly to Somalia since "Siad may be trying to play both us and the Soviets at the same time" (PRC, 11/04/1977: 2). Moreover, extending the relationship with Somalia could lead to alarming Kenya and encouraging Barre's territorial aspirations in Ethiopia and Djibouti.

---

14 The PRC was created by Presidential Directive 2 (PD-2) as the NSC standing committee responsible for dealing with department-specific issues which had repercussions for other departments or agencies.

The situation in the Horn of Africa deteriorated in July 1977 as about 5,000 Somali regular forces crossed the border into the Ogaden for a concerted attack on selected Ethiopian targets (Tareke, 2000). The Barre regime tried to justify the fighting by claiming that the only Somalis involved in the fighting were those living in Ethiopia wishing to attain self-determination (Jackson, 2007). However, information acquired by the superpowers attested to the contrary. In fact, by mid-summer there were almost 40,000 Somali troops in Ethiopia (Garthoff, 1985). Furthermore, the precarious political and military situation in Ethiopia allowed the Somali forces to achieve rapid victories and gain control of most of the Ogaden province by late-July (Jackson, 2010).

The Ogaden War presented the Carter administration with its first foreign policy crisis, providing the first "major test of the suitability and credibility of Carter's vision for American foreign policy" (Jackson, 2010: 28). It underscored the administration's new relationship with the Soviets, particularly regarding the Third World.[15] At the outset, Carter did not want to involve the US too deeply in the conflict, preferring a regionally negotiated settlement to the conflict, preferably framed within the OAU.[16] For that reason, the Carter administration did not overly emphasize Somalia's initial requests for military aid. In fact, during the first half of 1977, the State Department was reluctant even to supply defensive military equipment or to authorize allies and friends to supply Barre's regime with US weapons (Vance, 1983).

However, Carter also wanted to avoid the Soviets and its allies taking advantage of local conflicts. Carter believed that "outside powers should not be 'fueling' African territorial disputes" (cited in Jackson, 2010: 28). Therefore, when the PRC convened in late-August to review Somali and Eritrean advances in Ethiopia, Carter authorized stepping up US support to Sudan and Kenya and mobilizing African leaders to demand that outside powers refrain from supplying arms to the parties in conflict. Once again, the administration sought to try to accommodate both parties while placing the burden for the continuation of the conflict on the Soviets: "Since we do not want to supply arms to either Ethiopia or Somalia now but the Soviets are supplying them to both, an appeal for an arms embargo will dramatize the destructive role the Soviets are playing in the area" (Brzezinski to Carter, 26/08/1977: 1).

---

15 For a general outlook on Carter's ideas for Africa since his early Presidential campaign see Njølstad (1995: 168).

16 The OAU officially involved itself in the conflict after Ethiopia requested an emergency meeting to discuss the Somali invasion. Representatives of eight African nations met in August 1977, in Gabon, but talks failed as Somalia withdrew from the negotiations (Jackson, 2010).

American regional allies were equally concerned with the increasing Soviet involvement in the region. Many states feared that the Soviet Union was encroaching on the region and endangering their regimes. Officials from Egypt, Iran, Saudi Arabia, and Sudan approached the administration cautioning the US as to what they perceived as a dangerous Soviet scheme to destabilize their regimes and the security of the Gulf-Red Sea region (Njølstad, 1995). The Sudanese President had personally written Carter warning that the Soviets were "pursuing a sinister grand strategy in Africa" and hoped that the US "would respond favorably to requests of help from those countries ready and eager to defend themselves against the Soviet threat" (cited in Brzezinski, 1983: 179). In fact, several countries had endeavored to sway Somalia away from Soviet influence (Garthoff, 1985; Njølstad, 1995). In 1975, Iran, Egypt, and Saudi Arabia offered military and financial assistance to Somalia in return for it distancing itself from the USSR. America's reluctance to become directly involved in the conflict led its regional allies to request authorization to provide Somalia with military aid, including "cannibalized" Soviet weapons which they had in their possession, in order to compensate for the loss of Soviet assistance (Njølstad, 1995).

In mid-June 1977, the continued requests for aid from the Somali regime and the insistence of US allies led Carter to inform the Somali Ambassador that the US would ascertain the possibility of its regional allies helping Somalia sustain its defensive capabilities. Interpreting the President's words as a "forthcoming attitude", the Somalis made a specific request to the US for weapons on 9 July 1977 (Vance, 1983). The administration finally "concluded that 'in principle' we would help other countries to meet Somalia's needs for defensive equipment" (Vance, 1983: 73).[17]

The Soviets were in fact particularly active in the Somali-Ethiopian War. When the hostilities began, the Soviets continued to provide military assistance to both sides of the conflict. However, by the end of the summer the Soviets publicly condemned the Somali incursion and in October 1977 the Soviets announced the termination of all military supplies to Somalia (Jackson, 2010). Subsequently, the number of Soviet military advisors to Ethiopia was increased, totaling over a thousand, playing an important role in planning

17 There is speculation as to the amount of encouragement that regional allies actually received from the US for bolstering the Barre regime. The PRC meeting of April 1977 (PRC, 11/04/1977) had suggested that the US encourage regional allies, particularly Saudi Arabia, in assisting in the management of the conflict. While the level of responsibility the US had in persuading allies to act is debatable, there is no doubt that "there existed an explicit *interest* for such options on the US side several months before it was actually approved as US policy in July" (Njølstad, 1995: 173).

and commanding operations in the Ogaden (LeoGrande, 1980). The Soviets also coordinated their activities closely with Havana (Gleijeses, 2006). Cuba was directly involved in the conflict since it flared up in 1977. Initially, it dispatched military advisors to Ethiopia in May 1977. Subsequently, after Mogadishu broke off diplomatic relations with Cuba later that year, Cuban regular combat troops were deployed in the war. By early-1978, Cuba had dispatched nearly 17,000 regular soldiers to fight alongside Ethiopian troops in the Ogaden (LeoGrande, 1980).

With the active assistance of the Soviets and the Cubans, Barre's initial military triumphs were jeopardized. In an effort to try to attract Western aid, Barre renounced the Treaty of Friendship between Somalia and the Soviet Union in November 1977. In addition, all Soviet military and civilian advisors in Somalia were evicted and the Soviet naval bases on the Indian Ocean, including at Berbera, were closed (Jackson, 2007, 2010). Notwithstanding Barre's numerous requests and initiatives, Carter sought to maintain the US isolated from direct involvement in the conflict. After the ejection of the Soviets, the administration announced that it would maintain its official policy of refusing to supply arms to Somalia and continued to insist that regional problems should be resolved endogenously (Garthoff, 1985; Jackson, 2010).

The Carter administration was increasingly concerned with the growing Soviet involvement in the region. The administration was particularly worried that increasing Soviet (or one of its proxies) involvement in the Ogaden would prolong and exacerbate the war and destabilize the entire region (Jackson, 2007, 2010). As Soviet and Cuban support for Ethiopia continued to increase in the fall of 1977, the Carter administration continued to warn the different parties of the potential adverse outcomes such behavior could generate. Carter wrote a letter to Brezhnev on 21 December 1977 expressing "hope that the United States and the Soviet Union could collaborate in making certain that regional African disputes do not escalate into major international conflicts" (Carter to Brezhnev, 21/12/1977). The President informed his Soviet counterpart that the US was refraining from supplying arms to both parties and requested that the USSR adopt a similar policy in order to uphold the atmosphere of cooperation between the two superpowers.

Meanwhile, the Special Coordination Committee (SCC) convened on 26 January 1978, to reassess the developments in the Horn of Africa.[18] While acknowledging several problems relating to the conflict, the members of the SCC continued trying to downplay the confrontation with the Soviets in the

18 The SCC was created by Presidential Directive 2 (PD-2) and served as the NSC standing committee responsible for dealing with the crisscrossing issues that required coordination in developing the options and implementation of Presidential Decisions.

region. Accordingly, the SCC recommended a series of measures which sought to give the administration a high level of flexibility in dealing with both parties, without being liable for obstructing a resolution to the conflict, namely:

- "We will continue to seek advice from our allies and other friendly governments to enlist their aid in impressing upon the Soviets (and Cubans) [handwritten insertion by Carter] our serious concern, but we will be cautious about encouraging those who are inclined to help the Somalis to make commitments that they would expect us to back up;
- We will accelerate study of our own capabilities and those of other governments to intervene in the situation in ways that could complicate or make more costly the Soviet/Cuba intervention, but we will underwrite no action at this time; (...)
- Through military ----[blacked-out]---- the Iranian, Saudi, Egyptian and Sudanese governments will be sounded out on their capabilities and intentions for providing support to Somalia. We will not go beyond these discussions until we again talk to Sadat." (SCC, 27/01/1978: 2)

As the US weighed its options, the Soviet and Cuban commitment to the Mengistu regime allowed Ethiopia to launch a counter-offensive in early-1978 (Tareke, 2000). The lack of external support hindered Somalia's capability to fend off the attack and Somali troops quickly found themselves in retreat. Reports began reaching the administration that the communist bloc's continued military support of Ethiopia would eventually drive the Somalis out of the Ogaden (Jackson, 2010). This drive raised the possibility that Ethiopian and Cuban forces could potentially pursue Somali forces and launch an assault of their own against Somalia.

These events alarmed the administration and intensified the internal debate. The American policy of non-intervention was increasingly coming under question both outside and inside the administration. Congress was particularly vocal about the shortcomings of the Carter administration's policy for the Horn of Africa (Jackson, 2010). Similarly, in a report for the Committee on International Relations, submitted on 3 February 1978, the crisis in the Ogaden was considered the potentially most unstable and violent conflict in Africa. The most disturbing issue was the potential domino effect that could be set off due to the conflict: "By undermining the fragile governments that exist in the Horn, Soviet influence could rapidly spread throughout the region and along the entire East Coast of Africa" (Committee on International Relations, 1978: 1). According to the committee's final report, America's policy for Africa was in need of revision for a "laissez fair approach is simply untenable when our adversaries are involved so heavily in the internal and external conflicts of the area" (Idem: 4). While the report did recommend that the US should make clear its position of complete neutrality between the warring parties and continue to withhold, directly or indirectly, military aid to Somalia, it did reinforce the need for the administration to do more to educate the American people and particularly Congress on the political situation in the region.

President Carter had already raised the issue of public perception throughout the previous year. For instance, in the first National Security Council (NSC) meeting on Africa, convened on 6 October 1977, Carter stated he was worried that Soviet and Cuban involvement in Africa was creating the image domestically that he was not firm enough with the Russians (Vance, 1983). This idea was also pressed many times by Brzezinski. For example, in a Weekly Report to the President in late-1977, the National Security Adviser cautioned Carter that, despite the appropriateness of his initiatives, he felt that "we are confronting a growing domestic problem involving public perception of the general character of that policy", which was ultimately "seen as 'soft'" (Brzezinski to Carter, 18/11/1977).

For Brzezinski, Soviet involvement called for a more robust response from the US. The failure to respond would allow the Soviet Union to further strengthen its influence in Africa. In a memo to Carter on 18 January 1978, Brzezinski again warned the President of the possible consequences of the increased Soviet presence:

> Soviet leaders may be acting merely in response to an apparent opportunity, or the Soviet action may be part of a wider strategic design. In either case, the Soviets probably calculate, as previously in Angola, they can later adopt a more conciliatory attitude and that the US will simply again adjust to the consolidation of Soviet presence in yet another African country. (Brzezinski, 1983: 181)

More disconcerting still was the threat that this created for US interests in the broader Middle East region. The situation was becoming equally disturbing across the Red Sea in the Yemens. Since the late-1960s, South Yemen (i.e., the People's Republic of Yemen) had established friendly relations with the USSR, becoming the first Marxist Arab regime (Garthoff, 1985). During 1978 internal strife led Abd al-Fattah Isma'il to seize power in a coup and subsequently increase South Yemen-Soviet cooperation. In fact, South Yemen actively supported Soviet and Cuban involvement in the Horn of Africa. The prospect of another Soviet proxy in the region led Brzezinski (1983: 181) to warn the SCC that "if Ethiopia and South Yemen become Soviet associates, not only will the access to the Suez be threatened, and this involves the oil pipeline from Saudi

Arabia and Iran, but there will be a serious and direct political threat to Saudi Arabia". This prospective threat led the administration to send a delegation to North Yemen and Saudi Arabia to outline a new military aid program to counter growing Soviet influence in the Arabian Peninsula (Garthoff, 1985). Eventually, the US would supply North Yemen with a $390 million military aid package which included F-5 fighter aircraft, heavy artillery, and anti-tank weapons (Brzezinski, 1983; Smith, 1986).

In early-1978 the first serious disagreements within the administration over the policy for the Horn of Africa came to the forefront. The real issue was not the importance of the Horn of Africa. With the key foreign policy decision-makers' mental maps already fixated on the Middle East, the most pressing differences were on how best to safeguard US interests in the region. The main contention within the administration was whether to link US-USSR relations involving other issues to Soviet behavior in Africa. Brzezinski and the NSC favored linkage because it was a central principle of détente. However, Secretary of State Cyrus Vance rejected any idea that their actions in Africa were part of any Soviet grand design. On the contrary, Vance viewed Soviet behavior simply as the exploitation of emerging opportunities. In view of that, Vance rejected linking Soviet actions in the Horn of Africa on the ground that it would harm larger American interests, such as SALT negotiations, and have little or no effect on Soviet behavior in Africa (Vance, 1983).

The interagency debate confirmed this contrast. For instance, in a SCC meeting held on 22 February 1978, the discussion centered on the future role of the Soviets in the Horn of Africa and the US response. The discussion laid bare the internal differences on several key-issues regarding the ongoing conflict (SCC, 22/02/1978: 2). Besides the possibility of a resolution demanding Soviet and Cuban withdrawal from the conflict, the group discussed the illicit transfer of US weapons to Somalia by Saudi Arabia. While the group was in favor of US allies providing non-US military equipment, Secretary of Defense Harold Brown questioned whether the any such transfers should be supported without the prior withdrawal of Somali forces from the Ogaden. Secretary Vance argued that the US should not support the allies' arms transfers until Somalia had withdrawn. Nevertheless, Brzezinski was reluctant to counter Saudi Arabia's policy in the Horn of Africa, believing that Saudi support was essential to offset Soviet and Cuban advances.

The group also discussed the possibility of sending a US carrier task force to the region. Brzezinski defended the stationing of the task force in the Red Sea as a confidence-building measure and as a deterrent to further Soviet involvement. For Brzezinski, the task force would serve several purposes of which the most important would be for America to signal to "countries in the region that the US is present, stands with them, will protect the flow of arms, and will provide protection from the Russians" (SCC, 22/02/1978: 10). This argument met considerable opposition, particularly from Vance and Brown, who considered the initiative to be a bluff which the US could not enforce.

Unable to secure the placing of the task force in the region, Brzezinski inquired as to possible US actions which might influence Soviet behavior in the Horn of Africa. The possibility of linking other US-Soviet bilateral issues, such as the Indian Ocean talks, science and technology transfers, SALT II, or relations with China, to the Soviets' African policy were also discussed. However, the differences in orientation were evident in the meeting's final recommendations:

- "We should rely on the OAU to press for some sort negotiated settlement but not exclude the United Nations;
- We should approach the Saudis, Iranians, and Pakistanis to point out that arms transfers of US origin are illegal, that such illegal assistance could have a serious impact on future US arms sales, that we do not object to their providing non-US origin equipment to Somalia and that we would consider authorizing third country arms transfers if Somalia is threatened with invasion after withdrawing from the Ogaden;
- We are disagreed whether to recommend deployment of a US carrier task force but agree that we should proceed with consultations with regional powers; and
- With respect to other actions against the USSR and Cuba we see no direct linkage with other bilateral matters but are willing to consider further steps with respect to space cooperation and technology transfers to the Chinese. (Secretary Vance reserved his position on the latter)." (SCC, 22/02/1978: 15)

A few days later, President Carter issued Presidential Directive 32 (PD-32) setting the guidelines for US policy towards the Horn of Africa.[19] The directive seemed to validate the existing policies and the more accommodating attitude advocated by Vance and the State Department. In effect, it confirmed a regionally oriented resolution to the conflict in the Horn of Africa, namely through the initiatives of the OAU. It also reiterated the American policy of not authorizing allies to supply weapons of US-origin to third parties, particularly to Somalia. Providing Somalia with defensive non-US weapons was not disapproved, but PD-32 emphasized that Somalia should be pressed to withdraw

19 A Presidential Directive (PD) was implemented as a series used to promulgate presidential decisions on national security matters.

from the Ogaden. If Somalia did vacate the Ogaden, the US was prepared to initiate procedures to assure Congressional approval for the transfer of defensive US-origin weapons to assist in the defense of Somali territory. Furthermore, President Carter did not approve the deployment of a US carrier task force in the Red Sea.

However, PD-32 also endorsed considerable leeway in implementing a more assertive policy in case the need arose. For instance, while the carrier was not authorized in the Red Sea, the president did indicate willingness to move a carrier into the vicinity, namely to Diego Garcia.[20] What's more, the directive established that in the case of a Soviet and Cuban aided invasion of Somalia the US would consider authorizing its allies to transfer weapons to Somalia even in the absence of its commitment to withdraw from the Ogaden. More significantly, "in the event of an invasion of Somalia, should the countries of the region decide to deliver military equipment to Somalia, or to provide air cover or other units to counter Ethiopian or Cuban air capability, the United States would be prepared to offset Soviet threats or actions directed at such assistance measures" (PD-32: 2). The precise measures used to counterbalance prospective Soviet actions were not identified, but the directive clearly indicated US resolve to act more assertively in the Horn of Africa if circumstances so required.

Moreover, notwithstanding the recommendation resulting from the interagency debates against binding wider US-USSR relations to the Soviets' actions in the Horn of Africa, the President implicitly ended up linking them. One day after Brzezinski had stated to the press that Soviet military involvement in the Ogaden War could complicate efforts to achieve a new strategic-arms accord, the President declared at his 2 March 1978 News Conference that while SALT talks were currently in progress with the Soviets, they would have to be backed by the American people in order to be ratified by Congress.[21] The Soviet infringement of US principles regarding the conflict would, according to Carter (1978a), "lessen the confidence of the American people in the word and peaceful intentions of the Soviet Union, would make it more difficult to ratify a SALT agreement or comprehensive test ban agreement if concluded, and therefore, the two are linked because of actions by the Soviets.".

20 The carrier was never actually moved to Diego Garcia in accordance with the directive. Njølstad (1995) suggests that the proposal may have been put forward by the president simply to satisfy Brzezinski's more assertive demands.

21 In a breakfast for reporters hosted by Vice-President Mondale on 01 March, 1978, Brzezinski stated specifically that the "unwarranted intrusion of Soviet power into a purely local conflict ... will inevitably complicate the context not only of the (SALT) negotiating process itself but of any ratification that would follow the successful conclusion of the negotiations" (cited in Murphy, 1978: 4).

The President's statement reopened the debate within the administration regarding the appropriate policy for dealing with the situation in the Horn of Africa. On the same day the President spoke to the press, the SCC gathered to discuss the Horn of Africa. Secretaries Brown and Vance observed that it was wrong for the President to establish any linkage. Brzezinski, for his part, persisted in pushing the idea that the "Soviets are demonstrating a predisposition to exploit a local conflict for larger purposes" (SCC, 02/03/1978: 8). The US needed to act more assertively in order impress on the Soviets the cost of their actions, otherwise "this is going to be a continuation of our pattern of behavior of the last few months: noise but no follow-through" (SCC, 02/03/1978: 9). While Vance remained adamant in not jeopardizing US-Soviet relations any further, Brown suggested an overture to the Chinese to try to pressure Moscow. The majority of the group favored a closer relationship with China and Vance ultimately agreed that conversations on science and technology could proceed. However, Vance continued to caution that "we are on the brink of ending up with a real souring of relations between ourselves and the Soviet Union and it may take a helluva long while to change and may not be changed for years and I think that is a very important step to take" (SCC, 02/03/1978: 8).

3.3 *The Shaba II Conflict and the Consolidation of the Administration's Overarching Mental Maps*

The announcement of the end of the Ogaden War on 8 March 1978, settled the issue of how to convince Barre to withdraw his forces from Ethiopia. However, it did not resolve the discussion within the administration over Soviet and Cuban involvement in Africa. In fact, in May 1978 the situation in the Shaba province erupted once again. The FNLC invaded the Shaba province and was again able to achieve rapid advances into Zaire and conquer several strategic points in the area (Odom, 1992). This time, the Carter administration quickly denounced the situation. At news conference on 25 May, Carter (1978b) chastised the Neto regime and his Cuban associates. Brzezinski corroborated the President's claims a few days later on the NBC program *Meet the Press*. According to Brzezinski, the invasion "could not have taken place without the invading parties having been armed and trained by the Cubans and, indeed, perhaps also the East Germans, and we have sufficient evidence to be quite confident in our conclusion that Cuba shares the political and the moral responsibility for the invasion" (cited in Department of State, 1978: 26). The public denunciation of Cuban involvement continued throughout the following weeks and eventually the administration began implicating the Soviets for their responsibility in the crisis. More precisely, on 14 June, Carter (1978c) assailed both the Cubans and the Soviets for their responsibility in the Shaba conflict: "I think it's accurate to say that they [Cuba and the Soviet Union] take advantage of local disturbances and move in with massive intrusions, both of military weapons, which contribute to further bloodshed among Africans themselves, and when they are permitted by the local government, they send in large quantities of troops.".

Regardless of the actual facts concerning Cuban and Soviet involvement in the Shaba II crisis, by this time the Carter administration had transformed a Third World conflict into an East-West conflict.[22] The issue died down as direct European involvement – i.e., French and Belgian troops – and US air support helped to quickly defeat the FNLC forces (Odom, 1992). Nevertheless, by mid-1978, US policy was increasingly exhibiting a more assertive character. To begin with, the Ogaden and the Shaba II crises marked the end of the tentative rapprochement between the US and Cuba (Gleijeses, 2006). These conflicts also hardened the administration's attitude towards the Soviet Union, impairing the already strained relationship between the two superpowers. In particular, this toughened stance hindered increased cooperation with the USSR for, as Brzezinski (1983: 178) admitted, "it represented a serious setback to our attempts to develop with the Soviets some rules of the game in dealing with turbulence in the Third World". Ultimately, for the National Security Adviser, the Horn of Africa marked the beginning of the end of détente and the deterioration of US-USSR relations.

The espousal of a more assertive policy towards the Soviets was not, however, shared by all the administration's key foreign policy decision-makers. In fact, during the crises in Africa several different mental maps of the Middle East region coexisted within the Carter administration. While some were still optimistic about the possibility of cooperating with Soviets in managing Third World conflicts, others were increasingly pessimistic about the efficacy of the current US foreign policy, particularly regarding the relationship with the USSR in the Middle East region.

In particular, Brzezinski gradually became more critical of the Soviet behavior in the Third World. He repeatedly alerted the president to the detrimental effects of failing to stand up to Soviet expansionism. According to Brzezinski, the US could no longer afford to acquiesce to the Soviets. As he would incessantly remind Carter, "both for international reasons as well as domestic political reasons you ought to deliberately toughen both the tone and the substance of our foreign policy" (Brzezinski to Carter, 13/09/1979: 2). In contrast, Secretaries Vance and Brown were concerned that a more assertive approach could

22 For an account on the Cuban involvement in the Shaba conflict see Gleijeses (2006).

prove counterproductive to US interests. For Brown an excessive response could produce very few tangible results and possibly discredit future US initiatives. Vance, for his part, was apprehensive that a more robust approach could ultimately undermine détente and create further problems for US interests in the region.

In the end, it was the president who had the final word on US policy. Carter's judgment mirrored his advisors' divergent problem representations. As events unfolded in Africa, Carter maintained his principle of emphasizing non-intervention and non-military solutions to the crises. Despite Brzezinski's continued insistence for a more aggressive policy towards the Soviets, Carter rejected his advisor's more belligerent recommendations. PD-32 certainly seems to vindicate the opposing views, particularly those of Vance. All the same, Carter did modify his attitude towards the US-Soviet relationship. Not only did he come to link SALT to Soviet actions in Africa, he also made decisions which sought to get the USSR to appreciate the consequences of their actions. For instance, Carter suspended the Indian Ocean demilitarization talks in October 1978 and by the end of the year he relinquished the Conventional Arms Transfer (CAT) talks (Moens, 1990; Powaski, 1998).[23]

In this sense, Carter reflected the dynamic nature of his advisors' geographic mental maps. While still confident in the capability of regional actors to manage their local problems and in the ability of the US to cooperate with the USSR, Carter was increasingly apprehensive of the long-term implications of Soviet involvement in the Third World, particularly in the Middle East. His decisions embodied the greater concurrence within the administration's foreign policy decision-making group regarding the strategic importance of the Horn of Africa and the greater Middle East region. As he stated in a speech on US foreign and security policy in mid-March 1978:

> There also has been an ominous inclination on the part of the Soviet Union to use its military power – to intervene in local conflicts, with advisers, with equipment, and with full logistical support and encouragement for mercenaries from other Communist countries, as we can observe today in Africa. (…) We will match, together with our allies and friends, any threatening power through a combination of military forces,

23 The Indian Ocean demilitarization talks began in June 1977. The American proposal called for the US and the USSR to renounce increasing the existing level of their naval deployments, changing the general pattern of deployment, or attaining new bases in the Indian Ocean region (Powaski, 1998).

> political efforts, and economic programs. We will not allow any other nation to gain military superiority over us. (…) We shall implement this policy that I've outlined so briefly in three different ways: by maintaining strategic nuclear balance; by working closely with our NATO allies to strengthen and modernize our defenses in Europe; and by maintaining and developing forces to counter any threats to our allies and friends in our vital interests in Asia, the Middle East, and other regions of the world. (Carter, 1983d: 21–22)

As Carter later acknowledged, the Ogaden was not worthy of American military intervention. Rather, he admitted that he "always thought that the place for us to confront the Soviet Union, if necessary, was in the Middle East area" (cited in Njølstad, 1995: 177). This belief would grow as events in the region would once again concentrate the administration's attention.

4 Conclusion

The Carter administration came to Office placing considerable attention on the Middle East. The administration's main foreign policy decision-makers shared an optimistic outlook that the US could constructively engage the region and tackle many of the challenges. While diplomacy and cooperation were the favored means for dealing with regional issues, the administration also contemplated military options. As new challenges and threats surfaced, the decision-makers' geographic mental maps of the Middle East were continuously reconstructed. The region was increasingly viewed as a place of danger and potential military conflict. While diplomacy and cooperation were still political options, the administration gradually assumed a more assertive policy towards regional events, particularly towards Soviet involvement in the Middle East. Over time, small-scale, continuous adjustments to policy ultimately transformed America's engagement with the Middle East (da Vinha, 2017).

As this chapter illustrates, the crises in Africa during the first half of the Carter presidency revealed the growing assertiveness of US power in the Middle East region. When the Shaba I crisis broke out in early-1977, the administration initially framed the conflict within a regional framework. However, the Shaba I crisis set off a debate within the administration regarding Soviet and Cuban involvement in Africa. In March 1977, Carter issued PRM-21 requesting a general review of US policy towards the Horn of Africa. The policy review revealed a cautious attitude towards the warring parties. In particular, Carter did not want to involve the US too deeply in the conflict, preferring instead a regionally negotiated settlement. Nevertheless, the administration tried to mobilize African leaders in demanding that outside powers, particularly the USSR and its allies, refrain from interfering in the conflict and placing the burden for the maintenance of the conflict on the Soviets. However, as the conflict continued and the Soviets increasingly sided with Ethiopia, America's regional allies began requesting US consent for providing Somalia with military aid. The US eventually acquiesced to this request as concern mounted with the increasing Soviet involvement in the region.

The success of the Ethiopian counter-offensive in early-1978 led the administration to reassess its policy. The American policy of non-intervention increasingly came under question and the debate within the administration intensified. The main contention rested on the best policy to safeguard US interests in the region. The debate centered on whether to link US-USSR relations to Soviet behavior in Africa. While Brzezinski argued that linkage was a central principle of détente, Vance rejected linking Soviet actions in the Horn of Africa on the grounds that it would harm broader American interests.

The deliberation process led Carter to issue PD-32 which established the guidelines for US policy towards the Horn of Africa. The directive seemed to validate the more accommodating attitude, emphasizing a regionally oriented resolution to the conflict in the Horn of Africa. Nevertheless, PD-32 did confirm that in case the Soviets and Cubans aided in an invasion of Somalia, the US would consider authorizing the transfer of weapons to Somalia even in the absence of its commitment to withdraw from the Ogaden. More importantly, the directive determined that the US would be prepared to offset Soviet threats or actions directed at such assistance measures. Moreover, the president implicitly linked US-USSR relations with the Soviet involvement in the Horn of Africa, rearticulating the conventional terms of détente.

When the Shaba conflict erupted anew in May 1978, the Carter administration hurriedly denounced the situation. The inflamed rhetoric ultimately transformed the conflicts in Africa into East-West conflicts. In fact, by mid-1978, US policy was increasingly exhibiting a more assertive character. The Ogaden and the Shaba II crises marked the end of the tentative rapport between the US and Cuba and hardened the administration's attitude towards the Soviet Union.

The crises the administration later faced in the Middle East – e.g., the Iranian Revolution, the Iranian hostage crisis, and the Soviet invasion of Afghanistan – undoubtably contributed to further clouding the Carter administration's mental maps of the political environment in the Third World and of the superpower relationship. However, it is a mistake to claim that "prior to the invasion, the US public, moderates in the US government, and even the president were not sufficiently impressed by Soviet gains in Angola, Ethiopia, and South Yemen to promote a noticeable shift in what was widely viewed as a policy of accommodating Moscow" (Yetiv, 1990: 69).

After facing the crises in Africa, the administration's perception of the US-Soviet relationship was already dismal, reflecting a sense of fear and distrust regarding Soviet capabilities and intentions. By the time the crises unfolded in the Middle East and the president announced the Carter Doctrine, the administration had long altered its view regarding the potential for cooperation with the Soviets. In fact, the Administration had long been working to check Soviet power, namely by maintaining a strong rhetoric emphasizing the promotion of human rights, cooperating with China on intelligence, aiding Afghani insurgents and the Pakistani intelligence services, and strengthening US military capabilities (da Vinha, 2013; Gates, 1996, 2014). Therefore, rather than reveal a waning national determination, the Carter Doctrine represented a resolute reaffirmation of American power.

This view contrasts with many traditional assessments of the Carter administration's foreign policy. More significantly, it rebukes the standard rational actor centered explanations regarding the development of the Carter Doctrine and which emphasize episodic, revolutionary change. By employing geographic mental maps as an analytical concept, we can gain a better appreciation of the complex geographic and social dynamics involved in foreign policy decision-making. In other words, by focusing on mental maps we can gain a better understanding of how policy-makers develop a core set of shared geographic beliefs that inform foreign policy decisions.

Moreover, by analyzing decision-makers' mental maps we can acquire a more holistic and integrated view of foreign policy. On too many occasions, FPA has concentrated excessively on a particular region or country, obfuscating its relationship with other places. However, we need to understand a country's foreign policy in a more comprehensive framework. As this chapter illustrates, events in Africa were critical to defining the Carter administration's policy in the Middle East. Without this holistic approach, we run the risk of missing out on the complex interdependencies and trade-offs involved in foreign policy-making. This would be particularly unfortunate in the current period of transformation of the international system. As the liberal international order is increasingly challenged, understanding how decision-makers view the world is imperative. Using geographic mental maps as an analytical tool can help understand the perceptions driving policies and, potentially, help overcoming misperceptions and misunderstandings.

Bibliography

Barret, F., Thomas, G. & Hocevar, S. (1995). The Central Role of Discourse in Large-Scale Change: A Social Construction Perspective. *Journal of Applied Behavioral Science*, 31 (3), 352–372.

Bliddal, H. (2011). *Reforming Military Command Arrangements: The Case of the Rapid Deployment Joint Task Force*. Carlisle: US Army War College.

Brown, S. (1994). *The Faces of Power: The United States Foreign Policy from Truman to Clinton*. New York: Columbia University Press.

Brzezinski, Z. (1983). *Power and Principle: Memoirs of the National Security Adviser, 1977–1981*. New York: Farrar, Straus, & Giroux.

Brzezinski to Carter. (13 September, 1979). *NSC Weekly Report no. 109*. Jimmy Carter Library, Zbigniew Brzezinski Collection, Weekly Reports, Box 42.

Brzezinski to Carter. (26 August, 1977). *Memorandum from Brzezinski to President Carter, PRC Review of Situation in Horn of Africa*. The Carter-Brezhnev Project at the National Security Archive, George Washington University. Available at http://www2.gwu.edu/~nsarchiv/carterbrezhnev/docs_global_competition/Tab%202/19770826%20-%20PRC%20Review%20of%20the%20Situation%20in%20Horn%20of%20Africa.pdf (Accessed 20 January, 2013).

Brzezinski to Carter. (18 November, 1977). *NSC Weekly Report no. 37*. Jimmy Carter Library, Zbigniew Brzezinski Collection, Weekly Reports, Box 41, "Weekly Reports 31–41" folder.

Brzezinski to Carter. (11 March, 1977). *Memorandum from Brzezinski to President Carter*. Available at http://www.memo.ru/history/diss/carter/files/zb_daily_3-11-77.pdf (Accessed 30 August, 2012).

Carter, J. (1978a). *The President's News Conference* [02 March, 1978]. Available at The American Presidency Project http://www.presidency.ucsb.edu/ws/index.php?pid=30437 (Accessed 15 September, 2013).

Carter, J. (1978b). *The President's News Conference* [25 May, 1978]. Available at The American Presidency Project http://www.presidency.ucsb.edu/ws/index.php?pid=30852 (Accessed 15 September, 2013).

Carter, J. (1978c). *The President's News Conference* [14 June, 1978]. Available at The American Presidency Project http://www.presidency.ucsb.edu/ws/index.php?pid=30946 (Accessed 15 September, 2013).

Carter, J. (1977). *The President's News Conference* [24 March, 1977]. Available at The American Presidency Project http://www.presidency.ucsb.edu/ws/index.php?pid=7229 (Accessed 12 March, 2013).

Carter to Brezhnev. (21 December, 1977). *Letter*. The Carter-Brezhnev Project at the National Security Archive, George Washington University. Available at http://www2.gwu.edu/~nsarchiv/carterbrezhnev/docs_global_competition/Tab%20

2/19771221%20-%20Letter%20from%20Carter%20to%20Brezhnev.pdf (Accessed 20 January, 2013).

Committee on International Relations. (1978). *War in the Horn of Africa: A Firsthand Report on the Challenges for United States Policy: Report of a Factfinding Mission to Egypt, Sudan, Ethiopia, Somalia, and Kenya.* Washington, DC: US Government Printing Office. Available at http://catalog.hathitrust.org/Record/002943162 (Accessed 02 December, 2013).

Da Vinha, L. (2019). Maps of War and Peace: Rethinking Geography in International Affairs. *Brown Journal of World Affairs*, 25 (2), 73–89.

Da Vinha, L. (2017). *Geographic Mental Maps and Foreign Policy Change: Re-Mapping the Carter Doctrine.* Berlin: De Gruyter.

Da Vinha, L. (2015). Falling Dominos… Or the Role of Geographic Mental Maps in Foreign Policy. *European Journal of Geography*, 6 (4), 76–87.

Da Vinha, L. (2013). In Search of a Morally Pragmatic Foreign Policy: The Carter Administration's Human Rights Policy. In M. Costa (Ed.), *Democracia, Direitos Humanos e Justiça Global* (pp. 81–98). Braga: Universidade do Minho.

Department of State. (1978). Interview: National Security Adviser Brzezinski on "Meet the Press". *Department of State Bulletin*, 78 (2016), 26–28.

Dobson, A. & Marsh, S. (2001). *US Foreign Policy Since 1945.* London: Routledge.

Erforth, B. (2016). Mental Maps and Foreign Policy Decision-Making: Eurafrique and the French Military Intervention in Mali. *European Review of International Studies*, 3 (2), 38–58.

Ford, J. (1999). Organizational Change as Shifting Conversations. *Journal of Organizational Change Management*, 12 (6), 480–500

Ford, J. & Ford, L. (1995). The Role of Conversations in Producing Intentional Change in Organizations. *The Academy of Management Review*, 20 (3), 541–570.

Freedman, L. (2009). *A Choice of Enemies: America Confronts the Middle East.* London: Phoenix.

Gaddis, J. L. (2005). *Strategies of Containment: A Critical Appraisal of American National Security Policy during the Cold War.* New York: Oxford University Press.

Garthoff, R. (1985). *Détente and Confrontation: American-Soviet Relations from Nixon to Reagan.* Washington, DC: The Brookings Institution.

Gates, R. (2014). *Duty: Memoirs of a Secretary at War.* New York: Alfred A. Knopf.

Gates, R. (1996). *From the Shadows: The Ultimate Insider's Story of Five Presidents and How They Won the Cold War.* New York: Simon & Schuster.

Gleijeses, P. (2006). Moscow's Proxy? Cuba and Africa 1975–1988. *Journal of Cold War Studies*, 8 (2), 3–51.

Hunt, M. (2007). *The American Ascendency: How the United States Gained and Wielded Global Dominance.* Chappel Hill: The University of North Carolina Press.

Jackson, D. (2010). The Ogaden War and the Demise of Détente. *The Annals of the American Academy of Political and Social Science*, 632 (1), 26–40.

Jackson, D. (2007). The Carter Administration and Somalia. *Diplomatic History*, 31 (4), 703–721.

Kupchan, C. (1987). *The Persian Gulf and the West: Dilemmas of Security*. Boston: Allan & Unwin.

Lebow, R. & Stein, J. (1993). Afghanistan, Carter, and Foreign Policy Change: The Limits of Cognitive Models. In D. Caldwell & T. McKeown (Eds.), *Diplomacy, Force and Leadership: Essays in Honor of Alexander L. George* (pp. 95–127). Boulder: Westview Press.

LeoGrande, W. (1980) *Cuba's Policy in Africa, 1959–1980*. Berkley: Institute of International Studies.

Makinda, S. (1982). Conflict and the Superpowers in the Horn of Africa. *Third World Quarterly*, 4 (1), 93–103.

Michaels, J. (2011). Dysfunctional Doctrines: Eisenhower, Carter and US Military Intervention in the Middle East. *Political Science Quarterly*, 126 (3), 465–492.

Moens, A. (1990). The Carter Administration and Multiple Advocacy. *International Journal*, 45 (4), 913–948.

Moore, R. (1984). The Carter Presidency and Foreign Policy. In M. Abernathy, D. Hill, & P. Williams (Eds.), *The Carter Years: The President and Policy Making* (pp. 54–83). New York: St. Martin's Press.

Murphy, K. (1978). Brzezinski Pushed Linkage to Wreck SALT. *Executive Intelligence Review*, 5 (9), 3–4.

Njølstad, O. (2004). Shifting Priorities: The Persian Gulf in US Strategic Planning in the Carter Years. *Cold War History*, 4 (3), 21–55.

Njølstad, O. (1995). *Peacekeeper* and *Troublemaker: The Containment Policy of Jimmy Carter, 1977–1978*. Oslo: Norwegian Institute for Defense Studies.

Odom, W. (2006). The Cold War Origins of the US Central Command. *Journal of Cold War Studies*, 8 (2), 52–82.

Odom, T. (1992). *Shaba II: the French and Belgian intervention in Zaire in 1978*. Fort Leavenworth: US Army Command and General Staff College.

Palmer, M. (1999). *Guardians of the Gulf: A History of America's Expanding Role in the Persian Gulf, 1883–1992*. New York: Simon and Schuster.

PD-32. (24 February, 1978). *Presidential Directive 32, Horn of Africa*. Jimmy Carter Library website. Available at http://www.jimmycarterlibrary.gov/documents/pddirectives/pres_directive.phtml.

Powaski, R. (1998). *The Cold War: The United States and the Soviet Union, 1917–1991*. New York: Oxford University Press.

PRC. (11 April, 1977). *Policy Review Committee Meeting: Minutes*. The Carter-Brezhnev Project at the National Security Archive, George Washington University. Available at http://www.gwu.edu/~nsarchiv/carterbrezhnev/docs_global_competition/Tab%20 2/19770411%20-%20Summary%20of%20Conclusions%20of%20Policy%20 Review%20Committee%20Meeting,%20Ethiopia%20and%20Horn%20of%20 Africa.pdf (Accessed 20 January 2013).

PRM-21. (17 March, 1977). *Presidential Review Memorandum 21, The Horn of Africa.* Jimmy Carter Library website. Available at http://www.jimmycarterlibrary.gov/ documents/prmemorandums/pres_memorandums.phtml.

Quandt, W. (1986). *Camp David: Peace Making and Politics.* Washington, DC: The Brookings Institution.

Reisman, W. M. (1982). Critical Defense Zones and International Law: The Reagan Codicil. *The American Journal of International Law*, 76 (3), 589–591.

Rosati, J. (1994). Cycles in Foreign Policy Restructuring: The Politics of Continuity and Change in US Foreign Policy. In J. Rosati, J. Hagan, & M. Sampson (Eds.), *Foreign Policy Restructuring: How Governments Respond to Global Change* (pp. 221–261). Columbia: University of South Carolina Press.

Rosati, J. (1991). *The Carter Administration's Quest for Global Community: Beliefs and their Impact on Behavior.* Columbia: University of South Carolina Press.

SCC. (02 March, 1978). *Special Coordinating Committee Meeting: Minutes.* The Carter-Brezhnev Project at the National Security Archive, George Washington University. Available at http://www2.gwu.edu/~nsarchiv/carterbrezhnev/docs_global_competition/ Tab%202/19780302%20-%20SCC%20Meeting%20on%20the%20Horn%20of%20 Africa.pdf (Accessed 20 January, 2013).

SCC. (22 February, 1978). *Special Coordinating Committee Meeting: Minutes.* The Carter-Brezhnev Project at the National Security Archive, George Washington University. Available at http://www2.gwu.edu/~nsarchiv/carterbrezhnev/docs_global_competition/Tab%202/19780222%20-%20The%20Horn%20of%20Africa.pdf (Accessed 20 January, 2013).

SCC. (27 January, 1978). *Special Coordinating Committee Meeting: Summary of Conclusions.* The Carter-Brezhnev Project at the National Security Archive, George Washington University. Available at http://www.gwu.edu/~nsarchiv/carterbrezhnev/ docs_global_competition/Tab%202/19780127%20-%20Summary%20of%20Conclusions,%20SCC%20Meeting%20on%20Horn%20of%20Africa.pdf (Accessed 20 January, 2013).

Skidmore, D. (1996). *Reversing Course: Carter's Foreign Policy, Domestic Politics, and the Failure of Reform.* Nashville: Vanderbilt University Press.

Smith, G. (1986). *Morality, Reason and Power: American Diplomacy in the Carter Years.* New York: Hill and Wang.

Snyder, R., Bruck, H. & Sapin, B. (2002). *Foreign Policy Decision Making (Revisited).* New York: Palgrave Macmillan.

Sprout, H. & Sprout, M. (1960). Geography and International Politics in an Era of Revolutionary Change. *Journal of Conflict Resolution*, 4 (1), 145–161.
Sterman, J. (2001). System Dynamics Modelling: Tools for Learning in a Complex World. *California Management Review*. 43 (4), 8–25.
Sylvan, D. (1998). Introduction. In D. Sylvan & J. Voss (Eds.), *Problem Representation in Foreign Policy Decision Making* (pp.3–7). Cambridge: Cambridge University Press.
Taber, C. (1998). The Interpretation of Foreign Policy Events: A Cognitive Process Theory. In D. Sylvan & J. Voss (Eds.), *Problem Representation in Foreign Policy Decision Making* (pp.29–52). Cambridge: Cambridge University Press.
Tareke, G. (2000). The Ethiopia-Somalia War of 1977 Revisited. *International Journal of African Historical Studies*, 33 (3), 635–668.
Vance, C. (1983). *Hard Choices: Critical Years in Americas Foreign Policy*. New York: Simon and Schuster.
Vance to Carter. (01 October, 1977). *Telegram from Secretary Vance to President Carter.* The Carter-Brezhnev Project at the National Security Archive, George Washington University. Available at http://www2.gwu.edu/~nsarchiv/carterbrezhnev/docs_global_competition/TAB%203/doc06%20-%2019771001%20-%20Middle%20East%20Discussion%20with%20the%20Soviets.pdf (Accessed 20 January, 2013).
Vertzberger, Y. (2002). *The World in their Minds: Information Processing, Cognition and Perception in Foreign Policy Decisionmaking*. Stanford: Stanford University Press.
Weiss, J. (1989). The Powers of Problem Definition: The Case of Government Paperwork. *Policy Sciences*, 22 (2), 97–98.
Wittkopf, E., Jones, C. & Kegley Jr., C. (2008). *American Foreign Policy: Pattern and Process*. Belmont: Thomson Higher Education.
Yetiv, S. (1990). How the Soviet Military Intervention in Afghanistan Improved the US Strategic Position in the Persian Gulf. *Asian Affairs*, 17 (2), 62–81.

CHAPTER 9

Mapping Greed as a Conflict Motivation: Evidence from Armed Conflicts in Sudan and Libya on the Complexity of Armed Groups' Interactions with Natural Resources

Steven Spittaels

1 Introduction

The priorities of armed groups can be established and documented through the systematic analysis of their interaction with territorially embedded factors. Indeed, although it is not the exclusive determinant of their actions, geography will frequently influence their decision-making. When we plot both the actions of armed groups and the environment in which they operate on a map, we create a visualization of their interaction. It allows us to establish, and illustrate, links between conflict events and the geographic conditions within which they occur. When used in case studies, this can provide unique insights on armed group motivation as well as the opportunities for such groups to sustain themselves.

This contribution will focus specifically on the question of greed as a cause of armed conflict. Greed refers to the pursuit of material gain, which can be a potential motivation of armed groups. Such material gain is usually closely linked to the territory that armed groups control or attempt to control. The most important sources of armed group funding include income from their control over the extraction, production, transport and trade of goods and resources. All of these are territorially embedded factors and can therefore be plotted with relative ease on a map.

In the first part of this contribution, a short recap is provided on the concept of greed as a motivation for armed conflict. In the second, a methodology is presented to assess to what extent greed motivations drive the actions of armed groups. In the third, it is argued that, although they are rarely used in such a way, excellent tools for an analysis of armed groups' interests in material gain are readily available. In the fourth and final part, the methodological tools are applied to two cases. One from Sudan and one from Libya. In both cases,

 | DOI:10.1163/9789004432086_011

armed groups operated in or near important installations of the country's oil infrastructure. A detailed analysis of the groups' (lack of) interaction with these territorially embedded factors, shows that armed conflict in resource rich areas should not automatically be categorised as being driven by greed. Only a sustained effort to analyse these interactions can provide enough evidence to make an accurate assessment of the (changing) intentions of warring parties.

2 Greed Motivation as a Conflict Driver

A central cause of armed conflict within the relevant literature, which mostly discusses civil wars, is greed. Proponents of the greed theory argue that wars are driven by positive economic incentives. Parties to an armed conflict often control large areas, where they can run or tax economic activities. Targets which are particularly vulnerable to war profiting include mining areas, markets, main traffic arteries and border crossings. Armed groups' control over these areas is often sufficient for observers to raise suspicions of significant greed motivations.

The greed model originates from publications written by economists. Jack Hirshleifer was one of the pioneering economists on the issue of armed conflict and a passionate advocate of broadening the scope of economic research to all social processes (Hirshleifer, 2001). Hirshleifer developed a rational choice theory in which people in a society have to choose between producing the goods they need and taking them by force from others. The decision makers seek the optimal outcome for their own needs and their separate and private decisions result in an equilibrium situation (Hirshleifer, 1995).

Probably the best-known economic author on the causes of war is Paul Collier of the World Bank. His large-N research on civil wars sought to establish correlations between sets of greed and grievance-related variables and the incidence/duration of war. He conducted most of his initial research together with Anke Hoeffler and their publications initiated a lively academic discussion, which quickly became known as the 'greed vs. grievance debate' (Collier & Hoeffler, 2000; P. Collier, 2000a, 2000b, 2002). The running theme throughout these publications was the assertation that warring parties' grievance discourse is mostly window dressing. Instead, Collier argued that some small, identifiable groups do well out of war and have an interest in its initiation, perpetuation, and renewal (Collier, 2000a). The argument follows that grievance rhetoric of these groups is therefore primarily used to recruit followers, obtain diaspora financing, and maintain organisational cohesion.

By the mid-2000s, the emphasis of Collier's work shifted to some extent. Whereas previously they were lumped together, he now explicitly made a distinction between greed as a rebel motivation and greed as the potential viability of a rebellion. Increasingly, Collier would refer to greed as the *opportunity* for rebellion (Collier & Hoeffler, 2004). As a consequence, motivation (whether greed or grievance) became less important to him as a cause of war.

A third trendsetting author on greed motivations for participation in armed conflict is David Keen, whose arguments are based on qualitative analysis. As opposed to Collier, Keen doesn't reject the importance of grievances as a genuine motivation which drive people to violence. His main intention is to draw attention to the fact that armed conflicts can also generate economic benefits for certain people (Keen, 2000). Focusing on individual interests, Keen is one of the initial authors who inspired the study of greed motivations at a micro-level. He stressed that economic reasoning influences all those who are involved in an armed conflict (Keen, 1998). Both the military leader and the foot soldier have economic motivations driving their actions. Moreover, economics pervades in all aspects of warfare and all phenomena surrounding it. He points, for example, to relief aid's capacity to fuel violence.

In later work, Keen would explicitly distance himself from the main arguments promoted by greed authors, downplaying grievances as a motivation for armed conflict. Instead he argued that the related literature has received too much attention and has potentially negatively affected international policies (Keen, 2012).

Recent research into the relevance of greed motivations is often based on quantitative methods. Through statistical analysis of ever more specific hypotheses, existing models are confirmed or amended. Efforts to integrate the various findings have not yet resulted in a single theory on greed as a cause of war. They are hampered by the fact that the evidence on the functioning of greed mechanisms remains contested. One of the main areas of disagreement is whether the correlation between armed conflict and the availability of natural resources is direct or indirect (Lujala, 2010). The first hypothesis follows the argument of traditional greed authors that *valuable natural resources provide rebels with a motivation and/or opportunity to fight.* Proponents of the second hypothesis argue that *resource-rich countries tend to have weaker state institutions, while provoking grievances amongst population groups, thereby increasing the likelihood of armed revolt.* They reinterpret statistical findings thought to confirm the greed narrative as proof for pre-existing grievance theories. Rustad and Binningsbo (2012), for example, observe a correlation between the recurrence of armed conflict and conflicts over natural resources but only when the dispute revolves around the distribution of natural resources.

The thinking on greed described above remains relatively abstract and lacks a sufficiently comprehensive body of qualitative research to complement it. Although there is a significant volume of specialised literature that looks at the motivation of individual combatants and their households, the number of concrete case studies on greed as a driver of armed conflict at the armed group level is limited. Existing case studies on certain groups or zones sometimes highlight natural resource predation by warring parties, but they rarely analyse the scale, the relative importance and the evolution of the phenomenon. In fact, there are very few case studies that investigate whether pursuing material gain is an operational priority for specific armed groups. This is a crucial knowledge gap, preventing a complete understanding of the overall greed phenomenon. Specific analytic approaches have been successfully applied to bridge this gap between large-N research and case studies of armed conflict (Paul et al. 2013). They show how case-level insights are crucial to interpret the correlations found in the quantitative analysis of conflict datasets.

3 Conflict Motivation Mapping

As will be demonstrated below, case-level insights on the relative importance of material gain as a driver of armed group behaviour can be generated from applying conflict motivation mapping, a methodology which systematically analyses armed group interaction with territorially embedded factors. Conflict motivation mapping is based on the broader research methodology of process tracing. Ruzzene (2014) describes the approach as 'a method of within-case causal analysis that helps causal inference by detecting mechanisms'. Although process tracing is a relatively popular approach, he finds that there is no academic agreement on its application or merit. Therefore, the quality of any conclusions reached through process tracing are entirely dependent on the strength of the evidence supporting them. Process tracing is primarily a qualitative research method, but quantitative data can be used as evidence during the testing of causal inference (Collier, 2011). A conflict motivation mapping analysis does indeed rely on strong evidence, which consists of both qualitative and quantitative data, to reach its conclusions.

3.1 *Model*

Motivation mapping starts from the assumption that the motivations and objectives of parties to an armed conflict are reflected in their actions. Throughout the whole conflict cycle, military and political decisions by parties to an armed conflict will reveal their motivations, including any changes thereof. This implies that one should be able to analyse concrete military actions and decisions, and trace these back to what provoked them. The starting point of such analysis is the war(fare) itself:

- Who is fighting where? Where not?
- Which areas are most heavily defended?
- Which areas are most fiercely attacked?
- Are specific people targeted?
- Are specific landmarks targeted?
- Are the parties to the conflict using important military assets or only limited resources?
- Are they trying to take control over a territory or are they using hit and run tactics?

The answers to these questions can provide us with a lot of information on the interests and priorities of the warring parties.

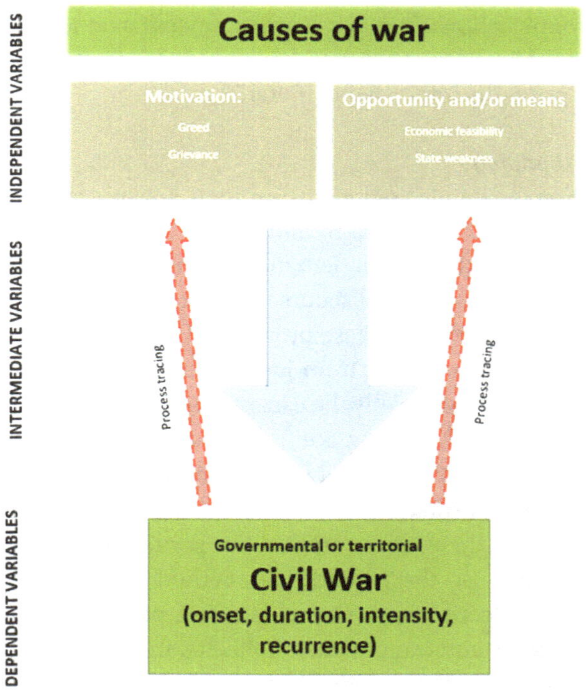

FIGURE 9.1
Model, causes of war, interpreted from literature

The above figure shows the basic research model used in the literature on the causes of war. The literature has identified a limited number of key independent variables, which can be grouped into two categories: opportunities and motivations. Evidently, conflict motivation mapping primarily focuses on the latter. However, although there is a clear relation between the motivations of warring parties and the outbreak/continuation of armed conflicts, it is not the only explanation. Warfare is also subject to opportunities to launch or sustain war efforts. For example, the military balance or access to conflict financing can have a significant impact on the behaviour of warring parties. Such opportunities include a myriad of circumstances. While some are structural, such as the presence of natural resources and difficult terrain, others are more haphazard, for example instability in a neighbouring country.

Greed, as a driver of armed conflict, can constitute both a motivation and an opportunity for armed groups. While this is an important distinction, it is not expected to have a major impact on how armed groups interact with profitable territorially embedded factors on the ground. For example, regardless of whether a certain natural resource constitutes an important means of enrichment or a key source of conflict financing, control over its deposits is expected to be a military priority for the armed group concerned and this should be visible from the armed group's actions. In other words, a process tracing based on the available evidence (the actions of armed groups), will help to assess whether these groups are primarily interested in material gain.

3.2 *The Mapping Methodology*

Warring parties will often make public statements on their reasons for starting an armed conflict or for participating in it. Sometimes they will write a detailed 'political program' that outlines their demands or ambitions, and they will frequently refer to their motivations in discourse used during public gatherings, in the media and on social media. These proclaimed motivations cannot be taken for granted. In fact, reporting from journalists or observers on armed groups' motivations, and more broadly the causes of a conflict, are often shaped by public discourse (Baum & Zhukov, 2015). Consequently, dominant narratives on armed conflicts do not necessarily reflect the real priorities of warring parties and the interests at stake.

Conflict motivation mapping therefore compares the public discourse of armed groups with their actions on the ground. The methodology relies on extensive and detailed data collection and tries to establish patterns revealing systematic behaviour. A large amount of data is collected from a variety of sources. It is then stored in a number of specifically designed databases. These databases allow for the automatic presentation of the data in visual tools to be used for qualitative analysis and the development of evidence.

A first tool is the **discourse file**, which is developed by collecting and archiving statements by key representatives of the armed group on their objectives. Of particular value are any 'official' documents such as laws, political declarations or founding acts, which will probably best reflect their self-proclaimed 'cause'. In an ideal scenario, armed groups have developed a detailed list of grievances. These are usually contained in some form of document that has been signed and adopted by the main representatives or commanders. The document can be a founding document, a response to important events, or the outcome of a high-level meeting. Additionally, social media such as Facebook, Twitter and YouTube have provided armed groups with a powerful public platform through which they can reach a broad audience, including sympathisers from within the diaspora, at a low cost and with minimal effort. As a consequence, communications from armed groups' representatives are often available in different formats, including recorded interviews and press statements. In cases where the armed group has participated in a negotiation process, related statements and demands should certainly be added to this file.

A second tool is a **map of conflict dynamics**, including systematic data on the position, behaviour and actions of the armed group on the ground. This set of maps visualises the areas in which the armed group concentrates its military efforts, as well as those it ignores. The data should contain details on the date of the incident, the geographic location and the unit involved and the type of event. A map of conflict dynamics will show conflict events as well as armed group positions. Conflict events can be combat-related incidents or other events that involve the use of force, both of which can be listed in a database or a spreadsheet. To understand the relevance of the incident, it is necessary to add a short description of each clash, with details on who initiated the fight and any information that could give an indication of the intensity of the fighting (See Figure 9.2 for an advanced example of a webmap of conflict dynamics). This could also include which weapons were used and how many casualties were reported. Data on combat incidents is often publicly available, for example in the press and on social media. However, the reliability of such reports is not guaranteed. It is therefore necessary to always add the sources of each reported incident.

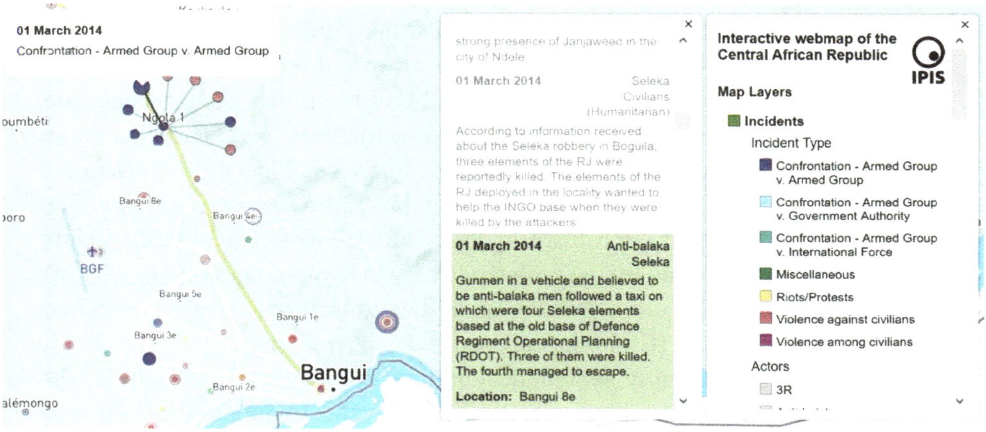

FIGURE 9.2 Screenshot of interactive map of conflict dynamics Central African Republic (IPIS, 2018)

Accurate data on the positions and strength of parties to an armed conflict are more difficult to obtain; often such data are classified. In addition, troop deployments are rarely very structured, especially in the case of armed groups. However, if sufficient information on deployments is available, it is useful to add them to the map. After all, large troop concentrations are likely to represent important military priorities.

In cases where the armed group has been involved in negotiations, and in which it has made territorial demands, these can be added on the map as well. Such demands could give a strong indication of the motivations and objectives of the negotiating party. All peace negotiations will at some point include territorial arrangements: the demarcation of (internal) borders, the ceasefire positions of opposing army units, the determination of buffer zones etc. During peace talks the parties to the armed conflict will probably compromise on certain issues but remain intransigent on others. This reveals a lot about their priorities.

Typically, a map of conflict dynamics consists of vector data layers. Vector data are a collection of drawn elements that mark locations on a map. The representations used in vector data are points, lines and polygons (shapes/areas). Incidents are often represented as points on a specific location. Army positions could be reflected in zones (polygons) or along roads (lines). Individual elements from a vector data layer can usually be clicked on to obtain further information.

A third tool used in a conflict motivation mapping is a **map of strategic interests**, which visualizes concrete military targets that physically represent the potential objectives and motivations of the conflict parties. The conversion of theoretical agendas and political ambitions into concrete physical targets is sometimes challenging but in the case of greed it is relatively straightforward. A war driven by profit will be located in an area that can generate economic benefits. Most of these profitable zones can be identified and because of their relatively fixed location, they can be pinpointed on a map.

The role of natural resources in fuelling armed conflict has received a lot of attention, with good reason. A number of army and rebel officers in conflict areas throughout the world have indeed become mining agents. Therefore, greed maps should indicate the location of extractives (See Figure 9.3 for an advanced example of a webmap of strategic interests). Most natural resources can be profitable to control and/or exploit, but some are more suitable than others. The Peace Research Institute Oslo (PRIO) previously identified eight resources of high value that are relatively easy to exploit: diamonds/gems, oil, natural gas, copper, gold, chromite, tantalite and timber – a list which is certainly not exhaustive (Gilmore et al., 2005).

Concessions currently exploited by mining companies should not be the only type considered; old concessions or deposits frequented by artisanal miners are also important. In the case of sites with industrial or semi-industrial mining, data could be collected from a geological institute or government service. Gathering data on artisanal mines is much more complex. If the war area has not been the subject of a specialised study, the information can only be gathered through extensive interviews with local experts/officials and terrain visits involving the collection of location coordinates. Natural resources can be indicated on maps as points or as areas (polygons). A point either refers to the precise location of a mining pit town or to the village from which the mining activity is run. An area either relates to a concession area or to a zone with evidence of mineral exploitation. Both points and areas can be combined on the same map layer. If relevant, the location of other key pieces of infrastructure of the mining business can be added to the same map, for example: warehouses; processing facilities (refineries); transport infrastructure (pipelines) and points of export.

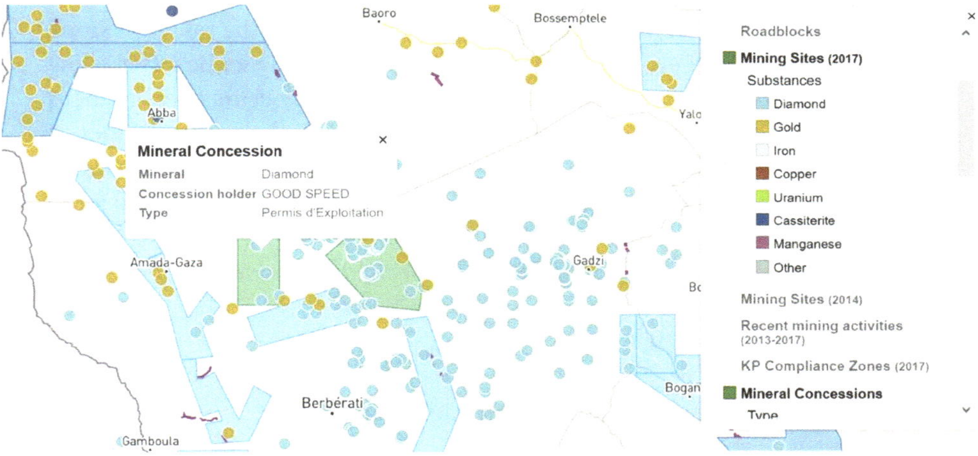

FIGURE 9.3 Screenshot of interactive map of strategic interests Central African Republic (IPIS, 2018)

Almost as notorious as the issue of so-called blood minerals, is the conflict-related production of drugs. Armed groups' income from drug trafficking sometimes largely exceeds the costs to sustain their organisation. If applicable, a map of strategic (greed) interests should seek to provide an overview of the major drugs production centres. In the framework of international policies, some areas have been covered by remote sensing. Very high-resolution satellite imagery can be used to track the cultivation of illegal crops. This method was for example applied by ISFEREA (Information Support for Effective and Rapid External Action), a research unit of the European Commission, to monitor poppy cultivation in Eastern Afghanistan.

Related to both minerals and drugs, as well as other goods, parties to an armed conflict can make profits from controlling trade routes where they can 'tax' all types of trade and facilitate smuggling operations. Therefore, a greed map should feature the local network of roads, rivers and transport hubs. Key infrastructure for maritime and air traffic includes ports and airports. For land routes, control over strategic crossroads and border crossings is essential. Many of these locations are readily available from existing commercial maps. If needed, additional information can be gathered from traders, transporters, (humanitarian) pilots and other professionals who use such routes on a regular basis and are likely to possess precise geographical data.

In summary, the conflict motivation mapping methodology compares the data from all three tools: a discourse file, a map of conflict dynamics and a map of greed-related strategic interests. Such a comparison will allow to falsify and/or confirm the hypothesis that a greed mechanism is driving armed group participation in a conflict. An important part of the process tracing analysis relies on visual interpretation. During the falsification process, the maps on strategic interests will be overlaid with the maps on conflict dynamics. This allows the visual confirmation of if and where heavy fighting occurs and whether it is linked to the presence of economic incentives. Hypothetical greed motivations are tested and confirmed or falsified through logical analysis. The logical inference is based on the formulation of necessary conditions, which all follow a similar format: *"if an armed group engages in ... actions, it is likely to be motivated by greed"* or *"if an armed group does not engage in ... actions, it is unlikely to be motivated greed".*

4 Current Use of Conflict Motivation Mapping

With the possible exception of some military organizations, conflict motivation mapping of armed groups does not yet feature in the research and analysis published by scholars or practitioners. Nevertheless, all the tools needed to analyse the impact of territorially embedded factors on the motivation and opportunities of armed groups are available: On the one hand digital mapping platforms allow maps to contain huge amounts of data, which can be organised, analysed and displayed by the users themselves. On the other, a lot of relevant data is already being collected.

4.1 *Maps/GIS Mapping*

There several types data visualizations that can be useful for conflict analysis (Rosenkranz & Jaillon, 2016). In this contribution, the focus is on maps. The use of maps in the analysis of armed conflict is not new. Costume dramas frequently feature scenes where army commanders are hunched over large table-top maps, with chess-like pieces, pondering over the positions and movements of their enemies. Students at military academies still study maps depicting battles that took place centuries ago. Such maps combine two types of data: *on the one hand* they show the relative strength of the opposing armies; *on the other*, they show the armies' positions within a wider geographic context.

GIS has made it much easier to accurately visualize the composition, movements and actions of warring parties against a geographic background, whilst also linking those features to an underlying database. GIS software is available from a wide range of applications, from basic user-friendly freeware to expensive specialized platforms used by a relatively small group of professionals. In terms of map use, technological solutions for online mapping and data exploration are increasingly accessible and their potential for research has only just started to become apparent (Smith, 2016).

GIS can be used to make and publish printed maps. However, its usefulness for qualitative analysis is best demonstrated in a digital output. Digital maps have several advantages. Most importantly, they render the geographic data interactive, allowing the user to generate hundreds or even thousands of different visualizations. Firstly, most digital maps provide a zoom function. As a consequence, developments can be reviewed in detail at a micro-level, but also as general trends within a larger geographic context. Secondly, many digital maps include filters, which enable the selection of data layers to be displayed. Such filters enable, for example, focusing on a single armed group, a specific type of event or a limited period in time. Thirdly, most digital maps include clickable elements, which will open in pop-up screens containing further information about the underlying data. Such data can be comprehensive and contain links to further information such as web articles or videos. Fourthly, in some cases the maps will provide summary statistics for the data displayed, allowing for basic quantitative analysis of the selected data layers.

4.2 *Data Collection*

Data on armed conflict is collected by a variety of sources. Some of it is publicly available; a lot of it is not. Some of the data is collected in the context of a specific conflict situation, some is collected regionally or globally. There are significant differences in the quality of the data collected.

Some of the most detailed conflict event data is gathered by those working in conflict areas. The most obvious organization to collect data on armed groups and their actions is the United Nations and its various agencies. MacGinty (2017) asserts that there are 37 datasets relevant to peacekeeping within the UN, which needed to be rationalized.

The UN's primary involvement in a (post-)conflict situation is through its Department of Peace Operations (DPO). UNDPO Missions show significant differences in the way conflict event data is collected. This is partly because there are multiple sections within each mission collecting data for their own specific purposes. In addition, collaboration and sharing between sections is not always optimal, especially between the UN military and civilians. In an attempt to bridge the gap between these two components, DPO missions now all include a dedicated Joint Mission Analysis Centre (JMAC) where information flows are centralized and complemented with additional information gathering and analysis. Data collected by the JMAC of the United Nations/African Union Mission in Darfur (UNAMID) in 2008 and 2009, show that there is enormous analytical potential. Duursma (2017) found that the JMAC data, largely based on human intelligence gathering, was much more comprehensive than datasets based on media reporting. He also concluded that the geographic referencing of the events by JMAC was more accurate.

The UN itself is aware that missions need to streamline reporting, improve information management and strengthen analytical capacities (United Nations General Assembly and Security Council, 2015). In addition, there is an increasing attention to the use of modern technology for monitoring, reconnaissance and reporting, including GIS. An expert panel appointed by the Under-Secretaries-General for Peacekeeping Operations and Field Support found that: "[*GIS*] *can provide a common operating picture used for situational awareness, analysis and modelling of relationships, patterns, trends, and process or planning potential course of actions*" (Expert Panel on Technology and Innovation, 2014). In addition, since 2014, the UN started rolling out a mission-wide digital web-based system, called the Mission Common Operating Picture (MCOP), which includes a platform for conflict event data collection and reporting (SAGE). The system should ultimately replace the separate databases managed by individual sections. While alternative databases and reporting systems are still in place, progress is relatively slow but its design and features are promising.

Other UN organizations collect relevant information as well, in particular: UNDSS, OHCHR, UNHCR and OCHA. At the UN headquarters in New York, the UN Operations and Crisis Centre (UNOCC) receives (only) some of the relevant conflict data from UN missions and agencies.

Besides the UN, other obvious gatherers of conflict data are deployed (national) armies. For intelligence officers, keeping track of armed groups' positions, their movements and the incidents in which they have been involved is part of their core business. Advanced armies have extensive GIS capacities and produce maps of conflict dynamics and strategic interests on a regular basis.

Their primary concern is often operational and they will gather a wide range of intelligence on the environment in which they are deployed. Key territorially embedded factors are usually visualized on maps to understand the wider politico-military environment, developments and trends. Such insights feed into the strategic and tactical decision-making at the command level. Unfortunately, the potential wealth of data collected by military organizations is only rarely made available to scholars or other conflict analysts.

Much easier to access is some of the data collected by specialised NGOs or research organizations. However, their coverage is limited. Indeed, most of these organizations focus on one or a small number of specific conflict areas for a limited period of time. One of the first organizations to get involved in conflict mapping has been the International Peace Information Service (IPIS). The Belgium-based research institute has published various conflict motivation mapping analyses based on the visual analysis of interactive maps on the IPIS website (https://ipisresearch.be/home/conflict-mapping/). The interactive maps allow the user to toggle on various map layers including conflict events and strategic interests. A zoom function is included and most of the map markers can be clicked for additional information.

Concerning academia, Gleditsch and Weidmann (2012) claim that a wealth of relevant datasets are available to social scientists. There are indeed a number of global conflict event datasets. These are publicly available and often used in academic settings, primarily for quantitative analysis. They include the publicly available Armed Conflict Location and Event Data Project (ACLED) (Raleigh et al., 2010), the Uppsala Conflict Data Program Georeferenced Event Dataset (UPCD GED) (Sundberg & Melander, 2013) and Braithwaite's Militarized Interstate Dispute Location (MIDLOC) (Braithwaite, 2010). Furthermore, the PRIO-GRID dataset (2.0) contains specific information on territorially embedded factors (Tollefsen et al., 2012). The dataset consists of quadratic grid cells that jointly cover all terrestrial areas of the world. Each grid cell contains cell-specific information on armed conflicts, socio-economic conditions, ethnic groups, physical attributes, climatic conditions and more. In other words, when integrated with geographic conflict event data, it allows for the discovery of correlations between such events and various geographic conditions.

The specialized georeferenced or grid-structured conflict data sets appear to be used almost exclusively for quantitative analysis. Indeed, they are developed with the specific purpose of detecting spatial variation when calculating related statistics (Gleditsch & Weidmann, 2012). The analysis of spatial disaggregation of conflict related data was introduced to refine and correct the results of country-level analyses of geographic characteristics related to armed conflict (Cederman et al., 2013).

Initially, spatial disaggregation was primarily applied in studies of global armed conflicts. However, because it captures variation within countries, such data can also be used for case studies of particular conflict areas or even armed groups. An increasing number of such case studies is being published (Dulic, 2018; Schutte, 2017; Martinez, 2017; Raleigh & De Bruyne, 2017).

The introduction of GIS and the trend of spatially disaggregating data have not led to an increase in the use of maps or related visualizations for qualitative research on the causes of war. When maps do feature in publications on the causes of war, they are usually used as illustrations. Notwithstanding the above, the value of data visualization is sometimes recognized. Gleditsch and Weidmann (2012) concede that visualization can help uncover details that would not be visible in tabular data.

The section above provided a short overview of the patchwork of actors collecting conflict-related data. While it appears that these organizations record and store a lot of information, it is less clear to what extent they use it for analytical purposes. international political organizations have the capacity to systematically produce visualizations based on 'big data'. However, the focus appears to be mostly on the production of static maps for quick and easy reference, rather than in-depth analysis. Fast points out a general sense that "data are often collected yet are not used or do not prompt action. Reports sit on shelves or in computer folders, while data sets remain buried in Excel spreadsheets or confined to sheets of paper in storage bins" (Fast, 2017).

5 Greed Motivation Mapping: The Case of Sudan and the SPLA-N (2011–2013)

The following case from Sudan is an armed conflict that was mostly 'framed' in the international (Western) press as the genuine fight of a rebel group, the SPLA-N (Sudan People's Liberation Army – North), against the oppression by a dictatorial regime. The issue of 'greed', as a potential cause of war, was never raised. The analysis below argues that while it is indeed unlikely that greed was an important motivation for the SPLA-N, that question should have been raised, given the group's various interactions with natural resources.

5.1 *Background*

Before South Sudan had voted for independence in its January 2011 referendum, the SPLA-N had not existed as a separate entity. Its members had been part of the wider Sudan People's Liberation Army (SPLA). However, when the SPLA became the standing army, of South Sudan, its members in North Sudan found themselves cut off (Gramizzi & Tubiana, 2013). Subsequently, they created a separate armed group, the SPLA-N.

The SPLA-N found itself in a precarious military position and in need of allies. Two developments ensued. On the one hand, the SPLA-N received significant support from its former brothers-in-arms of the SPLA (from here on referred to as South Sudanese army), at least until 2012 (Gramizzi & Tubiana, 2013). On the other, it played a key role in the creation a new coalition of Sudanese armed groups. On 11 November 2011, the Sudanese Revolutionary Front (SRF) was founded and besides the SPLA-N, it included the three main armed groups from Darfur.

Upon its creation, the SPLA-N itself had already been composed of two armed groups which largely operated independently, due to the fact that they were separated geographically. The two "divisions" of the SPLA-N would enter into an armed conflict with the Sudanese Army (SAF) on separate occasions and with almost three months in between.

In South Kordofan, The SPLA-N's 1st division and the SAF first clashed on the 5th of June 2011. Following the first clashes, the SPLA-N retreated to the mountains to the East of the State capital of Kadugli (See Figure 9.4.). While the SPLA-N controlled a lot of the countryside, the SAF controlled most of the town centres. The SPLA-N failed to capture or hold any additional large settlements after June 2011 (Spittaels & Weyns, 2013).

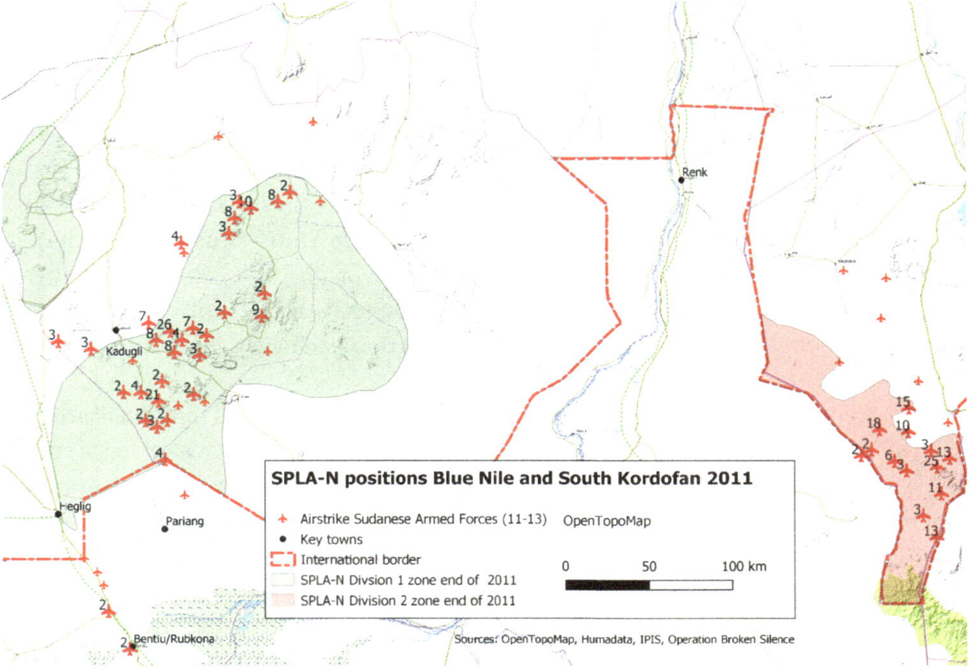

FIGURE 9.4 SPLA-N positions Blue Nile and South Kordofan (end of 2011)

In Blue Nile, the war between the SAF and the SPLA-N's 2nd division broke out on the 1st of September 2011. Fighting started in the State capital of Ad Damazin, from where it spread. During the first week of November 2011, the SPLA-N's traditional stronghold of Kurmuk was captured and the armed group was largely contained in the Southern tip of Blue Nile throughout the end of 2011 and 2012 (Harvard Humanitarian Initiative, 2013).

5.2 *SPLA-N Discourse*

It is crucial to first list the motivations advanced by the SPLA-N itself to justify its actions. The SPLA-N could count on some degree of sympathy from Western observers. The movement was more open than the Sudanese government, both in terms of providing information and allowing physical access. It also had a better human rights record. As a consequence, the SPLA-N discourse was seldom critically reviewed.

Generally speaking, SPLA-N discourse centred around grievances related to racism and political and economic marginalisation. The armed group and its political wing, the SPLM-N, linked these grievances directly to its participation in an armed conflict.

By December 2013, the SPLM-N had not issued a separate list of grievances or political agenda. On its now defunct website it had published the last SPLM manifesto, which dated from 2008 (SPLM, 2008). More importantly however, it had also co-signed a number of political declarations together with other armed groups and unarmed political opposition groups. In January 2013 the SPLM-N signed the "New Dawn Convention" (NDC) in Kampala (Izzadine, 2013). In November 2013 the SPLM-N chairman and its Secretary General travelled through Europe with a coalition of Sudanese armed groups under the umbrella of the Sudanese Revolutionary Front (SRF) promoting the October 2012 "Document of Restructuring of the Sudanese State" (DRSS) (SRF, 2012). There are some recurring themes in both texts.

Firstly, as co-signatory, the SPLM-N denounced the lack of development and it sought to review development policies that had negatively affected local populations.

Secondly, the armed group highlighted the issue of cultural marginalisation and what it called a culture of "supremacy and racism". It advocated for "a culture of love and coexistence" and a need of "separation of religious institutions from state institutions."

Thirdly, in the same texts, the SPLM-N denounced the problem of state repression and the lack of (political) freedom. Instead it demanded "the immediate annulment of laws and regulations which restrict freedoms" and "respect for human rights and insuring supremacy of rule of law

Throughout the texts, especially the DRSS, a strong demand for access to education featured prominently. The SPLM-N described the current system as an "ideological weapon" of the ruling party and called for free education to "close the education gap."

The discourse used in a series of interviews conducted with individual SPLA-N members in 2013, and the grievances interviewees raised, were largely similar to the language from the political texts: the lack of development in members' home areas; cases of discrimination, racism and general treatment as second-class citizens; political oppression and a lack of freedom (Spittaels & Weyns, 2013).

The SPLA-N's only solution to the above problems was regime change, which it very consistently advanced. Even in 2016, after five difficult years of war, the SPLA-N leadership would still maintain the same objective (Sudan Tribune, 2016).

Notwithstanding the above, the SPLA-N was not oblivious to the fact that Sudan had numerous valuable natural resources. This is clear from the one particular section in both the NDC and the DRSS, which does relate to economic control. Both documents argue that "all approved contracts regarding lands, mining, oil ... and public sector companies" should be revised. Even though this is only a short passage in a long text, it is significant because it is a public acknowledgement by an armed opposition group that economic control over natural resources mattered.

5.3 *Conflict Dynamics*

A closer look at the combined map layers on conflict dynamics and strategic interests (See Figure 9.5) shows a geographic situation that could have been indicative of a conflict motivated by greed, especially in South Kordofan. The map of strategic interests shows how the SPLA-N's 1st Division controlled a significant number of gold mines and a border crossing. In addition, other valuable resources: more gold, large scale agricultural projects and in particular oil, were located in relatively close proximity to their area of control. From the above it would appear that SPLA-N fitted the profile of an armed group that was trying to profit from war. Interestingly, such questions were almost never asked in mainstream reporting and analysis.

South Kordofan contains a number of gold mining sites. Some of these were controlled by the government and others by the SPLA-N. According to an SPLM-N mining official, in November 2013, an estimated 8,000 artisanal miners were working in the two main mining areas under the 1st Division's control, where they could work in relative safety from SAF attacks. Several other gold mines were not operational because of their proximity to the front lines or due to persistent air strikes by the SAF. The SPLA-N regulated artisanal mining in its

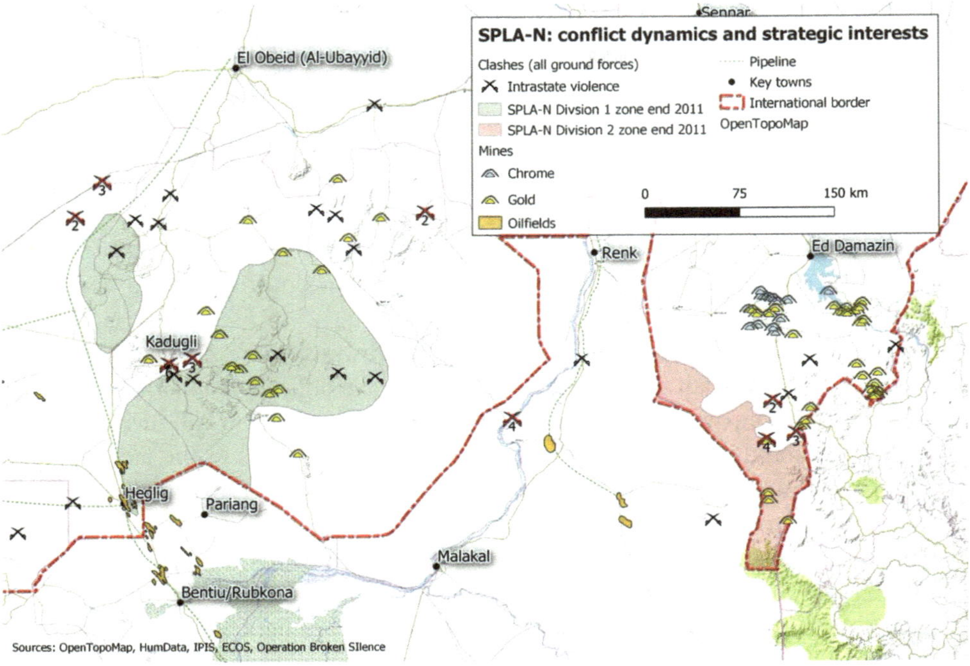

FIGURE 9.5 Strategic interests and conflict dynamics in/near SPLA-N zones (2011–2013)

areas. It did not allow buyers from Khartoum into its mining sites, explaining that these could be affiliated to their enemy. Instead, it encouraged miners to sell their production via an alternative channel over which it appeared to exert a high level of control (Spittaels & Weyns, 2013). Clearly, the SPLA-N's 1st Division recognised that income from mining could contribute to military victory or defeat.

Gold mines were also situated in neighbouring areas of South Kordofan under SAF control. Some were rather large operations, such as a semi-industrial site at Um Doual. However, the maps show that the SPLA-N did not target them. Although the SPLA-N controlled a number of gold mines and regulated the trade, capturing government-controlled mining sites was clearly not a strategic priority for the armed group between 2011 and 2013.

The SPLA-N's interaction with other strategic and geographically embedded targets, in particular oil, raises additional questions in terms of a potential greed motivation. In March and April 2012, the SPLA-N's current SRF allies and their former allies of the SPLA, jointly conducted a series of military operations in and around Heglig, Sudan's most important remaining oilfield. They seized the oil installations for several weeks. A spokesperson for the Justice and

Equality Movement (JEM), the main SRF coalition partner involved, stated on the radio that:

> We decided to also capture all the other oilfields. All Sudanese know that the income from the oilfields is not going to the people of Sudan, but to the army, the security and some powerful individuals. We want to stop this and we will continue to fight until the government of Al Bashir will be replaced. (Radio Dabanga, 2012)

Although there were no indications that the SPLA-N itself was directly involved, it certainly maintained operational ties with the JEM and some experts reported that the latter operated a command centre from Kauda, where the SPLA-N's headquarters were based (Small Arms Survey, 2012).

If the SPLA-N had been a Congolese, Colombian or Syrian armed group, the evidence presented above would have been enough to portray them in public reporting as a conflict party (partially) motivated by greed. However, the question was hardly raised, and the SPLA-N was generally presented as a movement entirely motivated by a political agenda. More out of luck than because of analytical rigour, this was largely an accurate assessment. A further analysis of the available data confirms that profiting from the war was not the SPLA-N's priority.

After the initial operations in and around Heglig, the SRF's (and the SPLA-N 1st Division's) focus shifted away from oil reserves. Comparing the map of conflict dynamics with the map of strategic interests, it is clear that the 1st Division's actions between July 2011 and December 2013 rarely focussed on targets from which they could generate a profit. In line with its discourse, economic interests were virtually absent from the SPLA-N's military actions.

The SPLA-N 1st Division retained positions in relatively close proximity to Sudan's remaining oilfields in the neighbouring state of West Kordofan. However, all active oil wells, such as Heglig, Bamboo and Neem, remained firmly under the control of the SAF and were never the subject of rebel attacks after April 2012. In fact, the most active frontline between the SPLA-N and the SAF moved away from the oil rich south(west) to the politically more relevant north under the impulse of the SPLA-N and its allies within the SRF. An overlay of the map of conflict dynamics and strategic interests clearly shows this shift.

The SPLA-N's 2nd Division showed even less interest in generating profits from natural resources. There were no oil wells in or near Blue Nile. There was some gold mining activity, including in areas held by the SPLA-N. Interviews with IDPs, a local trader and an international observer indicated that the number of miners in the 2nd Division's held area was not much more than

2,000. Their activities did not appear to be strictly monitored nor controlled by the armed group, although some individual SPLA-N combatants were digging themselves. The modest gold production appeared to be more a matter of survival than enrichment, and much of the mined gold was traded locally for basic products. The traders, who were often Ethiopian, were able to pay a relatively low price for the gold, compared to market rates in Uganda, Ethiopia or Khartoum.

The SPLA-N's 2nd Division did not show an interest in capturing other mining assets. The armed group remained mostly in a defensive position throughout the 2012–2013 dry season. It did attack Kurmuk, in an attempt to retake its former headquarters and gain control over an important border crossing with Ethiopia. Furthermore, the SPLA-N made no attempt to regain control over an important chromite mining area in the Ingessana hills. This is striking because they had only lost the area to the SAF in early 2012. In addition, many of the 2nd Division's combatants, including the SPLM-N (and SRF) chairman originated from the Ingessana hills.

5.4 *Diplomatic Actions*

There were no obvious economic motivations behind the SPLA-N's political and diplomatic actions either. The first negotiations between the SPLM-N and the government of Sudan started in Addis Abeba on 23 April 2013. It was a modest success to have both parties attending the talks, however they were suspended after less than two days because the starting positions of both delegations seemed to be too difficult to reconcile. In particular, the SPLM-N stressed its intention to extend the scope of the negotiations beyond South Kordofan and Blue Nile to include the countrywide issue of "misgovernance and institutional reform". The SPLM-N was very explicit in these demands, as shown by a public statement from their delegation leader at the outset of the talks (Radio Tamazuj, 2013). The leadership did not appear to be interested in a quick resolution, involving negotiations on positions or other personal benefits. Instead, the demand to broaden the geographical and political scope of the negotiations would remain unchanged for years, which is remarkable given the SPLA-N's precarious military situation and the ongoing humanitarian crisis in several of its areas.

Moreover, the SPLM-N helped build a broader politico-military coalition against the ruling National Congress Party (NCP) and the SAF. On the military side, the SPLA-N was one of the driving forces behind the creation of the SRF and held the alliance's most senior positions of 'Chairperson' and 'Chief of Staff'. The SPLM-N was also a strong supporter of the SRF's interaction with Sudan's political opposition. Already in July 2012, the SPLM-N's Secretary general, Yasir Arman, called for a common manifesto on democratic change between the political opposition, the SRF and civil society representatives (Arman, 2012). The envisaged manifesto was finally presented on the 5th of January 2013 in Kampala, Uganda, where the NDC was signed.

6 Greed Motivation Mapping: The Case of Libya and the LNA (2014–2017)

This second case discusses a more recent armed conflict: Libya and specifically the armed group 'Libyan National Army' (LNA). Contrary to the apparent public consensus on the SPLA-N, public reporting (and framing) of the LNA has followed very different narratives. For some, including US President Donald Trump, the LNA is a force involved in a legitimate fight against Islamic extremism (Reuters, 2019). This perception is helped by the fact that the LNA includes some (ex)regular army units and operates an airwing. Others present the LNA as a force operating for the personal interests of its leadership, and/or as a proxy group for the interests of regional countries. As a part of the latter representations, it is frequently argued that the LNA has a greed motivation, related to Libya's extensive oil reserves. The analysis below shows that, while this is a relevant angle, it is clearly insufficient to explain all of the LNA's actions.

6.1 *Background*

After the fall of the Qadhafi regime in 2011, Libya entered a transitional period that has been characterised by increasing insecurity and political instability. It is within this context that the Libyan National Army (LNA) appeared.

The LNA is a coalition of armed groups that includes 'regular units' from Libya's pre-2011-Armed Forces under Mumar Qadhafi and tribal militias. The inclusion of (ex) regular forces partially explains the LNA's considerable military capacity, which includes fighter planes. In addition, the LNA has also relied on assistance from regional countries, private military corporations and Sudanese armed groups (Delalande, 2018). Whereas some of its components are integrated into a military hierarchy, others are more loosely allied. Delalande (2018) reports that the LNA represents a force of 25,000 men, 7,000 of which are recruits from its regular ground forces.

The LNA and its main commander, Khalifa Haftar, came to the forefront of security reporting on Libya following the launch of the so-called 'Operation Dignity' in May 2014. During the operation, the LNA launched a series of attacks against strongholds of Islamist-leaning armed groups in the eastern city of Benghazi.

The start of 'Operation Dignity' was far from a success. The LNA's opponents also built a military coalition, the Benghazi Revolutionaries Shura Council (BRSC), which quickly seized control over several strategic areas during a counter-offensive (UN Panel of Experts, 2015). It would take the LNA three years to fully gain control over Benghazi. Throughout this whole period, the LNA's airwing, which was significantly strengthened through external support, was arguably the most visible part of its forces (UN Panel of Experts, 2017).

As the LNA's hold on Benghazi strengthened, it also started to increase its control over other territories. Partially through military operations, but mostly through deal-making and tribal recruitment, the LNA expanded its positions to the west and particularly the south. Although not populous, these were economically important areas because of oil reserves and terminals (ICG, 2016). At the end of 2017, the LNA was militarily in the strongest position it had been since its creation. On 4 April 2019 the LNA launched a large-scale offensive against the capital of Tripoli. These latest events are not covered in the below analysis, which is limited to the period 2014–2017.

6.2 *LNA Discourse*

Between 2014 and 2017, the LNA consistently presented itself as a purely military organization, not a political one. As a consequence, it did not involve itself with drafting political programs, manifestos, lists of grievances or similar documents. This did not mean that the LNA did not show any political ambition. Khalifa Haftar repeatedly confirmed that he was ready to take public office should the people "ask" him to do so (Mahmoud, 2014). Political positioning also appeared in the LNA's responses to events in Tripoli. For example, in July 2014, when a coalition of armed groups launched an attack against Tripoli International Airport, Haftar and the LNA repeatedly claimed they would take control of Tripoli from illegal political forces (Foreign Policy, 2014).

Notwithstanding the lack of a comprehensive political program, the LNA was very active on social media, where it provided regular updates on its operations, training and other activities. Various accounts were active, including from force components and its official spokesperson. See, for example, the Twitter account of the LNA spokesperson (https://twitter.com/spoxlna) or the Facebook account of the LNA Air Force (https://www.facebook.com/libyan.air.forces/). In addition, both its commander and spokesperson gave interviews for international media.

The media content focused a lot on military achievements and (international) prestige, such as visits of foreign militaries. The style of LNA communication is telling in itself. It made frequent use of military emblems and consistently referred to formal titles of its military hierarchy. Its soldiers and officers were often portrayed in impeccable uniforms while training, parading or being decorated. Clearly the media account managers were making a deliberate and coordinated effort to present the LNA as a regular force.

The LNA communication specifically related to its motivations can almost be considered as one-dimensional. Central to the whole discourse is the assertion that extremists were harming the people, the country and the region. In one of his first press appearances after the launching his 'Operation Dignity' in May 2014, Haftar emphasized that a security problem was at the root of his actions (Mahmoud, 2014). In his view, this security problem was both a national crisis and specific to Benghazi and eastern Libya (Corriere della sera, 2017). He accused the parliament and the Muslim Brotherhood of having facilitated the arrival of international terrorists into Libya. He describes his main mission as ridding Libya of this "disease".

In subsequent statements, these views would be repeated and remain the key justification for actions taken. In November 2014 he was quoted as having said that "the real danger comes from the fundamentalists who want to impose their will everywhere" (Al Arabiya, 2014). In a recorded interview from May 2016 he reiterated that the LNA was fighting terrorists from all over the world who had been invited in by the Muslim Brotherhood, and were committing atrocities against the civilian population (CNEWS, 2016). In July 2017, after he had become a regular invitee to political negotiations, he continued to insist that he was pursuing a military solution against a number of enemies that could not be dealt with in any other way (France 24, 2017). He specifically listed ISIL, Al Qaeda, the Libyan Islamic Fighting Group (LIFG), the Benghazi Defence Brigades (BDB) and the Muslim Brotherhood as enemies. In addition, the LNA repeatedly accused regional countries, such as Qatar, Turkey and Sudan of supporting these groups (Poole, 2017).

The counter-terrorism discourse was so dominant that it was used to explain virtually all of the LNA's political positioning and military actions. After March 2016, for example, when an internationally recognised executive branch of government was installed in Tripoli, Haftar would repeatedly challenge its authority. Haftar argued that the LNA's counter-terrorism strategy was still valid because the new government was under the influence of some of its members linked to ISIL and Al Qaeda (France 24, 2017).

Although the armed groups targeted by the LNA for causing security grievances are usually branded as terrorists or extremists, this has not always been the case. Interestingly, when the LNA explained its first major military takeover of oil infrastructure, it referred to the forces previously in control of the installations as an outlawed or illegal militia, a significant difference in the terminology applied (AFP, 2016). In subsequent seizures of oil installations, the LNA has provided a similar justification, presenting itself as a source of stability and statesmanship, in addition to an anti-terrorism force. In the same vein, it allowed oil operations to continue as normal, providing Tripoli with a steady and much needed flow of foreign currency.

6.3 *Conflict Dynamics*

A detailed analysis of the LNA's military operations between 2014 and 2017 shows a complex interaction with strategic geographically embedded factors. While the control over Libya's natural resources certainly was an important military objective, it mostly appeared to be a means, rather than an end in and of itself. If greed was the main consideration, the LNA's military offensives have turned out to be a long-term investment of which the returns are still uncertain and which has incurred enormous costs. As such, the LNA does not fit the profile of the typical rent-seeking armed group.

The first years after its creation, the LNA's military actions were mostly directed against militant Islamist groups and the group showed little interest in the country's wealth and resources. Data from the map of conflict dynamics shows that **in 2014, 2015 and most of 2016,** LNA ground forces were primarily active in eastern Libya, particularly in/around Benghazi and to a lesser extent Derna (See Figure 9.6 and Figure 9.7). Both eastern towns had a well-documented presence of Islamist extremists; initially only Ansar al-Sharia and allied groups, but later ISIL also, following its expansion to Libya in 2015. The map data suggests that the LNA could have done more to fight and contain ISIL, especially in relation to the latter's exodus from Derna to the town of Sirte, which would quickly become the extremists' stronghold in the country. The most important exception to the LNA's focus on Benghazi and Derna, was a series of bombing raids on major western towns in 2014. At the time, rival armed groups were battling over the control of Tripoli.

Throughout this first period, the economically critical 'Oil Crescent' area west of Benghazi, was under the control of another armed group, the Petroleum Facilities Guard (PFG), which was initially allied with the LNA until relations deteriorated in 2015.

In terms of LNA military action, **2016** appears to be a key year. ISIL violence peaked in the first months, but the LNA did not participate in an internationally supported operation against the extremists' stronghold in Sirte and surrounding areas. Only after ISIL had been virtually defeated, from September 2016 onwards, did the LNA suddenly expand its operations westwards. During this phase, it took control of the 'Oil Crescent', where the country's most important oil terminals are located. It stopped its advance before Sirte, where ISIL would retain a presence until December that year.

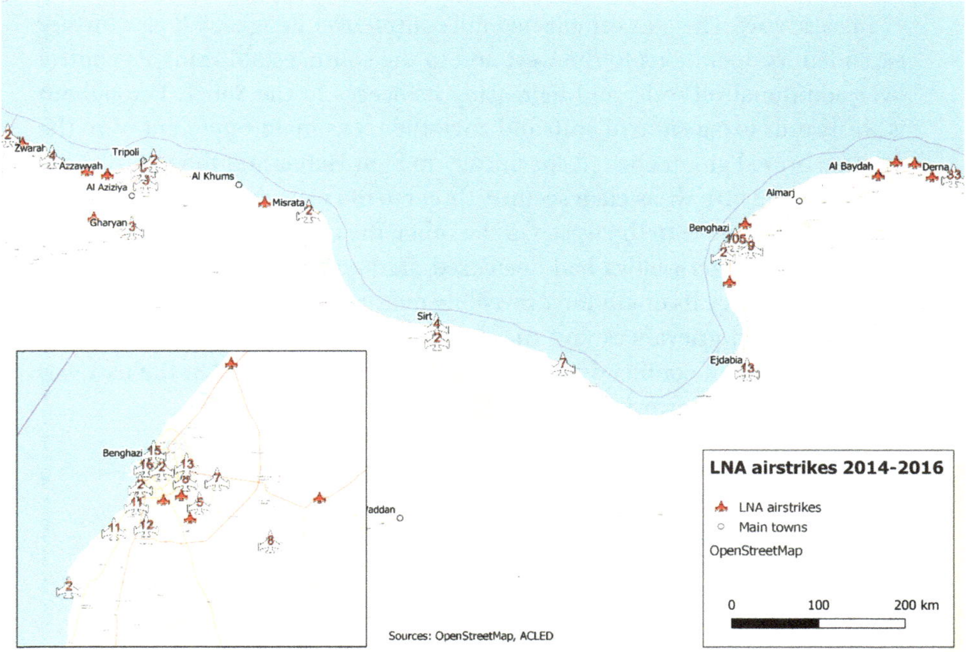

FIGURE 9.6 LNA airstrikes (2014–2016)

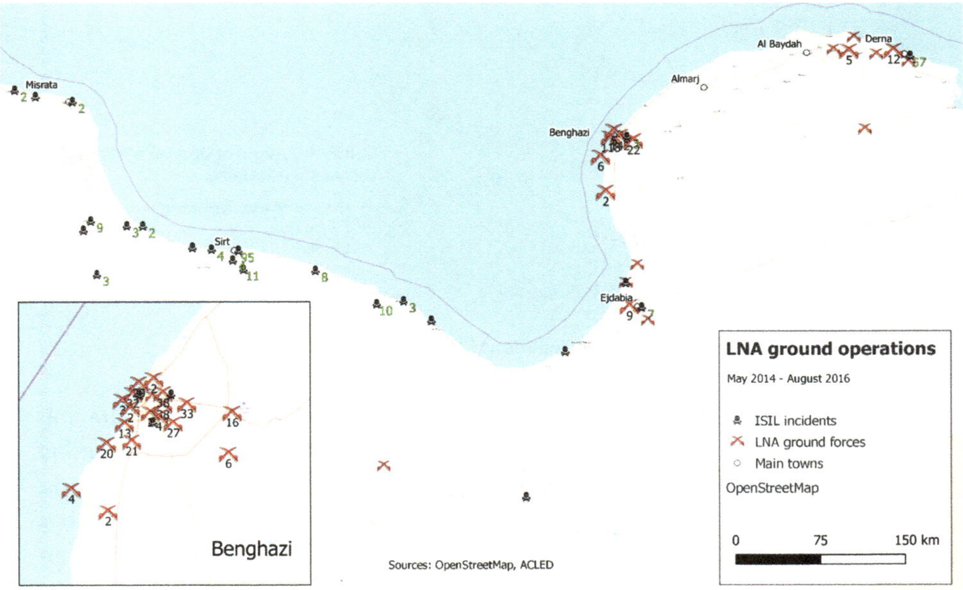

FIGURE 9.7 LNA Ground operations (May 2014 - August 2016)

In early 2017, The LNA established full control over Benghazi. It also further extended its operations to the west and to the south, establishing its control over additional oil wells and increasing its access to the Sahel. Throughout is westwards expansion, in 2016 and 2017, the LNA's main opponent were the BDB, an armed group created specifically to fight Haftar and the LNA. On the one hand, the BDB was a clear security threat to the LNA, providing some justification for its move to the west. On the other, the overall threat from extremist groups in eastern Libya had decreased dramatically by 2017. Yet, the LNA did not scale back its operations, revealing motivations and objectives beyond security-related grievances and the fight against extremist groups. In other words, the map of conflict dynamics (See Figure 9.8.) shows that the LNA was not purely an anti-terrorism force.

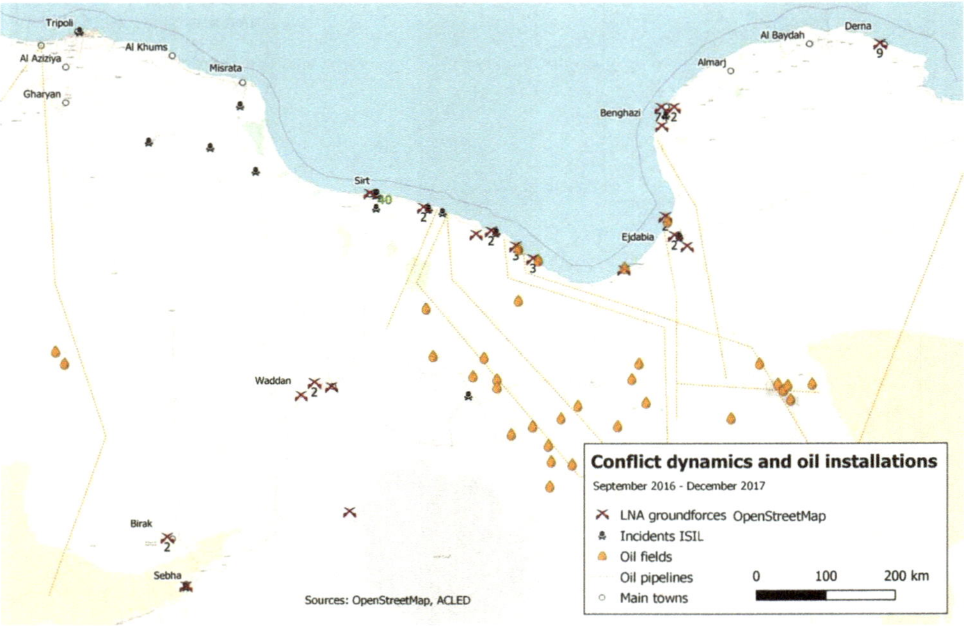

FIGURE 9.8 Conflict dynamics and Oil installations (August 2016 - December 2017)

Were these conflict dynamics sufficient proof to conclude that the LNA was (also) driven by greed? Comparing evidence from the map layer on conflict dynamics and one on Libya's economic interests largely refutes that hypothesis, at least in terms of short-term gains. Generally speaking, armed groups in Libya are reported to often engage in criminal activities, which are believed to generate significant profits. The armed conflict situation does indeed offer a number of lucrative opportunities, including trafficking of subsidized goods, migrant smuggling and extortion of a number of wealthy families. In addition, Libya is an important oil producer, which has fed the assumption that armed groups are trying to profit from the country's natural resources. However, in comparison to other groups, the LNA has shown little interest in pursuing (short-term) profit.

A defining event was the LNA's September 2016 capture of the 'Oil Crescent', which was, in some reporting, interpreted as a greed-motivated move (El-Gamaty, 2016). The operation was concluded relatively swift and with few casualties. Contrary to its usual rhetoric, the LNA leadership did not frame its actions as counterterrorism.

However, the greed interpretation of this (unexpected) move is not credible when taking a closer look at the events. Firstly, the LNA immediately returned control over the oil terminals to the civilian administration, knowing that oil trade-related profits would continue to flow to Tripoli. Secondly, as explained below, the LNA decided to work with the internationally recognised Libyan National Oil Corporation (NOC) in Tripoli, thereby ignoring its own parallel and unrecognised NOC based in Benghazi (International Crisis Group [ICG], 2018). Thirdly, the maps show that, militarily, there was also a strong rationale behind the action as the LNA was exposed to hostile armed groups operating in this area, in particular the PFG and the BDB.

On the map from 2017 above (See Figure 9.8.) the LNA's control over Libya's oil resources looks extensive. However, that control did not result in material gain, as the LNA still had no control over the financial transactions behind Libya's oil exports, which continued to go through the NOC in Tripoli and the Central Bank. Furthermore, although the LNA could have used its control over the oil industry's choking points to halt oil production and extort money (a practice previously applied by the PFG), no such instances were reported.

Looking at some of the other potentially lucrative opportunities created by the persisting situation of lawlessness, the LNA hardly appears to be involved. Armed groups in Libya are frequently involved in criminal activities, mostly related to smuggling (See Figure 9.9.). Migrant and fuel smuggling in particular are often mentioned as important sources of income. However, in both cases these activities appear to be largely concentrated at Libya's western coast. In the case of migrant smuggling, recent reports indicate that the city of Benghazi and the whole of the northeast are mostly avoided by the smugglers (Darme & Benattia, 2017).

Fuel smuggling also remained concentrated in the west, around the coastal towns of Zawiya and Zuwara, where local armed groups operate as the main security forces (UN Panel of Experts on Libya, 2016).

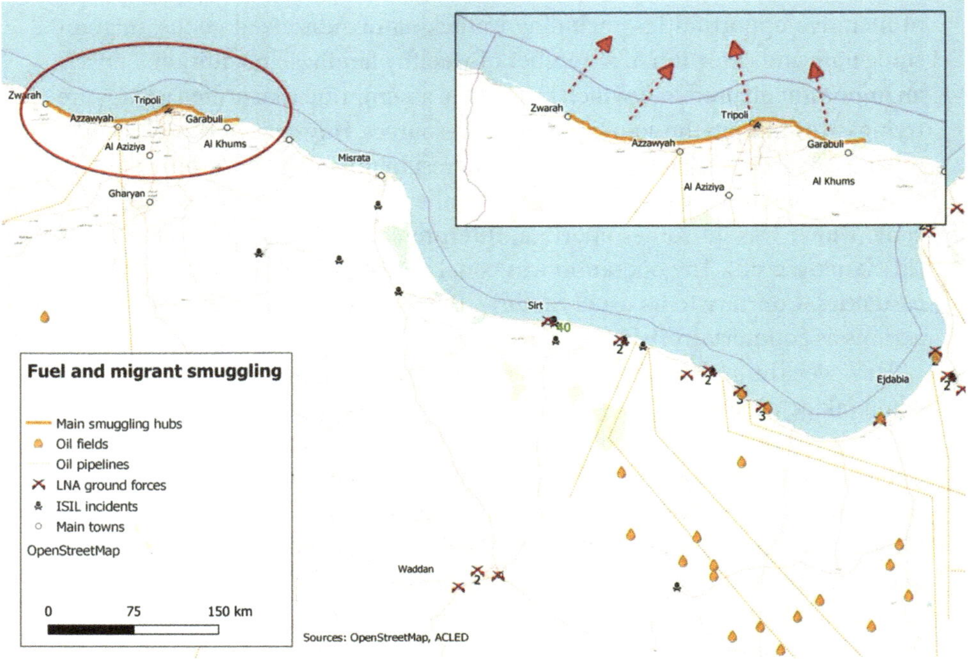

FIGURE 9.9 Main coastal strip for fuel and migrant smuggling

Finally, whereas there is ample evidence of the LNA's implication in human rights violations, the available incident data shows only little LNA involvement in reported crimes for profit, such as robberies or kidnappings. Also, instances of such crimes appear to be relatively low in areas fully under LNA control, especially in comparison to other towns and areas.

Arguably, the LNA did not urgently need the income from the oil sector or any of the other opportunities created by the armed conflict. Many of its recruits continued to receive salaries from the Central Bank in Tripoli. In addition, the displaced Interim Government, which supported the LNA, administered its own budget, based on loans from private banks. Finally, the LNA received material (and most likely financial) support from regional states.

6.4 *Diplomatic Actions*

The LNA's apparent focus on the oil sector, from 2016 onwards, was probably more related to its overall tendency to try to increase its power and influence. Oil is by far the most important source of income for the Libyan state. In 2016, oil sales represented 63% of the country's GDP (ICG, 2018). Whoever controlled these resources, could not be politically ignored.

At the negotiation table and in the political arena in general, the LNA frequently applied its military power to try to influence political processes. Haftar has shown a clear political ambition since he reappeared on the Libyan scene in 2011. Several episodes in 2014 suggested that, from Benghazi, he had his eye on the capital (Voltaire Network, 2014; Elumami & Laessing, 2014). These tendencies moved more to the background during the long war in Benghazi. However, they reappeared after September 2016, when the LNA increasingly started to act as a political force.

Since late 2016 the LNA directly and overtly involved itself in administering towns through the appointment of so-called military governors and the replacement of elected majors by its affiliates. Observers claimed that the LNA had more political power than the parliament and government to which it nominally responded.

Its political prominence was further underlined in 2017, when Haftar was frequently invited by foreign governments, often to discuss issues of a political nature. Cases in point include his visits to Cairo in February, to Paris in July, and to Rome in September. On his visit to Libya in August, British Foreign Minister Boris Johnson stated that "Field Marshall Haftar has a role to play in the political process" (McGuiness, 2017).

It would be incorrect however, to claim that the LNA did not show any short-term interest in Libya's wealth, economy and business. On the one hand, there have been reports of senior LNA figures involved in corruption (The New Arab, 2016). On the other, since 2017, the LNA has taken direct control over certain businesses, notably agricultural projects, under its newly created 'Military Authority for Investment and Public Works' (Libya Herald, 2017). This evolution merits a further analysis of developments in 2018 and 2019, and could indicate an increasing importance of greed-related motivations and objectives within the LNA leadership.

7 Conclusions

In public reporting, some armed groups are systematically depicted as greedy rebels, profiting from a war economy and therefore not very keen on the armed conflict to end. The analysis behind such assessments is often weak and rarely includes actual evidence. Conflict motivation mapping, an intuitive methodology for logical analysis through process tracing, allows for a more critical assessment of armed groups' interactions with natural resources and other strategic interests. As opposed to large quantitative studies, conflict motivation mapping is well-equipped to explain the intricacies of war motivations. Importantly, the underlying data of the methodology is also transparent. This allows the reader to assess how conclusions were reached, thereby opening up space for challenges to be levelled, and a public debate on the quality of both the evidence base and the analysis.

Basic conflict motivation mappings on Sudan and Libya show how armed groups' presence near potentially profitable geographically embedded factors does not automatically imply a strong greed motivation. The LNA captured key oil facilities and the SPLA-N organised a significant gold mining operation. However, neither of the groups appears to be primarily motivated by greed.

The motivation mapping convincingly demonstrated how short-term profits were only of minor importance to the SPLA-N. The LNA, on the other hand, mostly used its grasp over economic interests for political purposes and potentially long-term gains. Both groups clearly had different priorities, both unrelated to greed.

At the height of the 'greed vs. grievance' debate, academia had a significant and eye-opening impact on the public perception of armed groups' motivations. However, the debate has not yet reached a conclusion. Indeed, it may never. Instead of only trying to refine general insights through quantitative analysis, it might be more helpful if more scholars also prepare detailed case studies on the *motivation* of specific armed groups. Or, even better, they could hand interested stakeholders the tools to conduct their own analyses. Methodological tools, such as conflict motivation mapping, can help to improve the public reporting on armed groups. Many conflict areas around the world are inaccurately portrayed. In the Democratic Republic of the Congo for example, the persistence of its 150+ armed groups is often systematically linked to the country's many natural resources. While access to natural resources might motivate some, it may not be a primary or even significant motivation for many others.

Assessing the interaction between armed groups and greed-related geographically-embedded factors is a relatively straightforward exercise. However, a comprehensive conflict motivation mapping needs to go beyond the binary 'greed / not greed' question. In order to truly improve our understanding of armed groups' motivations, we need to look into alternative and/or additional explanations, including grievances and political ambitions. Including grievances and ambition in conflict motivation mapping analyses makes the exercise much more complex and challenging.

Bibliography

AFP (2016, September 12), *Libya unity govt loses third oil port to rivals.* https://www.business-standard.com/article/pti-stories/libya-unity-govt-loses-third-oil-port-to-rivals-116091200864_1.html

Al Arabiya (2014, November 28), *Libya's Haftar vows to 'take Tripoli' from Islamists,* http://english.alarabiya.net/en/News/middle-east/2014/11/28/Libya-s-Haftar-vows-to-take-Tripoli-from-Islamists.html

Arman, Y. (2012, July 9), *The SPLM-N Position on the National Consensus Forces Democratic Alternative Charter,* Sudan Tribune. http://www.sudantribune.com/spip.php?article43188

Baum, M. A. & Zhukov, Y. M. (2015), Filtering Revolution: Reporting bias in international media coverage of the Libyan civil war, *Journal of Peace Research, 52*(3), 384–400. https://doi.org/10.1177%2F0022343314554791

Bel, T. (2014, December 29), *'A ground invasion of the capital is imminent',* Foreign Policy. https://foreignpolicy.com/2014/12/29/a-ground-invasion-of-the-capital-is-imminent-libya-dawn-haftar-militias/

Braithwaite, A. (2010), MIDLOC: Introducing the Militarized Interstate Dispute Location dataset, *Journal of Peace Research, 47*(1), 91–98. https://doi.org/10.1177%2F0022343309350008

Cederman, L-E., Gleditsch, K. S. & Buhaug, H. (2013), *Inequality, Grievances and Civil War.* Cambridge University Press. https://doi.org/10.1017/CBO9781139084161

CNEWS. (2016, May 20). *ITELE Interview with Khalifa Haftar* [Video], YouTube. https://www.youtube.com/watch?v=xya11tWJgXg

Collier, D. (2011), Understanding Process Tracing, *PS: Political Science and Politics, 44*(4), 823–830. https://doi.org/10.1017/S1049096511001429

Collier, P. & Hoeffler, A. (2000), *Greed and Grievance in Civil War,* Policy Research Working Paper 2355, World Bank. https://doi.org/10.1596/1813-9450-2355;

Collier, P. (2000a), Doing Well out of War: An Economic Perspective, In M. Berdal & D. M. Malone (Eds.), *Greed and Grievance: Economic Agendas in Civil Wars* (pp. 91–112). Lynne Rienner Publishers.

Collier, P. (2000b), Rebellion as a quasi-criminal activity, *Journal of Conflict Resolution, 44*(6), 839–853. https://doi.org/10.1177%2F0022002700044006008

Collier, P. (2002), *Economic Causes of Civil Conflict and their Implications for policy,* World Bank, https://siteresources.worldbank.org/DEC/Resources/econonmic_causes_of_civilwar.pdf;

Collier, P. & Hoeffler, A. (2004), Greed and grievance in civil war, *Oxford Economic Papers, 56*(4), 563–595. https://doi.org/10.1093/oep/gpf064

Cremonesi, L. (2017, January 4), *General Haftar: "Italy has taken the wrong side in Libya"*, Corriere della sera. https://www.corriere.it/english/17_gennaio_03/general-haftar-italy-has-taken-the-wrong-side-libya-c8bea24e-d1dc-11e6-a55b-632cc5cf8e9f.shtml

Darme, M-C., & Benattia, T., E. (2017), *Mixed migration trends in Libya: Changing dynamics and protection challenges*, Altai consulting & Impact. http://www.altai-consulting.com/wp-content/uploads/2017/07/LIB-HCR-MAS-Final-Report.pdf

Dulic, T. (2018), The patterns of violence in Bosnia and Herzegovina: Security, geography and the killing of civilians during the war of the 1990s, *Political Geography*, *63*, 148–158. https://doi.org/10.1016/j.polgeo.2017.03.009

Duursma, A. (2017), Counting Deaths While Keeping Peace: An Assessment of the JMAC's Field Information and Analysis Capacity in Darfur, *International Peacekeeping*, *24*(5), 823–847. https://doi.org/10.1080/13533312.2017.1383567

El-Gamaty, G. (2016, September 14), *Haftar plays the oil card in Libya's conflict*, The New Arab. https://www.alaraby.co.uk/english/comment/2016/9/14/haftar-plays-the-oil-card-in-libyas-conflict

Elumami, A. & Laessing U. (2014, May 18), *Gunmen loyal to ex-general storm Libyan parliament, demand suspension*, Reuters. https://www.reuters.com/article/us-libya-violence/gunmen-loyal-to-ex-general-storm-libyan-parliament-demand-suspension-idUSBREA4G04A20140518

Expert Panel on Technology and Innovation in UN Peacekeeping (2014), *Final Report*. https://peacekeeping.un.org/en/final-report-of-expert-panel-technology-and-innovation-un-peacekeeping

Fast, L. (2017), Diverging Data: Exploring the Epistemologies of Data Collection and Use among Those Working on and in Conflict, *International Peacekeeping*, 24(5), 706–732. https://doi.org/10.1080/13533312.2017.1383562

France 24. (2017, July 27). *Interview with Libya's military strongman Khalifa Haftar* [Video]. YouTube. https://www.youtube.com/watch?v=7zSOzSuot5E

Gilmore, E., Gleditsch, N. P., Lujala, P., & Rod, J. K. (2005), Conflict Diamonds: A New Dataset, *Conflict Management and Peace Science*, *22*(3), 257–272. https://doi.org/10.1080%2F07388940500201003

Gleditsch, K. S. & Weidmann, N., Richardson in the Information Age: Geographic Information Systems and Spatial Data in International Studies, *Annual Review of Political Science*, *15*(1), 461–481. https://doi.org/10.1146/annurev-polisci-031710-112604

Gramizzi, C. and Tubiana, J. (2013), *New war, old enemies: Conflict dynamics in South Kordofan*, HSBA report. http://www.smallarmssurveysudan.org/fileadmin/docs/working-papers/HSBA-WP29-S.Kordofan.pdf

Hirshleifer, J. (1995), *Theorizing about Conflict*. UCLA Department of Economics

Hirshleifer, J. (2001), *The Dark Side of the Force. Economic Foundations of Conflict Theory*. Cambridge University Press.

International Crisis Group (2016), *The Libyan Political Agreement: Time for a Reset.* https://www.crisisgroup.org/middle-east-north-africa/north-africa/libya/libyan-political-agreement-time-reset

International Crisis Group (2018), *After the Showdown in Libya's Oil Crescent.* https://www.crisisgroup.org/middle-east-north-africa/north-africa/libya/189-after-showdown-libyas-oil-crescent

IPIS (2018), *Central African Republic: A Conflict Mapping.* https://ipisresearch.be/publication/central-african-republic-conflict-mapping/

Izzadine, A. (2013, January 5), *The New Dawn Convention* (unofficial English version), Sudan Tribune. http://www.sudantribune.com/spip.php?article45151

Keen, D. (1998), *The Economic Functions of Violence in Civil Wars*, Adelphi Papers, 38(320).

Keen, D. (2000), Incentives and Disincentives for Violence, In M. Berdal & D. M. Malone (Eds.), *Greed and Grievance: Economic Agendas in Civil Wars* (pp. 19–42). Lynne Rienner Publishers.

Keen, D. (2012), Greed and grievance in Civil War, *International Affairs*, *88*(4), 757–777. https://doi.org/10.1111/j.1468-2346.2012.01100.x

Libya Herald (2017, November 4), *Haftar extends LNA economic control.* https://www.libyaherald.com/2017/11/04/hafter-extends-lnas-economic-control/

Lujala, P. (2010), The spoils of nature: armed conflict and rebel access to natural resources, *Journal of Peace Research*, *47*(1), 15–28. https://doi.org/10.1177%2F0022343309350015

Mac Ginty R. (2017), Peacekeeping and Data, *International Peacekeeping*, *24*(5), 695–705. https://doi.org/10.1080/13533312.2017.1383561

Mahmoud, K. (2014, May 22), *Khalifa Haftar: My forces will reach Tripoli soon*, Asharq al-Aswat. https://eng-archive.aawsat.com/khalid-mahmoud/interviews/khalifa-haftar-my-forces-will-reach-tripoli-soon

Martinez, R. L. (2017), Transnational insurgents: Evidence from Colombia's FARC at the border with Chavez's Venezuela, *Journal of Development Economics*, *126*, 138–153. https://doi.org/10.1016/j.jdeveco.2017.01.003

McGuiness, A. (2017, August 24), *Boris Johnson meets military strongman Haftar on Libya trip*, Sky News. https://news.sky.com/story/boris-johnson-meets-military-strongman-heftar-on-libya-trip-11003992

Paul, C., Clarke, C. P., Grill, B. & Savitsky T. (2013), Between Large-N and Small-N Analyses. Historical Comparison of Thirty Insurgency Case Studies, *Historical Methods (Evidence Matters)*, *46*(4), 220–239. https://doi.org/10.1080/01615440.2012.732008

Poole, P. (2017, July 11), *Libyan army spox says Obama, Clinton 'abandoned the Libyan people to the terrorists'*, PJ Media. https://pjmedia.com/homeland-security/2017/07/11/exclusive-libyan-army-spox-says-obama-clinton-abandoned-the-libyan-people-to-the-terrorists/

Radio Dabanga (2012, April 11), *South Sudan Armed Forces says Heglig belongs to the South: 'We will not withdraw'.* https://www.dabangasudan.org/en/all-news/article/south-sudan-armed-forces-says-heglig-belongs-to-the-south-we-will-not-withdraw

Radio Tamazuj. (2013, April 25), *Press release: SPLM-N expectations for Addis talks.* https://radiotamazuj.org/en/news/article/press-release-splm-n-expectations-for-addis-talks

Raleigh, C., Linke, A., Hegre, H. & Karlsen, J. (2010), Introducing ACLED: An Armed Conflict Location and Event Dataset, *Journal of Peace Research, 47*(5), 651–660. https://doi.org/10.1177/0022343310378914

Raleigh, C. & De Bruyne, K. (2017), Where Rebels Dare to Thread: A Study of Conflict Geography and Co-option of Local Power in Sierra Leone, *Journal of Conflict Resolution, 61*(6), 1230–1260. https://doi.org/10.1177/0022002715603767

Reuters. (2019, 19 April), *Donald Trump spoke to General Haftar before US blocked British UN ceasefire resolution for Libya.* https://www.telegraph.co.uk/news/2019/04/19/donald-trump-spoke-general-haftar-us-blocked-british-un-ceasefire/

Rosenkranz, T. & Jaillon, A. (2016), Accessible and Interactive: New Methods of Data Visualization as Tools for Data Analysis and Information Sharing in Transitional Justice Research, *Transitional Justice Review, 1*(4). http://dx.doi.org/10.5206/tjr.2016.1.4.5

Rustad, S. A. & Binningsbo, H. M. (2012), A price worth fighting for? Natural resources and conflict recurrence, *Journal of Peace Research, 49*(4), 531–546. https://doi.org/10.1177%2F0022343312444942

Ruzzene, A. (2014), Process Tracing as an Effective Epistemic Complement, *Topoi, 33*(2), 361–372. https://doi.org/10.1007/s11245-013-9195-6

Schutte, S. (2017), Violence and Civilian Loyalties: Evidence from Afghanistan, *Journal of Conflict Resolution, 61*(8), 1595–1625. https://doi.org/10.1177%2F0022002715626249

The Signal Program on Human Security and Technology (2013), *Sudan: Anatomy of a Conflict,* Harvard Humanitarian Initiative. https://hhi.harvard.edu/sites/default/files/publications/sudan-anatomy-of-a-conflict.pdf

Small Arms Survey (2012, October 8), *Darfur Armed Opposition Groups.* http://www.smallarmssurveysudan.org/facts-figures/sudan/darfur/darfurs-armed-groups/darfurs-armed-opposition-groups.html

Smith, D. A. (2016), Online interactive thematic mapping: Applications and techniques for socio-economic research, *Computers, Environment and Urban systems, 57,* 106–117. https://doi.org/10.1016/j.compenvurbsys.2016.01.002

Spittaels, S. & Weyns, Y. (2014), *Mapping Conflict Motives. The Sudan – South Sudan border,* IPIS. https://ipisresearch.be/publication/mapping-conflict-motives-sudan-south-sudan-border/

SPLM (2008), *SPLM Manifesto.*

SRF (2012), *The Restructuring of the Sudanese State.*

Sudan Tribune. (2016, February 21), *SPLM-N leader urges international community to put pressure on Sudanese regime.* https://www.sudantribune.com/spip.php?article58069

Sundberg, R. & Melander, E. (2013), Introducing the UCPD Georeferenced Dataset, *Journal of Peace Research*, *50*(4), 523–532. https://doi.org/10.1177%2F0022343313484347

The New Arab (2016, January 22), *Libya's General Haftar accused of war crimes.* https://www.alaraby.co.uk/english/news/2016/1/22/libyas-general-khalifa-haftar-accused-of-war-crimes

Tollefsen, A. F., Strand, H. & Buhaug (2012), H., PRIO-GRID: A unified spatial data structure, *Journal of Peace Research*, *49*(2), 363–374. https://doi.org/10.1177%2F0022343311431287

United Nations General Assembly and United Nations Security Council. (2015), *Report of the High-level Independent Panel on Peace Operations on uniting our strengths for peace: politics, partnership and people* (United Nations official document No. S/2015/446). https://www.un.org/en/ga/search/view_doc.asp?symbol=S/2015/446

UN Panel of Experts on Libya (2015), *Final report of the Panel of Experts on Libya submitted in accordance with paragraph 13 (d) of Council resolution 2144 (2014)* (United Nations official document No. S/2015/128). https://www.undocs.org/S/2015/128

UN Panel of Experts on Libya (2017), *Final report of the Panel of Experts on Libya submitted in accordance with paragraph 13 of Council resolution 2278 (2016)* (United Nations official document No. S/2017/466). https://www.undocs.org/S/2017/466

Voltaire Network (2014, February 15), *Attempted coup d'état in Libya.* https://www.voltairenet.org/article182192.html

CHAPTER 10

Regional Diplomacy: Re-Territorialisation as a Piece in the Neo-Medieval Puzzle?

Manuel Duran

1 Introduction

Until recently, diplomacy has been regarded as the exclusive domain of the state. Recent evolutions in diplomatic practice, however, repudiate this state-centric exclusivity. By conceiving diplomacy as "the mechanism of representation, communication and negotiation through which states *and other international actors* (own italics) conduct their business (Melissen, 1999, p. xvii)" rather than "the official channels of communication employed *by the members of a system of states* (own italics) (Berridge, Keens-Soper, e.a., 2001, p. 1)", a new and more dynamic picture of diplomacy emerges. Looking back at past diplomatic practices might shed new light on contemporary diplomacy. Looking through the lens of neo-medievalism can prove to be a fruitful way of looking back.

The neo-medieval paradigm claims that we are entering a new global setting that in certain aspects resembles that of the Middle Ages. Neo-medievalism has a significant added value in that it introduces an historical, as well as a spatial – territorial - component in the current debate about the metamorphosis of the world. However, one important element seems under-researched in the literature on neo-medievalism: an analysis and comparison of the diplomatic relations between the various polities that form the constituent units of both the medieval and neo-medieval international system. When we see beyond the state-centric concept of diplomacy (Hoffmann, 2003, p. 541), a number of tendencies in today's diplomacy come to the fore showing a striking resemblance with medieval diplomacy, and regions play a paramount role in this process.

Globalisation led to fundamental changes in sovereignty, statehood and the territorial character of the state. These changes have resulted in a shift from the modern so-called Westphalian state-system to a new post-territorial or post-modern international system (Cooper, 1996, pp. 133–153).

 | DOI:10.1163/9789004432086_012

A number of scholars have been using the concept of neo-medievalism to map recent developments in international relations (Kratochwil, 2011, p. 15). Especially in the 1990s and the first decade of our current millennium, new medievalism has been presented as a framework to analyse the simultaneous processes of fragmentation and integration, associated with globalisation. States are at the same time integrating into larger units and disintegrating into smaller territorial ones, such as regional or local entities. Although not so much *en vogue* anymore, the neo-medieval paradigm has a significant added value in that it introduces an historical and spatial component in the current debate about the metamorphosis of the world.

As of late, diplomatic studies literature held a primarily state-centric view. According to the traditional canon diplomacy only came fully into being in the sixteenth and seventeenth centuries with the appearance of the territorial state with its foreign ministries, permanent embassies, diplomatic texts and a set of diplomatic norms and rules (Mattingly, 1955, p. 28). Pre-modern (medieval) diplomacy was depicted as infrequent, slow and undeveloped. *Prima facie*, comparing medieval and present diplomacy would thus enfeeble the historical analogy of the neo-medieval paradigm. However, when we consider diplomacy to be an activity instead of an organisation a new picture emerges. Diplomacy as an activity is a collection of social practices, roles, norms and rules. When we see beyond the state-centric concept of diplomacy and focus on the contrary on the diplomatic activities of other actors in the international arena, a number of tendencies in today's diplomacy come to the fore that show a striking resemblance with medieval diplomacy.

This chapter will first ponder the importance of territoriality as a guiding principle for political and diplomatic agency. We will then canvass the current international diplomatic environment, characterised by simultaneous and mutually influencing traditional and new territorial actors and modes of diplomatic practice and thinking. It will then focus on how this confluence of traditional and new diplomatic actors that deny the primacy of the nation-state can be regarded as a site of political re-territorialisation. Fourth, the neo-medieval paradigm will be sketched. It will be argued that to better analyse what is often referred to as the post-Westphalian international order, it might be adjuvant to consider the pre-Westphalian, medieval international system. Medieval and contemporary diplomacy will then be compared. The chapter argues that contemporary diplomacy resembles medieval diplomacy, and that regions play a paramount role in this respect. A final word of caution not to rely too much on historical analogy thinking will conclude this chapter.

2 The Importance of Territoriality

The concept of territoriality has been and is still being used time and again in so many different contexts that it has become an analytical *passe-partout*. According to Pierre Georges and Fernand Verger (2009), territoriality is defined as a geographic space, characterized by a legal membership (national territory), a natural specificity (for example, mountainous territory) or a cultural specificity (such as linguistic territory), while Claude Raffestin defines territoriality as 'a space transformed by human agency' (Raffestin, 1986). Territoriality, in other words, is physical territory (a geographical place, defined by its location on the earth's surface, delimitated by its longitude and latitude, and possessing certain physical characteristics, such as the nature of its coastline, its geological aspects, the presence of natural resources, etc.), plus both the social organization of this spatial setting and the value attached to this territory by humans, usually assembled in social groupings, be it a neighbourhood, village, region, or a state. This value can take different forms that can all be regarded as geopolitical parameters (Csurgai, 2005, p. 19; Agnew, 2009). They can be of a politico-legal nature (such as state and other boundaries, state sovereignty, or city limits), a cultural nature (for example, the territory of the Catalan language or the existence of an Adriatic cultural space), a historic nature (such as nostalgia for 'Greater Hungary' in the aftermath of the Versailles Treaty), an economic nature (for example, the economic dominance of northern Italy and its resentment of having to pay for the poor, southern *Mezzogiorno*), an ethnic or demographic nature (such as the dispersion of the Albanians in the western Balkans), and so on.

Territoriality thus possesses an objective and a subjective aspect, in other words: a physical–spatial and a human aspect. Making territoriality out of territory is important for politics, since this transformation furnishes the foundations of social and political life (Neumann, 2013, p. 5).

To describe the ongoing evolution of man's societal, political and economic and ecologic dealings with territoriality, we turn to Michel Foucault. The author asserted that, while the nineteenth century was principally concerned – even obsessed – with time, the twentieth and twenty-first centuries would be the age of space. He made this statement in 1984, a year when the term 'globalisation' had already found its way into mainstream media, which was exactly what Foucault had in mind when stating:

> [...] we are in the epoch of juxtaposition, the epoch of the near and far, of the side-by-side, of the dispersed. (Foucault, 1984, p. 46)

These juxtapositions, nears and fars, side-by-sides and dispersions signify a change in our dealings with space, including the political space. Recent decades have witnessed a number of evolutions, both on a global and local scale, in which society and politics have become less bound to territorial spaces (Criekemans, 2011). These evolutions have been labelled processes of 'deterritorialisation'. This is a somewhat fuzzy concept that has been used in a manifold of contexts. Gerard Ó Tuathail, one of the frontrunners of the critical school of geopolitics, labels its difficult tangibility as follows:

> Deterritorialisation is best interpreted, as Virilio remarks, as a question; it evokes the challenges posed to the status of territory and, by extension, our territorially embedded understandings of geography, governance and geopolitics, states, places and the social sciences, by planetary communication networks and globalizing tendencies. But it is deceptive when it becomes an answer polemically naming this challenge as a clear disappearance of territoriality. The problematic of deterritorialisation is therefore also the problematic of reterritorialisation; it is not the presence or absence of state territoriality but its changing status, power and meaning in relation to postmodern technological constellations, speed machines and global webs of capitalism. (Ó Tuathail, Dalby et al., 1998, p. 82)

The 'clear disappearance of territoriality' in contemporary political thought mainly concerns the diminution in importance, some might call it monopoly, of the territorial state. The territorial, modern or Westphalian state that succeeded the medieval feudal state can be described as 'a particular form of territoriality – disjointed, fixed and mutually exclusive – as the basis for organizing political life' (Ruggie, 1993, p. 168). The modern territorial state that replaced the overlapping, sometimes conflicting, jurisdictions of the Middle Ages was a centralizing endeavour, based on the theory of sovereignty. This theory claims the supremacy of the state's government over its people, resources and over all other authorities within the territory that it controls. Over time the territorial state came into being as 'a differentiated ensemble of governmental institutions, offices, and personnel that claims the exclusive power of authoritative political rule-making for a population within a continuous territory that has a clear, internationally recognized boundary' (Axtmann, 2004, p. 260). This exclusive state power has been put into question by the advent of numerous transnationally organized non-state actors and their involvement in world politics. Specifically, in Europe, new regionalism began in the 1970s mainly as a domestic phenomenon within a limited number of European (but also

North American) states. It gained momentum during the 1990s as a result of European integration and economic globalisation. Regionalism is both product and producer of a certain decomposition and recomposition of the territorial framework of public life (Keating, 1997). European regions are coherent territorial entities that are situated between local and national levels with a capacity for authoritative decision-making and are thus full-fledged sub-state entities. Their entry onto the global scene has challenged diplomacy as a state-only endeavour.

3 Diplomacy in a Changing World, Changing Diplomacies?

After the end of the Cold War and as a result of the accelerated globalisation, many authors argued that territoriality had ended as an organizing political principle. Ideas about the end of history (Fukuyama, 1992) and a borderless (Ceglowski, 1998) world went hand in hand with those of the waning importance or even the final end, of the state. There was talk of a post-territorial world (Van Staden and Vollaard, 2002), in which increasing regional integration (the European Union, but also the North Atlantic Free Trade Association NAFTA, the Southern Common Market MERCOSUR, the Association of Southeast Asian Nations ASEAN, etc.), the primacy of the market and liberal democracy were a teleological endpoint of history. In this new post-territorial world, the state would at most have a supportive and facilitating role, and thus be reduced to a "market-state" (Bobbitt, 2003). Diplomacy also seemed on its way out. Diplomacy, after all, was (and is) following one of its most generic definitions; the art and practice of negotiating, communicating and representing between sovereign states.

Some authors, such as Paul Sharp and Joe Clark, even talked about the end of diplomacy (Sharp and Clark, 1997), while Rik Coolsaet hinted at a new "post-territorial" diplomatic arrangement of international relations (Coolsaet, 1999).

A number of events have put territoriality back on the forefront since the beginning of the new millennium. First there were the 9/11 attacks and the subsequent wars in Afghanistan and Iraq, the Arab Spring and the civil wars in Libya and Syria. The European Union got hit by a serious migration crisis with considerable (domestic) political consequences. This followed the economic-financial crisis and the growing gap between the Southern and Northern EU Member States since 2007. Europe also met a growing Russian assertiveness at its western border. Territoriality, the way in which man defines and organizes space, was never really gone, as were various processes of territorialisation, the processes through which man exercises political power, wins or loses space.

To describe this withering away of the importance of the state and the consequent disappearance of territoriality, scholars returned to the concept of deterritorialisation, as it was formulated by French philosophers Gilles Deleuze and Félix Guattari in their 1972 book *L'Anti-OEdipe* (1972).[1] Deterritorialisation is the decline or even the blatant disappearance of the importance of territoriality in domestic politics or international relations. This de- or post-territorial international setting coincides with new forms of post-territorial diplomacy, characterized by the advent of new 'post-territorial' diplomatic actors, the rise of private multilateralism,[2] the erosion of the ministry of foreign affairs' central role and an increasing number of post-territorial global problems on the diplomatic agenda.

One of the manifestations of deterritorialisation is the process by which the state has been yielding certain aspects of its sovereignty to both supra- and sub-national authorities and non-state political actors (Rudolph, 2005, p. 1). Especially the second half of the twentieth century witnessed the emergence of new political actors as a result of dynamics of decentralization that changed not only the internal governmental structure of many a Western state, but also its party-political system and indeed its international agency and diplomatic practices. Coinciding with ongoing processes of economic and cultural globalisation, the (re-)emergence of new identities and a territorial realignment in which de- and reterritorialisation go hand in hand are witnessed (Newman, e.a., 2004), particularly affecting the ways in which old and new identities interrelate with each other – in other words, the ways in which they do diplomacy (Keating, 1999; Ó Tuathail and Luke, 1994; Sassen, 1996).

Reterritorialisation, or the (re)appearance of the importance of territoriality, can be narrowly defined as 'developments which occur when certain territorial entities lose their importance, in favour of other territorial configurations' (Scholte, 2005, p. 60). A broader definition is given by Michael Keating, who describes reterritorialisation as 'the emergence of new centres of power alongside the old ones' (Keating, 1998). These new centres of power can take the form of new independent states, international organizations, regional integration processes, or sub-national entities of different sorts. Sub-state entities are a particular category within these new centres of power, in that their characteristics approximate that of the state more than any other new centre

1 Originally used in a philosophical and psychoanalytical context, the term "deterritorialisation" soon became common property in anthropology, sociology and political science, much to the liking of both authors, who did not believe in an essentialist usage of their concepts.

2 The multilateral relations between multinational corporations and/or NGOs, and other non-state actors.

of power. Their diplomatic agency has become a global phenomenon, including European, American, Asian, Australian and African sub-state entities, and their diplomatic practice has increasingly become a governmental and institutionalized phenomenon (Duran and Criekemans, 2010, p. 6).

The popular American author Robert Kaplan held a challenging view on "the revenge of geography". The revenge of geography is an unmistakable warning for modern man, who thought he had eliminated the boundaries of space and time through a system of limitless economic globalisation, political homogenization and accelerated digitization (Kaplan, 2012). However, territoriality turned out only to have become more complex and multi-layered. The state had not withered away, as some authors had suggested only a decade before. It even had (re)gained strength, especially in the military and security domain. At the same time, in addition to states, other actors of territoriality had arisen: sub-national and local authorities, but also transnational or territorially embedded religious communities. They all fought for part of the political power that could be divided after the Cold War and the so-called post-territorial intermezzo of the 1990s. The new world order resembled a hybrid mixture of pre-modern, modern and post-modern overlapping power centres. This observation led several authors to define our world as "new-Medieval".

As in the Middle Ages, power in Europe was divided across several overlapping political centres: then they were counties and duchies, cities and towns, embryonic nation states like England and Hungary, but also the Holy Roman Empire of the German Nation or the Prince-Bishopric of Liège. Now they are states, supranational entities such as the EU, but also increasingly sub-entities, such as regions, urban governments, and even terrorist organizations, such as Islamic State.

4 The Emergence of Regional Diplomacy

Geography, territoriality and re-territorialisation also brought diplomacy back to the forefront. But it turned out that diplomacy now has a different outlook and dynamics compared to the past. The aforementioned multitude of diplomatic actors (states, regions, cities, etc.) also practiced a multitude of diplomatic forms in an equally complex diplomatic setting. In addition to traditional bilateral and multilateral diplomacy, public diplomacy, digital diplomacy, economic, commercial or mega-diplomacy also emerged (Khanna, 2011).

Regions are one of these new diplomatic actors. Their emergence as territorially embedded political agents coincided with global dynamics of regional integration, such as the EU, but also ASEAN, MERCOSUR, NAFTA, etc. As a result, the exclusivity of state-only political power corroded (Keating, 1998). Regions and other sub-national entities are granted considerable competences, including in the international domain. One important tool in the hands of these actors are their external relations and diplomatic activities, of which they make ample use so as to further expand their influence, be it domestic or global. This has been a truly global phenomenon, with regions, provinces, cities and other local authorities from every continent "going abroad". The sub-state and the supra-state policy level encounter one another in ever closer cross-border, transnational and inter-regional collaboration programmes and projects. Examples of these are the European Territorial Policies, or the inter-regional cooperation within the Union of South American Nations (UNASUR), and numerous other examples in all other continents.

There has been a proliferation of academic and policy-relevant literature on the topic of sub-national and regional diplomacy, often labelled paradiplomacy.[3] Most literature on regional diplomacy focuses on the judicial delimitations of regional diplomacy; on the foreign policy instruments; or on the division of power between the central state and the regional entity. It would lead us too far to delve into the vast richness of this paradiplomacy literature, but one of the most interesting analyses was made by Belgian scholar David Criekemans who developed an analytical matrix to analyze and evaluate the myriad of diplomatic instruments and variations in the organizational structure of diplomacy and foreign policy within different sub-state entities. This analytical model has not only advanced our knowledge of the concrete elaboration and development of paradiplomacy but has also given rise to a more historical conceptualization of paradiplomacy as an evolving practiced concept of political reality, subject to constant and contingent change. Criekemans distinguishes three phases or waves in the development of sub-state diplomacy.

> The first wave manifested itself from the 1980s onwards: a growing number of non-central governments tried to attract foreign direct investment through own initiatives [. . .] or to use culture and identity as a lever to place oneself on the international map. The second wave in the 1990s was characterized by the creation, within the sub-state entities of certain (European) countries, of a judicially grounded set of instruments for

3 Just to cite a number of recent examples: Kuznetsov, A. S. (2015), *Theory and practice of paradiplomacy: Subnational governments in international affairs*, Oxford, Routledge; Tavares, R. (2016), *Paradiplomacy: Cities and states as global players*, Oxford, Oxford University Press.; Criekemans, D. (ed.) (2010), *Regional sub-state diplomacy today*, Boston and Leiden, Brill.

> their own (parallel as well as complementary) diplomatic activities [...]. The current third wave is characterized by steps towards a 'verticalization' of the organizational structure of the administration or department of external/foreign affairs, a strategic reorientation of the geopolitical and functional priorities, and attempts to integrate the external instruments of a sub-state foreign policy into a well-performing whole. (Criekemans and Duran, 2010, p. 9)

Henry Kissinger once poignantly said that the "actual range of diplomatic innovations is heavily circumscribed by history, domestic institutions and geography" (Kissinger, 1994, p. 238). Attention towards the interaction between these three variables is frequently lacking in the study of international relations. To overcome this omission, this chapter proposes to take a closer look at the so-called neo-medieval paradigm.

5 A New Framework to Evaluate Diplomatic Changes? Neo-Medievalism

Neo-medievalism states we have now entered or are entering a new global epoch which resembles certain traits of the European Middle Ages. Proponents of neo-medievalism put forward that the beginning of the sixteenth century constituted the watershed between the medieval and modern eras. They claim we are again at the beginning or in the midst of a similar turning point; a transition to a new postmodern (or neo-medieval) era. These theorists state that looking back to medieval Europe may help us to understand the rough outlines of an emerging postmodern global setting. It allows us to think about other possible modes of political and economic organization (Friedrichs, 2001).

The concept of a new Middle Ages was first developed by Hedley Bull. In his classic book *The Anarchical Society* (Bull, 1977, p. 275), Bull draws a hypothetical picture of the dawn of a new Middle Ages characterised by an increasing regional integration of states, the internal disintegration of a number of states, the restoration of private international violence, the growing importance of transnational organizations, and the technological unification of the world. The world has changed since the publication of *The Anarchical Society* in 1977. One can safely state that the five criteria Bull cited are to be found in the present international system. It is not surprising then that a number of scholars took up the thread of Bull's work and further elaborated on and deepened the conceptualization of neo-medievalism and this from a number of vantage points. Such contributions ranged from literary criticism (Ferguson and Mansbach,

2008, p. 373), philosophy (Marschall, 2011) to social as well as political sciences. In an attempt to describe and explain the sequence of events that were rapidly altering the face of the world[4] they decided to look back. These authors presented the new Middle Ages in a number of ways. It could be envisioned as a purely aesthetic phenomenon, a spiritual-cultural given or a new framework to analyse international relations, as a complex system of overlapping authorities and loyalties which are in turn overarched by several universal claims.

Within IR-theory, we can distinguish between two takes on neo-medievalism. Some (neo-)realist scholars use it to describe the disturbing dark side of modern globalisation. The Middle Ages are represented here as the Dark Ages, a time when arbitrariness, political and social violence, and harsh conditions of living were the norm. Needless to say, that this depiction of the Middle Ages is too one-dimensional or even downright wrong. The dichotomy between modern order and medieval disorder does not stand the test of history. Medieval times on the one hand were also characterized by a strong tendency of ecclesiastical and secular universalism, while on the other hand modern times have witnessed some of the most horrifying examples of international violence and disorder.

The other approach to neo-medievalism ponders the aforementioned "globalisation" dynamics. New medievalism in this context constitutes a framework to analyze the simultaneous processes of fragmentation and integration. One of the best contributions to neo-medievalism stems from Jörg Friedrichs (2007). This German scholar presents the new Middle Ages as a complex system of overlapping authorities and loyalties, comparable to the situation before the Peace of Westphalia, which heralded the modern state system. Medieval territory differed fundamentally from modern territorial concepts in that the feudal world should be seen "as concentric circles of power projection" (Teschke, 2003, p. 66). Various competing power centres or systems of authority could all lay different but rightful claims to the same territorial configuration. The major divide was that between ecclesiastical and secular authorities, but even within these two a great multitude of sometimes opposing dominions existed, each of them trying to exert control over a given territory. Moreover, medieval territoriality was not exclusive nor perfect, but dependent on the personal ties between the lord and his vassal (Spruyt, 1994, p. 38). Vassals had different lords, secular or ecclesiastical, for different circumstances. The complexities of this system of overlapping, non-exclusive authorities are comprehensibly pictured

4 The end of the bipolar world of the Cold War after the events of 1989, the subsequent dissolution of the Soviet Union and Yugoslavia, the increasing number of "failed states" in the South, the perceived (at least by some) of a growing "clash of civilizations".

by Spruyt when he states that “one could simultaneously be the vassal of the German emperor, the French king, and various counts and bishops, none of whom necessarily had precedence over the other” (Spruyt, 1994, p. 39). We are today once again entering a world of overlapping, polycentric and competing authorities, where the modern “vassals” can be bound by multiple loyalties. As early as 1988 Lewis Lapham wrote a poignant article in *Harper’s Magazine* depicting the various societal forces pressuring the exclusivity of the state:

> The hierarchies of international capitalism resemble the feudal arrangements under which an Italian noble might swear fealty to a German prince, or a Norman duke declare himself the vassal of an English king. (Lapham, 1998, p. 10)

According to Friedrichs, neo-medieval overlapping authorities are overarched by several universal claims. After the fall of the Western Roman Empire in 476, the idea of a return of the Roman Empire survived in Western Europe. The coronation of Charlemagne in 800 was the consecration of the unification of the former Western Roman empire (minus Spain). After the death of Charlemagne and the division of his empire, the ideal still lived on. Soon the German emperor was considered Charlemagne’s heir to the title of Holy Roman Emperor. Although the empire was not Roman, was not holy and was not an empire, it still lived on as a political ideal. Competing with this ideal of *imperium* was the so-called *sacerdotium*. In Western Europe, every man and woman, regardless of the place he or she lived, considered him- or herself in the first place to be a Christian, belonging to the greater community of Christendom. The ecclesiastical hierarchy, with the pope at the top, the bishops, abbots, priests, formed a true transnational elite, unifying Western Europe, not in the least by means of their use of Latin, the *lingua franca* at the time.

To this neo-medieval paradigm a post-Westphalian conception of boundaries is added. This consists of a revival of the medieval boundaries, which more resembled a geographical zone than a fixed line. A notable example can be found in the European Union. With each enlargement of the Union, its borders have been shifting. Numerous unsolved debates have been raging on where one can pinpoint the exact border of the European Union and of Europe *tout court* (Christiansen, Petito, e.a., 2000). Instead of tying up a specific EU-border, the European Neighborhood Policy sets up a large frontier zone at Europe’s southern and Eastern border. This border includes the European neighbors in a number of cooperation programmes, and at the same time excludes them from the political decision making in Brussels.

6 Neo-Medievalism & Regional Diplomacy

Let us now take a closer look at how neo-medievalism might shed a new light on the subject of regional diplomacy. As Spruyt has shown in his book on political systemic change from the Middle Ages to the modern era, "the agents that make up the state system create a particular structure of interunit behaviour" (Spruyt, 1994, p. 17). Diplomacy being the means *par excellence* to engage in interunit exchange, a comparison between medieval and neo-medieval diplomacy might prove to be a valuable analysis.

Medieval diplomatic intercourse differed from modern diplomacy in that it was "spasmodic rather than continuous" (Anderson; 1998, p. 53). A fixed system of delegations and a standing body of resident ambassadors, the core elements of modern diplomacy did not come to light until the end of the fifteenth century, when a number of Italian city-states established the first permanent foreign representations. Yet this does not mean that medieval polities did not engage in diplomacy. On the contrary, medieval diplomacy was thriving. Political agents were communicating, negotiating and representing themselves, they were 'doing business with one another'. Out of medieval diplomacy emerged a prototype of diplomacy to mediate the newly articulated states that came to be during the late Middle Ages (Der Derian, 1987, p. 68).

One of the key features of medieval diplomacy was the existence of a vast range of diplomatic actors, comparable to the various non-state actors that currently are engaging in diplomatic intercourse. Nowadays, a great number of non-state actors are involved in diplomatic activities (Hocking, 2004). These include regional and local authorities, corporations, non-governmental organisations and international organisations. Therefore, sub-national diplomacy can be considered as one of the new postmodern diplomacies, alongside NGO diplomacy, city diplomacy, citizen diplomacy or corporate diplomacy. While NGO, corporate and citizen diplomacy assent to the post-territorial concept of diplomacy, sub-national and city diplomacy on the contrary support the reterritorialisation thesis, whereby alongside the state, other territorial configurations engage in diplomatic activities.

Over the years sub-national diplomacy has become a normalized and normal feature of the international environment (Cornago, 2010, p. 35). According to Robert Kaizer (2003, p. 18), sub-national diplomacy can be divided into three clusters of activities: horizontal cooperation, vertical cooperation, and promotion of interests. Horizontal cooperation are all forms of cross-border and interregional cooperation. These often take the form of bilateral or multilateral cooperation with neighboring regions but can also be found in a

European context. Vertical cooperation is the way in which regions participate in and design the foreign policy of the central or federal state. Germany does pioneering work in the way in which the representatives of the governments of the *Länder* delineate the foreign policy of the Federal Republic in the *Bundesrat*. The most striking form of interest promotion of sub-national entities is their own network of representatives or offices abroad. Regional entities also rely on a whole range of innovative policy tools like public diplomacy, informal networking, city diplomacy and an integrated international cultural policy.

One diplomatic site in particular of this new form of diplomacy shows great resemblance to medieval diplomacy: the importance of network diplomacy for regional authorities. "Network diplomacy" is, next to virtual diplomacy and e-diplomacy one of the elements of the new diplomatic paradigm, which was *inter alia* conceived in the concepts of transformational diplomacy and the development of the European External Action Service. Sub-national polities lack the diplomatic power international law grants to "traditional" nation-states (the *ius legationis* and the *ius tractati*).[5] They therefore had to resort to other means to go abroad, communicate and negotiate with international partners and to represent themselves. One of the most important tools in the hands of sub-national entities to overcome their relative weakness in this regard is the development of and adherence to a policy network. These networks can be formal or informal and have been paramount to the development of sub-national diplomacy. When considering the policy networks in which sub-national entities are involved, one is struck by the very diverse nature of the frameworks in which they operate. Some regions are involved in single issue networks (e.g. Scotland on maritime issues), others focus on broader policy-issues (e.g. Wallonia and Québec via the *Francophonie*, or Catalonia within the 'Four Motors for Europe'). Yet others have established global networks to bring together sub-state entities with a specific know-how (e.g. the 'Flanders Districts of Creativity'- network on creativity and the economy, referred to as the 'DC-network'). Network diplomacy allows polities of different levels (provinces, regions, sub-national entities) to develop structural or ad hoc contacts, without the need for physical embassies, although more and more sub-national entities are establishing an ever-vaster network of pseudo-diplomatic delegations (Tatham, 2008).

Before the establishment of resident ambassadors, medieval polities entered into diplomatic intercourse with each other by means of ad hoc or

5 The Belgian case can be considered an important exception in that the regional governments are granted by law the right to set up diplomatic offices abroad and are entitled (even obliged) to engage in international treaty-making within the area of their competences.

more permanent diplomatic networks. Donald Queller puts it eloquently when he states that "the modern notion that only a sovereign state can be represented by an ambassador was as inchoate in the Middle Ages as the concept of sovereignty itself" (Queller, 2005, p. 198). During the Middle Ages, there was no such thing as an international community of nation-states. The concept of territorial sovereignty only gained ground after the Peace of Westphalia. Since sovereign nation-states did not exist, the act to represent them could not be fulfilled. Instead, there existed a plethora of infra-statal institutions, starting from the hybrid "national" kingdoms like England, France, and Aragon, principalities, duchies, free counties, bishoprics, free cities, commercial alliances (like the Hanseatic League), baronies, petty lordships but also corporate bodies like guilds, military orders, and religious orders (Nigro, 2010, p. 174). All of these institutions sent diplomatic agents to all sorts of recipients (Queller, 2005, p. 194). Or as 13th century legal scholar William Durandus put it

> A legate is ... whoever has been sent from another ..., either from a prince, or from the pope to others..., or from some city, or province to a prince or to another... (Durandus, Speculum legatorum, 1, 1, cited and translated by Queller, 1967: 11)

These agents did not, as modern ambassadors do, reside in a particular place but were on the contrary of an ambulant nature. The Carolingian *missi* were later succeeded by the *nuncii* and the *procuratores*. *Missi*, *nuncii* and *procuratores* alike did not possess the prerogatives of the modern ambassadors. Instead, they acted as the moving mouths and ears, the magpie (Azo of Bologna) or the living letter of the sender (Queller, 1984, p. 201). In so doing, they allowed the feudal lords, the medieval cities, the popes and other clerics, the corporate bodies, etc. to communicate with one another, to negotiate treaties, to forge alliances and platforms for cooperation, simply said: to establish all sorts of functional, geographic, genealogical or other networks and do business with each other.

Network diplomacy enabled the various medieval polities to act diplomatically without possessing the 'traditional' or 'modern' prerequisites of a ministry of foreign affairs, an international network of embassies or a system of resident ambassadors. Likewise, new diplomatic actors such as European regions overcome their limitations regarding the *ius legationis* and the *ius tractati* by means of network diplomacy. They meet and negotiate with international partners, develop specific ad hoc projects and even set up institutional structures.

Still, we must be aware that any form of historical analogy thinking entails a number of conceptual dangers and pitfalls. We must guard ourselves not to fall into the Westphalian territorial trap.

7 The Westphalian Myth: Historical Analogy Thinking

Territorialisation deals with the way in which people organize territories and territorialities. These organizations are both inward- and outward-bound, and thus entail much more than just the possession or occupation of a certain place on this earth. All of us are territorializing actors, in that we all try to get a grip on the places we inhabit, work, love and eventually die in. We do this by buying or renting a house, by mapping a route to work, by consulting (Google)maps to plan our holidays. Not only individuals, but also groupings of humans, are actors of territorialisation, the most conspicuous being the state, which came into full maturity after the Peace of Westphalia and knew its apogee during the nineteenth century and early twentieth century. The state laid railways and motorways, initiated large urbanization programmemes, demarcated natural parks and opened foreign delegations called 'embassies'. For a long time, the state's ability to territorialize was strengthened because it put all other political agents in the shadow and/or subordinated them to the state's hierarchical domination. The territorializing voices of non- and sub-state actors were gradually silenced or grew mute. This is not to say that they vanished from the face of the earth completely, but they became invisible to the two fields of academic study – International Relations and Diplomatic Studies – that came into bloom when the state's territorializing power was at its peak; here lies the origin of both the 'Westphalian myth' and the 'territorial trap'. Both paradigms claim that the state is the only relevant political actor, at the domestic as well as the international level.

It is a truism that the Peace of Westphalia saw the emergence of the modern territorial state. The year 1648, so the somewhat simplified story goes, marked the end of the medieval territorial setting. As already mentioned, medieval territoriality differed fundamentally from modern territorial concepts in that the feudal world should be seen 'as concentric circles of power projection'. Authority during the Middle Ages was 'both personalized and parcelled within and across territorial formations (Ruggie, 1993)'.

Ruggie argues that the modern system of rule differentiated its subject collectivity into territorially defined, fixed, and mutually exclusive enclaves of legitimate domination, in this way depicting the traditional view on pre-modern and modern states. Ruggie, along with numerous other authors, argues that territoriality as the organizing principle of modern politics has been giving way since the end of the Cold War to a non-territorial organization of authority:

> In many respects, Ruggie's argument is simply one of the more subtle and provocative examples of an emerging genre arguing that the modern state and the modern state system are being challenged, and perhaps eroded,

> by a variety of forces ranging from domestic privatization to economic and cultural globalisation. The conventional argument runs roughly as follows. After steady expansion of the size and scope of states in the post-war era, a variety of social forces have sought to curtail and reverse this expansion. Waves of privatization of public services, deregulation of utilities and markets, and deconcentration or decentralization of service and authority to lower levels of government appear to have reversed the trend towards expansion of the state's role in the economy and the provision of social welfare. This 'retreat of the state' has coincided with a trend towards the internationalization of markets and the development of new information technologies that appear to 'shrink' space by allowing denser communication across national borders. (Ansell and Di Palma, 2004)

This so-called 'retreat of territoriality' had consequences for our thinking about diplomacy. Just as the modern international order evolved into a post-modern, 'neo-medieval (Kratochwil, 2011, p. 3)' order of overlapping, non-exclusive, non-territorial authorities, so diplomacy is being transformed into a new post-modern, post-territorial, non-territorial diplomacy (see chapters two and four).

This is, in a nutshell, the traditional narrative on (state) diplomacy and (state) territoriality: the modern state is a territorial area that grew out of the Treaty of Westphalia in 1648. Simultaneously and consequently, modern diplomacy surfaced, putting an end to pre-modern diplomacy. This pre-modern, medieval diplomacy was 'spasmodic rather than continuous (Anderson, 1998, p. 53)' and can at best be labelled as 'proto-diplomacy'.

Yet history disproves these conventional ideas, which unfortunately have gained the status of *idées reçues* in mainstream IR. The Treaty of Westphalia did not signify the sudden emergence of the modern territorial state and a new sovereignty-based international system. First, Westphalia did not mean the end of the universalist claims to power of the Church. Moreover, medieval territoriality – overlapping and non-exclusive – never totally withered away. Within the borders of the Holy Roman Empire, for example, a patchwork of authorities could be found. Italy, on the other hand, resembled a quilt of principalities, theoretically under Spanish (and later Austrian) control, but legally independent and bound to the Holy Roman Empire only by personal-dynastic ties. Although historically refutable, the Westphalian myth has served an epistemological function. It is:

> [...] a typical founding myth, it offers a neat account of how the 'classical' European system, the prototype of the present international system, came about. Conveniently and comprehensively, it explains the origin

> of what are considered the main characteristics of that system, such as territoriality, sovereignty, equality, and non-intervention. It fits perfectly with the accepted view of what international relations is about, or at least has 'traditionally' been about: relations of a specific kind (with the problem of war occupying a central position) among actors of a specific kind (territorial, sovereign, legally equal). While IR authors are divided on the applicability of this conventional model to current phenomena, very rarely do they question its applicability to the past. (Osiander, 2001, p. 266)

In the same vein, historical evidence shows that modern diplomacy did not materialize overnight in 1648. According to the traditional view of diplomacy, 'the Westphalian state order and modern diplomacy have co-evolved and remain mutually constitutive institutions (Batora, 2003, p. 1)'. This traditional view outlined diplomacy as 'the term given to the official channels of communication employed by members of a system of states (Berridge, 2005, p. 1)', or as 'the management of international relations by negotiation; the method by which these relations are adjusted by ambassadors and envoys; the business or art of the diplomatist (Nicolson, 1942, p. 15)'. Yet these definitions are too limited to describe the richness of pre-Westphalian -Medieval- diplomacy.

We can agree with James Caporaso when he claims that the Westphalian international order and modern diplomacy are to be regarded as ideal-types (Caporaso, 2000, p. 1). They facilitate our thinking and our ability to theorize international relations and diplomacy. At the same time, however, they restrict a sound heuristic and ontology of territoriality and diplomacy alike, both past and present. Indeed, painting an international setting in which territoriality is now being 'unbundled', thereby deterritorializing the modern state and the modern state system, is too much of an oversimplification. Territorialisation – the controlling and managing of a specific territory – has only temporarily vanished from the scholarly radar. It is therefore better to talk about a 'rebundling' instead of a disappearance of territoriality, whereby sub-national and supra-national entities gain increasing prominence in national and international affairs (Ansell and Di Palma, 2004), alongside states and other non-state actors. Just as the richness of the pre-modern diplomatic environment is not getting the attention that it deserves when one adheres to the Westphalian paradigm, the multiple facets of contemporary diplomacy cannot be adequately described by labelling them as 'post-Westphalian' or 'post-territorial'.

Indeed, the current diplomatic landscape is increasingly being populated by a multitude of new territorial actors, of which sub-state or regional authorities are the most conspicuous. German, Belgian, Italian and French regions, as well as Spanish autonomous communities, have over the last 30 years embarked on a mission to (re)claim their spot on the international map. Some of them, like Catalonia, have developed a diplomatic machinery that is increasingly emulating that of a small state. Others, such as the southern Italian region of Puglia, have set up a more modest model of diplomacy, mainly focusing on diaspora, cultural and economic diplomacy. The divergences, differences, commonalities and similarities that can be traced in each of their diplomacies find their origins in their specific geopolitical DNA. This consists of the interplay of political, economic, spatial, historical and cultural factors, on a regional and national – as well as on an international – level. This geopolitical DNA makes sub-state entities what they are. Yet it is only in their meetings, talks, dealings with and getting related to other political agents that their Self comes to full maturity. Sub-state entities have therefore all 'adopted basic diplomatic functions such as negotiation skills, visible representation, effective communication, filtered information, and political reporting from overseas and symbolism (Murray, 2008, p. 25)'. They all practice diplomacy for the same reason as other diplomatic actors: they want to mediate various degrees of estrangement between themselves and Others. In this process, engaging with the Others only reifies the Self, while the reification of the Self leads to more relations with the Others. In other words, diplomacy results in increasing degrees of agency. The more diplomatic Selves interrelate with diplomatic Others, the more they gain international actorness.

8 Conclusion

On 10 February 2016 a number of scholars from a variety of fields gathered at the *Academia Belgica* in Rome to ponder the possibilities of cross-fertilization between Medieval History, International Relations and Diplomatic Studies.[6] The title of the symposium "Back to the future, forward to the past?": Paradiplomacies as a site of neo-medievalism" could be read as an intellectual teaser for further research, of which this article is one of the first outcomes.[7] Changes in both the internal political structure of the state (decentralisation and devolution, as well as ceding political power to supranational institutions) and in

6 The author would like to thank all participants of this symposium for their inspiring and insightful contributions, as well as the lively debate with the audience: professors Isabelle Lazzarini, David Criekemans, Earl Fry and Jörg Friedrichs, as well as professor Wouter Bracke, director of the Academia Belgica and kind host to the symposium.

7 Another result of this symposium is Isabella Lazzarini: Storia della diplomazia e International Relations Studies fra pre- e post- moderno, in «Storica» 65 (2016), pp. 9–41

international relations (the interdependence of political, security, economic, environmental and developmental issues on a continental and even global scale) change the diplomatic interaction between international agents. In order to find out whether these are merely temporary and superficial changes, or on the contrary fundamental changes with a more permanent character, we need an historical approach (Van Kemseke, 2000, p. 11). As we have tried to show, a comparison between regional diplomacy and medieval diplomacy forms an additional piece in the neo-medieval puzzle by clarifying the relation between the constituent units of both the medieval and neo-medieval international system. All three generic dimensions of diplomacy, i.e. communication, representation and the reproduction (or socialization) of international society fitted the medieval feudal and city diplomacy and fit the current neo-medieval multi-layered diplomacy, in which networks and city diplomacy play an important role.

This comparison also enables us to move beyond the historical dichotomy between an undeveloped medieval system of "proto-diplomacy" (to use James Der Derian's expression) and the elaborate system of modern diplomacy, as depicted by Donald Queller and Garrett Mattingly. Both authors have been responsible for the linear teleological narrative concerning diplomatic history. This narrative repudiates the complexities of medieval diplomacy that, as John Watkins clearly indicates:

> still had an enormous impact on the shifting political, economic, religious, and cultural fortunes of European peoples and the emergence of national self-consciousness. Ironically, the divergent forms these contacts took sometimes provide striking analogues for the new practices that occupy a widening sector of our post-Cold War diplomatic practice. (Watkins, 2008: 4–5)

It also shows that

> It all comes down to alterity. For alterity does not exist in the singular: it does not reduce to how different 'they' all were from all of 'us'. Alterity is about the tremendous variety within and between medieval cultures. If, despite the allure of pop-cultural over-simplifications, despite the bludgeoning effect of unwieldy and unhelpful historical labels, despite the inadequacies and difficulties of the evidence, despite the distraction of demands for facile relevance, we still manage to find that medieval people were fascinatingly diverse, then the same must, thank goodness, be true of us as well. (Bull, 2005: 141)

In other words: looking back at the complexities of yesterday allows us to better understand the complexities of today. One of the sites of today's complex world is the way in which our current international diplomatic environment is characterized by the presence of both traditional (state) and new territorial (regional and local) actors and modes of diplomatic practice. This confluence of traditional and new diplomatic actors is an important expression of political reterritorialisation in that it gainsays the primacy of the nation-state, that has been so dominant since the Treaty of Westphalia. The neo-medieval paradigm is a means to better analyse what is often referred to as our current post-modern, post-Westphalian international order. When looking through the lens of the pre-Westphalian, medieval international system, we can see a significant resemblance with contemporary diplomacy, in which regions by virtue of their territorial but non-state situation play a paramount role. Neo-medievalism proposes an important added value in that it injects a temporal dimension to our otherwise static thinking about diplomacy. At the same time, it allows for a diachronic conceptualization of territoriality. Territoriality, from a neo-medieval vantage point, escapes both too narrow a state-only or an artificial non-territorial take on international relations.

Bibliography

Agnew, J. (2009). *Globalisation and Sovereignty*. Lanham: Rowman and Littlefield.

Anderson, J. (1996). The shifting stage of politics: new medieval and postmodern territorialities, *Environment and Planning*, Society and Space 14, 133–153.

Anderson, M.S. (1998). *The Origins of the Modern European State System, 1494–1618*. London: Longman.

Ansell, C. and G. Di Palma (2004). *Restructuring Territoriality: Europe and the United States Compared*. Cambridge: Cambridge University Press.

Axtmann, R. (2004). The State of the State: The Model of the Modern State and its Contemporary Transformation. *International Political Science Review* 25(3): 259–279.

Bátora, J. (2003). Does the European Union Transform the Institution of Diplomacy? *Discussion Papers in Diplomacy, 87*.

Berridge, G.R., Keens-Soper, M., et al. (2001), *Diplomatic theory from Machiavelli to Kissinger*. Basingstoke and New York: Palgrave.

Bobbitt, Ph. (2003). *The Shield of Achilles. War, Peace, and the Course of History*. New York: Anchor Books.

Bull, H. (1977). *The Anarchical Society: A Study of Order in World Politics*. London: MacMillan.

Bull, M. (2005). *Thinking Medieval: An Introduction to the Study of the Middle Ages.* Basingstoke and New York: Palgrave Macmillan.

Caporaso, J. (2000). Changes in the Westphalian Order: Territory, Public Authority, and Sovereignty. *International Studies Review* 2(2): 1–28.

Ceglowski, J. (1998). Has Globalisation Created a Borderless World? *Business Review,* march-april, Federal Reserve Bank of Philadelphia, 17–27.

Christiansen, T., Petito, F., et al. (2000). Fuzzy Politics Around Fuzzy Borders: The European Union's `Near Abroad'. *Cooperation and Conflict,* 35(4): 389–415.

Coolsaet, R. (1999). The Transformation of Diplomacy at the Threshold of a New Millennium. *Leicester Diplomatic Studies Programmeme: Discussion Papers,* 48.

Cooper, R. (1996). *The Postmodern State and the World Order.* Demos: London.

Cornago, N. (2010). On the Normalization of Sub-State Diplomacy In D. Criekemans (ed.). *Regional sub-state diplomacy today* (11–36). Boston and Leiden: Brill.

Criekemans, D. (ed.) (2010). *Regional sub-state diplomacy today.* Boston and Leiden: Brill.

Criekemans, D. (2011). Exploring the relationship between geopolitics, foreign policy and diplomacy. *International Studies Review,* 13(4), 713–716.

Csurgai, G. (2005). *La nation et ses territoires en Europe centrale: Une approche géopolitique.* Bern: Peter Lang.

Csurgai, G. (2009). Constant and Variable Factors of Geopolitical Analysis In G. Csurgai (ed.). *Geopolitics: Schools of Thought, Method of Analysis and Case Studies* (48–86). Geneva: Editions des Penthes.

Deleuze, G. and F. Guattari (1972). *Capitalisme et Schizophrénie: L'anti- Œdipe.* Paris: Les Editions de Minuit.

Der Derian, J. (1987). *On Diplomacy. A Genealogy of Western Estrangement.* Oxford: Basil Blackwell.

Duran, M., D. Criekemans et al. (2010). *Towards a "Third Wave" in Paradiplomacy?* Antwerp: Steunpunt Buitenlands Beleid.

Eco, U. (1986). Dreaming of the Middle Ages In *Travels in Hyperreality* (61–72). NY: Harcourt Brace, pp.;

Ferguson, Y.H. and Mansbach, R.W. (2008). Polities Past and Present. *Millenium: Journal of International Studies,* 37(2), 365–379.

Foucault, M. (1984). Des espaces autres. *Architecture–Mouvement–Continuité* 5 (October), 46–49.

Friedrichs, J. (2001). The Meaning of New Medievalism. *European Journal of International Relations,* 7(4), 475–502.

Friedrichs, J. (2007). New Medievalism In Scholte, J.A. and Robertson, R. (eds.). *Encyclopedia of Globalisation* (873–875). London and New York: Routledge..

Fukuyama, F. (1992). *The end of history and the last man.* New York: Free Press.

Georges, P. And Verger, F. (2009). *Dictionnaie de la géographie.* Paris: Presse universitaires de France.

Hamilton, K. and Langhorne, R. (2005). *The Practice of Diplomacy: Its evolution, theory and administration.* London: Routledge.

Hocking, B. (2004). Privatizing Diplomacy? *International Studies Perspectives* 5, 147–152.

Hoffmann, J. (2003). Reconstructing Diplomacy, *British Journal of Politics and International Relations* 5(4), 525–542.

Kaizer, R. (2003). Paradiplomacy and Multilevel Governance in Europe and North America : Subnational Governments in International Arenas. *Participation* 27(1), 17–19.

Kaplan, R.D. (2012), *The Revenge of Geography.* New York: Random House.

Keating, M. (1997). *The Political Economy of Regionalism* In: M. Keating and J. Loughlin (eds). The Political Economy of Regionalism (17–40). London: Frank Cass.

Keating, M. (1998). *The New Regionalism in Western Europe: Territorial Restructuring and Political Change.* Cheltenham Glos: Edward Elgar.

Keating, M. (1999). Regions and International Affairs: Motives, Opportunities and Strategies In: F. Aldecoa and M. Keating (eds). *Paradiplomacy in Action: The Foreign Relations of Subnational Governments* (1–16). London: Frank Cass.

Khanna, P. (2011). *How to Run the World: Charting a Course to the Next Renaissance.* New York: Random House

Kissinger, H. (1994). *Diplomacy.* New York: Simon & Schuster.

Kratochwil, F. (2011). *Of Maps, Law, and Politics: An Inquiry into the Changing Meaning of Territoriality*, DIIS Working Paper 03 (27 pages).

Kuznetsov, A. S. (2015). *Theory and practice of paradiplomacy: Subnational governments in international affairs.* Oxford: Routledge

Lapham, L. (1988). Leviathan in Trouble. *Harper's Magazine*, September, 8–11.

Lazzarini, I. (2016). Storia della diplomazia e International Relations Studies fra pre- e post- modern. *Storica* 65 (2016), pp. 9–41.

Lukes, D. (2014). Comparative neomedievalisms: A little bit medieval. *Postmedieval: a journal of medieval cultural studies* (2014) 5, 1–9.

Marschall, D.W. (2011). Neomedievalism, Identification, and the Haze of Medievalisms In Fugelso, K. (ed.). *Defining neomedievalim(s)* (11–20). Cambridge: Studies in Medievalism XX.

Mattingly, G. (1955). *Renaissance Diplomacy.* New York: Dover.

Melissen, J. (1999). Introduction In J. Melissen (ed.), *Innovation in Diplomatic Practice* (i-xxiii). Basingstoke: Palgrave Macmillan.

Murray, S. (2008). Consolidating the Gains Made in Diplomacy Studies. *International Studies Perspectives* 9(1): 22 – 39.

Neumann, I. (2013). *Diplomatic Sites. A Critical Inquiry.* Columbia: Columbia University Press.

Newman, D. et al. (2004). *Boundaries, Territory and Postmodernity.* London: Frank Cass.

Nicolson, H. (1942). Diplomacy. Oxford: Oxford University Press.

Nigro, L. (2010). Theory and Practice of Modern Diplomacy: Origins and Development to 1914 In Bartholomees, J.B. (ed.). *Theory of War and Strategy* (173–186). Carlisle: Strategic Studies Institute.

Ó Tuathail, G. and T.W. Luke (1994). Present at the (Dis)integration: Deterritorialisation and Reterritorialisation in the New Wor(l)d Order. *Annals of the Association of American Geographers* 84: 381–398.

Ó Tuathail, G., S. Dalby et al. (1998). *The Geopolitics Reader*. London: Routledge.

Osiander, A. (2001). Sovereignty, International Relations and the Westphalian Myth. *International Organization*, 55(2): 251–287.

Queller, D. (1984). Medieval Diplomacy In J.R. Strayer (ed.). *Dictionary of the Middle Ages* (201–214). New York: Scribner.

Queller, D. (2005). *Medieval Diplomacy*. London: Sage.

Raffestin, C. (1986). Ecogénèse territoriale et territorialité. *Espaces, jeux et enjeux* (pp. 173–185).

Riggirozzi, P. (2012). Region, Regionness and Regionalism in Latin America: Towards a New Synthesis. *New Political Economy*, 17:4, 421–443.

Rudolph, C. (2005). Sovereignty and Territorial Borders in a Global Age. *International Studies Review* 7(1): 1–20.

Ruggie, J. (1993). Territoriality and beyond: Problematizing modernity in international relations. *International Organization*, 47(1), 139–174.

Sassen, S. (1996). *Losing Control? Sovereignty in an Age of Globalisation*. New York: Columbia University Press.

Scholte, J.A. (2005). *Globalisation: A critical introduction*. London: Macmillan.

Sharp, P. and Clark, J. (1997). The End of Diplomacy *International Journal*, 52(4), 539–736.

Spruyt, H. (1994). *The Sovereign State and Its Competitors*. Princeton: Princeton University Press.

Tatham, M. (2008). Going Solo: Direct Regional Representation in the European Union. *Regional and Federal Studies* 18(5), 493 — 515.

Tavares, R. (2016). *Paradiplomacy: Cities and states as global players*. Oxford: Oxford University Press.

Teschke, B. (2003). *The Myth of 1648: class, geopolitics, and the making of modern international relations*. London and New York: Verso Books.

Van Kemseke, P. (2000). Inleiding. Diplomatie: een kwestie van cultuur In Van Kemseke, P. (ed.). *Diplomatieke Cultuur* (9–34). Leuven: Universitaire Pers Leuven.

Van Staden, A. and Vollaard, H. (2002). The Erosion of State Sovereignty: Towards a Post-Territorial World? In Kreijin, G. (ed.) *State, Sovereignty, and International Governance* (164–184). Oxford: Oxford University Press.

Watkins, J. (2008). Toward a New Diplomatic History of Medieval and Early Modern Europe. *Journal of Medieval and Early Modern Studies* 38(1), 1–14.

PART 4

Conclusions

Geopolitics and International Relations: From 'Living Apart Together' to 'Friends with Benefits'

David Criekemans

During the past decades, Geopolitics and International Relations have at best been 'living apart together'. But world events and intrinsic academic debates are gradually bringing both fields back together. This book aimed to contribute to the academic re-integration of both fields into a mutually beneficial, scholarly rewarding and fruitful journey. It introduced readers to the geopolitical literature; from the basic variables of geopolitical analysis, over the main theoretical approaches in Geopolitics to examples of more practical geopolitical analyses. In many ways that academic journey is just getting started as this constitutes the first foundational book in a much wider academic endeavour as Brill's book series *'Geopolitics and International Relations'*. Geopolitical risks can be analysed in many different sectors; economy, environment, energy, strategy and technology. The upcoming book series aims to become a unique platform where a debate is possible between and within schools of thought in Geopolitics and International Relations. This foundational book has tried to set the scene so as to create a zone where Geopolitics and IR can connect with each other, rather than closing themselves off into existing publications in their respective fields. This foundational book as well as the upcoming book series will also be open to contributions from scholars in other fields such as historians, geographers, economists, political scientists, psychologists, specialists in international law, etc. Perhaps, through this, Geopolitics and International Relations can again become at least 'friends with benefits'. Both have much to offer to each other, but hurdles at the conceptual, theoretical or methodological level may lie in between. Both have similar interests; to make sense of a world which is in transition in many domains; economic, energy, technological, environmental and in terms of power politics. Both are also different; Geopolitics asks attention for territorially embedded variables and provides a more holistic view of world problems and their interconnectedness. International Relations is a broader, multi-disciplinary endeavour which also encapsulates approaches coming

 | DOI:10.1163/9789004432086_013

from diplomatic history, economic theory, international law, etc. Moreover, IR has branched out in many different areas around crucial concepts such as power (Realism), interdependence (Liberalism), inequality (Marxism), and identity and international norms (Constructivism). Similar theoretical developments have taken place inside the field of Geopolitics. But because of all these theoretical branches and different schools of thought, it has become less apparent for outsiders where respective theories of Geopolitics and IR can be mutually strengthening each other's ontological views and epistemological insights.

The renewed attention for territorially embedded factors in several schools of thought nevertheless connects numerous scientific approaches. By better understanding these contributions, academics, students and practitioners can learn from each other. Hence it is possible to develop more comprehensive analyses on the geopolitical challenges which affect many dimensions of politics today and tomorrow (security, economy, energy, environment, technology, diplomacy & foreign policy).

1 Western and non-Western Approaches

An ongoing challenge within the literature of Geopolitics remains that most of the publications are Western in nature (Parker, 2015; Rona, 1982). Mainstream literature could however be enriched to also discover more local, non-Western approaches from Central and South America, Africa, Russia and the post-Soviet area, Asia, etc. Only gradually are these trickling into the mainstream geopolitical literature. Confronting Western and non-Western approaches with regard to basic geopolitical concepts and their political application at home may prove very insightful, both from a fundamental and a more practical point of view. It may give us a better insight into basic sources of contention and potential areas of agreement. It may help us to identify misunderstandings or fundamental differences in opinion. It may also help us in the "decolonization" of key geopolitical concepts and approaches. Through such a scientific endeavour, a critical attitude can be developed which may inform a rethinking of North-South relations (Slater, 2004). At the same time, as this book has shown, Geopolitics itself also has an opportunity to move beyond mere critical approaches into an 'analytic' Geopolitics, for instance in reflecting about national myths. In any event, this new book series will thus give room to both Western and non-Western geopolitical approaches and insights.

2 Towards a Joint Research Agenda

Bringing the scholarships of Geopolitics and International Relations more actively together may result, over time, in the development of a joint research agenda. It may be guided by and facilitated through the fascinating process of learning from different schools of thought and of academic fields. The most obvious elements of such a research agenda are affected by the times in which we are living. Clearly, global power centres are shifting and territorial entities around the world (states, macro-regional entities, cities and regions) are trying to deal with these realities. The drivers of these shifts are multiple; demography, technology, economy, energy, military, etc. Each of these variables offer us a 'way into' better understanding the fundamental geopolitical shifts which we are experiencing, and how world actors are responding to them. Through a chapter on the main components of geopolitical analysis, this book has given the reader some handles to try to grasp them. In an additional chapter, this book has illustrated how geopolitical factors interact with technology, creating new 'geotechnical ensembles' with which the world needs to deal. An additional insight which is relevant to develop in a new research agenda is that a changing geopolitics cannot be seen separate from developments in geo-economics and geostrategy. If China rises geo-economically, there will be consequences in the geopolitical and geostrategic theatres (An, 2020). Conversely, the cause of current tensions between the West and Russia may lie in a fundamental misunderstanding between both concerning their respective geopolitical and geo-economic aspirations or values. Specialists in law can also help us to understand what the legal boundaries or interpretations are in which policy practitioners can operate. There is much to learn from one another.

Geopolitical analyses can be developed at a global, macro-regional or local level. For instance, the French geopolitical tradition has shown how a geopolitical analysis may also be relevant inside states themselves, in addition to their foreign policy (*'géopolitique interne'* vs. *'géopolitique externe'*) (Lacoste, 1976; Lacoste, 1982). Geopolitical developments at the local level may also change regional equations. Conversely, global geopolitics may limit what is possible at the regional or local level. Specialists in Geography and International Relations can also help each other in making sense of some of these dynamics.

Geopolitical analyses can be historical in nature, contemporary or even include scenario analysis. Historical analyses can help us to better understand key geopolitical concepts of the past. In this book we for instance discussed the origins and interpretations of the concept of 'containment'. Such an analysis can still be relevant to today's world. Another domain to be further developed lies in extrapolating key geopolitical variables into the future for the purpose of developing better policy or even investment choices. Both military planners and financial specialists have, over the last years, become quite interested in combining the insights of forecasting with geopolitical analysis (Papic, 2021). This area clearly also constitutes a domain which can be of future relevance to both academia and practitioners.

3 The Interaction between Geopolitics, Foreign Policy and Diplomacy

Another aspect to further explore is the changing relationship between Geopolitics, Foreign Policy and Diplomacy. How can diplomatic studies develop further from an empirical and theoretical point of view? For one thing, by engaging with other IR-subfields and social sciences, and by contributing to a more complete view on the forces reshaping modern world politics.

One neglected yet promising area to be developed within diplomatic studies is the relationship between geopolitics and diplomacy. At the beginning of the 1990s, influential IR scholars focused their attention on globalisation and its impact. Some believed the world would gradually become one village, with no borders. They argued that myriad processes of de-territorialisation were occurring, in which society and politics were less bound to territorial spaces.[1] During the 1990s, it seemed this process would continue.[2] However, as the twenty-first century dawned, it became clear that territoriality had not vanished as

1 Different authors in IR but also in Political Geography focused on other aspects of de-territorialization. Ó Tuathail (1998) made some very important remarks in this regard: "Deterritorialization is best interpreted, as Virilio remarks, as a question; it evokes the challenges posed to the status of territory and, by extension, our territorially embedded understandings of geography, governance and geopolitics, states, places and the social sciences, by planetary communication networks and globalizing tendencies. But it is deceptive when it becomes an answer polemically naming this challenge as a clear disappearance of territoriality. The problematic of deterritorialization is therefore also the problematic of reterritorialization; it is not the presence or absence of state territoriality but its changing status, power and meaning in relation to postmodern technological constellations, speed machines and global webs of capitalism" (82).

2 A seminal contribution can be found in the work of Ruggie (1993). He spoke of a process of "unbundling" of territoriality: "in the modern international polity an institutional negation of exclusive territoriality serves as the means of situating and dealing with those dimensions of collective existence that territorial rulers recognize to be irreducibly transterritorial in character. Nonterritorial functional space is the place wherein international society is anchored." (165).

a potential explanatory variable of international relations and diplomacy.[3] In fact, quite the opposite has occurred.

Today, multiple processes of re-territorialisation can be identified. This concept can be understood as a series of "developments which occur when certain territorial entities diminish in importance, in favour of other territorial configurations" (Scholte 2000: 60).[4] Thus, geopolitics has not vanished: different types of re-territorialisation are altering the fabric of international relations and, inevitably, such processes are also influencing the practices and conduct of modern diplomacy (Criekemans 2009). Four occurrences of re-territorialisation highlight these processes and suggest a promising area of scholarship for both diplomatic and IR scholars.

The first occurrence concerns changing spheres of political influence, both at a regional and global level. The BRIC countries – Brazil, Russia, India and China – are of particular relevance here. They all combine steady economic growth (somewhat hampered by the economic crisis of 2008–09) with a more prominent geopolitical role, both individually and as a group (for example, via the new G-20 regime). In some cases, there is even a desire to translate this newfound geo-economical and geopolitical influence into a more prominent geo-strategical one. Via diplomacy, countries such as China or Brazil 'test' their relationship vis-à-vis each other and, more importantly vis-à-vis the hegemon, the United States of America. Today, diplomacy constitutes an integral part of the geopolitical and geo-economical shifts taking place both at a regional and global level and thus demand academic attention. More recently, Western countries are responding to the changes in spheres of influence. Whereas the former American President Donald Trump developed an *'America First'*-policy, the new Biden-administration wishes to bring Western powers together under the umbrella of the G7 and NATO to develop a strategic answer to a rising China, thereby combining geo-economics and geostrategy. The jury is still out on whether Americans and Europeans will see eye to eye with regard to their respective interests in Asia. Nevertheless, this global re-territorialisation and shift in global power seems to produce new geopolitical, geo-economic, technological and diplomatic patterns in the years to come. Scholars in both Geopolitics and International Relations are developing relevant insights in

3 Scholte (2000) argued: *"The end of territorialism as a consequence of globalisation does not mean the end of territoriality."* (59).

4 The concepts *'deterritorialization'* and *'reterritorialization'* originally stem from the psychoanalytical work *'A Thousand Plateaus. Capitalism and Schizofrenia'* by Deleuze and Guattari on the impact of capitalism (1988). In today's geopolitical literature, both concepts are often utilized as metaphors for cultural, social and spatial change.

order to better understand these dynamics (Young, 2020). The Indo-Pacific Region may well become one of the key geopolitical areas in the coming decades in which this changing power struggle between the West and China will take place (Kapur, 2020; Berkofsky et al., 2019; Markey, 2020).

The second example of re-territorialisation relates to the first. The international relations system is evolving from a uni-multipolar world (which saw its dawn in 1991, when the Soviet Union disintegrated) to a possible duo-multipolar world (the US and China) or perhaps a multipolar world. What implications will these tectonic shifts have on diplomacy? In addition, how will the diplomatic apparatus of Western countries cope with the changing international order? In most cases, one can detect a serious "lagging behind-effect," in which the national diplomats still consider Paris, Vienna, London or Berlin more important than Beijing, New Delhi or Brasilia. Some countries seem to adapt better and in more flexible ways to the changing geopolitical and geo-economical currents, while others seem to have a diplomatic network and priorities which more resemble the world in 1945 instead of 2021. Re-territorialisation will also affect multilateral diplomacy, but in some fora such as the WTO[5] or IMF the 'translation process' of geopolitical and geo-economic power shifts seems to move quicker than in the UN Security Council. When and under what conditions do changing power relations affect the rules and practices of diplomacy itself? These trends will force diplomatic studies to reduce its traditional Western focus and contemplate an emerging world beyond the doorsteps of Washington and London.

A third form of re-territorialisation concerns the increasing role which scarce resources (oil, gas, coal and other natural deposits of various kinds), located in specific territorial places, have on international relations and diplomacy. As more people enter the global economy, they will have a profound impact. The demand for natural resources will increase, making some countries or regions relatively more important than others (Criekemans, 2018b). The ongoing energy transition will create a new geopolitical struggle over natural gas as a 'transition fuel' towards a renewable energy future (Criekemans, 2018a). At the same time, the renewable energy future in which electrification stands central is already today creating scarcity issues and geopolitical struggles over access to rare earth metals, but also to more basic natural resources such as copper, silver, lithium and cobalt (Pitron, 2020; Hafner & Tagliapietra, 2020; Mehmet & Yorucu, 2020). The resulting power shifts may be facilitated or slowed down by diplomacy. An area for future theoretical and practical

5 Some important, yet at this time unpublished work on this phenomenon, has been developed by Braz Baracuhy, a diplomat at the WTO Agricultural Desk of the Permanent Mission of Brazil to the WTO in Geneva (published in *Global Policy*, 2012).

exploration, therefore, would be to study how these shifts in power relations impact the diplomatic strategies of producer, transit and consumer countries in a world with ever scarcer resources.

The fourth and final example concerns the relationship between re-territorialisation and non-state actors. Both above and beneath the state level, territorial entities become relevant, and generate their own external relations, foreign policy and diplomatic practices. Europe constitutes an interesting testing ground in this regard. On the one hand, the Lisbon Treaty in 2010 has led to the establishment of the European External Action Service (EEAS). European diplomacy is still in its infancy, but with the new Commission under the leadership of Ursula von der Leyen, it has expressed an ambition to think more in a geopolitical and geostrategic fashion. Many institutional hurdles, such as the need for unanimity and the compartmentalisation of dossiers over different policy-matters, are obstacles to achieving that goal. Nevertheless, the EU's *Global Strategy* developed under the former High Representative for Foreign Affairs Mogherini, constitutes an important milestone in this ongoing ambition. One of its added values is that it tries to identify the root causes of problems such as migration, terrorism and instability in Europe's near and far abroad. At the same time, national diplomatic services are adapting to this new geopolitical reality. They often sent their brightest diplomats to the European External Action Service. Gradually, a new division of work between the EU level and the member states will materialise on the wide variety of foreign policy dossiers. This experiment will impact European and possibly global diplomatic practices.

On the other hand, Europe has been and still is a nursery for sub-state diplomacy. Different regional sub-state entities in Europe such as Flanders, Wallonia, Catalonia, Scotland, Bavaria and others engage in international relations on their own merits, and conduct a foreign policy parallel, complementary or sometimes in conflict with their diplomatic state counterparts. The days when diplomacy was exclusively associated with national states are gone. Since the late 1990s, the spectrum of diplomatic instruments and the strategies that accompany sub-state entities have become more diverse and complex (Criekemans 2010a; Criekemans 2010b). To a certain extent, today's diplomatic practices resemble a pre-Westphalian world in which realms of different territorial sizes generate their own diplomatic identity and practices. Diplomacy has become a multi-level endeavour, in which different policy levels (macroregional, national, cross-border, substate: regions and cities) each generate specific types of diplomatic activities reflecting specific needs felt at their respective territorial levels. The question here then is *when* and *under what conditions* are diplomats of the macro-regional, national and sub-state level *able* and *willing* to cooperate with one another? This line of thinking mirrors the complexity of societal questions relating to the EU experiment and would add another layer of knowledge to diplomatic studies.

Re-territorialisation challenges the study of diplomacy, particularly in terms of its research questions and objectives. The potential for exploring the geopolitics-diplomacy-nexus is valuable but multifarious.

4 Geopolitics, Towards a New 'Geographical Consciousness' of Foreign Policy?

'Geopolitical scientists' underline that although today we may perhaps mainly be living in a social world, this does not necessarily mean that territorially embedded variables have lost all their explanatory power. These still generate an influence upon today's 'foreign policy' & 'international relations'. From our comfortable position in the 'North', in the 'West', or in the 'developed world', we sometimes seem to forget this. But as we already mentioned in the beginning of this book, territorially embedded explanatory factors often form the beginning of an answer to very acute questions regarding development, or even to (partially) explain the difficult political relations within countries. The most important and potentially most dangerous conflicts in the world are often exactly those in which 'territoriality' plays a crucial role (van Staden 1999: 615). One can think of such recent examples as the war in Syria, the situation in Iraq and Yemen, the race for resources and power in areas such as the South China Sea or the North pole region, the continued fragility of the Balkans, the situation in Libya, etc. The examples are numerous.

Even in the 21st century, physical-geographical obstacles such as mountains or deserts can explain why certain, relatively speaking 'nearby' peoples throughout their history and today barely maintained contact, or could not be integrated within 'nation-states'. The American IR-specialist Adam Garfinkle employs an interesting saying to summarize all this; "we become where we are" (Garfinkle, 2003). Both local social patterns and the human-political interaction between peoples, are unmistakably also influenced by 'territoriality' (both in its physical-geographical, in its human-geographical, as in its spatial dimensions).

Some areas are more 'endowed' by nature than others, as a result of which they have more opportunities for development. From this stems –according to 'Geopolitics'– also a relative power balance within and between societies, which can be 'translated' by politicians and policymakers into a vague, yet at least implicitly recognized 'geopolitical influence' emanating from states, regions or cities. In our opinion, 'Geopolitics' as a field of research could also in the current juncture play an important scientific research role and societal sensibilization-function in developing the awareness that the many global-ecological challenges which announce themselves today, can/will generate forceful consequences for foreign policy & for the global political relations. After having been ignored for some decades, it seems as though environmental variables are back with a vengeance within the study of Geopolitics. A simple enumeration is already revealing; increasing water scarcity in highly populated areas (worsened by global warming), increasing scarcity of oil and natural gas, which causes a politicization of these issues, the endangering of global biodiversity, etc. In each of these dossiers, 'territoriality' & foreign policy interact. These are crucial geopolitical questions; their outcome could literally influence the future of humanity. The problem is however that politicians do not always appreciate the level of interdependence which exists between & within these dossiers. Foreign policy-elites will in first instance always defend their own 'national interest'. Only when offered more insight into the complex relationship between 'nature' and 'society' (Matthew 1999: 298), will politicians be inclined to re-formulate their own 'national interest' in another, more creative way (e.g. the Paris Accord and the further need for a global road towards CO2-neutrality in 2050 in order to stave off the dire environmental consequences of a 2 degrees Celsius global warming scenario).

For foreign policy elites, it is crucial to gain a better insight into the dependence of societies upon the 'changing' environmental variables; to include them into their political 'calculations' in order to better understand the viewpoints they have to defend in their foreign policy 'the day after tomorrow'. In our opinion, it is exactly here where there still lies a yet to be explored terrain for 'Geopolitics' – to grow into a 'geographical consciousness' of foreign policy, but then in a whole different way compared to what the German geopolitical thinker Karl Haushofer had in mind during the interwar years of last century. Central in this endeavour is the issue of how the questions mentioned above could best be 'politicized' in the arena of international relations. By analogy with Ellsworth Huntington one could state that humanity can only become really politically free if one is conscious of the limitations which nature has imposed and the finiteness of what is possible on this earth.

Bibliography

An, N. (2020). *Confucian Geopolitics. Chinese Geopolitical Imaginations of the US War on Terror.* Singapore: Springer.

Baracuhy, B. (2012) Running into a Brick Wall: The WTO Doha Round, Governance Gap and Geopolitical Risks, *Global Policy*, 3(1): 108–110.

Berkofsky, A., & Miracola, S. (2019). *Geopolitics by Other Means. The Indo-Pacific Reality.* Milan: Ledizioni LediPublishing.

Criekemans, D. (2010a). Regional sub-state diplomacy from a comparative perspective: Quebec, Scotland, Bavaria, Catalonia, Wallonia and Flanders, In *The Hague Journal of Diplomacy*, 5 (1): 37–64.

Criekemans, D. (Ed.) (2010b). *Regional Sub-State Diplomacy Today.* Leiden, Martinus Nijhoff Publishers.

Criekemans, D. (2018a). Geopolitiek van aardgas: brug naar de toekomst? *Karakter : tijdschrift van wetenschap* (Katholieke Universiteit Leuven. Vlaamse Leergangen), 62(16): 25–27, Retrieved at: https://www.tijdschriftkarakter.be/geopolitiek-van-aardgas-brug-naar-de-toekomst/ .

Criekemans, D. (2018b). 'Geopolitics of the Renewable Energy Game and its potential impact upon global power relations', In Scholten, D. (et al.) (2018). *The Geopolitics of Renewables* (Lecture Notes in Energy, 61), Springer: 37–73.

Deleuze, G. & Guattari, F. (1988). *A Thousand Plateaus. Capitalism and Schizophrenia.* London: Athlone Press.

Garfinkle, A. (2003). Geopolitics: Middle Eastern Notes and Anticipations, *Orbis: a journal of world affairs*, 47(2).

Hafner, M., & Tagliapietra, S. (2020). *The Geopolitics of Global Energy Transition.* Cham: Springer.

Kapur, A. (2020). *Geopolitics and the Indo-Pacific Region.* Abingdon & New York: Routledge.

Lacoste, Y. (1976). *Geographie, ça sert, d'abord, à faire la guerre*. Paris: Maspero.

Lacoste, Y. (1982). Editorial. D'autres géopolitiques. *Hérodote. Revue de Géographie et de Géopolitique* (25): 3–9.

Markey, D. (2020). *China's Western Horizon. Beijing and the New Geopolitics of Eurasia.* Oxford: Oxford University Press.

Matthew, R. A. (1999). Conclusion, In D. H. Deudney & R. A. Matthew. *Contested grounds: Security and conflict in the new environment politics* Albany, State University of New York Press: 291–301.

Mehmet, O., & Yorucu, V. (2020). *Modern Geopolitics of Eastern Mediterranean Hydrocarbons in an Age of Energy Transformation.* Cham: Springer.

Ó Tuathail, G. (1998). Political geography III: dealing with deterritorialization, In *Progress in Human Geography. An international review of geographic work in the social sciences and humanities*, 22(1): 81–93.

Papic, M. (2021). *Geopolitical Alpha. An Investment Framework for Predicting the Future.* Hoboken, New Jersey: John Wiley & Sons.

Parker, G. (2015) *Western Geopolitical Thought in the Twentieth Century.* Abingdon: Routledge.

Pitron, G. (2020). *The Rare Metals War. The Dark Side of Clean Energy and Digital Technologies.* London: Scribe.

Rona, T. (1982) *Our Changing Geopolitical Premises.* New Brunswick & London: Transaction Books.

Ruggie, John Gerard (1993) 'Territoriality and Beyond: Problematizing Modernity in International Relations', In *International Organization*, Vol. 47, No. 1. (Winter, 1993), pp. 139–174.

Scholte, J. A. (2000). *Globalization. A Critical Introduction.* London, Mac Millan Press, Ltd.

Slater, D. (2004). *Geopolitics and the Post-Colonial. Rethinking North-South Relations.* Oxford: Blackwell Publishing.

van Staden, A. (1999). Economisering van de internationale betrekkingen?, In *Internationale Spectator*, 53(11): 612–616.

Young, J. (2020). *Structural Realism and Geopolitical Thought. An Approach to International Political Development.* Chisinau, Moldova: Eliva Press.

Index

Page numbers in **bold** refer to tables; page numbers in *italics* refer to figures; 'n' after a page number indicates the footnote number.